ORIGINS OF NEW TESTAMENT CHRISTOLOGY

AN INTRODUCTION
TO THE TRADITIONS AND TITLES
APPLIED TO JESUS

STANLEY E. PORTER
AND BRYAN R. DYER

Baker Academic
a division of Baker Publishing Group
Grand Rapids, Michigan

© 2023 by Stanley E. Porter and Bryan R. Dyer

Published by Baker Academic
a division of Baker Publishing Group
Grand Rapids, Michigan
www.bakeracademic.com

All rights reserved. No part of this publication may be reproduced, stored in a retrieval system, or transmitted in any form or by any means—for example, electronic, photocopy, recording—without the prior written permission of the publisher. The only exception is brief quotations in printed reviews.

Library of Congress Cataloging-in-Publication Data
Names: Porter, Stanley E., 1956– author. | Dyer, Bryan R., author.
Title: Origins of New Testament Christology : an introduction to the traditions and titles applied to Jesus / Stanley E. Porter and Bryan R. Dyer.
Description: Grand Rapids, Michigan : Baker Academic, a division of Baker Publishing Group, [2023] | Includes bibliographical references and index.
Identifiers: LCCN 2022033455 | ISBN 9780801098710 (paperback) | ISBN 9781540966476 (casebound) | ISBN 9781493440146 (ebook) | ISBN 9781493440153 (pdf)
Subjects: LCSH: Jesus Christ—History of doctrines—Early church, ca. 30–600. | Bible. Gospels—Criticism, interpretation, etc. | Christianity—Origin.
Classification: LCC BT198 .P6755 2023 | DDC 232—dc23/eng/20220914
LC record available at https://lccn.loc.gov/2022033455

Unless indicated otherwise, Scripture quotations are from the New Revised Standard Version of the Bible, copyright © 1989 National Council of the Churches of Christ in the United States of America. Used by permission. All rights reserved.

Scripture quotations labeled NIV are from THE HOLY BIBLE, NEW INTERNATIONAL VERSION®, NIV® Copyright © 1973, 1978, 1984, 2011 by Biblica, Inc.® Used by permission. All rights reserved worldwide.

Some material taken from *Sacred Tradition in the New Testament* by Stanley E. Porter, copyright © 2014. Used by permission of Baker Academic, a division of Baker Publishing Group.

Baker Publishing Group publications use paper produced from sustainable forestry practices and post-consumer waste whenever possible.

23 24 25 26 27 28 29   7 6 5 4 3 2 1

"Porter and Dyer offer an excellent introduction to New Testament Christology, organized around the titles used of Jesus, including Lord, Messiah, Son of Man, and Son of God. The approach is not a simple catalogue but rather a sophisticated reading of literary and social contexts, in illuminating dialogue with contemporary scholars. Examination of each title leads students through a close reading of key texts toward a more general evaluation of the title's significance. Introductory courses will find in the work an extremely valuable resource."

—**Harold Attridge**, Yale Divinity School

"This is not just another book on christological titles. Instead, Porter and Dyer offer a vital bridge from biblical interpretation to theological reasoning through a hermeneutically rich and historically informed study of the traditions applied to Jesus. Insightful and clear, this book will be an essential resource for students, pastors, and scholars interested in constructing an exegetically informed Christology."

—**Elizabeth E. Shively**, St. Mary's College, University of St. Andrews

"Stanley Porter and Bryan Dyer have written a learned book on an important and complicated topic, and they have done so in a remarkably clear and compelling fashion. What makes the book so good is how well they contextualize every aspect of New Testament Christology with the relevant biblical and extrabiblical texts. This book will become the foundational study of biblical Christology."

—**Craig A. Evans**, Houston Christian University

"Porter and Dyer's *Origins of New Testament Christology* offers thoughtful guidance to and wisdom about the titles used for Jesus. Wonderfully immersed in the historical and sociocultural traditions of Jesus's time, this book is a fantastic textbook for any New Testament Christology classroom! Porter and Dyer avoid the pitfalls of past works on this topic and instead offer the best of recent scholarship with their own unique flair."

—**Beth M. Stovell**, Ambrose University

"Orienting readers to the world of the New Testament and its claims about Jesus in the midst of that world, *Origins of New Testament Christology* provides a rich perspective for all who desire to contemplate the question 'Who is this man?' By respecting both the complexity of the traditions in their own settings and the complexity with which they manifest in the New Testament writings, Porter and Dyer's presentation allows the arresting nature of the biblical claims about Jesus to shine forth with fresh power. Students of the New Testament with historical and theological interest will come to rely on this volume as a treasured resource."

—**Amy Peeler**, Wheaton College

"In the tradition of Oscar Cullmann's classic *The Christology of the New Testament*, Porter and Dyer provide a fresh, up-to-date study of Christology through the lens of titles. This work is particularly helpful in contextualizing the titles historically and exegetically. The authors rightly conclude that Jesus is presented as divine in the New Testament. This is an important topic indeed!"

—**Brandon D. Crowe**, Westminster Theological Seminary

For Craig L. Blomberg

CONTENTS

List of Sidebars ix
Preface xi
Abbreviations xiii
Introduction xvii

1. Jesus the Lord 1
2. Jesus the Prophet 23
3. Jesus the Son of Man 47
4. Jesus the Son of God 65
5. Jesus the Suffering Servant 91
6. Jesus the Passover Lamb 111
7. Jesus the Messiah 135
8. Jesus the Savior 157
9. Jesus the Last Adam 169
10. Jesus the Word 189
11. Jesus the High Priest 211

Conclusion: *Jesus as God* 227
Bibliography 237
Modern Authors Index 259
Ancient Sources Index 264

SIDEBARS

Onias's Plea to King Ptolemy Philometor   5
Ignatius to the Smyrnaeans (Early 2nd Century CE)   20
The Anticipation of the Prophet Elijah's Return   27
Jesus the "Archprophet of the Prophets"   33
Moses and Jesus in the *Epistle of Barnabas*   41
"Son of Man" in Daniel 7   52
1 Enoch's Son of Man   54
The Elect One on God's Throne   61
The Achievements of the Divine Augustus   68
The Qumran "Son of God" Text   74
Hippolytus on the Adoptionist Heresy   88
The Servant as Israel in the Zohar   98
The *Epistle of Barnabas* on the Suffering Servant and Jesus   109
Hyssop and the Passover Lamb   125
Melito of Sardis's "On the Passover"   133
The Messiah in *4 Ezra*   141
Ignatius on "Our God, Jesus the Christ"   156
"Savior of Those without Hope"   160
"Savior" in *2 Clement*   168
Sirach 15:13–15   173
Origen on Romans 5   182
Irenaeus on Recapitulation   187
Plutarch on *Logos*   191
Justin Martyr on Jesus the *Logos*   207
High Priests More Important Than Kings   217
Jesus the High Priest in *1 Clement*   225

PREFACE

This volume began to take shape as we were working on the manuscript for *Sacred Tradition in the New Testament: Tracing Old Testament Themes in the Gospels and Epistles*—Stan as the author and Bryan as his teaching assistant, editor, and contributor of a chapter. Since that is a rigorously researched academic monograph, we dreamed up the possibility of writing a more accessible book that expands on the traditions under consideration while focusing on New Testament Christology. Five of the chapters from *Sacred Tradition in the New Testament* provided some basis for chapters in the present volume. Although some sections are recognizable, all the material was rethought, often rewritten, and, in many places, expanded with this Christology volume in mind. These chapters include the following: "'Jesus Christ' in Paul's Letters" was used in small part in chapter 1 of this volume; "Daniel 7:13 and the Son of Man" was adapted for chapter 3; "Isaiah 42–53 and the Suffering Servant" was adapted for chapter 5; "The Son of God and the Messiah and Jesus" was adapted for chapters 4 and 7; and "Exodus 12 and the Passover Theme in John" was adapted for chapter 6. We highlight this here so that if any reader is interested in a more rigorous defense of the ideas presented in these chapters, they may consult those earlier versions in *Sacred Tradition*.

    We chose the title for this book, *Origins of New Testament Christology: An Introduction to the Traditions and Titles Applied to Jesus*, in order to explicitly identify the book as an introduction to the traditions that are foundational to the Christology of the New Testament. We examine eleven key traditions that reflect responsible scholarship while making the material accessible to the nonspecialist. As we explain in the introductory chapter, we believe that an appreciation of these traditions and how the New Testament writers utilized them is an important initial step in the study of Christology. In this way, these traditions can be viewed as the "origins" of the Christology of the New Testament. We wanted to produce a usable volume that assists readers who are new to the field to navigate the traditions and imagery that are applied to Jesus in the New Testament.

With this audience in mind, we wish to explain one decision that we have made throughout the book: our decision to retain the biblical languages and not use transliteration. Despite the assumption that transliteration is more accessible for readers without Greek or Hebrew, we are not convinced that transliteration offers any assistance. If someone does not read Greek, for instance, it is unclear how a transliteration of a term is any more helpful than simply writing the term in Greek. We believe that incorporating the actual Greek or Hebrew language, when necessary, is important for the study that we are engaged in. We always provide English translations and trust that our readers can follow along with us. Throughout this volume, unless otherwise indicated, we use the NRSV as our translation.

This book was in all important respects a fruitful collaborative effort on the part of both authors. We divided up the task of writing the individual chapters. They were then read, commented on, and edited by the other author, and then revised and checked again until we were both sufficiently satisfied with the final product. Many other people also helped bring the manuscript to book form. These include those who helped do research for this volume (Jason Jung and Jackson Theune) and who read early drafts of chapters (including Madison Pierce and Wally Cirafesi). We also wish to thank the folks at Baker Academic (R. David Nelson, Brandy Scritchfield, and Tim West) as well as an anonymous reviewer who made helpful comments. We are grateful for their help and contributions while acknowledging that any shortcomings of the book are our own. We are thankful for the ongoing support of our spouses, Wendy Porter and Anna Dyer, who have been a source of encouragement and love. We dedicate this book to Craig L. Blomberg, who recently retired from a prolific teaching career at Denver Seminary. Stan first met Craig when Stan was completing his PhD, and they spent many hours discussing and, as one might expect, challenging each other on various issues regarding interpretation of the New Testament. Bryan studied with Craig while an MA student and is grateful for his initial investment and continued encouragement in his research. We both consider Craig to be a good friend and colleague and have benefited from his many contributions to New Testament scholarship.

ABBREVIATIONS

1–2 En.	1–2 Enoch
1–4 Macc.	1–4 Maccabees
2 Bar.	2 Baruch
AB	Anchor Bible
AGJU	Arbeiten zur Geschichte des antiken Judentums und des Urchristentums
Ant.	Josephus, *Jewish Antiquities*
Apoc. Mos.	Apocalypse of Moses
AT	authors' translation
AYB	Anchor Yale Bible
Bar.	Baruch
BBR	*Bulletin for Biblical Research*
BECNT	Baker Exegetical Commentary on the New Testament
BGU	*Aegyptische Urkunden aus den Königlichen Staatlichen Museen zu Berlin, Griechische Urkunden.* 15 vols. Berlin: Weidmann, 1895–1937.
BNTC	Black's New Testament Commentaries
BSac	*Bibliotheca Sacra*
b. Sanh.	Babylonian Talmud tractate *Sanhedrin*
CBQ	*Catholic Biblical Quarterly*
cf.	*confer*, compare
chap(s).	chapter(s)
CurBR	*Currents in Biblical Research*
DSS	Dead Sea Scrolls
esp.	especially
ExpTim	*Expository Times*
FC	Fathers of the Church
HBT	*Horizons in Biblical Theology*
HTR	*Harvard Theological Review*
ICC	International Critical Commentary
IG	*Inscriptiones Graecae. Editio Minor.* Berlin: de Gruyter, 1924–.

IGR	*Inscriptiones Graecae ad res Romanas pertinentes*. Edited by R. Cagnat et al. Rome, 1964.
JBL	*Journal of Biblical Literature*
JETS	*Journal of the Evangelical Theological Society*
JGRChJ	*Journal of Greco-Roman Christianity and Judaism*
JSNT	*Journal for the Study of the New Testament*
JSNTSup	Journal for the Study of the New Testament Supplement Series
JSP	*Journal for the Study of the Pseudepigrapha*
JSPSup	Journal for the Study of the Pseudepigrapha Supplement Series
JTS	*Journal of Theological Studies*
Jub.	*Jubilees*
J.W.	Josephus, *Jewish War*
L.A.E.	*Life of Adam and Eve*
LCL	Loeb Classical Library
LNTS	Library of New Testament Studies
LXX	Septuagint
m. B. Metzi'a	Mishnah tractate *Bava Metzi'a*
MBSS	McMaster Biblical Studies Series
Midr. Ps.	*Midrash on Psalms*
MNTS	McMaster New Testament Studies
m. Sanh.	Mishnah tractate *Sanhedrin*
m. Sotah	Mishnah tractate *Sotah*
NA^{28}	Nestle-Aland, *Novum Testamentum Graece*. 28th ed.
NAC	New American Commentary
NCB	New Century Bible
NICNT	New International Commentary on the New Testament
NIGTC	New International Greek Testament Commentary
no.	number
NovTSup	Supplements to Novum Testamentum
n.s.	new series
NTM	New Testament Monographs
NTS	*New Testament Studies*
OGIS	*Orientis Graeci Inscriptiones Selectae*. Edited by W. Dittenberger. 2 vols. Leipzig: Hirzel, 1903–5.
OTL	Old Testament Library
OTP	*The Old Testament Pseudepigrapha*. Edited by James H. Charlesworth. 2 vols. New York: Doubleday, 1983–85.
par(s).	parallel(s)
PNTC	Pillar New Testament Commentary
Pss. Sol.	*Psalms of Solomon*
PTMS	Princeton Theological Monograph Series
RB	*Revue Biblique*
SB	*Sammelbuch griechischer Urkunden aus Aegypten*. Edited by Friedrich Preisigke et al. Vols. 1–21. Wiesbaden: Harrassowitz, 1915–2002.
SBLDS	Society of Biblical Literature Dissertation Series
SBLMS	Society of Biblical Literature Monograph Series
SBLSS	Society of Biblical Literature Symposium Series

SBT	Studies in Biblical Theology
Sib. Or.	Sibylline Oracles
SIG³	Sylloge Inscriptionum Graecarum. Edited by W. Dittenberger. 4 vols. 3rd ed. Leipzig: Hirzel, 1915–24.
Sir.	Sirach
SJT	Scottish Journal of Theology
SNTSMS	Society for New Testament Studies Monograph Series
SP	Sacra Pagina
SPhiloA	Studia Philonica Annual
STDJ	Studies on the Texts of the Desert of Judah
TDNT	Theological Dictionary of the New Testament. Edited by G. Kittel and G. Friedrich. Translated by G. W. Bromiley. 10 vols. Grand Rapids: Eerdmans, 1964–76.
TJ	Trinity Journal
TNTC	Tyndale New Testament Commentaries
Tob.	Tobit
TynBul	Tyndale Bulletin
UBS⁵	United Bible Societies, The Greek New Testament. 5th ed.
WBC	Word Biblical Commentary
Wis.	Wisdom of Solomon
WUNT	Wissenschaftliche Untersuchungen zum Neuen Testament
y. Ta'an.	Jerusalem Talmud tractate Ta'anit
ZNW	Zeitschrift für die neutestamentliche Wissenschaft

INTRODUCTION

"Who Is This?"

Luke's Gospel contains the account of a woman anointing Jesus with oil and washing his feet with her tears and hair (Luke 7:36–50). This woman hears that Jesus is dining at the house of a local religious leader and so brings an alabaster jar of oil to anoint him. The host of the dinner, seeing what is happening, comments that this woman is a "sinner" and that Jesus, if he were truly a prophet (the Greek wording indicates that the leader doubts this), should know that about her and, it is inferred, not allow her to touch him. Jesus responds to this comment with a parable and then declares that the woman's sins have been forgiven. This provokes murmurs among those dining with Jesus, and the Gospel writer tells us that "those who were at the table with him began to say among themselves, 'Who is this who even forgives sins?'" (7:49).

This is not the only time that Jesus says or does something that prompts the question "Who is this?" At several points in all four Gospels, the question of Jesus's identity surfaces and a variety of responses is given.[1] Just prior to this event with the woman anointing Jesus, Luke describes an interaction that Jesus has with disciples of John the Baptist. John had heard about Jesus's ministry, so he sends two of his disciples to ask, "Are you the one who is to come?" (Luke 7:19; cf. Matt. 11:3). Two chapters later, Luke describes King Herod hearing about Jesus and pondering, "Who is this about whom I hear such things?" (Luke 9:9). John's Gospel presents a lengthy conversation between Jesus and the religious leaders that continually revolves around the

---

1. Matt. 11:2–4; Mark 2:6–8; 11:27–28; Luke 23:39; John 7:25–31; 18:33–38.

identity of Jesus, prompting the leaders to ask, "Who are you?" (John 8:25) and "Who do you claim to be?" (8:53). Matthew's Gospel, when describing Jesus's entrance into Jerusalem, tells us that "the whole city was in turmoil, asking, 'Who is this?'" (Matt. 21:10).

The question is so persistent that the first three, or Synoptic, Gospels each contain an account of Jesus asking his disciples what people have been saying about his identity: "Who do people say that I am?" (Matt. 16:13–17; Mark 8:27–30; Luke 9:18–20). The disciples provide several answers, including John the Baptist, Elijah, Jeremiah, or some other prophet. Jesus then asks his disciples who *they* say that he is. Peter responds that he is the Messiah (Mark 8:29; Luke 9:20) and the Son of God (Matt. 16:16). What is interesting about this interaction is that the responses to Jesus's questions attempt to place Jesus's identity within familiar categories or traditions. The crowds, according to the disciples, seem to place him among the tradition of Israel's prophets, while Peter draws from traditions regarding the Messiah and the Son of God.

This question concerning the identity of Jesus is not limited to the Gospels but is present throughout the New Testament. These writings do not always ask the question as directly as the characters in the Gospel narratives do, but they all take up this question in some way—either in the words they use to describe Jesus's actions or in the names and titles he is given. Since the New Testament is a diverse collection of writings, Jesus is not always described in the same way, but each text contributes to the question of Jesus's identity. And just like Jesus's disciples, the New Testament writers draw from familiar traditions and categories to help them articulate their understanding of Jesus. At different points in the New Testament, Jesus is presented as the Suffering Servant from Isaiah, the elusive Son of Man figure described in Daniel 7, the king-priest Melchizedek, the lamb slaughtered at Passover, and so forth. The early Christian writers turned to these traditions to shed light on the person of Jesus Christ, sometimes identifying these figures or traditions with Jesus and other times finding important points of connection between the two. What is clear is that as the writers of the New Testament formulated their answers to the question "Who is this?" they looked to various traditions of their time to help articulate their answers.

The Importance of Traditions for New Testament Christology

Christology, or the doctrine of Christ, is the name given to the theological inquiry into the identity of Jesus. Christology is defined differently depending on the theologian and the questions they are asking, but it typically concerns the "person of Christ," even though the "work of Christ" (soteriology) is intricately tied to it. Many fine theologians throughout the centuries have produced excellent articulations of Christology, either as a dedicated study or as a part of a larger systematic theology. The question of Christology was especially prominent during the patristic period as theologians attempted to fend off heretical christological movements such as Nestorianism, Arianism, and Apollinarism.[2] Yet the question of Jesus's identity remains as important today as it was for the early Christian church since "the person of Jesus Christ is of central importance to Christian theology."[3]

Christian theology upholds Scripture as a primary source for doctrine, and the doctrine of Christology must begin by asking how the New Testament portrays Jesus; any good articulation of Christology must consider the Christology *of* the New Testament. This book is an attempt to clarify the New Testament's portrayals of Jesus. We believe this is a worthy endeavor, but we also hope that this study might serve as a solid foundation for theological treatments of the doctrine of Christ.

There are any number of ways to go about producing a New Testament Christology, and the history of scholarship demonstrates the merits and shortcomings of the variety of approaches.[4] Some move book by book through the New Testament to emphasize each writing's unique contribution while tending to the overall portrait that emerges.[5] Others take a chronological approach, looking at what are deemed the earliest writings in an effort to situate them historically within the development of christological ideas.[6] Others take a "titles approach," which examines the titles or attributions given to Jesus by the New Testament writers in order to unpack the christological significance behind them.[7] These studies have all contributed in valuable ways, but each brings its own difficulties. A book-by-book approach can sometimes lose the forest for the trees or lose sight of the cohesive ties that unite the New Testament canon on the matter of Christology. Book-by-book approaches are also sometimes redundant, as they treat the same topic on multiple occasions. The chronological or developmental approach forces one to make determinations of dating and frequently designates some writings (i.e., the earliest) as more reliable and others of less significance. The result is often an approach that overlooks how the New Testament presents itself to its readers,

---

2. See Norris, *Christological Controversy*.
3. McGrath, *Christian Theology*, 347.
4. We will not offer a history of research in this chapter, but we engage with a great deal of this scholarship throughout the book. In our conclusion we engage with some key thinkers and approaches to New Testament Christology in order to situate the contribution we hope to make.
5. Matera, *New Testament Christology*; Tuckett, *Christology and the New Testament*.
6. Dunn, *Christology in the Making*.
7. Cullmann, *Christology of the New Testament*.

not with historical development but with urgency. The titles approach can easily fall victim to imposing too much theological weight on a title, or even an individual word, and can hardly account for the full complexity of the New Testament's Christology by just focusing on christological titles. Narrative elements may be overlooked by the search for specific titles.

Our task in this book is more modest than these studies, as we are not attempting to write a fulsome New Testament Christology. We believe that just as articulations of Christology must start with the New Testament, those attempting a New Testament Christology must also understand the religious and cultural traditions behind the early Christians' portraits of Jesus. In this book we ask the question of what traditions or previous cultural thought the New Testament writers drew from as they attempted to address the question of Jesus's identity. Since the earliest Jesus movement was a Jewish movement and the New Testament writings are essentially early Jewish writings, we frequently turn to the Old Testament and other Jewish literature to inform our understanding of how these writers portray and understand Jesus. Equally important is the fact that Christianity developed within a Hellenistic culture and under Roman rule. The New Testament is written in Greek with many of its original recipients being gentile converts living in Greek cities throughout the Roman Empire. The New Testament writers frequently turned to Greco-Roman ideas, in addition to Jewish ones, to help convey their understanding of the person of Jesus.

We have identified eleven key traditions that the New Testament writers incorporate into their presentations of Jesus. Most of these are also "titles" that are given to Jesus in the New Testament, including Son of Man, high priest, Lord, and others. Some, such as the Suffering Servant and Passover Lamb, do not function as titles like the others do, but they nonetheless identify Jesus with a specific tradition or theological concept. For each tradition, we examine the relevant Jewish and/or Greco-Roman uses of the concept to better understand how the New Testament writers are applying it to Jesus. As will become clear, these traditions are often complex, sometimes with several different views or interpretations coexisting even within the same time period or individual thinker. We do not wish to see them as a disjunction but as a complex interplay of factors that coincided within the ancient world out of which the New Testament emerged. After this initial investigation, we turn to the New Testament's engagement with the tradition or title to better understand its use. Not surprisingly, it is frequently the case that these traditions are used or understood differently by the different biblical authors depending on the context in which they appear. We attempt to identify this complexity while also describing lines of cohesion in the uses of these traditions in the entire New Testament canon. We end each chapter with a brief articulation of the contribution that each tradition makes to the larger Christology of the New Testament.

To appreciate the full christological complexity of the New Testament, readers will have to go beyond the traditions presented here, but they must not neglect them. Since our approach overlaps with the "titles approach" that was prominent in the twentieth century through scholars such as Vincent Taylor, Oscar Cullmann, and Ferdinand Hahn,[8] it is also susceptible to the shortcomings of such an orientation.[9] We will address some of those concerns below, but here we wish to situate our study as a contribution to New Testament Christology and not as a Christology itself. Readers wishing to move beyond the groundwork that we provide here would be wise to take into account the multifaceted ways that the New Testament expresses its Christology. This would include, as David Capes has identified, "messianic exegesis, patterns of nontitular language, patterns of behavior, historical studies, and various narrative strategies."[10]

The Contribution of This Study

We acknowledge the difficulty in writing a book like this one given the abundance of scholarly work and the variety of opinions on New Testament Christology. With this in mind, we wish to highlight some features of this book that will help situate it within the larger study of Christology while also narrowing our focus and stated aims. We will first identify key features of our study to set some parameters on our endeavor. Then some specific caveats will be raised to bring further clarity to our task and help to avoid the pitfalls of previous studies.

First, this book is written to serve as an introductory textbook in New Testament Christology. Both of us teach in Christian higher education, and we have kept our students as the primary readership for this book. We assume that our readers have some familiarity with the New Testament but may not be familiar with the traditions that we explore in this volume. That being the case, we have chosen to keep our discussions at a level that someone new to the field can benefit from. Each chapter engages with centuries of scholarly discussion, and it is easy to get bogged down in debate and

---

8. V. Taylor, *Names of Jesus*; Cullmann, *Christology of the New Testament*; Hahn, *Titles of Jesus in Christology*. See the engagement with these and other studies in Marshall, *Origins of New Testament Christology*, 11–31.

9. See the discussion in Tuckett, *Christology and the New Testament*, 10–11.

10. Capes, "New Testament Christology," 163.

secondary literature. We have attempted to point interested readers to these discussions in the footnotes. The inclusion of sidebars hopefully contributes to the accessibility of the material and allows us to focus on key passages or interpretations of the tradition under examination.

Second, this book is concerned with *New Testament* Christology and so is focused exclusively on the canon of the New Testament. While we may occasionally refer to the later christological controversies of the patristic era, we are not concerned with the development of Christology outside the New Testament. In fact, this study will spend little time attempting to document the development of christological concepts, either in the New Testament or beyond it. Instead, we approach the task from a canonical perspective. The question that lies behind our study is this: How does this collection of twenty-seven writings that we now call the New Testament draw from various traditions in order to articulate its view of the person of Jesus Christ? By adopting this canonical approach, we leave behind questions of authorship or historicity. We use the names of the writers traditionally attributed to each New Testament text (e.g., Matthew, Luke, James, Paul) without assuming actual authorship, even if good cases can be made for or against. These questions lie outside our examination of the Christology of the New Testament writings. In addition, we are concerned here not with the so-called historical Jesus but rather with how Jesus is understood within this collection of texts. This means that the question of Jesus's own self-understanding (for example, whether he viewed himself as the Messiah) often goes beyond our study, although it is impossible to ignore altogether. In short, we are concerned with how the New Testament writings—as we have them today—express the identity of Jesus.

Third, we use the language of "tradition" since we believe that it best expresses the focus of our study. The term is not easy to define, but here it refers to a belief or pattern of thought that is given meaning within a group of people, often passed down from a point of origin that is given special meaning. We believe that the eleven traditions we have identified are essential for the study of Christology. Some of these traditions are titles given to Jesus, while others function as conceptual imagery that the New Testament writers incorporate into their compositions.[11] All these traditions developed prior to and independent of the early Jesus movement and must be taken on their own terms. That is to say, we must understand the traditions in all their complexity before we ask how the New Testament writers understood and utilized them. Our goal is to preserve these traditions within their own history while at the same time highlighting how they were understood around the time of

---

11. Longenecker, *Christology of Early Jewish Christianity*, 23.

the New Testament. In this way, we wish to avoid reading into the traditions later Christian exegesis or thought.

In light of this previous point, allow us to register four caveats that will, we believe, allow us to avoid the pitfalls of previous studies of New Testament Christology. First, in addition to understanding each tradition on its own terms, we must also be careful not to imply that these traditions, especially those of ancient and early Judaism (and certainly not those of the Greco-Roman world), were on a trajectory leading toward Christ. We can appreciate how the New Testament portrays Jesus Christ as the fulfillment or culmination of a certain tradition, but we must not do so to the detriment of how that tradition was understood in its own religious and cultural context. In many cases, the New Testament does something unique with these traditions, and we will fail to appreciate how this is so if we study the traditions simply as roads that were inevitably headed toward the person of Christ. We must uphold the integrity of these traditions before we can grasp the New Testament's use of them. It is true that many traditions anticipated a coming figure that the New Testament writers identify as Jesus Christ. But we must also acknowledge that it is nearly always the case that Jesus is seen as fulfilling such anticipation in unexpected ways. It is therefore of vital importance that we first appreciate what those traditions were by the time of the first century before we understand how the New Testament incorporates them.

A second caveat concerns the relationship between a term and a concept. Since many of these traditions are connected to specific words or phrases (e.g., Savior, Lord, *Logos*), we must be careful not to conflate the term with the tradition or concept that is associated with it. Previous studies on christological titles were rightly criticized for assuming that titles carried certain ideas forward to Christ. While it is necessary for us to examine how a particular word or phrase is used in Jewish or Greco-Roman literature, this is done to better understand how a tradition was commonly expressed using specific language. One cannot assume that the use of a term in one context will mean or signify the same thing in a different context. We do not wish to commit the fallacy of assuming that a concept is imbedded in a term or phrase and that this can be simply carried over by the reproduction of that term.

Third, a limitation of a "titles approach" to New Testament Christology is that such studies have sometimes failed to account for how titles are given meaning within the narrative or argumentation within which they appear.[12] We must appreciate the contribution that studies into narrative Christology

---

12. We are grateful to the outside reader of this manuscript for pointing out this criticism of a "titles approach" to us.

have provided—especially how christological titles often function within a much larger framework created by the New Testament authors.¹³ C. Kavin Rowe, for example, argues that, through narrative development, Luke uses the term κύριος (Lord) in order to bring history and theology together and bind the identity of Jesus with the God of Israel.¹⁴ In some ways, this point is related to the previous one. We must appreciate that these traditions and titles always appear embedded within a larger narrative or argument. We have tried to account for this—especially when the larger discourse has direct bearing on our understanding of the tradition or title; we ourselves have even used such an approach in some instances (see chap. 6)—but we acknowledge that full appreciation of this dynamic lies outside the limited scope of our study. We also believe, however, that a narrative approach has limitations that mean a title-based approach still has a place. Narrative approaches, at least the most convincing ones, are usually confined to a single narrative. When one is attempting to render a full-orbed view of a particular christological title in the New Testament, a titles approach can arguably better synthesize the results of study that transcends several narratives.

Finally, the examples taken from the Gospel narratives at the beginning of this chapter point to another important aspect of our approach that we must consider: rarely are these traditions or titles applied to Jesus in isolation from other traditions. Rather, the New Testament writers commonly combine titles or traditions. For example, in the opening thanksgiving of his Letter to the Romans, Paul refers to Jesus as "Son of God," "Christ," and "Lord" (Rom. 1:4). Is this combination significant, and does it communicate a meaning for each title that would be different were the title to appear on its own? By organizing this volume using chapters dedicated to each individual tradition or title, we risk neglecting the interplay of traditions within a particular New Testament text. We attempt to address this phenomenon in our chapters but rely on others to build on our study to address this dynamic more fully.

Moving Forward

Like the many characters who engage or hear about Jesus in the Gospels, the New Testament writers were concerned with the question "Who is this?" One important way that they answered this question was by reexamining and reinterpreting various religious and cultural traditions in light of the person

---

13. See Malbon, *Mark's Jesus*.
14. C. Rowe, *Early Narrative Christology*. See also Henrichs-Tarasenkova, *Luke's Christology of Divine Identity*.

of Christ. The study of these traditions, frequently encapsulated as titles for Jesus, offers important evidence for an appreciation of the Christology of the New Testament. While this type of approach has fallen out of vogue in recent decades, we hope to reestablish the foundational contribution that the examination of traditions—and, yes, christological titles—offers for the study of the New Testament. It is our hope that readers will come to a greater appreciation of the traditions that are so powerfully interpreted in light of Jesus Christ by the New Testament writers. The contribution that this makes toward an understanding of the Christology of the New Testament is of great significance. We hope that this book will serve as a springboard for further study of how the New Testament understands and communicates its Christology.

CHAPTER I

JESUS THE LORD

Introduction

In Matthew 10, Jesus offers aphoristic advice to his disciples as they go out on his behalf. One of the statements he makes is that "a disciple is not above the teacher, nor a slave above the lord" (Matt. 10:24 [NRSV altered]). In Matthew 8:5, a centurion comes to Jesus as he enters Capernaum. The centurion says, "Lord, my servant is lying at home paralyzed, in terrible distress." After Jesus responds that he is willing to come and heal the servant, the centurion states, "Lord, I am not worthy to have you come under my roof." In Matthew 7:21–23, as part of the Sermon on the Mount, Jesus speaks to his audience—including his disciples but probably also a large crowd around him—about the characteristics of discipleship. He says, "Not everyone who says to me, 'Lord, Lord,' will enter the kingdom of heaven." Finally, in Matthew 1:20, an "angel of the Lord" appears to Joseph and tells him to take Mary as his wife.

These four examples provide a range of understandings of κύριος, the Greek word often translated "lord" in the New Testament. We selected all of them from the Gospel of Matthew because Matthew's Gospel provides an example of some of the confusion this terminology can engender. In the first example, Jesus's statement uses the word translated "lord" apparently to refer to a master in relationship to a servant (the NIV in fact translates κύριος as "master" rather than "lord"). In such an instance, κύριος has the sense of someone who has a place of authority or status above another. The example of the centurion is more difficult. The centurion comes to Jesus because he knows something about Jesus as a healer, and he asks Jesus to heal his paralyzed servant. At first sight, we might wish to think that the centurion is attributing more than just respect to Jesus—that he is recognizing Jesus as possibly a divine healer. However, in explaining his reticence to have Jesus visit his home, the centurion explains that, although he has a servant and soldiers under him, he is not just a person of authority (a lord) who is able to give orders but also a person under authority. In this instance, it is more difficult to know the sense in which the centurion uses the term translated "lord." In the example in Matthew 7, Jesus is speaking about disciples and their characteristics. He notes that not all of those who might claim to be his followers—that is, those who call him "Lord"—will be recognized by him. Although the sense of respecting one of authority is evident in this passage, the question is how much more may be indicated by those disciples who call out "Lord, Lord." That is, do they mean "master, master" or something more, such as "God, God"? The final example, with a sense repeated in several ways at the beginning of Matthew's Gospel (e.g., Matt. 1:22, 24; 2:13, 15, 19; 3:3; 4:7, 10; 5:33), indicates that the "Lord" here is the God of the Old Testament, who possesses divine qualities. He is the one who sends angels and speaks through prophets—the object of worship who is depicted as being above temptation.

Many studies of "Lord" in the New Testament frame the issue in relation to the word κύριος having two primary senses: the first one is that of human preeminence, such as a position of authority; and the second is as a title of Jesus that attributes to him the characteristics of the divine being. We do not doubt that the Greek term is used to indicate humans who are worthy of respect (whether positional or earned) or that it is used to refer to Jesus by appropriating language used elsewhere in the Jewish Scriptures for God and hence to attribute to Jesus divine characteristics. However, these are not two opposed senses.[1] This is a case of semantic expansion, whereby a term used for a person due respect is then expanded to encompass one who is due ultimate respect because of the attribution of divine qualities. Thus, κύριος has one sense, even if that sense is applied in different ways depending on the context. The examples above illustrate some of the difficulties of making such a determination, but they also provide the kinds of contextual indicators that help us to make such distinctions on the basis of the wider context. In this chapter we will examine the use of "Lord" language in the New Testament to determine what is christologically indicated when Jesus is said to be Lord, not just as one worthy of respect but as one who is seen to be God. Before we

---

1. See C. Rowe, *Early Narrative Christology*, esp. 45–47. He uses a narrative interpretive method but begins from the same lexical starting point as many earlier studies. We believe that our approach overcomes some of the limitations of previous studies of the language of "Lord."

examine the New Testament, however, we must understand the use of "Lord" in Jewish and Greco-Roman literature.

Old Testament and Greco-Roman Use of "Lord"

"Yahweh" appears in the Old Testament roughly 6,580 times and is translated into English as "Lord." There are only a small number of exceptions to this rendering (e.g., Gen. 6:5). Although other names or titles of God in the Old Testament are sometimes rendered as "Lord" in English, they are comparatively fewer (just under 700 instances). However, what distinguishes these predominant uses is that they all refer to the God of the Old Testament, even if that God is also known by some other names. When other figures of authority are addressed (e.g., Gen. 18:3, 12), they are addressed not as Yahweh but with other terms of respect.

When the Hebrew Bible was translated into Greek, an appropriate rendering for the Hebrew name of God, Yahweh (the Tetragrammaton), had to be found. Scholars have long posited that "Yahweh" was translated as "Lord" (κύριος), thus equating the God of the Old Testament, Yahweh, with the language often used of Jesus in the New Testament. However, more recent scholarship has argued that the earliest manuscripts of the Hebrew Bible in Greek did not translate the Tetragrammaton with κύριος. It appears that in the earliest Greek texts of the Hebrew Bible, the scribes utilized the Hebrew letters YHWH to avoid making a translation.[2] It was only in the later fourth- and fifth-century CE majuscule biblical manuscripts that YHWH was consistently translated using κύριος, to the point that κύριος was said to render YHWH throughout the Septuagint.

The question that arises is when the transition from referring to God as YHWH to referring to God as Lord occurred within Jewish literature. Some have thought it impossible to conceive of such a transition occurring. Despite this, it nevertheless appears to be the case that, in the final two centuries BCE, Palestinian Jews began to think of God as Lord and translate their manuscripts accordingly. There are many possible reasons for this and many theories as well. It is unlikely that the use of "Lord" for God was simply on the basis of translational equivalence, since the Hebrew אֲדֹנָי (Adonai), which might have been the natural equivalent of κύριος, is not consistently rendered with κύριος. However, "Adonai" was used in Hebrew worship for God, so

---

2. E.g., P.Fuad. 266 and 8HevXIIgr (Greek Scroll of the Minor Prophets), the first from Egypt and the second from Palestine. See Fitzmyer, "κύριος," 2:328–31, esp. 330, who is used in this section.

this may have contributed to it.³ The explanation is probably more complex, involving larger cultural issues. This conception of God as Lord, however, is found in a number of manuscripts of the period—both Aramaic and Hebrew.⁴

More surprising is that the same phenomenon of God being thought of as Lord (κύριος) is also evident in several Greek-writing Jewish authors. These examples include Josephus, *Jewish Antiquities* 20.90; 13.68 (quotation of Isa. 19:19); *Testament of Levi* 18.2; and *1 Enoch* 10.9. As Joseph Fitzmyer points out, these latter examples do not necessarily prove when YHWH was finally translated as κύριος—although we might note that Paul's use of κύριος when citing some Old Testament passages confirms that by the first century the practice was apparently widespread. These examples do show, however, that since they eventually translate YHWH as κύριος, there must have been a time when the rendering became relatively fixed. This practice seems to have originated in instances in which God is referred to with κύριος and then was extended to the point of becoming a firm and almost invariable tradition among Greek manuscripts of the Bible.⁵

This brief recounting of the development of reference to God as Lord is related to Wilhelm Bousset's belief that early Christianity was a Lord-cult, or a community that came to revere Jesus as Lord, not unlike other pagan groups who divinized various figures.⁶ Bousset argues that there was no precedent for this kind of thought within Judaism and that this exalted view of Jesus as Lord came about through the influence of the Septuagint and Hellenistic Christianity. Instead of looking to the Old Testament for the foundation of the Lord-cult, therefore, Bousset looks to Hellenistic influence. For him, this includes especially the Eastern ruler cults and the various mystery religions and cults. Bousset must admit that an important text such as the Rosetta Stone does not refer to "absolute κύριος,"⁷ but it does still use the designation κύριου βασιλείων (*OGIS* 90.1), "lord of crowns." However, he does cite several other inscriptions from Hellenistic and later Roman times that use "Lord," many of them from Adolf Deissmann's *Light from the Ancient East*.⁸ These include (we have added additional references):

---

3. This is the explanation found in Cullmann, *Christology of the New Testament*, 200–201. Cf. Moule, *Origin of Christology*, 36–41.

4. Aramaic manuscripts include 11QtgJob 24.6–7; 1QapGen 20.12–13; 4QEnᵇ 1, iv.5; Hebrew manuscript: 11QPsᵃ 28.7–8.

5. Fitzmyer, "κύριος," 2:330.

6. Bousset, *Kyrios Christos*, esp. 119–52.

7. Bousset, *Kyrios Christos*, 140. Bousset defines this as use of κύριος without genitive modifiers.

8. For references, see Bousset, *Kyrios Christos*, 140–41; Deissmann, *Light from the Ancient East*, esp. 349–57 but also cross-references (whose translations tend to be followed); Evans,

> **ONIAS'S PLEA TO KING PTOLEMY PHILOMETOR**
>
> This passage in Josephus is significant because it shows that κύριος was used in reference to Yahweh in the first century. The quotation from Isaiah 19:19 demonstrates that κύριος was an adequate translation for "Yahweh" in the Greek language.
>
> > I desire, therefore, that you will grant me leave to purge this holy place, which belongs to no master, and is fallen down, and to build there a temple to Almighty God, after the pattern of that in Jerusalem, and of the same dimensions, that may be for the benefit of thyself, and thy wife and children, that those Jews who dwell in Egypt may have a place whither they may come and meet together in mutual harmony one with another, and be subservient to thy advantages; for the prophet Isaiah foretold, that "there should be an altar in Egypt to the **Lord God** [κυρίῳ τῷ θεῷ]:" and many other such things did he prophesy relating to that place.[a]
>
> a. Josephus, *Jewish Antiquities* 13.67–68. Translation from Whiston, *Works of Flavius Josephus*, 339.

- an inscription from 62 BCE referring to Ptolemy XIII as τοῦ κυρίου βασιλέος θεοῦ ("lord king god")[9]
- an inscription from 52 BCE that refers to Alexandria Ptolemy and Cleopatra as τοῖς κυρίοις θεοῖς μεγίστοις ("the lords the greatest gods")[10]
- an inscription from 13 BCE that refers to both τὴν κυρίαν βασίλισσαν and κύριος Ἑρμῆς ("the lady queen" and "lord Hermes")[11]
- a papyrus referring to Augustus regarding sacrifices ὑπὲρ τοῦ θεοῦ κυρίου Αὐτοκράτορος ("for the god and lord Emperor")[12]
- inscriptions referring to the various Herods as lord[13]
- a Syrian inscription referring to Tiberius and Livia as τῶν κυρίων Σεβαστῶν ("the lords Augusti")[14]

Mark 8:27–16:20, lxxxii–lxxxiii; and Fantin, *Lord of the Entire World*, esp. 192–204 (cf. 77–148 on the imperial cult).
9. *OGIS* 186.8.
10. Wilamowitz-Moellendorff, "Alexandrinische Inschriften," 1096.
11. Wilcken and Mitteis, *Grundzüge und Chrestomathie*, 1.2, no. 4, p. 11.
12. P.Oxy. 1143.4.
13. *OGIS* 415, 418, 423, 425, 426.
14. *OGIS* 606.

- Claudius (41–54 CE) being referred to on a papyrus from 49 CE as Τιβερίου Κλαυδίου Καίσαρος τοῦ κυρίου ("Tiberius Claudius Caesar the lord")[15] and on different ostraca as Τιβέριος Κλαύδιος Καῖσαρ Σεβαστὸς αὐτοκράτωρ ὁ κύριος ("Tiberius Claudius Caesar Augustus Emperor the lord")[16] and ὁ κύριος ("the lord")[17]
- Nero (54–68 CE) being referred to in multiple papyri and ostraca as Νέρων ὁ κύριος ("Nero the lord"),[18] Νέρων κύριος ("Nero lord"),[19] Νέρων Καῖσαρ ὁ κύριος ("Nero Caesar the lord"),[20] ὁ τοῦ παντὸς κόσμου κύριος Νέρων ("Nero lord of the entire world"),[21] and τοῦ κυρίου Σεβαστοῦ [Νέρωνος] ("the lord Augustus [Nero]")[22]

Acts even refers to Nero as "lord" (Acts 25:26). Josephus says that Jewish martyrs were killed because of their failure to call Caesar "lord" (*J.W.* 7.418–19). There are later references as well, including to "lord" Serapis[23] and to the emperor as "lord."[24]

This evidence may be interpreted in several ways. Bousset sees it as indicating that Christianity was a Lord-cult—that is, that it adopted the use of "Lord" for Jesus Christ on the basis of the parallel usage in the Hellenistic literature. There is no doubt that "Lord" language was used for figures of importance, including divine beings and rulers such as emperors, within the ancient Mediterranean world around the first century. Not all of it was the titular usage that Bousset seeks in order to make his point, as some of it seems more honorific and respectful than titular. However, Deissmann, who marshals much of the evidence relied on by Bousset and who himself was very much interested in the history of religion, has a different interpretation of the data.[25] Deissmann sees the evidence as, at best, incomplete and fragmentary. He notes the significant increase in the use of "Lord" language with Nero. He attributes this to the fact that Nero was proclaimed lord of the city of Alexandria when he became emperor. Further, Deissmann reminds us that

15. P.Oxy. 37.6.
16. Wilcken, *Griechische Ostraka*, 268 (no. 1038).
17. O.Petr. 209.
18. P.Lond. 1215; P.Oxy. 246.30; Wilcken, *Griechische Ostraka*, 268 (no. 1038); P.Meyer II.22.2–3; 23.3–4; 24.2–3; 25.2–3; 36a.3; 37.3–4; 76.4–5.
19. P.Meyer II.39.4.
20. O.Petr. 288; P.Oxy. 246.36–37.
21. *SIG*³ 814.31.
22. *SIG*³ 814.55.
23. P.Oxy. 110.2–3; BGU 423.6.
24. *Martyrdom of Polycarp* 8.2; P.Oxy. 1439; SB 1927; Wilcken, *Griechische Ostraka*, 126 (no. 439); 153 (no. 563).
25. See Deissmann, *Light from the Ancient East*, 352–53, 365.

much of the evidence for the Lord-cult originated in Egypt, where close contact between Semitic and Egyptian culture already coincided, to the point that he sees similar developments as "another instance of the parallelism already insisted on between Egyptian and Palestinian culture."[26] This accounts for why "Lord" language was integrated into the Greek translation of the Hebrew Bible in Egypt. Deissmann believes, therefore, that it is "in accordance with Egyptian or Egypto-Semitic custom that in numerous Greek papyri, inscriptions, and ostraca of the earliest Imperial period the title 'lord' is attached also to the Caesars by Egyptians and Syrians."[27] Paul had, therefore, written his letters by the time the Lord/emperor cult had strongly emerged in the Roman world in 54 CE with the investiture of Nero. Deissmann goes so far as to see Paul using the language of "Lord" as a protest against the language used of the emperor and others in positions of authority, especially the emperor.

Deissmann provides a much more satisfactory explanation of the emergence of exalted "Lord" language than Bousset. "Lord" language in the New Testament appears to be interconnected with its development within the Greco-Roman world but is probably best seen as originating with later Septuagint influence dependent upon a mix of Semitic and Egyptian factors. Rather than Christianity being a Hellenistic Lord-cult, dependent upon so-called oriental thought (as Bousset imagines),[28] Christianity, if it can be said to be a Lord-cult (and the attribution is doubtful), came to use the language of "Lord" for Jesus Christ on the basis of emerging septuagintal and biblical tradition that captured what the New Testament authors wished to say about who they believed Jesus Christ to be—the Lord God.

Κύριος in the New Testament

The use of κύριος occurs throughout the New Testament. This is not surprising in light of what we have already discussed regarding the range of usage of this term. This has been one of the most important terms in the development of New Testament Christology. Not only is the usage widespread, but it also has nuances within the various subcorpora of the New Testament that merit further differentiation. As a result, we divide this section into three parts: the Gospels and Acts; Paul and his letters; and Hebrews, the General Epistles, and Revelation.

---

26. Deissmann, *Light from the Ancient East*, 353.
27. Deissmann, *Light from the Ancient East*, 353; cf. 365n2.
28. One cannot help but wonder how much Bousset and others were influenced by stereotypes of the "Orient," what we would now call the ancient Near East. The reaction to such colonialist tendencies was led by Said, *Orientalism*.

The Gospels and Acts

There are many instances in the Gospels and in Acts in which "lord" is used simply as a term of respect for one who is held in high esteem. Jesus is so regarded by a wide variety of people and even addressed as κύριος by his disciples,[29] including Peter.[30] Many of these instances, as Bousset rightly points out, are in the vocative, an appropriate use of the term for address. They probably should not figure largely in estimating the christological implications of the use of κύριος.[31] The major question is whether there are places in which κύριος, in reference to Jesus, is more than simply a term of respect for a teacher and religious figure, even a miracle worker. The problem has to do with how one goes about showing this without presuming the conclusion. Much study of "Lord/lord" in the Gospels has employed a prior understanding based on other New Testament authors (especially Paul) and later church writers to interpret Gospel uses. One proposed way forward is to examine citations of the Old Testament in which, in the original context, reference is made to God but in which in the New Testament context the reference is to Jesus. We already know that κύριος is understood as a reference to God in the Gospels. Matthew 1:20, 24 and 2:13, 19 and Luke 1:11 and 2:9 contain references to the "angel of the Lord," invoking that enigmatic figure in the Old Testament who is God's emissary (e.g., Exod. 3:2). There are other references to entities that originate with God by use of the term κύριος, such as Scripture (Matt. 1:22; 2:15), name (Matt. 21:9; Acts 2:21), commandments (Luke 1:6), temple (Luke 1:9), law (Luke 2:24, 39), and day (Acts 2:20). There is also the phrase "Lord God,"[32] or parallelism that makes clear that the Lord is God (e.g., Luke 1:46–47, 68). The question is whether Jesus is ever viewed in this way in the Gospels.

Several instances of κύριος in the Gospels, including some of the examples that Bousset attempts arbitrarily to dismiss, do indicate Jesus as God. Only one instance, however, is clearly taken from an Old Testament passage that refers to God. This provides a good starting point for discussion. In Matthew 3:3 and Luke 3:4 (cf. John 1:23), John the Baptist cites Isaiah 40:3 to describe

---

29. E.g. Matt. 8:25; 26:22; Luke 10:17; 11:1; 17:37; 22:38, 49; John 6:34; 11:12.
30. Matt. 14:28, 30; 16:22; 17:4; 18:21; Luke 5:8; 12:41; 22:33; John 6:68; 13:6, 9, 36, 37; 21:15–17, 21.
31. However, to say that they have no role to play in the discussion probably goes too far, once one is able to establish the implications of the other usage. For an example of a scholar who overreacts to the vocative, see Moule, *Origin of Christology*, 35.
32. Matt. 4:7, citing Deut. 6:16; Matt. 4:10, citing Deut. 6:13; Matt. 22:37, citing Deut. 6:5; Mark 12:29, 30, citing Deut. 6:5; Luke 1:16, 32; 4:8, citing Deut. 6:13; Luke 4:12, citing Deut. 6:16; Luke 20:37; John 20:28.

himself as one calling in the wilderness to "prepare the way of the Lord," a passage that in its original context refers to God as Lord. This is anticipated in Luke's Gospel in Luke 1:17, where Zechariah is told that his son, John, will go before the Lord. Throughout the Gospels, Jesus is the one for whom John is preparing the way, as the baptism episode makes clear. When Jesus emerges from the waters, God proclaims him as his Son, with whom he is pleased (Matt. 3:17//Mark 1:11//Luke 3:22). The references to Jesus as son continue throughout the Gospels, whether he is seen as "Son of God" (Matt. 4:3, 6; 8:29; 14:33; 17:5; 27:54; Mark 1:11; 3:11; 9:7; 15:39; Luke 1:35; 8:28; 9:35; 22:70), "son of Abraham" (Matt. 1:1, 20; Luke 19:9), or "son of David" (Matt. 1:1; 9:27; 12:23; 15:22; 20:30, 31; 21:9, 15; 22:45; Mark 10:47, 48; 12:35, 37; Luke 18:38, 39).

This pattern helps us to understand more fully what is being said in the parallel passages in Matthew 22:44//Mark 12:36//Luke 20:42 (cf. Acts 2:33–35). Jesus initiates a discussion with the Pharisees in which he asks them about whose son the Messiah is. They state that he is the "Son of David." Jesus then asks how this can be when David refers to the Messiah not as "son" but as "Lord" in Psalm 110:1: "The Lord said to my Lord, 'Sit at my right hand until I put your enemies under your feet.'" There is no reply to Jesus's question, because the statement has three potentially troubling implications. The first is that this quotation from the Psalms depicts the Lord, God in the Old Testament, saying to another Lord that he is to sit as his fellow judge while he conquers and subjects the second Lord's enemies. In other words, the second Lord is depicted as God's equal, sitting at the right hand (the place of judgment) while God exercises his divine prerogatives. The second implication is that, because the Messiah is the Son of David, and this messianic figure of the psalm is placed in the position of equality with God, the Messiah is to be seen as a divine figure. The third implication, and most important for our discussion in this chapter, is that Jesus clarifies that the Son of David is not an inferior to David (which is indicated by his messianic status as well) but is in fact Lord. What once may have been simply a form of address is now clearly a title of one equal with God—the second Lord equal with the Lord God.

This makes sense of Mark 5:19, in which Jesus heals a demon-possessed man. Jesus tells him, "Go home to your friends, and tell them how much the Lord has done for you." Mark then states in verse 20 that the man went away, telling others "how much Jesus had done for him." In this passage the statement about "what the Lord has done for you" is reminiscent of Old Testament language regarding God's provision, except that here Mark specifies that Jesus has done this. Luke makes this even more explicit in his Gospel, where Jesus tells the demon-possessed man to "declare how much God has done for you" and the man tells "how much Jesus had done for him" (Luke 8:39).

Several times in John's Gospel and Acts, Jesus is referred to by others in the narrative as Lord after the resurrection.[33] The equation is made more explicit when Jesus is referred to as the Lord Jesus.[34] The language used here, with reference to the name and word of the Lord Jesus and to being baptized into him and believing in him for salvation, is similar to the language used of God. The use of "Lord" in these contexts recognizes Jesus as Lord God because of the testimony and power of the resurrection. The postresurrection context makes it much more understandable how an Old Testament passage that uses "Lord" can be understood as referring to Jesus as Lord, meaning Jesus as the Lord God. In Acts 2:25–28, Peter says he saw the Lord, the God of the Old Testament, before him, and he is confident that God will not abandon him to the dead. This reference to Jesus's resurrection indicates that Peter understands the risen Jesus to be the Lord.

The relatively few clear statements regarding Jesus as Lord indicate that there may be other instances in the Gospels that assume that Jesus is equivalent to the God of the Old Testament. One major example has to do with events in which Jesus is addressed as Lord and depicted as performing divine actions, such as healings. In Matthew 8:5–13, Jesus heals the centurion's servant. The centurion addresses Jesus as Lord (8:6), but he does not request that Jesus come to his house because he has faith that Jesus, as Lord, can heal him from a distance. In Matthew 14:22–32, Jesus walks on the water to join the disciples in their boat. Peter wishes to walk on the water as well and asks, "Lord, if it is you, command me to come to you on the water" (14:28). However, he is not able to and sinks because he does not have enough faith, and he cries out, "Lord, save me!" (14:30). In Matthew 15:22, a Canaanite woman cries out to Jesus, "Lord, Son of David," requesting his mercy because her daughter is demon-possessed. She repeats her request—"Lord, help me" (15:25)—and is commended for her faith. In Luke 5:12–15, a leprous man approaches Jesus with the request that the Lord heal him if he is willing, and Jesus does. In Luke 9:54, the disciples ask Jesus, as Lord, whether he wants them to call down fire to destroy his opposition.

The evidence from the Gospels is not as definitive as it is in other places in the New Testament, but the use of "Lord" for Jesus is found in a variety

---

33. E.g., John 21:12, 15, 16, 17, 20, 21; Acts 1:6, 24; 7:59, 60; 9:10, 13; 22:19. Cf. Rainbow, *Johannine Theology*, 187–88, but he downplays the significance of "Lord" in John's theology because he wishes to distance John's Gospel from Hellenistic influence.

34. Acts 1:21; 7:59; 8:16; 11:17, 20; 15:11, 26; 16:31; 19:5, 13, 17; 20:24, 35; 21:13.

of contexts. This suggests that, even in those instances in which the use of κύριος does not have any clear indicators, when it is used of Jesus—whether addressed to him or used with reference to him—the honorific sense may be extended to include reference to God. What is also worth noting is that, if Bousset were correct, one would expect the Gospels, probably written later than the Pauline Letters, to have an abundance of clear references to Jesus Christ as Lord, reflecting the growth of the Lord-cult. But the opposite is the case. The Gospels appear to reflect the emerging recognition among the early followers of Jesus that he was indeed Lord, and they began to formulate this using biblical language with which they were familiar. It required someone else—Paul—to make this equation clear and pronounced in light of the power of the death and resurrection of Jesus.

Paul and His Letters

The use of κύριος in Paul's Letters offers clearer evidence of how to interpret Paul's understanding of who Jesus is as Lord. In treating Paul's references, we examine several different sets of evidence, although some of them overlap.

Words of Jesus cited by Paul make up the first body of evidence. Paul probably quotes words of Jesus in 1 Corinthians 7:10 (cf. 7:12); 9:14; possibly 11:24–25; and perhaps a few other places.[35] In all three passages in which explicit quotation is made, Paul refers not to words of Jesus but to words or commands of "the Lord." But what does "Lord" mean to Paul? In the Gospels the term "Lord/lord" may be used in a variety of ways, as we have seen, sometimes simply as a form of respectful address and sometimes in an extended way with more theological weight. But this does not seem to be a sufficient explanation in Paul's Letters, especially in quotations from Jesus, whom Paul sees as the crucified and risen Jesus—that is, the Jesus who has triumphed over death, has ascended to God, and is now worshiped and reigning in power as the Lord God (e.g., Rom. 1:24). It is hard to imagine Paul not having the more theological meaning in mind. In Paul, κύριος is consistently (though not invariably) used as a title, often in the form "Lord Jesus Christ" or a variant of it.[36]

---

35. See Wenham, *Paul*, 4. Cf. Kim, "Jesus, Sayings of," who tries to argue for more clear allusions to Jesus's words. The secondary literature on these passages is large. On 1 Cor. 7:10, see Beattie, *Women and Marriage in Paul*, 27–31.

36. Rom. 1:4, 7; 5:1, 11, 21; 6:23; 7:25; 8:39; 13:14; 15:6, 30; 16:24; 1 Cor. 1:2, 3, 7, 8, 9, 10; 6:11; 8:6; 15:31, 57; 2 Cor. 1:2, 3; 13:13; Gal. 1:3; 6:18; Eph. 1:2, 3, 17; 3:11, 14; 5:20; 6:23, 24; Phil. 1:2; 2:11; 4:23; Col. 1:3; 2:6; 1 Thess. 1:1, 3; 5:9, 23, 28; 2 Thess. 1:1, 2, 12; 2:1, 14, 16; 3:12, 18; 1 Tim. 1:2, 12; 6:3, 14; 2 Tim. 1:2; Philem. 3, 25. See Hurtado, "Lord," 560–61. This material is incorporated into his fuller treatment in Hurtado, *Lord Jesus Christ*. Besides others

By the time of the New Testament, the Old Greek manuscripts appear to have been in the process of translating "Yahweh" as "Lord" (κύριος),[37] which was also used to translate other words used for God. Paul cites several Old Testament passages with "Lord," indicating that, at least by the time Paul wrote, it was commonplace for "Yahweh" to be rendered with κύριος. Therefore, it is not surprising that Paul would interpret several Old Testament passages as referring to God that use the word "Lord" (κύριος in the Septuagint), even when the Hebrew text may not use the word "Yahweh."

These passages include the following:

- Romans 4:8, citing Psalm 32:2 (31:2 LXX): "Blessed is the one against whom the Lord will not reckon sin."
- Romans 9:28–29, citing Isaiah 28:22; 1:9: "For the Lord will execute his sentence on the earth quickly and decisively. . . . If the Lord of hosts had not left survivors to us, we would have fared like Sodom and been made like Gomorrah."
- Romans 10:16, citing Isaiah 53:1: "Lord, who has believed our message?"
- Romans 11:3, citing 1 Kings 19:1: "Lord, they have killed your prophets . . ."
- Romans 11:34, citing Isaiah 40:13: "For who has known the mind of the Lord?"
- Romans 12:19, citing Deuteronomy 32:35: "Vengeance is mine, I will repay, says the Lord."
- Romans 15:11, citing Psalm 117:1: "Praise the Lord, all you Gentiles . . ."
- 1 Corinthians 3:20, citing Psalm 94:11: "The Lord knows the thoughts of the wise, that they are futile."
- 1 Corinthians 14:21, citing Isaiah 28:11: "'By people of strange tongues and by the lips of foreigners I will speak to this people; yet even then they will not listen to me,' says the Lord."
- 2 Corinthians 6:17–18, citing Isaiah 52:11; 2 Samuel 7:14: "Come out from them, and be separate from them, says the Lord. . . . I will be your father, and you shall be my sons and daughters, says the Lord Almighty."

What is perhaps even more noteworthy and more significant for our understanding of the use of "Lord" in the New Testament, however, is that there

---

of his works cited below, see Hurtado, *At the Origins of Christian Worship*; and *How on Earth Did Jesus Become a God?*

37. See Fitzmyer, "κύριος," 2:330.

Jesus the Lord 13

are several passages in which Paul appears to apply Old Testament verses referring to Yahweh to Jesus Christ. We begin with two examples that may not be as clear as the others, though they still reflect this pattern. First, in Romans 14:11, citing Isaiah 49:18 and especially 45:23, after stating that Christ died and returned to life so that he might be the Lord of both the dead and the living (Rom. 14:9), Paul cites the Old Testament passage in a combined formulaic quotation: "As I live, says the Lord, every knee shall bow to me, and every tongue shall give praise to God." In this passage Paul understands that the Lord to whom every knee will bow is Jesus Christ, acknowledging him as God. This passage has obvious similarities with Philippians 2:6–11, in which a three-stage Christology moves from Jesus Christ having the divine nature, to incarnation, to exaltation and elevation to a place of equivalence with God. Paul states that God exalted Jesus to a place where the divine creation worships him and acknowledges that "Jesus Christ is Lord" (Phil. 2:11). This is a passage in which the evidence for "Lord" and "Christ" as a coequal with God seems entirely convincing.[38] Second, in 1 Corinthians 2:16, Paul cites Isaiah 40:13 in a direct quotation: "For who has known the mind of the Lord [i.e., God] so as to instruct him?" and he follows this by saying that "we have the mind of Christ." The parallel lines and parallel constructions in Greek (νοῦν κυρίου and νοῦν Χριστοῦ) indicate that, for Paul, the mind of the Lord—God—and the mind of Christ, who for him is the risen and exalted Christ Jesus, are the same.

Although these passages may be somewhat ambiguous, there are also several New Testament passages in which Paul clearly applies "Lord" to Jesus Christ as the one risen from the dead and reigning with God and through whom comes salvation. An early Christian confession captures this. This confession may be the earliest creedal affirmation upon which Christians drew in affirming their faith. In Romans 10:9, Paul states that if one confesses that "Jesus is Lord" and believes that God raised him from the dead, one will be saved. Then in Romans 10:13, Paul directly quotes Joel 2:32, which states, "Everyone who calls on the name of the Lord shall be saved" (cf. also 1 Cor. 1:2).[39] A similar confession is found in 1 Corinthians 12:3 but without the Old Testament quotation in support of it (cf. Phil. 2:11, mentioned above, where a slightly expanded form is found, "Jesus Christ is Lord," as part of an allusion to Isa. 45:23). In 1 Corinthians 1:31, after speaking of being in Christ Jesus, Paul cites Jeremiah 9:24 in a formulaic quotation: "Let the

---

38. For discussion, see Fewster, "Philippians 'Christ Hymn.'"
39. See Davis, *Name and Way of the Lord*, 103–40. Cf. Goppelt, *Theology of the New Testament*, 2:79–81.

one who boasts, boast in the Lord." The same quotation is used in 2 Corinthians 10:17 but without the quotation formula. In 1 Corinthians 10:26, Paul quotes Psalm 24:1 and applies it to Christ: "The earth and its fullness are the Lord's." And in 2 Timothy 2:19, Paul first cites Numbers 16:5 in a direct quotation and then paraphrases one or more Old Testament passages (e.g., Num. 16:26; Isa. 26:13; 52:11; Ps. 6:8), stating, "The Lord knows those who are his" and "Let everyone who calls on the name of the Lord turn away from wickedness."[40]

In several instances, Paul also probably alludes to Old Testament passages that use "Lord" to refer to God in the original context but that refer to Jesus Christ in the Pauline context. These passages include the following:[41]

- 1 Corinthians 10:21, alluding to Malachi 1:7, 12, with reference to the Lord's table
- 1 Corinthians 10:22, alluding to Deuteronomy 32:21, with reference to the Lord's jealousy
- 2 Corinthians 3:16, alluding to Exodus 34:34, with reference to Moses's veil and turning to the Lord or being in the Lord's presence
- 1 Thessalonians 3:13, alluding to Zechariah 14:5, with reference to the coming of the Lord
- 1 Thessalonians 4:6, alluding to Psalm 94:2, with reference to the Lord punishing those who take advantage
- 2 Thessalonians 1:7–8, alluding to Isaiah 66:15, with reference to the coming of the Lord with fire and accompanied by his angels
- 2 Thessalonians 1:9, alluding to Isaiah 2:10, 19, 21, with reference to exclusion from the "presence of the Lord"
- 2 Thessalonians 1:12, alluding to Isaiah 66:5, with reference to the glorification of the Lord

We do not wish to say that Paul conflates Jesus Christ with God so that he simply equates the two in an uncritical or unreflective way. However, it is

---

40. For discussion of the above passages in detail, see Capes, *Old Testament Yahweh Texts in Paul's Christology*, esp. 115–49; and now Capes, *Divine Christ*, esp. 111–50. Cf. Wright, *Paul and the Faithfulness of God*, 701–6. A similar approach but often with different results is found in Bates, *Hermeneutics of the Apostolic Proclamation*, who uses what he terms "prosopological exegesis."

41. See Hurtado, "Lord," 563, for discussion of most of the following passages and a response to Capes (564). Capes's case may have been helped, however, by publications from Cave 4 at Qumran, in which there appear to be places where human and divine figures are interchanged. See, e.g., 4Q521 and the discussion in Evans, *Jesus and His Contemporaries*, 127–29.

certainly true that, for Paul, there is the sense of a close relationship between these two figures as reflected in the terms used of them—if not in essence or ontology, then at least in function.[42] It probably represents what Larry Kreitzer calls "conceptual overlap between Christ and God."[43] In that sense, images and actions of Jesus Christ are, for Paul, also in some ways images and actions of God, to the point that he often depicts Jesus Christ using the biblical imagery of the God of the Old Testament.

This same pattern is found in another kind of imagery. One of the commonplace images of Jewish apocalyptic is the intervention of God in history. It has been increasingly recognized in Pauline studies that Paul was an apocalyptic thinker[44] and that he anticipated the wrath of God (Rom. 1:18; 2:5; 3:5; 5:9; Eph. 5:6; Col. 3:6; 1 Thess. 1:10) and God's retributive judgment upon sin in the last day—that is, the day of the Lord.[45] The Aramaic expression *maranatha* (1 Cor. 16:22), translated "The Lord comes," is probably part of this apocalyptic orientation, in which the Lord is invoked to come and bring his judgment and salvation.[46] Paul shares the eschatological framework of the Old Testament, except that there is what Kreitzer calls a "referential shift"[47] from "Lord" referring to God to its referring to Jesus Christ in a number of apocalyptic judgment passages. Besides Romans 10:13 (see above), several passages utilize Old Testament citations to speak of the return of Christ. Some of these passages worth noting are:

- Philippians 2:10–11, invoking Isaiah 45:23 (cf. Isa. 51–52): "so that at the name of Jesus every knee should bend, in heaven and on earth and under the earth, and every tongue should confess that Jesus Christ is Lord," whereas Isaiah 45:23 says that every knee will bow "to me," the God of the Old Testament
- 1 Thessalonians 3:13, invoking Zechariah 14:5: "at the coming of our Lord Jesus with all his saints"

---

42. See Hurtado, *One God, One Lord*, esp. 93–124. Cf. Tilling, *Paul's Divine Christology*, who emphasizes the relational dimension in Pauline Christology, in the sense that the relationship that Jesus Christ has with believers is similar to that of Yahweh with Israel.

43. Kreitzer, *Jesus and God in Paul's Eschatology*, 116.

44. For a survey of work, see de Boer, *Defeat of Death*, 21–37. There is a long tradition of this type of interpretation. See, e.g., Schweitzer, *Mysticism of Paul the Apostle*. For a popular recent treatment, see Pate, *Apostle of the Last Days*.

45. See Morris, *Apostolic Preaching of the Cross*, 179–84, for a survey of the issues.

46. See Cullmann, *Christology of the New Testament*, 209; cf. 209–14. Contra Bousset, *Kyrios Christos*, 126–27.

47. Kreitzer, *Jesus and God in Paul's Eschatology*, 113.

- 1 Thessalonians 5:8, invoking Isaiah 59:17: "Put on the breastplate of faith and love, and for a helmet the hope of salvation" at the time of the day of the Lord (1 Thess. 5:1)
- 2 Thessalonians 1:6–12, invoking Isaiah 66:4–6, 15: the day of the Lord

By way of illustration, in 2 Thessalonians 1:6–12, alluding to Isaiah 66:4–6 and 15 (and possibly other passages), Paul speaks of the Lord Jesus being revealed from heaven in blazing fire and with his powerful angels, punishing those who do not know God and obey the gospel with everlasting destruction.[48] As Kreitzer says, "It appears clear that for Paul, the fact that christology and eschatology are so closely linked is what determines his use of 'Day of the Lord' texts from the Old Testament as a means of expressing his understanding of the Christian faith. For Paul, the Day of the Lord Yahweh has become the Day of the Lord Jesus Christ."[49]

Hebrews, the General Epistles, and Revelation

Hebrews, the General Epistles, and Revelation develop similar patterns that we have observed above in their referring to Jesus Christ as Lord. These postresurrection works use "Lord" to speak of Jesus Christ as God, but they also use "Lord" for the God of the Old Testament. Sometimes it is hard to differentiate them. Nevertheless, at several significant places, these books indicate that Jesus is Lord—an affirmation of his divinity. These authors who use "Lord" for Jesus Christ see him as Lord in the same way that the God of the Old Testament is Lord.

Hebrews is an example of the potential ambiguity of the meaning of "Lord" because of its direct use of Old Testament imagery and institutions. As a result, some instances of "Lord" refer to the God of the Old Testament and some refer to Jesus Christ. In Hebrews, most of the passages in which the Greek word κύριος is used are quotations from the Old Testament. The author sometimes cites the passage with reference to the Old Testament context, although some of the passages are ambiguous regarding "Lord." However, in several of them, the Lord of the Old Testament, Yahweh, becomes the Lord Jesus Christ, which is sufficient to affirm that the author of Hebrews sees Jesus Christ as divine.

There is one example in Hebrews in which an Old Testament quotation applies the title "Lord" to Jesus. In Hebrews 1:10 the words of Psalm 102:6 are placed on the lips of God the Father as he speaks to the Son (see Heb.

---

48. See Kreitzer, *Jesus and God in Paul's Eschatology*, 113–28.
49. Kreitzer, *Jesus and God in Paul's Eschatology*, 129.

1:8)—"In the beginning, Lord, you founded the earth"—thereby attributing divine creative attributes to Jesus Christ.[50] In 2:3, Hebrews uses the title "Lord" for Jesus when discussing the salvation announced by the Lord—a reference to Jesus's gospel proclamation.[51] In 7:14, the author addresses the issue of Jesus's lineage: "For it is evident that our Lord was descended from Judah." In the benediction, the author writes, "Now may the God of peace, who brought back from the dead our Lord Jesus, the great shepherd of the sheep, by the blood of the eternal covenant, make you complete in everything good so that you may do his will" (13:20–21a).

James refers to the Lord Jesus Christ at the beginning of the letter (James 1:1; 2:1), and to his coming (5:7, 8), but he also refers to God as Lord (e.g., 3:9; 4:10; 5:4, 10, 11). The result is that there are several ambiguous passages regarding who is Lord (1:7; 4:15). In some ways, James reflects a similar ambiguity as is often found in the Gospels, apart from the fact that it was written in and reflects a postresurrection context of divine exaltation of Jesus and affirms Jesus's resurrection lordship in its use of the full name Lord Jesus Christ at the outset of the letter and later.

The Petrine Letters evidence different ways of treating references to "Lord." First Peter refers to the Lord Jesus Christ (1 Pet. 1:3). However, in 1 Peter, most of the instances occur in Old Testament quotations. Several of these refer to the God of the Old Testament (e.g., 1:25; 3:12), but two clearly appropriate them to refer to Jesus Christ. The first is 1 Peter 2:3, in which the author invokes Psalm 34:8, regarding tasting the Lord and finding him good. The second is 1 Peter 3:15, invoking Isaiah 8:13, which encourages the recipients to "sanctify Christ as Lord."

Second Peter, by contrast, does not contain any Old Testament citations, whether quotations or allusions, that use "Lord." However, there are numerous references to Jesus as Lord (2 Pet. 1:2), or to the Lord Jesus Christ (1:8, 11, 14, 16; 2:20; 3:18), or to the Lord and Savior, indicating Jesus (3:2). There are also some instances in which "Lord" is probably applied to God (2:9, 11; 3:8, 9), although these may be ambiguous. Finally, the book refers to the "day of the Lord," probably understood here as the day of Christ's coming in divine glory (3:10). Jude contains some clear instances of "Lord" in reference to Jesus Christ (e.g., Jude 17, 21, 25) and some that appear to refer to the God of the Old Testament (e.g., Jude 4, 5, 9, 14).

---

50. See Cullmann, *Christology of the New Testament*, 234, who believes that this passage is not given sufficient recognition in christological discussions: "The writer of Hebrews does not hesitate to address [Jesus] with the words of the psalm, and thus to designate him the Creator of heaven and earth." See also Jamieson, *Paradox of Sonship*, 59–66.

51. Attridge, *Hebrews*, 66.

Finally, the book of Revelation, by using the language of "Lord God" or its equivalent, makes clear that in some instances the Lord is seen as the God of the Old Testament (e.g., Rev. 1:8; 4:8, 11; 11:17; 15:3; 16:7; 18:8; 19:6; 21:22; 22:5, 6, 20), but it does have one reference to the Lord Jesus (22:21). There are probably a few other references to the God of the Old Testament (e.g., 11:4, 15; 15:4). Reference to the God of the Old Testament constitutes most of the instances in the book. Jesus, however, is also designated as the Lord of lords and King of kings (17:14; 19:16), appropriating Old Testament language for God (e.g., Deut. 10:17; Dan. 2:47). Revelation 11:8 refers to the place where the Lord was crucified and to those who died in the Lord (14:13). There is also one instance of a form of respect (7:14). Revelation, despite being written relatively late, refers much more frequently to God as Lord than it does to Jesus as Lord,[52] although it also equates Jesus with the Lord of lords, with Jesus seen as the God of the Old Testament.

Passages that use the term "Lord" in Hebrews, the General Epistles, and Revelation include a mix of references to Jesus Christ and to the God of the Old Testament. Whereas some of these references are ambiguous, one of the results of this intermingling of terminology is the recognition that for these authors to say that God is Lord and that Jesus is Lord is to say that Jesus is God. This is supported by several key examples in these books that make such an equation clear.

Contribution to New Testament Christology

Three times in his letters the apostle Paul identifies a basic confession of the early Christian movement as "Jesus is κύριος" (Rom. 10:9; 1 Cor. 12:3; Phil. 2:11 states "Jesus Christ is Lord"). Early Christians, so it would seem, could distill their confession of faith down to one simple yet extraordinarily profound statement. The discussion of what is meant by declaring that Jesus Christ is Lord was an important one in the early church and continues to be so to this day. However, if we examine the New Testament passages in which "Lord" is found, we see a variety of uses, some of them simply honorific and some of them much more exalted. As we have shown in this chapter, the uses of κύριος in contexts such as the verses cited above—and many others in the New Testament—move beyond an honorific title toward a declaration of the divinity of Jesus. Among the many contributions that the New Testament's use of κύριος makes to Christology, we wish to highlight three: the connection of Jesus to the God of the Old Testament, the implication

---

52. See Rainbow, *Johannine Theology*, 188.

regarding earthly powers and authorities, and the content and extent of the lordship of Jesus.

In the New Testament, we can see that the affirmation that Jesus is Lord means much more than simply that he is one to be respected. Of course Jesus is to be respected, but this is because he is exercising the divine prerogatives of the God of the Old Testament. This occurs to the point that what is said about the God of the Old Testament can be said of Jesus Christ in the New Testament. The biblical authors cite passages in the Old Testament that refer to the Lord God acting, but they indicate that they believe that Jesus Christ is that figure in his own actions and even person.[53] The connection of Jesus to God is therefore made implicitly by applying the title κύριος to Jesus in contexts in which it had previously been applied to God.

This divine status is reinforced by the combination of other titles or traditions with κύριος, especially when the New Testament authors combine κύριος with another designation of divinity, such as "Son of God" or "God." Paul, for instance, writes that "Jesus Christ our Lord" was "declared to be Son of God" (Rom. 1:4). During an exchange with Martha in John's Gospel, Jesus is declared "Lord," "Messiah," and "the Son of God" (John 11:27). In Luke 2:11, an angel of the Lord (a clear reference to God; 2:9) announces Jesus as "Savior," "Messiah," and "Lord." Significant also is the account of Jesus's postresurrection appearance to Thomas in John 20:24–29. When in verse 28 Thomas is confronted with the resurrected Christ, he declares, "My Lord and my God!" (ὁ κύριός μου καὶ ὁ θεός μου).

Another important contribution of the title "Lord" to Christology is what it communicates about Jesus's status above any earthly rule or power. We noted that κύριος was often used of Roman rulers, especially of Emperor Nero but also of Claudius, Augustus, and others. There has been a great deal of attention paid in recent years to the influence of the Roman imperial cult on the composition of the New Testament, including multiple studies on anti-imperial rhetoric in various New Testament texts.[54] Understood within this

---

53. Many scholars recognize that one must be careful formulating the relationship of Jesus to the God of the Old Testament. The terminological shift regarding κύριος pushes toward substitution, in which Jesus becomes the God of the Old Testament. There is a sense in which this is what some of the New Testament writers seem to indicate on occasion. However, they also do so within the larger context of recognition of the God of the Old Testament. Hence, we have formulated the language in terms of Jesus as equivalent to the God of the Old Testament, without sacrificing either his or God's individual personhood. See Cullmann, *Christology of the New Testament*, 236; Fitzmyer, "κύριος," 2:330; Capes, *Divine Christ*, 1–45.

54. For an overview and sampling of recent scholarship, see the essays in McKnight and Modica, *Jesus Is Lord, Caesar Is Not*; Porter and Westfall, *Empire in the New Testament*; and especially Fantin, *Lord of the Entire World*.

> ### IGNATIUS TO THE SMYRNAEANS (EARLY 2ND CENTURY CE)
>
> This early Christian epistle, likely written just prior to Ignatius's martyrdom in the early second century, demonstrates how the designation "Lord" was applied to Jesus in combination with other christological titles to convey both his humanity and his divinity.
>
>> I glorify Jesus Christ, the God who made you so wise, for I observed that you are established in an unshakable faith, having been nailed, as it were, to the cross of **the Lord Jesus Christ** in both body and spirit, and firmly established in love by the blood of Christ, totally convinced with regard to **our Lord** that he is truly of the family of David with respect to human descent, Son of God with respect to the divine will and power, truly born of a virgin, baptized by John in order that all righteousness might be fulfilled by him.[a]
>
> a. Ignatius, *To the Smyrnaeans* 1.1. Translation from Holmes, *Apostolic Fathers*, 249.

context, the early Christian confession "Jesus is Lord" carried the implication that Caesar is not lord. By attributing the term κύριος to Jesus, the early Christians may have been making both a political and a theological statement.

Any such anti-Roman imperial statements are (possibly out of necessity) not explicit in the New Testament.[55] There are, however, clear references to Jesus being Lord over all earthly powers and rulers. The New Testament envisions Jesus seated at the right hand of the Father and reigning until his enemies are defeated (1 Cor. 15:25; Heb. 1:13; 10:13; cf. Matt. 22:44; Mark 12:36). The Christ hymn of Colossians 1:15–20 declares that all things—whether "thrones or dominions or rulers or powers"—are under Jesus's rule since "in him all things hold together" (1:17). Later, Paul states that Jesus is "the head of every ruler and authority" (2:10). The book of Revelation identifies Jesus Christ as "the ruler of the kings of the earth" (Rev. 1:5).

Finally, the declaration that Jesus is Lord begs the question of what exactly Jesus is Lord of. Or, put differently, what does Jesus's lordship consist of? This question is not always addressed in the passages that attribute the title κύριος to Jesus. Just prior to the statement that "every tongue should confess that Jesus Christ is Lord" in Philippians 2, Paul declares that this includes everyone "in heaven and on earth and under the earth" (Phil. 2:10). In Romans,

---

55. However, John's Gospel does highlight that Jesus's designation as a king by others would be seen as one who "sets himself against the emperor" (John 19:12; cf. Acts 17:7).

Paul lists all the things that cannot separate believers from Christ Jesus "our Lord," establishing Jesus's superiority and lordship over them. These include death, life, rulers, powers, "nor anything else in all creation" (Rom. 8:38–39). In Revelation, Jesus is called the "Lord of lords" (cf. 1 Tim. 6:15) and "King of kings" (Rev. 17:14; 19:16), establishing his rule over earthly rulers. Other passages that do not include the term κύριος provide further insight into the lordship of Jesus. In Colossians, Paul writes that Jesus is above "all things in heaven and on earth," including "things visible and invisible" (Col. 1:16). Matthew's Gospel has Jesus declare, "All authority in heaven and on earth has been given to me" (Matt. 28:18).

Some New Testament passages understand Jesus's lordship as being over the church and the individual believer. Ephesians 1:22 states that Jesus is the head "over all things for the church." Similarly, Colossians 1:28 declares that Jesus is "the head of the body, the church." Yet the lordship of Jesus is not limited to just the church. All of creation is said to be under Jesus's lordship—both that which is seen and that which is invisible. Further, this lordship is not only a present reality but also a future reality. The New Testament presents Jesus as currently reigning until he has "put all his enemies under his feet" (1 Cor. 15:25) but also states that he will "reign forever and ever" (Rev. 11:15).

CHAPTER 2

JESUS THE PROPHET

Introduction

Each of the Synoptic Gospels tells the story of Herod inquiring about Jesus after Jesus's reputation begins to grow (Matt. 14:1–12; Mark 6:14–16; Luke 9:7–9). Jesus's name and actions catch Herod's attention, and he asks those around him about Jesus's identity. The response is a summary of some of the rumors swirling around Jesus's ministry. Mark's Gospel puts it this way:

> Some were saying, "John the baptizer has been raised from the dead; and for this reason these powers are at work in him." But others said, "It is Elijah." And others said, "It is a prophet, like one of the prophets of old." But when Herod heard of it, he said, "John, whom I beheaded, has been raised." (Mark 6:14b–16)

Each of the three suggestions for Jesus's identity in this passage understands him to be a kind of prophet. The question is which or what kind of prophet he is. John the Baptist is depicted as a prophetic figure in the Gospels, even though in one instance he is portrayed as rejecting the title (John 1:21). However, Matthew's Gospel makes clear that the crowds around John the Baptist considered him to be a prophet (Matt. 14:5). The suggestion that Jesus is Elijah may appear odd at first, but it fits within a tradition of awaiting the prophet Elijah's return to earth in the last days. Elijah was not the only prophet thought to return at the end of days; several interpretive traditions included the anticipation that specific prophetic figures would return to earth. These traditions may stand behind the third option concerning Jesus's identity, that he is a prophet like those of old. In Mark's Gospel the suggestion is simply that Jesus represents a return to the time of the prophets—a notion steeped in eschatological expectation. In Matthew's and Luke's Gospels the suggestion is that Jesus is an ancient prophet other than Elijah ("One of the ancient prophets had arisen"; Luke 9:8; cf. Matt. 16:14).

According to the crowds and those around Herod, then, Jesus is widely understood as a kind of prophet. But this answer stops short of a solution, for disagreement continues about which kind of prophet or which specific returning prophet Jesus is. The three suggestions to the question of Jesus's identity—John the Baptist, Elijah, another of the prophets—reemerge when Jesus asks his disciples the same question that Herod asked: Who do people say that Jesus is? Luke's Gospel goes to great lengths to connect these two events by placing them just verses apart (Luke 9:7–9, 18–20). After the three suggested options are repeated to Jesus, he asks his disciples who *they* say that he is. This culminates in Peter's confession: you are "the Messiah of God" (9:20).

As we will see, the failure of the crowds is not that they are wrong in their assessment of Jesus. The Gospel writers intentionally present Jesus as a prophetic figure. Various threads of sacred tradition regarding an eschatological prophet are utilized in the New Testament's portrayal of Jesus. Yet, as with many of these titles and sacred traditions, it is not the complete picture. Jesus is not just a prophet; he is the Messiah of God.

Prophets in Israel's Sacred Scriptures

Ancient Israel emerged in a world full of diviners, magicians, and other individuals offering oracles, prophecies, and divinations. Israel's prophets overlapped with their contemporaries but were uniquely called by Israel's God to serve as his messengers. Reaching their peak during the divided monarchy of Israel and Judah, the prophets served as Yahweh's mouthpiece to speak against injustice and provoke Israel to covenant faithfulness. A prophetic tradition emerged during this time with some figures leaving behind a written tradition. After the exile and return to Jerusalem, the prophets faded in the literature of the Second Temple period. There was no shortage of people identifying as prophets, yet it was commonly understood that the age of the prophets was in the past. This led to the anticipation of a reemergence of prophetic activity and even the return of specific prophets in the last days. By the first century, many prophetic figures existed—often modeling their proclamations and actions on the great prophets of the past. This anticipation of the return to the age of the prophets influenced how many people of the time—including the writers of the New Testament—understood Jesus.

Prophets in the Old Testament

The prophets play an important role both in the history of Israel and in its literary tradition—with a major section of its sacred Scriptures containing examples of prophetic literature (נביאים, "the Prophets"). The role of a prophet was diverse, with numerous figures taking on characteristics that can be identified as "prophetic." While today a prophet might be closely associated with visions of the future, this was just a small aspect of their function and ministry in the ancient world. One significant prophetic role involved calling for Israel's repentance after unfaithfulness to Yahweh or the covenant. Prophets also typically offered oracles—solicited or unsolicited—that conveyed the word of God into a specific context.[1] One element that connects all the prophets is their role as intermediaries between humans and the divine.[2]

The terminology used to refer to the prophets is also diverse.[3] The phrase "man of God" (איש האלהים) appears frequently in the Old Testament for prophetic figures: Moses (Deut. 33:1), Samuel (1 Sam. 9:8), Elijah (2 Kings 1:10), Elisha (2 Kings 4:7), and others (1 Sam. 2:27; 1 Kings 12:22; 13:1; 20:28). Those given this title were connected to such prophetic activities as performing miracles and predicting the fulfillment of events.[4] Two terms often translated as "seer" (ראה and חזה) are sometimes used to describe prophetic activity (1 Sam. 9:9; 2 Sam. 24:11). Yet the word commonly translated "prophet" (נביא) (or "prophetess" [נביאה]) is most frequent and appears to be the default term for prophets and their activity. In fact, in 1 Samuel the author clarifies, "The one who is now called a prophet [נביא] was formerly called a seer [ראה]" (1 Sam. 9:9). Numerous Old Testament figures, from Abraham (Gen. 20:7) and Moses (Deut. 18:15, 18) to Isaiah (Isa. 38:1) and Jeremiah (Jer. 1:5), were given the title "prophet."

The title "prophet" reaches as far back as the patriarch Abraham, with some prophets serving as judges prior to Israel's monarchy. This was the case with the prophetess Deborah, who was sought out for her wisdom and instructed Israel's military leaders (Judg. 4:1–10). However, the role and ministry of the prophets reached their apex during the divided monarchy of Israel. Some prophets were located among the king's court, while many others pointed their messages of repentance toward the royal court. The prophets Nathan and Gad, for example, served in King David's court (2 Sam. 7:2–17; 22:5).

---

1. See Aune, *Prophecy in Early Christianity*, 81–102.
2. Petersen, *Prophetic Literature*, 7.
3. See Mead, "Biblical Prophets in Historiography," 263–66; Petersen, *Prophetic Literature*, 5–6.
4. Mead, "Biblical Prophets in Historiography," 264.

Other prophets had a cultic connection, either coming from a priestly family (Jer. 1:1) or confronting the cultic system of Israel (Mal. 1:6–2:17). While a repeated message of the prophets was one of repentance, many prophets also had a message of hope, with visions of a future restoration of Israel and the temple after the Babylonian exile (Zech. 8:1–8; Hag. 1:15–2:9).

Prophecy and Expectation in the Second Temple Period

By the time of the Second Temple, prophecy and the vocation of the prophet as seen in the Old Testament had taken on different forms. This is not to say that persons identifying as prophets ceased to exist, but there was a general sense that the time of the prophets of old had passed. The author of 1 Maccabees, likely written in the late second century BCE, remarks that after the death of Judas Maccabeus "there was great distress in Israel, such as had not been since the time that prophets ceased to appear among them" (1 Macc. 9:27). The historian Josephus, while discussing the composition of Israel's history, comments that there "has not been an exact succession of prophets" since the reign of Artaxerxes in the fourth century BCE (*Against Apion* 1.40). The author of *2 Baruch*, writing in the early second century CE but describing events from the sixth century BCE, declares, "Further, know that our fathers in former times and former generations had helpers, righteous prophets and holy men.... But now, the righteous have been assembled, and the prophets are sleeping" (*2 Bar.* 85.1, 3).[5] While prophetic activity had quieted down by the first century CE, Josephus does document several figures identifying as prophets during this time (*Ant.* 20.97; *J.W.* 2.261). Thus, a prophet was still a "viable category" for religious figures in Second Temple Judaism.[6] In fact, it is likely that prophets continued to appear throughout the Second Temple period. As a result, prophetic activity did not necessarily cease altogether. Rather, this literature reflects a more nostalgic belief that there were no longer any prophets like those of old.[7]

It makes sense that figures in the first century CE took on the title of "prophet," since a revival of prophetic activity was an anticipated eschatological event attested in numerous sources. While formally dormant for centuries, prophecy of old was believed to become resurgent as a part of God's intervention at the end of days. The prophet Joel speaks of a time when "your sons and daughters shall prophesy, your old men shall dream dreams, and your young men shall see visions" (Joel 2:28). The author of 1 Macca-

---

5. Translation by A. F. J. Klijn in *OTP* 1:651.
6. Dunn, *Jesus Remembered*, 660.
7. Hooker, *Signs of a Prophet*, 6.

> ## THE ANTICIPATION OF THE PROPHET ELIJAH'S RETURN
>
> The Second Temple Jewish text Sirach illustrates that, for some, the prophet Elijah was expected to return. This event is closely connected to an eschatological day of judgment in which Elijah will help "restore the tribes of Jacob" (Sir. 48:10).
>
> > How glorious you were, Elijah, in your wonderous deeds!
> >   Whose glory is equal to yours? . . .
> > You anointed kings to inflict retribution,
> >   and prophets to succeed you.
> > You were taken up by a whirlwind of fire,
> >   in a chariot with horses of fire.
> > At the appointed time, it is written, you are destined
> >   to calm the wrath of God before it breaks out in fury,
> > to turn the hearts of parents to their children,
> >   and to restore the tribes of Jacob.[a]
>
> a. Sirach 48:4, 8–10.

bees anticipates a time when a "trustworthy prophet should arise" (1 Macc. 14:41; see also 4:46).

Various other Second Temple texts demonstrate a belief not only in the eschatological revival of prophecy but also in the appearance of an eschatological prophet. Who this figure would be and what they would accomplish vary within the literature. At times, the anticipated person overlaps with expectations regarding the anticipated messiah. One well-documented expectation of the eschatological prophet was the return of the prophet Elijah (Mal. 4:5; Sir. 48:10; *4 Ezra* 6.26). It was reasoned that, since Elijah was taken up to heaven without dying (2 Kings 2:11), he would return to the earth at some future date.[8] Elijah's anticipated return is explicitly stated in Malachi 4:5: "Lo, I will send you the prophet Elijah before the great and terrible day of the Lord comes." According to Malachi, Elijah's return will serve the function of preparing the way for the Lord (cf. Mal. 3:1). Further, the return of Elijah will bring reconciliation between parents and children. Ben Sira repeats this

---

8. Enoch, who is described as walking with God and then being taken by God and not dying in Gen. 5:22–24, was also anticipated to return at the end of days in certain lines of interpretation (*1 En.* 90.37).

latter claim and adds that Elijah's return will also restore the tribes of Jacob (Sir. 48:10). In *4 Ezra*, Elijah and other figures who did not die will return to the earth when the Messiah is revealed (*4 Ezra* 6.26; 7.26). This tradition appears also in the literature from Qumran (4Q558; 4Q382) and later in the Mishnah (*m. B. Metzi'a* 1:8; 2:8; 3:4–5; *m. Sotah* 9:15).[9]

Another line of tradition regarding the eschatological prophet in Second Temple literature is the expectation of a prophet like Moses. The basis for this anticipated figure is Deuteronomy 18:15, where Moses states that "the LORD your God will raise up for you a prophet like me from among your own people." This is followed by the Lord speaking in verse 18: "I will raise up for them a prophet like you from among their own people; I will put my words in the mouth of the prophet, who shall speak to them everything that I command." Some scholars have interpreted these passages as referring to a series of prophets (such as those during Israel's monarchy) or a special line of prophet-kings.[10] Significant for our study is a line of interpretation that understood these verses as speaking of an eschatological figure. As we will see, the New Testament writers often connected this anticipated prophet to Jesus.

The literature discovered at Qumran reflects a similar interpretation when it mentions a time when "there shall come the Prophet and the Messiahs of Aaron and Israel" (1QS 9.11).[11] This passage is clarified when read alongside 4QTestimonia, which connects Deuteronomy 18:18–19 (prophet like Moses) to Deuteronomy 33:8–11 (referring to the Messiah of Aaron) and Numbers 24:15–17 (the Davidic Messiah).[12] It may also be that the Teacher of Righteousness, the commonly understood founder of the Qumran community, was regarded as an eschatological prophet like Moses.[13] Similarly, the Samaritans held a belief that a prophet like Moses, later called "Taheb" (the returning one), would appear at the end of days.[14] This is likely behind the Samaritan woman's comment to Jesus in John's Gospel: "I know that Messiah is coming" (John 4:25). Further, as Dale Allison has argued, the various accounts in Josephus of would-be prophets show that these individuals modeled their prophetic ministry after Moses and his successor, Joshua. Therefore, the anticipation of a prophet like Moses was prevalent in the Second Temple period, with aspiring prophets "provok[ing] speculation regarding the fulfillment of Deuteronomy 18:15 and 18."[15]

9. See Joynes, "Elijah."
10. See Allison, *New Moses*, 74–75.
11. Translation from Vermes, *Complete Dead Sea Scrolls in English*, 110.
12. See Meeks, *Prophet-King*, 168–69; Allison, *New Moses*, 74–75.
13. Meeks, *Prophet-King*, 170; Teeple, *Mosaic Eschatological Prophet*, 51–52.
14. See Pummer, *Samaritans*, esp. 63.
15. Allison, *New Moses*, 78–84 (82).

Prophets in the New Testament

We now turn to the New Testament to examine the evidence for prophets. We will examine two significant prophetic figures in the New Testament: John the Baptist and Jesus.

John the Baptist

Before commenting on the New Testament writers' presentation of Jesus as a prophet, we must consider the role of John the Baptist in the Gospels and Acts. This is because John, as represented in the Gospels, reveals something significant about Jesus. All four Gospels agree that John had a ministry of baptism for repentance leading up to the ministry of Jesus (Matt. 3:1–12; Mark 1:2–8; Luke 3:1–20; John 1:19–28; also Acts 19:4).[16] Likewise, each of the Gospel writers identifies John as a prophet of sorts. The crowds clearly understand him to be a prophet, which is one reason Herod is said to fear putting John to death (Matt. 14:5). Jesus considers John to be a prophet (Matt. 11:9; Luke 7:26), and John's father calls him a "prophet of the Most High" when he is still in the womb (Luke 1:76). John the Baptist looks and behaves much like the prophets from the Old Testament. Luke's Gospel tells us that "the word of God came to John" (3:2), placing him within the prophetic tradition (see Jer. 2:1; Ezek. 3:16; Hosea 1:1; Jon. 1:1; Mic. 1:1). His clothing looks like a prophet's clothing (Mark 1:6; 2 Kings 1:8), and his message of repentance follows an established tradition. In many ways, the Gospel writers present John the Baptist as a prophet of old, which is itself an eschatological claim: John's ministry is evidence of a revival of the prophetic word.

But John is not just *a* prophet; the Gospel writers understand him to be a *specific* prophet. When Jesus asks a crowd what they saw when they visited John, he rhetorically answers his own question: "A prophet? Yes, I tell you, and more than a prophet" (Matt. 11:9; Luke 7:26). He goes on to identify John as the one written about by the prophet Malachi who will come ahead of the Lord (Matt. 11:10; Luke 7:27; see Mal. 3:1). John is understood by Jesus in the Gospels as the eschatological prophet who will prepare the way of the Lord. Indeed, all four Gospels depict John's ministry within the context of Isaiah 40:3 (the "voice of one crying out in the wilderness" to "prepare the way of the Lord"), with John's Gospel putting these words in the Baptist's

---

16. That John was associated with the ritual of baptism is also supported by Josephus (*Ant.* 18.116–19). On the historicity of John the Baptist, see Meier, *Marginal Jew*, 2:19–62; Aune, *Prophecy in Early Christianity*, 129–32.

own mouth (Matt. 3:3//Mark 1:3//Luke 3:4//John 1:23).[17] According to the Gospels, John's primary prophetic role was to prepare the way for Jesus, the Messiah. The words of John in the Gospels reinforce this point: "The one who is more powerful than I is coming after me; I am not worthy to stoop down and untie the thong of his sandals. I have baptized you with water; but he will baptize you with the Holy Spirit" (Mark 1:7–8; cf. Matt. 3:11; Luke 3:16; John 1:26–27).

Furthermore, the Synoptic Gospels portray John as the return of the prophet Elijah, anticipated by Malachi and other Second Temple sources. In Luke's birth narrative of John the Baptist, an angel of the Lord tells Zechariah, John's father, "With the spirit and power of Elijah he [John] will go before him, to turn the hearts of parents to their children" (Luke 1:17a). This clearly recalls Malachi's prophecy regarding the return of Elijah, who will "turn the hearts of parents to their children" (Mal. 4:6). Mark details an exchange between Jesus and his disciples about why scribes say that Elijah will return (Mark 9:11–13). Jesus agrees that Elijah indeed must return before the Son of Man appears. He then states, "But I tell you that Elijah has come, and they did to him whatever they pleased, as it is written about him" (9:13). What is implied in Mark's Gospel is made explicit in Matthew's: "Then the disciples understood that he was speaking to them about John the Baptist" (Matt. 17:13). Also unique to Matthew's Gospel is an earlier exchange in which Jesus explicitly states that John is Elijah returned: "For all the prophets and the law prophesied until John came; and if you are willing to accept it, he is Elijah who is to come. Let anyone with ears listen!" (11:13–15).

Curiously, in the Fourth Gospel, John the Baptist outright rejects being identified as Elijah returned or as the awaited eschatological prophet (John 1:21). Instead, he identifies himself in the role of the voice in the wilderness preparing the way of the Lord. This fits with the Gospel's emphasis on John's importance as a precursor to Jesus while clarifying that Jesus is of greater significance (1:6–9, 25–28; 3:25–30). Similarly, the Fourth Gospel does not directly mention Jesus being baptized by John. Oscar Cullmann proposes that the Fourth Gospel is attempting to address a group of John's disciples who believe that he is the Messiah. Thus, the Gospel writer attempts to clarify John's role as the forerunner to the true Messiah.[18] Whether this is the case or not, the Gospels present a tension in how John the Baptist is perceived

---

17. Interestingly, John identifies himself in this way to argue against being identified as Elijah or "the Prophet." It does not necessarily follow that the Baptist is refusing to be identified as *a* prophet.

18. Cullmann, *Christology of the New Testament*, 28–29. Cf. Williams, "Jesus the Prophet," esp. 93–95.

in relation to Jesus. All the Gospel writers portray him as an eschatological prophet in the tradition of Isaiah's prophecy regarding the one who will come to prepare the way for the Messiah. The Synoptic Gospels frame John as Elijah returned to fulfill this role; the Fourth Gospel discards this connection but has John essentially fulfilling the same eschatological role.

For the Gospel writers, then, John the Baptist serves an important function within their larger presentation of Jesus. John represents the revival of prophecy in the tradition of the prophets of old—which Jesus himself will continue. As the eschatological prophet preparing the way of the Lord, John initiates the in-breaking of God's kingdom at the end of days. Further, the early church interpreted Elijah's return as a necessary element of the Messiah's appearance. In short, before the Messiah appears, Elijah must return. John the Baptist fulfills this expectation and points to the true identity of Jesus.

Jesus the Prophet

The two episodes recounted in the beginning of this chapter reveal that, for the crowds who heard about or experienced Jesus, the most obvious religious category into which to place him was that of a prophet. When Herod inquires about Jesus, he is told that some say he is John the Baptist back from the dead, others that he is Elijah returned, and others that he is a prophet of old (Mark 6:14–15). This account parallels Jesus asking his disciples the same question, to which they respond by repeating the same public opinion. Clearly, in the Gospels Jesus is considered a prophetic figure by many beyond his immediate circle. This demonstrates that the anticipation of an eschatological prophetic figure was widespread in the first century. By suggesting that Jesus is the return of Elijah or another of the prophets of old, the crowds are placing him within the category of eschatological prophet.

That the larger population considered Jesus a prophet is supported elsewhere in the Gospels. According to Luke, the people cry out, "A great prophet has risen among us!" when Jesus raises a person from the dead (Luke 7:16). Later, a Pharisee is scandalized that Jesus would allow a sinful woman to wash his feet, stating, "If this man were a prophet, he would have known who and what kind of woman this is" (7:39). While arguing that Jesus is not a prophet, the Pharisee identifies that this is the popular opinion.[19] Upon Jesus's entering Jerusalem, the crowds in Matthew's Gospel declare, "This is the prophet Jesus

---

19. Luke's Gospel, in particular, goes to great lengths to characterize Jesus as a prophetic figure. To see the variety of ways that Luke does this, see McWhirter, *Rejected Prophets*, esp. chap. 1. Cf. also the earlier study of Minear, *To Heal and to Reveal*; and, more recently, L. Johnson, *Prophetic Jesus, Prophetic Church*.

from Nazareth in Galilee" (Matt. 21:11; cf. 21:46). In the Gospel of John, numerous people identify Jesus as a prophet. The crowds respond to Jesus by saying, "This is indeed the prophet who is to come into the world" (John 6:14) and "This is really the prophet" (7:40). Both declarations likely connect Jesus to the anticipated eschatological prophet. During Jesus's interaction with the Samaritan woman at the well, she declares, "Sir, I see that you are a prophet" (4:19). Similarly, when a man healed by Jesus is interrogated by the Pharisees, he states about Jesus, "He is a prophet" (9:17).[20] When Jesus is mocked during his crucifixion, he is blindfolded and instructed to "prophesy" (Matt. 26:67–68; Mark 14:65; Luke 22:64). As Craig Evans writes, "The jeering demands that Jesus prophesy make sense only if Jesus came to them with the reputation of being a prophet."[21]

That the crowds around Jesus understand him to be a prophet is clear from the Gospel narratives. While the Gospel writers clarify that Jesus is much more than a prophet, the New Testament does present Jesus in prophetic terms. The title is particularly pronounced in Luke's two volumes. Luke's Gospel contains two important episodes that identify Jesus as a prophet. The first occurs early in Jesus's ministry when Jesus reads from the scroll of Isaiah in the synagogue in Nazareth (Luke 4:16–30). Those in attendance are reluctant to take him seriously since he grew up in that town. Jesus responds, "Truly I tell you, no prophet is accepted in the prophet's hometown" (4:24) and goes on to illustrate this by appealing to Elijah and Elisha. Here Jesus identifies himself with the prophets of old. The second episode occurs at the end of the Gospel when two of Jesus's disciples meet the risen Jesus, although they do not recognize him (24:13–35). When asked what they are discussing while they walk, the disciples respond, "The things about Jesus of Nazareth, who was a prophet mighty in deed and word before God and all people" (24:19).

Twice in the Acts of the Apostles, in speeches by Peter and Stephen, the promise of a prophet like Moses from Deuteronomy 18 is quoted and applied to Jesus (Acts 3:22; 7:37). In Acts 3:22–23, Peter quotes Deuteronomy 18:18–19 to identify Jesus as the "prophet like Moses."[22] Peter here addresses fellow Israelites. While they did not follow Jesus prior to his death, now that they properly understand his identity they should repent and embrace Jesus as the Messiah (3:11–26). In quoting Deuteronomy 18:18, Peter proclaims that Jesus is indeed the long-awaited prophet who was promised long ago. In quoting the following verse, Deuteronomy 18:19, Peter warns of the consequences of

---

20. Cf. Williams, "Jesus the Prophet," 96–103.
21. Evans, "Prophet, Sage, Healer," 1222.
22. Keener, *Acts*, 2:1112–17.

> ## JESUS THE "ARCHPROPHET OF THE PROPHETS"
>
> In the following passage, Eusebius reflects on the title "Christ" and argues that the earlier prophets not only foretold of Jesus Christ but also became "type[s]" referring to Christ as prophet.
>
> > We have also learned through tradition that some of the Prophets themselves had already through anointing become Christs in type, so that all these have reference to the true Christ, the divine and heavenly Word, who really is the only High Priest of all, the only King of all creation, and the Father's only Archprophet of the Prophets.[a]
>
> a. Eusebius, *Ecclesiastical History* 1.3.6. Translation from Deferrari, *Eusebius Pamphili*, 48.

not listening to the Mosaic prophet. In Stephen's speech, Deuteronomy 18 appears within his retelling of Israel's history—with the culmination being Jesus Christ. Stephen's audience is primarily Jewish, and Deuteronomy 18:18 serves as an indictment that they missed the prophet like Moses when he was on earth. These two speeches indicate that, for some early Christians, Jesus was understood, among many other things, as the long-awaited Mosaic prophet promised long ago who would appear at the end of days.

As we have seen, in the Gospels, people saw Jesus as a prophet. But what did Jesus think about himself? Did he identify himself as a prophet or as the eschatological Mosaic prophet? The closest that the Gospels come to Jesus's self-identification as a prophet is when he places his ministry within the context of a prophet's. All three Synoptics recount Jesus's rejection in his hometown of Nazareth. They each quote Jesus as responding to this rejection by saying, "Prophets are not without honor, except in their hometown" (Mark 6:4; cf. Matt. 13:57; Luke 4:24). Here Jesus compares himself to a prophet and seems to understand his ministry within this context. Luke's Gospel contains another example. When Jesus is informed of Herod's desire to have him killed (Luke 13:31–35), he responds, "Today, tomorrow, and the next day I must be on my way, because it is impossible for a prophet to be killed outside of Jerusalem" (13:33). For the Gospel writers at least, Jesus understood his ministry and identity as parallel to those of the prophets of old.

The Gospels depict Jesus as a prophetic figure in other ways. In 1930, C. H. Dodd articulated fifteen aspects of the Gospels' portrayal of Jesus's ministry that would have led to his being understood as a prophet.²³ Like the prophets of old, Jesus has a special calling, has a mission to Israel, speaks and acts like a prophet, and plays a role in the fulfillment of God's promises. Three aspects of Jesus's portrayal are worth exploring: (1) his speeches frequently recall the prophets, (2) his actions often invoke the imagery of the prophets, and (3) his suffering and death are often interpreted through the examples of the prophets.

First, Jesus's speeches or proclamations in the Gospel tradition have a prophetic quality.²⁴ While the Old Testament prophets used a typical introductory formula for their speeches ("Thus says the LORD"), this formula is never present on the lips of Jesus. Instead, Jesus uses the phrase "I say to you" (often, "Truly, I say to you"), which appears over ninety times in the Gospels. As David Aune points out, the phrase "is not a functional equivalent of the Old Testament prophetic messenger formula, but rather an expression which defines the social relationship of the speaker and audience."²⁵ Variations of this phrase are used by biblical figures, but usually the speaker is established as having authority over those listening. While the Old Testament prophets grounded their message in the authority of Yahweh, Jesus's message is authorized by himself. Like the prophets, then, Jesus spoke words that carried divine authority and "had the same absoluteness" as those of the Old Testament prophets.²⁶

The content of Jesus's speeches often takes on a prophetic character, especially when it has a predictive element. Jesus predicts the arrival of the kingdom of God (Mark 1:15), the destruction of the temple (Matt. 24:2; Mark 13:2; Luke 21:6), the destruction of Jerusalem (Luke 19:41–44), his own suffering and death (Mark 10:33–34), and the arrival of the Son of Man (Luke 17:26–30). The Olivet Discourse (Matt. 24:1–36; Mark 13:1–32; Luke 21:5–33) is Jesus's lengthiest documented speech regarding the end times. Elsewhere, Jesus describes visions (Luke 10:18) and pronounces judgments (Matt. 11:21–22; Luke 6:24–26).²⁷ Jesus, like John before him, is a preacher of repentance who speaks a harsh word to perpetrators of injustice (Matt. 4:17; 23:2–28). These elements of Jesus's speech are all closely associated with the messages of the Old Testament prophets.

Second, many of Jesus's actions in the Gospels can be understood as prophetic acts, even when he is not directly called a prophet. Morna Hooker argues that Jesus was considered a prophet not only because he *spoke* like a

---

23. Dodd, "Jesus as Teacher and Prophet," 57–65.
24. See Aune, *Prophecy in Early Christianity*, 163–69.
25. Aune, *Prophecy in Early Christianity*, 169.
26. Dodd, "Jesus as Teacher and Prophet," 57.
27. On Jesus's oracles of judgment, see Wright, *Jesus and the Victory of God*, 182–86.

prophet but also because he *acted* like a prophet.[28] In the Gospels, Jesus rejects the demand to offer a prophetic sign (Matt. 12:39; 16:4; Luke 11:29). Yet the numerous miracles of Jesus are to be understood as signs of his identity. They are not offered to authenticate his prophetic ministry, but, as Hooker writes, they do present him as a prophet, because he acts like a prophet.[29] Jesus's healings demonstrate God's power working in him, while his exorcisms demonstrate the breaking of God's kingdom into the world. Like the prophets of old, Jesus is often seen as embodying or acting out prophetic images in his ministry. His choice of twelve disciples, for example, is intended to communicate the restoration of Israel. As such, it is a prophetic sign.[30] Similarly, the account of Jesus instructing Simon to let down his fishing nets one more time after a frustrating day of fishing (Luke 5:1–11) is presented as a prophetic sign. Simon's net overflows with his catch, signifying the bountiful mission of the disciples of Jesus. Jesus's initiation of the Lord's Supper is also a prophetic action (Matt. 26:20–29; Mark 14:17–25; Luke 22:14–23; 1 Cor. 11:23–26). Through the simple breaking of bread and pouring of wine, Jesus enacts the coming of the kingdom of God and the future messianic banquet.

The episode of Jesus cursing a fig tree is another prophetic action (Matt. 21:18–22; Mark 11:12–21). After finding no fruit growing on the tree, Jesus curses it and it withers. This is intended to convey a meaning beyond fruit and trees. The reader is meant to see in this action what will happen to those who do not bear good fruit in their lives. Mark's Gospel wraps this episode around Jesus's entrance and heated clearing of the temple. That event itself is a prophetic action with deep significance. By clearing out the temple, Jesus declares, or warns about, its destruction (Matt. 23:37–24:2).[31]

Third, Jesus's suffering and death are often interpreted through the examples of the prophets.[32] Among the many prominent features of the prophets of old is the pattern of experiencing great suffering and a violent fate. The Old Testament frequently details the persecution and martyrdom of the prophets: Uriah is killed (Jer. 26:20–23), Zechariah is stoned (2 Chron. 24:21), Micaiah is imprisoned (1 Kings 22:27–28), Jeremiah is beaten (Jer. 20:2). New Testament writings such as the Epistle of James and Revelation refer to this tradition (James 5:10; Rev. 18:24; cf. Rom. 11:3; Heb. 11:36–38). At numerous places in the material shared by Matthew and Luke, Jesus appeals to this tradition (Matt. 5:11–12//Luke 6:22–23; Matt. 23:34–36//Luke 11:49–51). Jesus calls

---

28. Hooker, *Signs of a Prophet*, esp. 16.
29. Hooker, *Signs of a Prophet*, 36.
30. Hooker, *Signs of a Prophet*, 39.
31. Hooker, *Signs of a Prophet*, 44–47.
32. Aune, *Prophecy in Early Christianity*, 157–59.

Jerusalem "the city that kills the prophets" (Matt. 23:37; Luke 13:34), and in Luke's Gospel he places himself within this tradition (Luke 13:33). In Acts 7, Stephen also places Jesus's death within the tradition of the prophets: "Which of the prophets did your ancestors not persecute? They killed those who foretold the coming of the Righteous One, and now you have become his betrayers and murderers" (Acts 7:51–52). In 1 Thessalonians, Paul makes a similar connection by referring to those "who killed both the Lord Jesus and the prophets" (1 Thess. 2:15). The early Christians' understanding of Jesus as a prophet helps make sense of his violent passion and death. Just as many former prophets experienced a violent fate, so too Jesus was persecuted and killed.

The New Testament writers drew from prophetic traditions and the expectation of a renewal of prophecy and an appearance of an eschatological prophet in their presentation of Jesus. During his earthly ministry, it seems that the category of "prophet" was the best fit for what Jesus was saying and doing. His speeches have prophetic characteristics, and his numerous miracles are depicted as prophetic acts. This prophetic tradition is also applied to John the Baptist. For the Synoptic writers, John is Elijah redivivus who prepares the way for the Messiah. John serves an important role in pointing to the identity of Jesus. Parts of the New Testament draw from the tradition that before the Messiah would appear, Elijah would first return. Any prophetic features of Jesus's ministry serve the purpose of clarifying his identity as the Messiah. It then makes sense that some New Testament writers present Jesus as the eschatological Mosaic prophet, who in some lines of interpretation had both messianic and prophetic features.

Jesus as a Prophet like Moses

In his 2005 monograph *Jesus and His Death*, New Testament scholar Scot McKnight laments the "persistent absence in modern reshapings of Christology" of "appealing to Moses as a prototype for Jesus."[33] Moses is not completely ignored in modern discussions of Christology, but McKnight is correct to identify the lack of attention that this specific tradition is often given. Some work has been done in recent decades to correct this imbalance and to offer nuanced studies of how Jesus is portrayed as a Moses-like figure or a "new Moses."[34] Alongside Abraham, Moses is arguably one of the most

---

33. McKnight, *Jesus and His Death*, 199.
34. The leading figure in this regard is Dale Allison, who in 1993 wrote a detailed study of Matthew's Moses typology (*New Jesus*). See also Allison, *Constructing Jesus*, 270–73; Pitre, *Jesus and the Last Supper*, 53–147.

important figures within Judaism. Certainly, by the time of the New Testament writers, Moses was a prominent figure who had taken on a variety of roles. He led the Israelites through the exodus, serving as both a prophet and a king (Philo, *Life of Moses* 2.3–4). Moses had a special relationship with God and spoke with God "face to face" (Exod. 33:11). He was the giver of the law (Bar. 2:28; Sir. 24:23; 2 Macc. 7:30) and inaugurated the covenant between God and his people (Exod. 24:8). In later Jewish writings, claiming that Moses said or wrote something is essentially the same as saying that God said or wrote something (4 Macc. 17:19; cf. Matt. 19:6–8; Mark 7:9). In addition, as we have seen, several lines of tradition within Second Temple Judaism anticipated the return of Moses or a prophetic figure like Moses. The appearance of this Mosaic figure was sometimes linked to the arrival of the Messiah (1QS 9.11).

We argued above that Jesus is portrayed in the Gospels as a prophet. We further claimed that some of the New Testament writers interpret Jesus as the eschatological Mosaic prophet. In this section we hope to strengthen that argument by placing Jesus within the larger tradition of Moses that is present in the New Testament. Moses was an important figure in first-century Judaism, and an entire chapter of this book could have been devoted to how the New Testament writers develop this sacred tradition. We chose to place the discussion here because it contributes to an understanding of how Jesus is presented as a prophetic figure.

The New Testament's engagement with Moses is complex, and he is often invoked for multiple purposes. The following sections examine two elements of the New Testament's use of the figure of Moses. First, the New Testament frequently uses Moses as a point of comparison to Jesus—often to demonstrate Jesus's superiority to the earlier figure. Second, Moses is used as a *type* for Jesus. In this sense, Jesus is portrayed as a Moses-like figure or a new Moses.

Jesus and Moses Compared

Moses often appears in the New Testament as a point of comparison to Jesus—ultimately to reveal how Jesus is superior to his predecessor. At certain points the two figures are contrasted (John 1:17; Heb. 3:3–6), but more frequently the comparison is between what the two individuals represent. In these cases, Moses stands for the entire Mosaic law, the Jewish cultic system, and the old covenant. Jesus, by contrast, represents the new covenant of the Spirit. Paul frequently discusses the Mosaic law in contrast to the work of Jesus to demonstrate how Jesus has fulfilled the law and that Christians are no longer bound by law (Rom. 3:19–31; Gal. 3:10–14). While these discussions about the law would conjure up the figure of Moses, we will limit our discussion here to places in the New Testament where Moses is invoked by name.

At the close of the prologue to John's Gospel (John 1:1–18), the author compares what was accomplished through Jesus to what was accomplished through Moses. Referring to the incarnation, John writes that "the Word became flesh" and "we have seen his glory," which is "full of grace and truth" (1:14). He goes on: "The law indeed was given through Moses; grace and truth came through Jesus Christ" (1:17). When the law was given to Moses, God's character was revealed (Exod. 34:6–7). But now, the author reasons, that character is made fully available through Jesus.[35] Both Moses and Jesus are understood as revealers of God, but Jesus is understood as offering a more complete revelation. Further, the law "was given" (ἐδόθη) through Moses, indicating that it was given by God to Moses, while grace and truth "came" (ἐγένετο) through Jesus Christ himself.[36] The comparison continues into the next verse, where John writes, "No one has ever seen God. It is God the only Son, who is close to the Father's heart, who has made him known" (John 1:18). While Moses had a close relationship with God, speaking with him "face to face," Exodus states that Moses was not able to see God's face directly (Exod. 33:17–23). Yet through Jesus, God's Son, God has been made known.

The status of Jesus as God's Son is an important point of contrast between Jesus and Moses in the Epistle to the Hebrews. While both Moses and Jesus were faithful to God, "Jesus is worthy of more glory than Moses" (Heb. 3:3). According to the author, Moses served God's house as a servant, but Jesus serves as a son (3:5–6).[37] Using imagery from the exodus narrative, the author contrasts the wilderness generation, under Moses's leadership (3:16), who failed to enter God's rest, with those who now compose God's house and have an opportunity to enter that rest through Jesus (3:6–4:16). Elsewhere in Hebrews, Jesus's ministry as a high priest is contrasted with Moses and the Levitical priesthood (Heb. 7–10). While the Levitical priests served in the tabernacle, which was a sketch offered to Moses of the heavenly reality, Jesus serves in the real thing (8:1–7). Further, when Moses oversaw the inauguration of the covenant by the sprinkling of blood, he was necessarily bound by the limitations of such sacrifices (9:19–23). By comparison, Jesus offers a better sacrifice—his own blood and not that of animals—when he inaugurates a better covenant (9:23–28). Throughout his exposition, the author stresses

---

35. Keener, *Gospel of John*, 1:421.
36. Michaels, *Gospel of John*, 90–91.
37. On the use of "servant" to describe Moses, see Attridge, *Hebrews*, 110–11.

that Moses's law and the covenant that he inaugurated are only shadows and sketches of the true law and covenant now available through Christ (10:1).

Moses as a Type

Being such a significant and foundational figure for Judaism, Moses was often used as a type for various persons in both Jewish and Christian literature.[38] This is seen in the Old Testament's presentation of Moses's successor, Joshua, as a new Moses-like leader. In the book of Joshua, Joshua experiences his own theophany (Josh. 5:13–15) in which he is told to remove his sandals, like Moses before the burning bush (5:15; see Exod. 3:5). Further, Joshua leads the Israelites through a parted Jordan River (Josh. 3:9–17), renews the covenant between God and the people (24:25), and writes in the Book of the Law (24:26). These and many other events and descriptions are intended to portray Joshua in a way that is reminiscent of Moses. Moses serves as the type after which Joshua is modeled. Similar typological presentations exist for Elijah (2 Kings 2:8), Josiah (2 Kings 23:6), Jeremiah (Jer. 1:5–16), and several others. Indeed, we find a similar typological treatment between Jesus and Moses in the Gospels.

This typology is present in all four Gospels, but the Moses typology is most pronounced in the Gospel of Matthew.[39] We do not have space for a fulsome treatment, so we will examine three episodes in the First Gospel: the birth narrative, Jesus's temptation, and the Sermon on the Mount.

Matthew's birth narrative (Matt. 1:18–2:23) clearly uses a Moses typology in its presentation of Jesus.[40] Elements of the narrative recall events surrounding Moses, and specific language is used to connect Moses and Jesus. We could offer numerous examples but will mention only four:

1. Herod's order to kill all male infants in Bethlehem (Matt. 2:16–18) parallels Pharaoh's order to kill all male Hebrew children (Exod. 1:16).
2. Jesus being taken away from his homeland because Herod wants to kill him (Matt. 2:13–14) recalls Moses fleeing from Pharaoh, who seeks to kill him (Exod. 2:15).
3. After Herod's death, an angel tells Joseph, "Go to the land of Israel, for those who were seeking the child's life are dead" (Matt. 2:19–20); after Pharaoh's death, God commands Moses, "Go back to Egypt; for all those who were seeking your life are dead" (Exod. 4:19).

---

38. See Allison, *New Moses*, chaps. 2–3.
39. The best treatment of this is Allison, *New Moses*. This section is indebted to his work.
40. See Allison, *New Moses*, 140–65; R. Brown, *Birth of the Messiah*, 111–19.

4. Matthew directly quotes Hosea 11:1, a text about the exodus: "Out of Egypt I have called my son" (Matt. 2:15).

The way that Matthew constructs his narrative of Jesus's birth is intended to recall the story of Moses and the exodus.

Matthew's account of Jesus's temptation in the wilderness (Matt. 4:1–11), also recounted in Luke's Gospel (Luke 4:1–13), similarly draws upon the Moses and exodus traditions. Each of Jesus's responses to Satan is drawn from Deuteronomy's description of the exodus. Jesus's response in Matthew 4:4 (Luke 4:3) that "one does not live by bread alone" is a quotation from Deuteronomy 8:3. Jesus goes on to quote Deuteronomy 6:16 and 13 in response to the following two temptations (Matt. 4:7//Luke 4:12; Matt. 4:10//Luke 4:7). Here Matthew is depicting Jesus, like Moses and Israel, as experiencing an extended time of testing in the wilderness. Additional points of connection include the following: Jesus fasting for "forty days and forty nights" (Matt. 4:2) parallels Moses's own fast of "forty days and forty nights" (Exod. 24:18; Deut. 9:18); Jesus being led up a mountain and overlooking all the kingdoms of the earth (Matt. 4:8–9) recalls Moses on Mount Nebo being shown all the land that he will not enter (Deut. 34:1–4); Jesus being ministered to by angels (Matt. 4:11) parallels Moses and Israel receiving manna from heaven (the "bread of angels"; Ps. 78:25) during the wilderness wandering (Exod. 16).

Finally, Matthew's Sermon on the Mount draws upon the Mosaic tradition to show Jesus as the giver of a new law.[41] The image of Jesus on a mountain, sitting and teaching, is immediately reminiscent of Moses on Mount Sinai. In a key section of the sermon (Matt. 5:21–48), Jesus paraphrases and engages with the teaching of Moses in the Torah. While being clear that he is not attempting to abolish what Moses said (5:17), Jesus moves past the letter of the Mosaic law to hold his listeners to a higher standard. Interacting with six areas of Moses's law (murder, adultery, divorce, oaths, retaliation, neighborly love), Jesus upholds the law while adding to it. In each case, Jesus uses a formula: "You have heard / It was said [Moses's command], . . . but I say to you [new command]." Jesus's teaching takes the original command and turns it inward. Murder is still prohibited, but Jesus now teaches that the heart issue (i.e., anger) is also subject to judgment. The same is true of the other five commands: adultery/lust, divorce/fidelity, oaths/honesty, retaliation/good works, neighborly love/love of enemies. In light of Matthew 5:17–20, Jesus's words here should not be understood as replacing the Mosaic law. Rather, he

---

41. See Allison, *New Moses*, 172–94; Pennington, *Sermon on the Mount*, 138–41; McKnight, *Sermon on the Mount*, 21–24.

> ## MOSES AND JESUS IN THE *EPISTLE OF BARNABAS*
>
> In this influential early Christian epistle, the author compares Jesus and Moses in terms of the covenant that was initiated through them by God. Whereas Moses received the covenant as a servant, Jesus gave the new covenant directly.
>
> > For the prophet says: "And Moses was fasting on Mount Sinai forty days and forty nights in order to receive the Lord's covenant with the people." . . . So Moses received it, but they were not worthy.
> >
> > But how did we receive it? Learn! Moses received it as a servant, but the Lord himself gave it to us, so that we might become the people of inheritance, by suffering for us. And he was made manifest in order that they might fill up the measure of their sins and we might receive the covenant through the Lord Jesus who inherited it, who was prepared for this purpose, in order that by appearing in person and redeeming from darkness our hearts, which had already been paid over to death and given over to the lawlessness of error, he might establish a covenant in us by his word.[a]
>
> a. *Epistle of Barnabas* 14.2a, 4–5. Translation from Holmes, *Apostolic Fathers*, 425.

is adding to Moses's teaching and essentially *internalizing* the earlier commandments. As Allison has pointed out, Matthew not only portrays Jesus as a new Moses here but also demonstrates how Jesus inaugurates a new covenant that internalizes the law (Jer. 31:31–34).[42] Finally, the description of Jesus's descent from the mountain (Matt. 8:1: καταβάντος δὲ αὐτοῦ ἀπὸ τοῦ ὄρους) parallels the description of Moses's descent from Mount Sinai in Exodus 34:29 in some versions of the Septuagint (καταβαίνοντος δὲ αὐτοῦ ἐκ τοῦ ὄρους).[43]

Moses typology is applied to Jesus beyond Matthew's Gospel. Each of the Gospels emphasizes that Jesus appoints twelve disciples and serves as their leader (Matt. 10:1–4; Mark 3:14–16; Luke 6:13; John 6:70). The twelve disciples represent the twelve tribes of Israel, and Jesus's role in appointing these individuals recalls Moses's similar role. In the book of Numbers, Moses is instructed to appoint twelve men—one from each tribe—to assist in taking a census (Num. 1:4–16). Moses's successor, Joshua, similarly appoints twelve men to assist in crossing the Jordan River (Josh. 3:12). Each of the Gospels also contains the account of Jesus miraculously feeding a multitude of people with

---

42. Allison, *New Moses*, 189.
43. Allison, *New Moses*, 180.

limited supplies—a miracle steeped in Moses imagery (Matt. 15:13–21; Mark 6:30–44; Luke 9:10–17; John 6:1–13).[44] In the Synoptics, the setting of this miracle is the wilderness ("deserted place"), which recalls Israel's wanderings in Exodus. John's Gospel places this miracle on a mountain, which alludes to the Moses tradition as well (John 6:3; note the Moses comparison introduced just prior to this in 5:45–47). The miraculous provision of bread recalls the provision of manna to the Israelites during their desert wandering. Mark's Gospel draws another parallel when he states that the crowd was divided into "groups of hundreds and of fifties" (Mark 6:40; cf. Luke 9:14)—recalling the division of the Israelites into "thousands, hundreds, fifties, and tens" (Exod. 18:25). John's Gospel provides the only glimpse into the crowd's reaction to this miracle (John 6:14–15). They interpret the miracle as a sign of Jesus's identity as a prophet like Moses ("the prophet who is to come"; 6:14) and intend to make him king (6:15). As we have seen, some Jewish traditions understood Moses to be a king (Philo, *Life of Moses* 2.3–4).[45]

The Gospel of Luke inserts a reference to Moses in Jesus's response to those who accuse him of casting out demons by the power of Beelzebul. Jesus states that "it is by the finger of God" that he casts out demons (Luke 11:20). This recalls the exodus narrative and the ten plagues. At God's command, Moses directs Aaron to strike the dust with his staff, miraculously transforming it into gnats and leading Pharoah's magicians to proclaim, "This is the finger of God" (Exod. 8:19). Thematically, Jesus is linked to Moses in that they both were challenged on the origins of their miracles and both performed such miracles by the same authority.[46]

The transfiguration of Jesus, appearing in each of the Synoptics (Matt. 17:1–8; Mark 9:2–8; Luke 9:28–36; cf. 2 Pet. 1:16–18), is another example of Moses typology being used in the Gospel writers' portrayal of Jesus. The parallels between this episode and Exodus 24 and 34 are numerous. Allison notes seven parallels:[47]

- a high mountain (Mark 9:2 par. Exod. 24:12, 15–18; 34:3)
- a descending cloud that overshadows the mountain (Mark 9:2 par. Exod. 24:15–18; 34:5)
- a voice from the cloud (Mark 9:7 par. Exod. 24:16)
- the central figure radiating (Mark 9:2–3 par. Exod. 24:29–30, 35)

---

44. Allison, *Constructing Jesus*, 273; Pitre, *Jesus and the Last Supper*, 66–90; L. Johnson, *Miracles*, 210.
45. Michaels, *Gospel of John*, 352; R. Brown, *Gospel according to John*, 1:234–35.
46. See McKnight, *Jesus and His Death*, 197–200; Allison, *Constructing Jesus*, 271.
47. Allison, *New Moses*, 243–44.

- the fear of those witnessing the radiance (Mark 9:6 par. Exod. 34:29–30)
- the presence of a special group of individuals (Mark 9:2 par. Exod. 24:1)
- the occurrence of six days (Mark 9:2 par. Exod. 24:16)

These parallels all create the impression that Jesus's transfiguration is modeled after Moses on Mount Sinai. Jesus, of course, is seen talking with Moses and Elijah during this episode. Both figures are prophets, and both conversed with God on Mount Sinai (1 Kings 19:8–18). The transfiguration episode places Jesus squarely in this prophetic tradition and is told in a way to recall the narrative of Moses.

Lastly, an event that is steeped in Moses typology is the institution of the Last Supper (Matt. 26:26–29; Mark 14:22–25; Luke 22:14–20; 1 Cor. 11:23–26).[48] The Moses imagery is clear: Jesus's reference to "my blood of the covenant" (Matt. 26:28; Mark 14:24) parallels Moses's "blood of the covenant" (Exod. 24:8); in both narratives the blood is said to be "poured out" (Matt. 26:28; Mark 14:24; Exod. 24:6 LXX: προσέχεεν πρός); in both narratives the event takes place within the context of a banquet (Exod. 24:11); and Jesus's breaking of bread recalls the "bread of the Presence" of Exodus 25:30. In the New Testament accounts, Jesus is not renewing the Mosaic covenant but is inaugurating a *new covenant* with his *own* blood (not the blood of animals). The anticipation of a new covenant is present in Jeremiah 31 (cf. Ezek. 16:59–63; Zech. 9:11–17):

> The days are surely coming, says the LORD, when I will make a new covenant with the house of Israel and the house of Judah. It will not be like the covenant that I made with their ancestors when I took them by the hand to bring them out of the land of Egypt—a covenant that they broke, though I was their husband, says the LORD. (Jer. 31:31–32)

Jeremiah explicitly contrasts the new covenant with the Mosaic covenant. The New Testament's presentation of Jesus, the new Moses, inaugurating a new covenant, draws from this tradition. As Brant Pitre states, "In the Last Supper, Jesus is therefore recapitulating the well-known covenant-making actions of Moses but reconfiguring those actions around his suffering and death."[49]

In the Last Supper, then, Jesus is portrayed not just as a Moses-type or even as superior to Moses. Instead, Jesus is presented as a Mosaic figure inaugurating a new eschatological covenant. Other New Testament writers draw upon

---

48. Here we are indebted to Brant Pitre's recent study *Jesus and the Last Supper*, 90–147. See also McKnight, *Jesus and His Death*, 303–21; Allison, *New Moses*, 256–61.

49. Pitre, *Jesus and the Last Supper*, 95.

and further develop the inauguration of a new covenant by Jesus's blood. The author of Hebrews, contrasting the new covenant with the Mosaic covenant, writes, "[Jesus] is the mediator of a better covenant, which has been enacted through better promises. For if that first covenant had been faultless, there would have been no need to look for a second one" (Heb. 8:6b–7).

The New Testament writers, especially in the Gospels, understand Jesus to be a Moses-like figure. Being the most important person in the history of Israel, Moses is compared to Jesus with the intention of demonstrating how the latter is superior to the former. This is not intended to disparage Moses but rather to promote Jesus to his proper position. In the Gospel narratives, Jesus is often portrayed as Moses-like and following a script put forward by Moses. Jesus's words, actions, and circumstances are cast as being in tandem with the life of Moses. In Matthew's Gospel, Jesus's birth is recounted with details that are reminiscent of the life of Moses. Similarly, Jesus's miracles, teaching, transfiguration, and Last Supper are depicted in ways that are intended to recall Moses. In this way, Jesus is presented as a new Moses who offers a new Torah and inaugurates a new covenant.

Contribution to New Testament Christology

Taking our cue from the exchange that Jesus has with his disciples in the Synoptic accounts (Matt. 16:13–20; Mark 8:27–30; Luke 9:18–21), we must affirm that while the title and tradition of "prophet" help us understand the earthly ministry and eschatological role of Christ, they fall short of capturing Jesus's full identity. Yet, as with many of these titles and sacred traditions, understanding Jesus as a prophet offers some helpful contributions to a fulsome Christology of the New Testament. In this section we will explore three contributions of the prophetic tradition that help us better understand the identity of Jesus: (1) it offers a helpful category for comprehending his earthly ministry; (2) it reveals his eschatological significance; and (3) it overlaps with and helps us better appreciate other sacred traditions applied to Jesus.

There is a reason why those around Jesus in the Gospels repeatedly identify him as a prophetic figure. In his earthly ministry, Jesus speaks and acts like a prophet of old. His speeches have the character of a prophetic message: a message of repentance and eschatological hope spoken with the authority of God. Like the prophets of old, Jesus teaches compassion for the outcast, confronts the religious authorities, and makes predictive statements regarding the kingdom of God. In addition, many of Jesus's miracles and actions can be understood as prophetic acts. The in-breaking kingdom is demonstrated by Jesus's miracles—which often take on deep spiritual significance. The miraculous feeding of a multitude of people reveals God's provision for his people. The Passover meal is given new meaning through the Last Supper and points to the eschatological banquet of God's people.

The Gospel writers did not shy away from placing Jesus's earthly ministry within the prophetic tradition. It is difficult to believe that the perception of Jesus as a prophet recounted in the Gospels did not have a historical precedent. Whether or not this is case, the Gospel writers clearly drew from the prophetic tradition in their presentations of Jesus. The more that we as readers understand this tradition, the better equipped we are to fully appreciate the Gospel portraits.

Yet Jesus is not understood as just another prophet; he is *the* prophet. The New Testament writers portray Jesus as a prophet like Moses—an anticipated prophetic figure. This contributes to a larger presentation of Jesus as a Moses-like figure whose life follows a script similar to that of the Jewish hero. Alongside the ministry of John the Baptist, Jesus's prophetic activity is itself an eschatological event. The New Testament draws from sacred traditions that expected a Mosaic prophet who will usher in the kingdom of God in the end of days. Jesus is understood as the fulfillment of this expectation and the ultimate prophetic authority.

Finally, Jesus as eschatological prophet contributes to and overlaps with several other sacred traditions utilized to understand his identity.[50] As we have seen, the eschatological prophet was sometimes understood as a messianic figure. Several lines of Jewish interpretation expected the Messiah to be an eschatological figure who would usher in the kingdom of God. The Synoptic tradition appears to play with these overlapping expectations but ultimately sides with Jesus's identity as the Messiah. This is not to say that Jesus was not a prophet or even *the* prophet; the Synoptic writers seem to understand the role of Messiah as capable of folding these traditions into one person. Another point of overlap is the prophetic experience of suffering and death and the Suffering Servant described in Isaiah. The Gospels present Jesus's role as one of suffering and see in the prophets a precursor for this fate. As we will see, Jesus's suffering and death are also interpreted through the figure of the Suffering Servant of God (see chap. 5), who suffers at the hands of sinners for the redemption of Israel.

---

50. Cullmann, *Christology of the New Testament*, 44.

CHAPTER 3

JESUS THE SON OF MAN

Introduction

After Jesus's arrest, he is taken before the ruling group of priests, called the Sanhedrin, and interrogated. All three of the Synoptic Gospels record this encounter (Matt. 26:57–68//Mark 14:53–65//Luke 22:63–71). The goal of this interrogation, led by the high priest Caiaphas (Matt. 26:57), is to seek grounds for putting Jesus to death (Mark 14:55). The Sanhedrin hears testimony from several witnesses, but the testimony does not agree and so no charges can be found. Next, several people give false testimony about Jesus, claiming that he will destroy the temple and build another one not made by human hands. Even then, the testimony does not agree and is insufficient. The high priest then stands and asks Jesus whether he is going to respond to such accusations, but Jesus is silent. The high priest asks, "Are you the Messiah, the Son of the Blessed?" (Mark 14:61; similarly Matt. 26:63 but with "Son of God"; cf. later Luke 22:70: "Are you, then, the Son of God?"). This is a theologically loaded question. The high priest is uniting two christological titles of significance. The first is Messiah, God's chosen and anointed agent to do his work in the world, and the second is the Son of God, one who has a unique filial relationship with God. We note that the high priest is not quoted as using the name of God but refers to him as "the Blessed." A claim by Jesus to either of these titles would arouse controversy, since they suggest a special and even unique relationship with God.

At this point, Jesus does answer the high priest, but perhaps not in the way that he might have desired. Jesus says two things. The first is "I am," and the second is "and 'you will see the Son of Man seated at the right hand of the

Power,' and 'coming with the clouds of heaven'" (Mark 14:62 pars.). This is probably the most important Son of Man statement in the New Testament. The reason it is so important is that it firmly establishes the identity of the Son of Man as Jesus—it clearly links the "Son of Man" title to the Old Testament (especially Dan. 7:13) and directly invokes an eschatological use of a Son of Man statement.[1]

In this chapter we examine the title "Son of Man" in light of its origins in Daniel 7 and other relevant Jewish literature. "Son of Man" (in the New Testament, the Greek phrase ὁ υἱὸς τοῦ ἀνθρώπου, almost invariably) is used consistently in statements by Jesus. At first sight this seems like an awkward expression, as Jesus uses the third person and so appears to be referring to another person and not to himself. Yet in the Gospels, Jesus's favorite designation for himself is "Son of Man," and its use is consistent with the Old Testament and Jewish background of this title as one who in his humanity is also positioned alongside God himself.[2] In other words, "Son of Man" is a title that attributes humanity to Jesus, but it also attributes divinity to him, and it recognizes his divinity by means of his performing divine functions.[3] The "Son of Man" language invokes episodes in the Old Testament as well as alluding to a well-known figure from Jewish sacred tradition. As a result, there is some conceptual theological overlap with other titles for Jesus in the New Testament, such as "Messiah" and "Son of God," as is present in the Gospel story recounted above.[4] There are several possible reasons for this overlap. Some might look to the common Palestinian origin within the Jewish Aramaic-speaking church, their common eschatological orientation, and their lack of emphasis on preexistence.[5] Others find a more likely explanation is the common theological tradition found within the Jewish Scriptures, since the earliest records of Christianity already recognize the divinity of Christ.[6] In any case, the "Son of Man" language has led to little consensus among scholars as to its origins, meaning, and interpretation because there has been widespread disagreement about the context of early Christianity.[7]

1. Cf. Hooker, *Son of Man in Mark*, 163.
2. The convention of referring to oneself in the third person, illeism, is discussed at greater length in Elledge, *Use of the Third Person for Self-Reference by Jesus and Yahweh*, esp. 122–40, where he notes that "Son of Man" is the most frequent of Jesus's uses of this feature, but that it is also occasionally used with other christological titles, such as Christ, Son (of God), and so forth.
3. Cf. Hurtado, *Lord Jesus Christ*, 305–6.
4. See Cullmann, *Christology of the New Testament*, 290; Dunn, *Christology in the Making*, 7.
5. See Braun, "Meaning of New Testament Christology," 96.
6. Bauckham, *Jesus and the God of Israel*, 19.
7. Borsch, *The Christian and the Gnostic Son of Man*, 1. Cf. Longenecker, *Christology of Early Jewish Christianity*, 90.

To understand the title "Son of Man," we will examine the use of the phrase in other literature, especially other Jewish literature, and then turn to the New Testament to discuss the meaning of the phrase. We will discuss the various types of "Son of Man" statements in the Synoptic Gospels and then John's Gospel and their implications for understanding Jesus.[8] We recognize that scholars continue to argue about the terminology. We are not attempting to provide a solution to all the issues but to clarify the title's christological implications.

"Son of Man" in Jewish Literature

Before we can examine more closely what it means that Jesus is identified as the Son of Man, we must examine the language that may have inspired or stimulated the Gospel writers' use of this terminology. Some scholars looked to supposed ancient Near Eastern mythology, especially of a universal or first human, as the source to which Jesus refers in the Gospels.[9] This view was more typical of those influenced by the history of religion, but the parallels are imprecise, and the tradition's relationship to Jesus or the early church is uncertain.

For its possible origins, we instead must turn to the Old Testament and other Jewish traditions. "Son of Man" terminology is used in a variety of ways and in reference to various figures. It appears at least 161 times in the Old Testament as well as several times in related literature. The most common form of the expression is the Hebrew phrase rendered literally as "son of man" (בן אדם) or its plural form. Together they occur 154 times (106 times in the singular, 48 times in the plural). The equivalent Aramaic expression is also used (בר אנשׁ) but without apparent distinction in sense from the Hebrew form. In all but three instances, the Septuagint renders these Hebrew and Aramaic phrases using the Greek equivalent of "son of (the) man" (υἱὸς [τοῦ] ἀνθρώπου) or its plural equivalent, or simply "man" (ἄνθρωπος) or its plural form.[10]

Psalms, Wisdom, and Other Old Testament References

Most instances of "son of man" in the Old Testament are relatively insignificant for establishing the conceptual orientation and background of the

---

8. There have been many studies of the Son of Man title—so many, in fact, that there are now surveys of the studies. One of the best studies of this topic remains Caragounis, *Son of Man*, whom we rely upon in the following discussion. See also Hurtado and Owen, "Who Is This Son of Man?"

9. See, e.g., Kraeling, *Anthropos and Son of Man*, vii.

10. See Caragounis, *Son of Man*, 49–53, for the data, with a helpful chart on 49.

term. The term is used once each in Genesis (11:5), Numbers (23:19), Deuteronomy (32:8), 1 Samuel (26:19), 2 Samuel (7:14), 1 Kings (8:39), 2 Chronicles (6:30), Joel (1:12), and Micah (5:7 [5:6 MT]); three times in Job (16:21; 25:6; 35:8) and Isaiah (51:12; 52:14; 56:2); and five times in Jeremiah (32:19; 49:18; 49:33; 50:40; 51:43). All these instances refer to a human being or human beings, often drawing analogies between "man" or humanity and "the son of man." This phrasing is noticeably redundant: "son" and "man" are semantically overlapping in ways that other "sons of . . ." statements in the Old Testament are not.

In the Psalms and Wisdom literature, the term "son of man" is used thirty-nine times, again with reference to a human being or human beings. There is one passage (Ps. 80:17), along with possibly one other (45:2), that Chrys Caragounis categorizes as positive in its context, with reference to relying on a "son of man."[11] Other uses have a neutral context, speaking of the transience of human life (Pss. 89:47; 90:3), the weakness and frailty of humanity (146:3), and the weakness of humanity (8:4; 49:2; 62:9; 144:3). Negative uses of the term are far more abundant, speaking of sons of men as fools (14; 53:1–2), as liars and deceivers (12:1–2), and as having an evil heart (Eccles. 8:11; 9:3, 12). Further, the Old Testament says that God protects sons of men from their evil ways (Ps. 31:19–20), that they are unable to save themselves (146:3), and that their evil leads to their death and destruction (Prov. 15:11).[12]

Ezekiel

In Ezekiel the term "son of man" is used over ninety times. Some scholars dismiss this frequent usage as being nontechnical, meaning that God addresses Ezekiel as a "son of man" in order to stress his humanity or weakness.[13] This is what the NRSV does by rendering the wording as "mortal." The numerous instances of this term in Ezekiel to refer to humanity in its weakness are seen by most scholars as having little or no influence on the New Testament usage.

However, Caragounis notes two factors showing that Ezekiel has more importance for discussion of the son of man than has been usually thought.[14] First, it is significant that God addresses Ezekiel as "son of man." In other

---

11. Caragounis, *Son of Man*, 55.
12. Caragounis, *Son of Man*, 55–57.
13. See Burkett, *Son of Man Debate*, 57–60. See also Bauckham, *Jewish World around the New Testament*, 95.
14. Caragounis, *Son of Man*, 60.

words, "son of man" is used as some form of consistent and pervasive title for addressing the purported author of the book. Second, how the term "son of man" is introduced in the book of Ezekiel itself is significant. Caragounis notes that the book of Ezekiel opens with a vision of the chariot throne of God (Ezek. 1:4–28) and that God's first words of address to Ezekiel are "son of man" (2:1). This son of man, Ezekiel, is appointed to bring a message to the rebellious nation of Israel (2:3). The book depicts the symbolic tasks that the prophet is to perform to bring the people to repentance. The prophet is addressed throughout as "son of man." Caragounis rightly concludes,

> The role which the prophet has assumed among his people is one of representative, intercessor and substitute. The appellation "son of man" is, therefore, not a characterization of him as a rebellious person, but is indicative of his identification with the wicked nation which he serves. Thus, the status of son of man is transferred from those to whom it properly belongs to one who has identified himself with them and becomes their substitute.[15]

The use of "son of man" in Ezekiel is significant because it is used not simply as a description of the character of humanity but rather as a term that designates a mediatorial role or function between God and sinful sons of men.

Daniel

"Son of man" language is commonly associated with the book of Daniel. There are at least four instances of "son of man" language in Daniel, but Daniel 7:13 (in Aramaic) will be our focus here.[16] In a dream, Daniel sees four beasts, and while thinking about them he sees that "thrones were set in place, and an Ancient One took his throne" (7:9). In Daniel 7:13 (similar in sense to 10:18), and by implication 8:17, since the same son of man is addressed, the text does not say that Daniel saw explicitly the son of man, but that he saw one "like a son of man."[17] This simple use of a preposition may go unnoticed in interpretation of these instances in Daniel, but it is significant for our understanding of the figure.

There are at least four different interpretations by scholars of the identity of the son of man in Daniel 7:13 (involving vv. 1–14). Some scholars have thought that the term refers to Daniel himself. In 8:17, Daniel is addressed

---

15. Caragounis, *Son of Man*, 60.
16. The other uses of "son of man" language include Dan. 8:17; 10:16, 18.
17. NRSV: "one like a human being." We retain the language of "son of man" in this chapter and elsewhere.

> ## "SON OF MAN" IN DANIEL 7
>
> As I watched in the night visions,
> I saw one like a son of man
> coming with the clouds of heaven.
> And he came to the Ancient One
> and was presented before him.
> To him was given dominion
> and glory and kingship,
> that all peoples, nations, and languages
> should serve him.
> His dominion is an everlasting dominion
> that shall not pass away,
> and his kingship is one
> that shall never be destroyed.[a]
>
> a. Daniel 7:13–14 (NRSV altered).

as "son of man" (hence the NRSV's "mortal") and told to understand that the vision concerns the time of the end. Some have further said that perhaps Daniel will be that son of man and that the usage in Daniel 8:17 looks a lot like the usage in Ezekiel and other places in the Old Testament. Yet the usage in Ezekiel and elsewhere does not do justice to the imagery in Daniel 7:13. A second position is that the son of man is an anticipated future leader or king of Israel, possibly some sort of messiah figure. A third interpretation is to equate the term "son of man" with the "holy ones of the Most High" (Dan. 7:18)—that is, the Israelite people, possibly one individual anointed out of the group. Others have argued a fourth option, that the son of man is a divine figure (possibly angelic), distinct from God, who is elevated to heavenly status and given God's authority.[18]

The text of Daniel does not tell us much more about the identity of the son of man in 7:13. To conclude this matter, a possible way forward is to look at some other Jewish literature, including some literature that is roughly contemporary with the New Testament, to see how this type of language has been interpreted.

---

18. For a survey of the various views, see Goldingay, *Daniel*, 167–72; J. Collins, *Daniel*, 280–94, 304–10.

Other Jewish Literature

One section of the Second Temple text *1 Enoch* is called the Similitudes (*1 En.* 37–71). Scholars have suggested various compositional dates for the Similitudes—from the first century BCE to as late as the third century CE. As a result, it is impossible to determine whether the text might have influenced the New Testament—or even if the influence moves in the opposite direction.[19] While we might side with those who date the Similitudes to the turn of the millennium, this is far from certain.[20] Nevertheless, the Similitudes of Enoch does give us an idea of how such language was being interpreted around the New Testament era, perhaps suggesting how Daniel 7:13 was being interpreted by the New Testament authors.

The Similitudes portrays a highly complex view of the son of man, quite possibly dependent upon and expanding the use of "son of man" in Daniel 7.[21] For example, *1 Enoch* 46.1–2 says that his face was "like that of one among the holy angels."[22] Elsewhere, it says that he was chosen by God, named in the presence of God and before time and creation, hence preexistent (48.2, 3, 6). He is repeatedly called the "Elect One" (49.2; 51.3; 52.6; 53.6; 55.4; 61.8; 62.1) and even "Messiah" (48.10; 52.4). He performs many functions, including coming in judgment against the rulers of the world and all other powers (46.4–5; 62.11; 69.27–29), destroying evil (69.29), and ruling the world in peace (52.8–9; 71.17).

Considering the dating of and roughly contemporary context in *1 Enoch*, we probably have a figure similar to that in Daniel 7: an individual who is humanlike, heavenly, and possibly angelic, standing in contrast to the beasts mentioned in Daniel 7:1–8. This being enters into God's presence with the clouds of heaven and is brought before God (the Ancient One) to receive authority, glory, and sovereign power. Whereas this could be merely a human being, there are a few indicators that he is more than this. One indicator is that all of humanity worships him, and another is that his dominion and power are said to be eternal and will never pass away. This is the language used for the worship of God in his sovereignty (Dan. 2:44–45).[23]

Fourth Ezra, written after the destruction of the Second Temple, reinterprets Daniel's vision so that his fourth beast represents the Roman Empire (*4 Ezra* 12.11).[24] In a vision, Ezra views "something like the figure of a man,"

---

19. See J. Charlesworth, "Can We Discern the Composition Date of the Parables of Enoch?"
20. See Hannah, "The Elect Son of Man of the *Parables of Enoch*," esp. 133–34.
21. So J. Collins, *The Scepter and the Star*, 177.
22. Translation by E. Isaac in *OTP* 1:34.
23. See A. Collins and J. Collins, *King and Messiah as Son of God*, 75–100.
24. Here we are following Gurtner, *Introducing the Pseudepigrapha*, 45.

> ## *I ENOCH'S* SON OF MAN
>
> The appearance of the Son of Man in *1 Enoch* is significant for a variety of reasons—specifically, the figure is understood as preexistent ("prior to creation") and eternal ("for eternity").
>
> > At that hour, that Son of Man was given a name, in the presence of the Lord of the Spirits, the Before-Time; even before the creation of the sun and the moon, before the creation of the stars, he was given a name in the presence of the Lord of the Spirits. He will become a staff for the righteous ones in order that they may lean on him and not fall. He is the light of the gentiles and he will become the hope of those who are sick in their hearts. All those who dwell upon the earth shall fall and worship before him; they shall glorify, bless, and sing the name of the Lord of the Spirits. For this purpose he became the Chosen One; he was concealed in the presence of (the Lord of the Spirits) prior to the creation of the world, and for eternity.[a]
>
> a. *1 Enoch* 48.2–6. Translation by E. Isaac in *OTP* 1:35.

which is a clear reference to Daniel's son of man figure.[25] The man flies in the air "with the clouds of heaven; and wherever he turned his face to look, everything under his gaze trembled" (13.3). While *4 Ezra* was written after the Gospels, its "son of man" is clearly influenced by Daniel 7, and it identifies the figure with the Messiah, who oversees eschatological judgment (cf. 13.25–38).

"Son of Man" in the New Testament

In the New Testament the language of "Son of Man" is mainly contained in the Gospels. Paul never uses the designation,[26] and it is used outside the Gospels in only four places in the New Testament: Stephen's speech in Acts 7:56; Hebrews 2:6–8 (quoting Ps. 8); and Revelation 1:13; 14:14. The reference to a "son of man" in Hebrews 2:6 (NRSV: "mortals"), as in Psalm 8, is used in a neutral context and so is typically translated as "mortal" or "human being."[27]

25. See Stone, *Fourth Ezra*, 384.
26. Some scholars, however, believe that Paul's "last Adam" and "man from heaven" are from the same tradition as "Son of Man." See Hengel, *Studies in Early Christology*, 170.
27. See, however, the discussion by Moffitt (*Atonement and the Logic of Resurrection*, 120–29), who argues that a christological interpretation of the phrase is likely in play alongside an anthropological reading of the psalm.

The uses of the term in Acts and Revelation are linked in that they refer to Jesus appearing in a vision. In Acts, Stephen sees "the heavens opened and the Son of Man standing at the right hand of God!" (Acts 7:56). This use is closer to how the Gospels use the term since the two instances in Revelation instead refer to "one like the Son of Man" (Rev. 1:13; 14:14). This figure is described as "the first and the last" and "alive forever and ever" (1:17–18). In Revelation 14, the Son of Man is seated upon a cloud and enacts judgment upon the earth (14:14–16).

The Synoptic Gospels

We begin with a discussion of the Synoptic Gospels before we turn to the Son of Man in John's Gospel. Nearly every reference to the Son of Man appears on the lips of Jesus as a self-referential designation.[28] The two times that someone else utters the term, they are repeating the words of Jesus (Luke 24:7; John 12:34). In the Synoptics, Son of Man sayings are traditionally delineated into three categories: (1) Jesus's earthly ministry; (2) his suffering, death, and resurrection; and (3) his future, exalted apocalyptic return.[29]

The first category of Son of Man sayings pertains to Jesus's earthly ministry. Two instances are found in all three Synoptics: one on the Son of Man having authority on earth to forgive sins (Matt. 9:6//Mark 2:1//Luke 5:24) and one on being Lord of the Sabbath (Matt. 12:8//Mark 2:28//Luke 6:5). Other references include the Son of Man having nowhere to lay his head (Matt. 8:20//Luke 9:58), the Son of Man coming eating and drinking (Matt. 11:19//Luke 7:34), and one who says a word against the Son of Man being forgiven (Matt. 12:32//Luke 12:10). Elsewhere, Jesus states that the Son of Man "came to seek out and to save the lost" (Luke 19:10), is identified as the one who sows the good seed within a parable (Matt. 13:37), and may be the cause of his followers being hated (Luke 6:22).

The second category of sayings, regarding the Son of Man's suffering, death, and resurrection, appears in all three Synoptics and is featured quite prominently in Mark's Gospel. Jesus repeatedly states that "the Son of Man is to be betrayed into human hands, and they will kill him, and three days after being killed, he will rise again" (Mark 9:31 pars.). Similar statements are made at least six more times in Mark's Gospel.[30] In Mark 10:45, Jesus

---

28. On the authenticity of these statements, see Porter, *Sacred Tradition in the New Testament*, 51–77; cf. Grindheim, *God's Equal*, 289–304.

29. This categorization apparently originated with Bultmann, *Theology of the New Testament*, 1:30.

30. Mark 8:31; 9:9, 12; 10:33; 14:21, 41. Outside of the parallels to Mark's uses, see also Matt. 26:2; Luke 24:7.

states that "the Son of Man came not to be served but to serve, and to give his life a ransom for many" (cf. Matt. 20:28). Both Matthew and Luke include a saying comparing the Son of Man to Jonah, since he will "be in the heart of the earth" for "three days and three nights" (Matt. 12:40//Luke 11:30). In Luke's Gospel, Jesus asks Judas, "Is it with a kiss that you are betraying the Son of Man?" (Luke 22:48).

The third category of Son of Man sayings appears most prominently in Matthew's and Luke's Gospels. When Mark includes references to the Son of Man's apocalyptic return, there are always parallels with the other two Synoptic Gospels. This includes the Son of Man coming in glory (Mark 8:38 pars.), coming in the clouds with power and glory (Mark 13:26 pars.), and sitting at the right hand and coming with the clouds (Mark 14:62 pars.). Three instances that appear in both Matthew and Luke have the Son of Man coming like lightning (Matt. 24:27//Luke 17:24), as in the days of Noah (Matt. 24:37//Luke 17:26), and at an unexpected hour (Matt. 24:44//Luke 12:40). There are also twelve instances found in only one Gospel, either Matthew or Luke.[31] Matthew's seven instances include the Son of Man coming before Jesus's hearers go through the towns of Israel (Matt. 10:23), sending his angels (13:41), coming in his kingdom (16:28), sitting on his throne (19:28), as a sign in the sky (24:30), coming as in the days of Noah's flood (24:39), and coming in glory with his angels (25:31). Luke's five instances include the Son of Man confessing anyone who acknowledges him (Luke 12:8), not being seen in his days (17:22), coming as in the day of Lot when he left Sodom (17:29–30), coming and seeing whether he will find faith (18:8), and judging humanity standing before him (21:36).

Each of these categories of Son of Man sayings appears in all three Synoptic Gospels. Some appear more frequently in one Gospel than in others—Mark's Gospel has more references to the Son of Man's suffering, death, and resurrection (category 2), for example. Some Son of Man sayings appear in all three Synoptics, while some occurrences are unique to a particular Gospel. Nonetheless, the Son of Man sayings appear throughout the Synoptics and in a variety of contexts.[32]

---

31. While some of these instances have Synoptic parallels, they do not include a reference to the Son of Man.

32. From a narrative perspective, the "Son of Man" title takes on unique significance since it appears only on the lips of Jesus and is not used by other characters or the narrator. In Mark's Gospel, e.g., Jesus uses the title at key points in the narrative (8:29–33; 14:62) to essentially correct other characters' declarations of his identity. See Malbon, *Mark's Jesus*, 199–210; also Kirk, *Man Attested by God*, 269–339, although we disagree with Kirk's conclusion that the title in the Gospels identifies Jesus merely as an idealized human (356–57).

John's Gospel

"Son of Man" occurs thirteen times in John's Gospel (John 1:51; 3:13–14; 5:27; 6:27, 53, 62; 8:28; 9:35; 12:23, 34 [2×]; 13:31). Some of the occurrences are similar to usage in the Synoptic Gospels, and others are distinct.[33] John's Gospel has a more fluid and varied portrayal of the Son of Man, who can be depicted as functioning in one or more categories (if we use those from the Synoptic Gospels). He can be the earthly and the apocalyptic one or the suffering and the apocalyptic one. Whereas the three categories of the Synoptic Gospels appear adequate for those texts (at least for our purposes), the same categories do not correspond completely with "Son of Man" in John's Gospel. There is some overlap, but not full congruity. The apocalyptic type of statement appears most frequently in John's Gospel, but there are instances that more closely resemble the earthly activity category and the death and resurrection category, with some evidencing features of both.

The first Son of Man saying in John occurs when Jesus tells Nathanael, "Very truly, I tell you, you will see heaven opened and the angels of God ascending and descending upon the Son of Man" (John 1:51). This clearly has apocalyptic elements, but it is curious that the Son of Man is positioned on earth with the angels visiting him. Another significant occurrence is in John 5:27, where Jesus states that God "has given him authority to execute judgment, because he is the Son of Man [υἱὸς ἀνθρώπου]." This is the only occurrence in any of the Gospels in which "Son of Man" is not preceded by the Greek article (often translated "the") and so more closely mirrors the uses in apocalyptic literature.[34] Three occurrences take place within Jesus's "bread of life" discourse (6:22–70; cf. 6:27, 53, 62). Jesus explains that the Son of Man will offer "food that endures for eternal life" and that "you [must] eat the flesh of the Son of Man" (6:27, 53). When some disciples grumble at this teaching, Jesus asks them, "What if you were to see the Son of Man ascending to where he was before?" (6:62). This is clearly apocalyptic, but there are also hints of the Son of Man's suffering and death.

Interpretive Issues

When examining the use of "Son of Man," especially in the Synoptics, one is faced with some significant interpretive issues. Given the depth of scholarly

---

33. See Moloney, *Johannine Son of Man*; Burkett, *Son of Man in the Gospel of John*; Reynolds, *Apocalyptic Son of Man in the Gospel of John*; and Reynolds, "Jesus the Son of Man," esp. 127–33.

34. English translations insert "the," but in the Greek there is no article.

debate, understanding what this phrase means is no easy task. Determining its christological significance is even harder. However, an explanation of the use of the Greek phrase and then the treatment of a crucial instance found in all three Synoptics should help clear the way.

How Are the Son of Man Sayings to Be Understood?

One of the major issues in this discussion is whether the term "Son of Man," especially in the Synoptics, designates a title. In Jewish literature prior to the composition of the Gospels, "son of man" was not a recognized messianic title—although it could be understood to function in such a way given how Daniel 7 was interpreted.[35] Scholars often point out that the Greek phrase rendered "Son of Man" in the Gospels is a rendition of an Aramaic phrase used by Jesus. Most think that the phrase meant something like "one" or "a human being," meaning it was a generic or impersonal term.[36] There is the possibility that some of this generic usage appears in the Gospels; however, Caragounis is right that such an explanation is ultimately unsatisfactory, as it does not do justice to several New Testament uses.[37] For example, the Gospel of Mark states that the Son of Man has authority to forgive sins (Mark 2:10) and that the Son of Man is the Lord of the Sabbath (2:27–28). These are clearly not references to a generic human being. In addition, Matthew 12:31–32 discusses blasphemy against the Spirit and the Son of Man—again, certainly a generic person is not in mind here. These examples could be multiplied, especially within the Son of Man sayings detailing the suffering and death of Jesus (category 2) and his apocalyptic return (category 3).

There are also examples that identify Jesus as the Son of Man. In the account in which Jesus asks his disciples who people say he is, Matthew reads, "Who do people say that the Son of Man is?" (Matt. 16:13), but Mark has "Who do people say I am?" (Mark 8:27). The first may appear to be generic, but the parallel in Mark makes clear that Jesus is referring to himself. This would indicate that the Gospel authors understood that "the Son of Man" and the specific "I" referred to the same person. This alternation between "Son of Man" and personal reference to Jesus can be identified in several other places as well.[38] These examples indicate that in some way "Son of Man" was an indirect way that Jesus referred to himself, not to a generic person.

---

35. See Hengel and Schwemer, *Jesus and Judaism*, 559.
36. Vermes, "'Son of Man' Debate"; Casey, *Solution to the "Son of Man" Problem*, 56–81.
37. Caragounis, *Son of Man*, 33.
38. See Luke 6:22 and Matt. 5:11; Luke 12:8 and Matt. 10:32; Matt. 8:31//Luke 9:22 and Matt. 16:21.

Another interpretive issue concerns the Greek phrasing itself. Many scholars have argued that the Greek phrase ὁ υἱὸς τοῦ ἀνθρώπου, translated "son of man," is awkward Greek.[39] This is likely due to the semantic clash of "son" and "man" and to the repetition of the Greek article with each element of the construction. Yet, this is not awkward Greek at all, and the syntax—including the double use of the article—is not unusual.[40] However, the use of the article is indeed noteworthy, since the article is not present in the Hebrew or Aramaic equivalent term in the Old Testament and Second Temple literature,[41] nor in the usual translation of the Hebrew into Greek in the Septuagint renderings (υἱὸς ἀνθρώπου, found only in John 5:37 in the Gospels). Yet, to put it simply, the article is used in the Gospels because the syntax requires it. That does not mean, however, that the phrase does not refer to earlier usage, such as is found in Daniel or possibly in Ezekiel or the Similitudes. It probably does, with the initial article having scope over the entire phrase as a single unit, "the Son of Man." Therefore, while "Son of Man" is not used as a title in Daniel, the Gospel writers use it as an overt designation for Jesus and with reference to "the son of man" found in earlier tradition—and in that sense as a title or quasi-title.[42]

The question, however, remains: What do the Gospel writers mean by using the term "Son of Man"? The generic, impersonal use does not satisfactorily answer the question, especially when the Son of Man is described in terms that go beyond generic actions or when the pronoun "I/me" is used. The best answer is that the Gospel writers are alluding to the Old Testament tradition of the son of man, possibly the one who mediates between God and humanity as in Ezekiel, but more likely the son of man in Daniel and the Similitudes of Enoch. Perhaps they did not have the full force of Daniel 7 in mind in the earthly ministry and even betrayal, death, and resurrection passages. But the influence of Daniel 7 is assured in the so-called apocalyptic passages[43] such as Mark 8:38 (and parallels), where Jesus speaks of the Son of Man coming in his Father's glory with the holy angels. This is reminiscent of the "one like a son of man" in Daniel 7:13 (NIV). Another passage is Mark 13:26 (and parallels), where Jesus says (quoting Dan. 7:13–14) that people will see the Son of Man coming in clouds with great power and glory. In Matthew 13:41,

---

39. E.g., Dunn, *Jesus Remembered*, 726.
40. See Porter, "Adjectival Attributive Genitive in the New Testament." There is a tradition of making too much of the two articles in this construction (often referred to as definite articles, with emphasis on definite). See, e.g., Moule, *Origin of Christology*, 10, followed by many, such as Marcus, "Son of Man as Son of Adam."
41. Gathercole, "Son of Man in Mark's Gospel," 368.
42. See Marshall, "Synoptic 'Son of Man' Sayings in the Light of Linguistic Study," esp. 94.
43. Cf. Zacharias, "Old Greek Daniel 7:13–14 and Matthew's Son of Man."

the Son of Man is associated with the sending out of angels. In Matthew 19:28, the Son of Man sits on his glorious throne, judging Israel. Finally, in Matthew 25:31, the Son of Man comes in glory and sits on his throne in heavenly glory. He is an individual who is humanlike, heavenly, and probably more than angelic, who reflects God's glory in his coming, is accompanied by angels, and has the authority to sit on a heavenly throne and judge humanity. This interpretation—even if not overt in all instances of "Son of Man"—is confirmed in the title's climactic use during the trial of Jesus.

The Son of Man in Mark 14:62 and Parallels

At the beginning of this chapter, we set the stage for discussion of the term "Son of Man" by describing Jesus's interrogation by the high priest. Jesus's answer offers the fullest exposition of his understanding of being the Son of Man and brings together the various christological elements in one description. When the high priest asks Jesus, "Are you the Messiah, the Son of the Blessed?" (Mark 14:61) or "the Son of God" (Matt. 26:63; asked later in Luke 22:70), Jesus answers, "I am; and 'you will see the Son of Man seated at the right hand of the Power,' and 'coming with the clouds of heaven'" (Mark 14:62; similarly Matt. 26:64; Luke 22:69). At this point, the high priest tears his clothes and declares that Jesus has spoken blasphemy.

How do we explain this scene? As we can see from the above discussion, the high priest is asking whether Jesus claims to be the Messiah and, by extension, the Son of God. This pairing is also found in Matthew and Luke. He is asking Jesus if he is the Messiah, God's anointed one, one of whose characteristics at the time was that of claiming a special relationship with God, described here as being the Son of God. (We will discuss "Son of God" language in chap. 4.) Jesus affirms that he is the Messiah (we will discuss the Messiah in chap. 7), but he does so by introducing "Son of Man" language, especially as found in Daniel 7:13. Jesus's response prompts the high priest to do four things that have been identified as marking a proper response to blasphemy: the high priest tears his robes (*m. Sanh.* 7:5, 8, 10; 2 Kings 18:37; 9:1), asks the rhetorical question regarding the need for further witnesses (*m. Sanh.* 7:5), claims that blasphemy was committed (*m. Sanh.* 7:5), and condemns Jesus as deserving death (*m. Sanh.* 6:4; 7:5).[44] However, there is little if any ancient biblical or extrabiblical evidence to indicate that simply claiming to be the Messiah was a cause for a charge of blasphemy and being killed. For example, Josephus does not accuse any of those he discusses as messianic pretenders as being blasphemers, and Rabbi Aqiba, though not believed, was not accused

---

44. Evans, *Jesus and His Contemporaries*, 411.

> ## THE ELECT ONE ON GOD'S THRONE
>
> Jesus's indication that he will sit at the "right hand of the Power" (Mark 14:62) carries serious theological weight since only God sits on God's throne. However, some passages, such as this one from *1 Enoch*, present an image of another figure on God's throne.
>
> > In those days, (the Elect One) shall sit on my throne, and from the conscience of his mouth shall come out all the secrets of wisdom, for the Lord of the Spirits has given them to him and glorified him. In those days, mountains shall dance like rams; and the hills shall leap like kids satiated with milk. And the faces of all the angels in heaven shall glow with joy, because on that day the Elect One has arisen.[a]
>
> a. *1 Enoch* 51.3–4. Translation by E. Isaac in *OTP* 1:36–37.

of blasphemy when he proclaimed Simon bar Kosiba as Messiah. Therefore, something else must have prompted the high priest's demonstrative reply.

Craig Evans proposes that what provokes the charge of blasphemy is Jesus's combination of allusions from Daniel 7 and Psalm 110. When the two passages are combined, which Jesus does, the result is that one sees the "son of man" (Dan. 7:13) seated at the right hand of power (cf. Ps. 110:1 [109:1 LXX]) and "coming with the clouds of heaven" (Dan. 7:13).[45] By stating that he is seated at the right hand of the Mighty One, Jesus claims divine status. The joining of these two passages into a collective reference is not surprising, since they are similar passages. Both are clearly messianic, in which Israel's enemies are subjugated and someone nominated by God rules over and judges God's people. These two passages are indeed combined in the later *Midrash on Psalms*: "And in one place in the Writings it is written, 'the Lord said to my lord, "Sit at my right hand" [Ps. 110:1],' and it is also written: 'Behold, one came with the clouds of heaven, as a son of man' [Dan. 7:13]" (*Midr. Ps.* 2.9 [on 2:7]).[46]

Thus, it appears that Jesus as the Son of Man depicts himself not only as the Messiah—that is, God's anointed Son who comes from the line of David to judge and deliver Israel—but also as a figure equal with God himself, the Son of God. As Rabbi Aqiba is believed to have said, there are two thrones, one for God and one for his co-regent from the line of David.[47] The indication

---

45. Evans, *Jesus and His Contemporaries*, 422.
46. Evans, *Jesus and His Contemporaries*, 419.
47. See Hengel, *Studies in Early Christology*, 194, with references to the rabbinic literature.

is that Jesus is implying, even if subtly, that he will sit on God's throne. Only God sits on God's throne. It is this implicit though obvious claim that provides a plausible rationale for the reaction of the high priest. But is this sufficient to lead to Jesus's subsequent death at the hands of the Romans? The deification language regarding the emperor that was prominent and growing in the Roman Empire left little room for rival divine kings. As Evans has pointed out, the image of another figure sitting on a throne by God is found not only in other Jewish literature of the time (e.g., *1 En.* 51.3; Philo, *On Flight and Finding* 101) but also in a Greco-Roman milieu, as illustrated by a coin from 55 CE minted in Rome with Claudius sitting to the right of the divine Augustus on a chariot pulled by four elephants.[48] This interpretation is confirmed by the *titulus* placed above Jesus's head on the cross. It read, "The King of the Jews" (Mark 15:26 pars.), showing that Jesus was perceived by the Romans as having made claim to at least messianic status, but probably more than that—to status as the Son of Man who is seated next to God and comes in apocalyptic glory and judgment. It is this position of divine prerogative—seated next to God, coming in divine glory and judgment—that Jesus seems to take upon himself, and that leads to his death.[49]

"Son of man" terminology is used of a variety of figures in the Old Testament and other related Jewish literature, and in a variety of ways. It is often simply a reference to a human being or humanity in general. However, when Jesus, in the Gospels, uses the term for himself, he goes further and is drawing from Daniel 7 and *1 Enoch*. In Daniel 7:13, the "one like a son of man" approaches God, is led into his presence, and is given authority of the same order. Jesus makes a similar claim as one who, as the Son of Man, is seated next to God and exercising God's own apocalyptic and judgmental authority. Therefore, the high priest Caiaphas tears his robes and accuses Jesus of blasphemy. If Jesus was simply claiming to be human, Caiaphas's response would be unusual, even inexplicable. But Jesus is making a direct claim by his use of "Son of Man" and his allusion to Daniel 7:13, one fully consistent with how the son of man is interpreted in *1 Enoch* 37–71. There, the son of man is *the* one who not only is able to approach God but also sits alongside God and shares God's authority to judge and rule the world—that is, *the* one who is in every sense identifiable with God. In sum, by alluding to Daniel 7—and consistent with the Similitudes of Enoch—Jesus claims to be *the* Son of Man who has the authority, power, and even status of God.

---

48. Evans, *Jesus and His Contemporaries*, 420, citing Mattingly, *Augustus to Vitellius*, 201 + plate 38.

49. On this topic, see Evans, "Historical Jesus and the Deified Christ," 58–67.

Contribution to New Testament Christology

The New Testament—especially the Gospels and Revelation—understands Jesus in terms of the Son of Man figure from Daniel 7 and other apocalyptic texts. This figure was bound up with Jewish apocalyptic hopes of a heavenly being who would bring salvation and judgment to the world. This hope overlaps with expectations of a Davidic kingly messiah who would rule over Israel and restore its glory. By tapping into the tradition of the Son of Man, the New Testament writers present Jesus as this kind of salvific figure. Yet, as with virtually every aspect of messianic expectation, Jesus's identity as the Son of Man requires a reconceptualization of people's expectations.

Of the three types of Son of Man sayings, the sayings referring to his future, apocalyptic return most clearly align with how the Son of Man is presented in Daniel and *1 Enoch*. Yet the sayings that highlight the Son of Man's suffering and death instigate a reorientation of how the figure's mission is understood. Before he comes in glory, riding in the clouds and administering judgment, the Son of Man must be betrayed and handed over for death by human hands. Those hoping that the Son of Man's appearance will lead to a conquest of Israel's enemies and the establishment of a Davidic kingdom will have to wait.

The title "Son of Man," certainly at its simplest level, communicates something of Jesus's humanity and of his relationship with humankind. The phrase could be used to refer to a human individual or humanity itself (Gen. 11:5; 1 Kings 8:39; Isa. 51:12). Jesus's use of this phrase as a self-designation in the Gospels implies more than this basic interpretation, but we must not miss how the title connects Jesus with humanity. It may be that this title and the tradition of Adam (see chap. 9), applied to Jesus, work together to communicate a similar idea regarding Jesus's full humanity.

There are also clear implications regarding how the New Testament understands Jesus's divinity by this connection to the Son of Man. While the term could simply refer to a human being—like much of the usage in the Old Testament—the use of the term in Daniel 7 and other apocalyptic literature establishes a divine figure of heavenly origin. The Similitudes of Enoch takes this even further by assigning preexistence (*1 En.* 48.2, 3, 6), messianic status (48.10), and the ability to enact judgment against all powers (46.4–5; 62.11; 69.27–29). Therefore, when the New Testament writers identify Jesus as the Son of Man, they are claiming something beyond human status. As we have argued, this notion is supported by the fact that Jesus's self-identification as the Son of Man seated at the right hand of God (the Power) and coming in judgment incited charges of blasphemy by the high priest.

CHAPTER 4

JESUS THE SON OF GOD

Introduction

Two passages in the New Testament provide a suitable introduction to a discussion of Jesus as the Son of God. The first is perhaps not too surprising, and it is one of several in which followers of Jesus proclaim him the Son of God. In an episode in all three Synoptic Gospels, Jesus's disciples are in a boat on the Sea of Galilee. A huge storm on the lake arises, and their boat is tossed about. In the night, while at sea, the disciples see Jesus walking on the water. They are frightened and think he may be a ghost, but he speaks to them and calms them. In Matthew's account, Peter wants to join Jesus by walking to him, but when he tries, he becomes afraid and needs to be rescued by Jesus. When all are safely in the boat, the storm subsides. The disciples in the boat proclaim, "Truly you are the Son of God" (Matt. 14:33).

More surprising are instances in which those who are not Jesus's followers make a similar exclamation. Early in each of the Synoptic Gospels, Jesus is pursued by crowds of people who have heard of his healings. Mark's Gospel says that during these healings Jesus sometimes confronts unclean spirits. When he does so, they fall down before him and cry out, "You are the Son of God" (Mark 3:11; cf. Luke 4:41). Jesus tells the unclean spirits not to make known who he is.

We will discuss in detail many passages regarding Jesus as the Son of God. However, the range of such references is worth noting. No claim regarding Jesus has been more controversial than the claim Christians have traditionally made that Jesus is the Son of God—that he has a unique and filial relationship with God and in some way participates in the divine nature and character.[1] For

---

1. Cullmann, *Christology of the New Testament*, 275.

the modern person, making such a claim about a *human being* seems outrageous. This is true even of some modern Christian theologians and biblical scholars who have been hesitant to see any affirmation of Jesus as the Son of God in the earliest writings of the New Testament.[2] Yet the designation "Son of God" is used consistently throughout the New Testament in reference to Jesus. All the Gospels record Jesus being called the Son of God—sometimes even the authors themselves use the title for Jesus (Mark 1:1; John 20:31).[3] The title "Son of God" (in the New Testament often ὁ υἱὸς τοῦ θεοῦ, or some variation of it; see below for further discussion) occurs not only in the Gospels but also in Acts (9:20), Paul's Letters (e.g., Rom. 1:4), Hebrews (e.g., 4:14), 1 John (e.g., 4:15), and Revelation (2:18), with related sonship language in 1–2 Peter (e.g., 1 Pet. 5:13) and 2 John (v. 3). Reference to Jesus as the Son of God is found in a surprisingly wide swath of the New Testament.[4] Jesus is referred to as the Son of God by himself and by others. There are also passages in which Jesus addresses God as his Father, God calls Jesus his "Son," and others call Jesus "Son." This abundance and diversity of evidence—all of which has in common the assertion that Jesus is the Son of God—requires further examination as to its origins and meaning.

"Son of God" in Greco-Roman Writings

We begin by exploring some of the Greco-Roman traditions that may have contributed to the meaning of "Son of God." In the chapter on Jesus as Lord we briefly examined Wilhelm Bousset's understanding of Christianity as a Lord-cult.[5] Even if Bousset's major theses have been disputed, he brings attention to the fact that the origins of Christianity must be sought in and beyond Jesus's contemporary Judaism. These factors involve the surrounding religio-cultural context, in which various religious cults, including official ones, deified individuals and used language that is surprisingly similar to that found in early Christianity.

In the first-century world, politics and religion were not and could not be distinguished in the way that we in the modern world have done (or have tried to do). It has been argued, in fact, that the concept of religion is a modern

---

2. See, e.g., Dunn, *Christology in the Making*; the debate among theologians of all types in Hick, *Myth of God Incarnate*; and Goulder, *Incarnation and Myth*.
3. Mark 1:1 has some textual variants, which we will discuss below.
4. According to traditional Gospel source criticism, "Son of God" is found in both Markan and Q material in the Synoptic Gospels. Such appellations also appear in John's Gospel, Paul's Letters, and other New Testament writings, as will be discussed below.
5. Bousset, *Kyrios Christos*.

invention.⁶ If by "religion" we mean a separable compartment of human experience, then this is true, because for the ancients the world was a complex of religious practices that encompassed daily life and were especially entwined with politics and culture. As a result, the attribution of deity to various humans has a long tradition in the ancient world.⁷ In the Hellenistic world, since at least the time of Alexander the Great (see Plutarch, *Alexander* 28.1),⁸ it was not unknown for various figures of political significance to be "deified" or recognized as "gods" in various ways. This includes the growing emperor cult in the Roman Empire during New Testament times, begun especially during the time of Augustus (27 BCE–14 CE), and spreading from the east to the west during the first century. This was the world into which Jesus of Nazareth was born.

As a result of this environment, several ancient Greek texts directly speak of a ruler as "god."⁹ For example, in Greece, Julius Caesar was heralded as a god. This description of Julius Caesar appeared also at Lesbos, Mytilene, and Ephesus in Asia Minor. The divinization of Augustus was widespread throughout the Roman Empire, including in Neapolis, where he is listed along with all the other gods and goddesses to which one was to swear allegiance. Similar designations have been found with subsequent emperors. Tiberius was heralded as "god" and "the son of the god Augustus" at Lapethus in Cyprus, and as "god" at Myra in Lycia. Gaius Caligula was called "the new Ares" at Athens, a "new god" at Halasarna, "god" at Mytilene, and "god" in an inscription near Lake Askania in Asia Minor. Nero was called "Lord Nero," "the one with foreknowledge," "savior," "Zeus the savior," and "Zeus the liberator." Nero was also called the "good god Asclepius Caesar" and "the new Apollo" in Athens. Additional evidence exists among the Flavian emperors (68–96 CE). It is difficult to avoid the evidence that throughout the Greco-Roman world at the time of the emergence of Christianity, divinization of the Caesars was widespread. Various Caesars—especially Augustus but also others from Julius Caesar to the end of the first century—were heralded

---

6. See Nongbri, *Before Religion*.

7. See Lattey, *Texts Illustrating Ancient Ruler-Worship*, 9–10, for those that precede the Hellenistic period.

8. See Scott, *Adoption as Sons of God*, 16–18. Cf. Peppard, *Son of God in the Roman World*, esp. 35–85.

9. See L. Taylor, *Divinity of the Roman Emperor*, 267–83; Ehrenberg and Jones, *Documents Illustrating the Reigns of Augustus and Tiberius*, 81–97; M. Charlesworth, *Documents Illustrating the Reigns of Claudius and Nero*; McCrum and Woodhead, *Documents of the Principates of the Flavian Emperors*, 52–59; Smallwood, *Documents Illustrating the Principates of Gaius, Claudius and Nero*, 60–65. Many other honors indicating divinization are also given that we do not cite here, such as savior, benefactor, and creator.

> ## THE ACHIEVEMENTS OF THE DIVINE AUGUSTUS
>
> The following passage is taken from *Res Gestae Divi Augusti* (The Achievements of the Divine Augustus), an inscription attributed to the Roman emperor Augustus. The claim that Augustus's name was added to the hymn of the Salii is significant not only because the Salii were priests of the divine but also because, as Quintilian points out, the words of the hymn were seen as sacred things (*Institutio oratoria* 1.6.41).
>
> > My name was inserted in the hymn of the Salii by a decree of the senate, and it was enacted by law that my person should be inviolable for ever and that I should hold the tribunician power for the duration of my life.[a]
>
> a. *Res Gestae Divi Augusti* 10.1. Translation from Brunt and Moore, *Res Gestae Divi Augusti*, 23.

as gods who occupied a place within the Roman pantheon. Even if this constituted a form of civic or folk religion within Greco-Roman culture, there appears to have been an exaltation, represented as deification, of the ruler in both official and unofficial religious belief.

An abundance of textual evidence employs terminology closer to the kind of language that we find in the New Testament regarding Jesus, in which a filial relationship to God is asserted. This includes a number of ancient papyri and inscriptions roughly contemporary with the New Testament that use various forms of "son of god" language, demonstrating that this constituted a recognized tradition for those of the Greco-Roman world.[10] For example, the well-known Rosetta Stone (196 BCE) from the Hellenistic period calls Ptolemy V Epiphanes "god from god and goddess, just as Horus is son of Isis and Osiris" (line 10), illustrating the link between the Greek ruler tradition and the Egyptian tradition regarding "sons of god."[11] Julius Caesar, in a 48 BCE inscription found at Ephesus, is called "manifest god from Ares and Aphrodite." The Thespiaen people called Augustus "Caesar, son of god,

---

10. These examples are mostly taken from Deissmann, *Bible Studies*, 166–67; Deissmann, *Light from the Ancient East*, 344–47; L. Taylor, *Divinity of the Roman Emperor*, 267–83; Ehrenberg and Jones, *Documents Illustrating the Reigns of Augustus and Tiberius*, 81–97; M. Charlesworth, *Documents Illustrating the Reigns of Claudius and Nero*; and Smallwood, *Documents Illustrating the Principates of Gaius, Claudius and Nero*, 60–65. The usual phrasing in the ancient Greek texts for "son of god" is υἱὸς θεοῦ, with a few variations.

11. For a full presentation of sources with citations, see Porter, *Sacred Tradition in the New Testament*, 108–9.

savior" (30–27 BCE), and the Tarsians called him "Emperor Caesar, son of god [θεοῦ υἱόν], Augustus." Augustus was called "son of god" in Athens, Nicopolis, and Thera (31–27 BCE).[12] An inscription from after 9 BCE from Myrina Caesarea refers to Augustus as "Caesar, god, son of god, Augustus." Similar is an inscription from Pergamum that refers to "emperor, Caesar, son of god, the god Augustus" (line 1 on the base of a pedestal); one from Sardis that refers to "Caesar, son of god, emperor" (5–2 BCE); one from Myra in Lycia that calls Augustus "god Augustus, son of god, Caesar, ruler of the earth and sea, benefactor and savior of the whole world"; one in Ilium that calls him "emperor Caesar, son of god, god Augustus"; and one from Halicarnassus similar to the calendar inscription that describes Augustus in relation to father Zeus. Several texts refer to Augustus as "god of god." An inscription erected by the guild of bakers in the Fayum, dated to February 3, 19 CE, refers to Caesar as "son of God."

Nero was called "the son of the god Claudius" and "the son of the greatest of gods." An inscription found at Magnesia (50–54 CE) refers to Nero as "the son of the greatest of gods, Tiberius Claudius" (lines 1–3); the link is now between divinized Caesars and their sons. The affirmation of a significant figure as "son of god" was not surprising at all in the Greco-Roman world but constituted a cultural-religious tradition that continued to develop over the course of the first century.

One of the major questions regarding this evidence concerns how the Greco-Roman world viewed such language of divinization.[13] It is easy to be dismissive of such declarations—as were some leading thinkers in the ancient world of the time—but the dismissive statements themselves tell us that the declarations were to be reckoned with because many people were wary of their larger sociocultural and even political and religious implications.[14] The reason for their expressed caution was that the Greco-Roman pantheon, or group of gods, was not based on a limited number of essentially spiritual beings. The Greco-Roman pantheon had always functioned as a range of beings who were deeply embedded within their sociocultural context and constituted

---

12. The Greek reads: τοῦ Αὐτοκράτορος θεοῦ υἱοῦ Καίσαρος. Ulrich von Wilamowitz-Moellendorff suggested that the article may have indicated divinity. See L. Taylor, *Divinity of the Roman Emperor*, 271.

13. This question is directly related to the question of how the Greeks and Romans viewed what we would call religion within their cultures. See, e.g., Veyne (*Did the Greeks Believe in Their Myths?*), who answers yes to the question posed in the title of his book, in the same sense that we believe myths.

14. See Bird, *Jesus the Eternal Son*, 38–49, esp. 43–49; Longenecker, *Christology of Early Jewish Christianity*, 98; Hurtado, *Lord Jesus Christ*, 102–3, who characterizes the Greco-Roman language as simply honorific or uncommon.

a flexible group that sometimes added and sometimes subtracted members.[15] Earlier gods were directly derived from nature, first as basic elements (e.g., local gods of nature, such as rocks and springs) and then as elemental powers (e.g., Prometheus as the god of fire), hence the thought that some of these gods were eternal. They were eternal only so far as they were equated with such primal elements. Even the most exalted and fully developed gods, those thought to be genuinely eternal, were still identified with nature (e.g., Zeus/Jupiter and the thunderbolt), but they also were anthropomorphized and had very human characteristics. In other words, the Greco-Roman pantheon was a set of posited divine beings who had many human and various nonmaterial characteristics. There was even a place for humans who had attained divinity, the so-called heroes (e.g., Heracles/Hercules, who was the son of Zeus and a woman and attained divine status, as did Dionysus).[16] This also included the founders of Rome (e.g., Romulus), who set a precedent for human divinization.

The Greek and Roman gods functioned as the kinds of divine beings that the cultural-religious milieu demanded, living lives that many might admire and even wish to emulate or benefit from. This may well have been accelerated during the principate of Augustus, under whom there was a politico-religious revival. The divinized emperors fit comfortably within such a scenario as a political expansion of the category of divine beings, much as some philosophers, teachers, and miracle workers would (e.g., Apollonius of Tyana). Christianity could not avoid confronting this cultural-religious environment and responding to it.

This reality may help to explain, at least in part, some of the "Son of God" language in the New Testament. Before we provide an extended discussion below, we cite two important passages in the New Testament that may reflect the influence of Greco-Roman conceptions of "son of god." The Greco-Roman tradition regarding the divinization of important people may help us to understand why Mark's Gospel begins with the words "The beginning of the good news of Jesus Christ, the Son of God," especially if the traditional ascription of the Gospel to authorship in Rome is historically reliable.[17] There are two issues to consider here. First, there is no major reason why the

---

15. For Greco-Roman views of the gods, see Rose, *Religion in Greece and Rome*, esp. 254–72; Ferguson, *Religions of the Roman Empire*; Liebeschuetz, *Continuity and Change in Roman Religion*; Beard, North, and Price, *Religions of Rome*, esp. 2:26–59; cf. Burkert, *Greek Religion*; Price, *Religions of the Ancient Greeks*, esp. 143–58; Bremmer, *Greek Religion*.

16. See Kerényi, *Heroes of the Greeks*.

17. On this issue, see Guelich, *Mark 1–8:26*, xxix–xxxi; cf. Turner, *Gospel according to St. Mark*, 3–6; Lane, *Gospel according to Mark*, 12–17; and Hengel, *Studies in the Gospel of Mark*, 1–30.

textual variant "Son of God," found in all the best early codices,[18] should not be accepted as genuine to the Gospel itself. The author of the Gospel, especially if writing in Rome and familiar with growing Greco-Roman deification tendencies throughout the empire, could have used similar language to proclaim Jesus as the (from the author's perspective) only and true Son of God. The evidence above indicates that such an attribution need not have arisen in later church reflection on who Jesus is but could have been an early (authentic?) reflection of who the earliest Christians believed Jesus to be. This would have been in keeping with the cultural-religious propensity toward the divinization of major leaders.

A second consideration is that Mark 1:1 associates Jesus Christ's divinity (υἱοῦ θεοῦ) with "good news," language reminiscent of the Priene calendrical inscription regarding the "good news" of the birth "of the god" Augustus. The concept of "good news" is a controlling idea for Mark's Gospel. This idea is carried forward by the unmodified use of the word by Jesus in Mark 1:15; 8:35; 10:20; 13:10; and 14:9, proclaiming the good news to his hearers. The Markan emphasis on good news is not only introduced in Mark 1:1 but also explicitly reiterated by the Roman centurion at Jesus's death in Mark 15:39. The conjunction of "good news" and "son of god" in the Priene inscription indicates a suitable historical precedent for the juxtaposition of these two ideas in Mark's Gospel as well. Their use at the beginning of the Gospel provides a controlling motif developed throughout, even to the point of the proclamation of Jesus as the Son of God at his death by none other than a Roman centurion. A Roman thus declares that Jesus, not Caesar, is the Son of God. The author of Mark appears to be stating—using the religious and political tradition of his day—that Caesar has been replaced with the genuine Son of God, Jesus Christ.[19]

The second passage is Romans 1:1–4, the opening of Paul's letter to Rome, the heart of the empire. In the above discussion, we mentioned the Tarsian inscription in honor of Augustus Caesar that reads, "Emperor Caesar, son of god [θεοῦ υἱόν], Augustus." In the words of Adolf Deissmann, referring to this early first-century inscription, "Perhaps the young Paul may have seen here the expression *Son of God* for the first time—long before it came to him with

---

18. The variant "Son of God" (υἱοῦ θεοῦ) or similar is found in ℵ[a] A B D K L W and others. The evidence against the variant is quite weak, apart from the original hand of ℵ (and a few later manuscripts), which omits "Son of God" *but* which is changed by the first corrector. See Cranfield, *Gospel according to Saint Mark*, 33–38, on the opening statement, with its textual variant. Cf. also Evans, "Mark's Incipit and the Priene Calendar Inscription." Against the reading "Son of God," see A. Collins, "Establishing the Text."

19. See Porter, "Literary Approaches to the New Testament," 122, in which this idea was first developed.

another meaning."²⁰ This other, later meaning that Paul learned is perhaps reflected in his Letter to the Romans when he speaks of his being called as an apostle and set apart for the good news of God concerning his Son, who was declared the "Son of God" with power "by his resurrection from the dead" (Rom. 1:1, 3, 4 NIV). Romans 1:4 is often taken as indicating adoptive sonship from the time of, or even by, the resurrection,²¹ but this is much too simplistic an analysis of the verse's Greek and of the rest of Paul's Letters.²² Paul frames his Letter to the Romans²³ to indicate that Jesus Christ's public declaration as the fully empowered "Son of God" *was* the resurrection, not that this status was simply given to him at the resurrection. In this analysis the Letter to the Romans, along with the Gospel of Mark, may, at least at this point, directly confront the power of Rome with affirmation of a "Son of God" other than the emperor, one who brings a different kind of good news.

Thus, Deissmann concludes, "it is established that the expression υἱὸς θεοῦ [son of God] was a familiar one in the Graeco-Roman world from the beginning of the first century"²⁴—and would have been known to the writers of the New Testament as well. More than that, it constituted a fundamental category within the Greco-Roman cultural-religious world—to the point that people were called upon to worship the emperors to whom such titles were addressed—that evoked a direct response by the New Testament authors. They do not appropriate this tradition in the same way they appropriate the Old Testament or other Jewish traditions (or the way that other Greco-Roman authors did), but they clearly invoke such traditions in their use of "Son of God" language.

"Son of God" in Jewish Literature

There is, however, another strong tradition that helps us to understand the use of "Son of God" language in the New Testament and how it might be used of Jesus Christ. We find this in the ancient Jewish literature, especially the Old Testament. While most recognize at least some verbal and even conceptual parallels between the Greco-Roman and New Testament evidence, there has

---

20. Deissmann, *Bible Studies*, 167.
21. For a recent statement, see Peppard, "Adopted and Begotten Sons of God," esp. 99 with references; cf. also Peppard, *Son of God in the Roman World*, 132–72.
22. See Porter, *Letter to the Romans*, 41–46; cf. Porter, *Sacred Tradition in the New Testament*, 227–46.
23. See Porter, "Paul Confronts Caesar with the Good News," esp. 173–89, based on a narrative analysis of the so-called Priene inscription (*OGIS* 458).
24. Deissmann, *Bible Studies*, 167. He is followed by, e.g., Kümmel, *Theology of the New Testament*, 76.

been a hesitance to find the origin and major source for the concept in this Greco-Roman tradition, at least as it is found in the New Testament.[25] We will address this further below. Consequently, most scholars have turned to the Jewish background of the New Testament.[26] This material, as a possible source of understanding the use of "Son of God" in the New Testament, merits close examination.

Various Jewish writings have similar "Son of God" language.[27] Psalm 2:7 speaks of the anointed king of Israel as in some sense God's son when it says, "You are my son; today I have begotten you," and 2 Samuel 7:14 quotes God as stating of the Davidic king that God "will be a father to him, and he shall be a son to me." Similar sentiments are found in Psalm 89:26 (89:27 MT): "He shall cry to me, 'You are my father, my God . . .'"; Psalm 110:1: "The LORD says to my lord, 'Sit at my right hand . . .'"; and 1 Chronicles 29:23: "Solomon sat on the throne of the LORD . . . as king." Of note here is the equation of sonship with the Davidic kingship, quite possibly with messianic connotations based on Psalm 2:2, 7: "[Yahweh's] anointed." In Sirach 4:10, the reward of one helping the unfortunate is to "then be like a son of the Most High" (υἱὸς ὑψίστου), and in Wisdom 2:18, "the righteous person is a son of God" (υἱὸς θεοῦ) (AT). Despite the conceptual sonship language, the use of the specific wording υἱὸς θεοῦ, so common in the Greco-Roman literature (and in various expanded forms in the New Testament), does not appear very much in the Greek Old Testament, and then only in literature from the Hellenistic period.[28] Although this evidence is highly suggestive, it is still a far cry from the "Son of God" language of the Gospels.

Another significant source is the so-called Qumran "Son of God" text (4Q426).[29] This is a late first-century BCE Aramaic text that was published in 1992.[30] In a prophetic utterance given to a vexed king, the prophet apparently says that the king will have a son who "shall be great upon the earth"

---

25. See, e.g., Fitzmyer, "Contribution of Qumran Aramaic," esp. 103–4, one of whose major "arguments" seems to be simply that Bousset (*Kyrios Christos*) did not go as far as Deissmann in this regard. See, similarly, Scott, *Adoption as Sons of God*; and Capes, *Old Testament Yahweh Texts in Paul's Christology*, with regard to "Lord."

26. See the introduction on why we continue to use this language while also seeing it as a false disjunction, on the basis of the fundamental work of Hengel, *Judaism and Hellenism*.

27. See Evans, "Historical Jesus and the Deified Christ," 50–57.

28. "Sons of God" (or equivalent) appears in Gen. 6:2, 4; Deut. 32:43; Pss. 81:6 LXX; 88:7 LXX; Wis. 5:5; 3 Macc. 6:28.

29. See Evans, *Jesus and His Contemporaries*, 107–11, whose translation is followed unless otherwise indicated. For a fuller examination of this text, see Porter, *Sacred Tradition in the New Testament*, 112–15.

30. The official publication is in Puech, "Fragment d'une apocalypse en Araméen." A preliminary edition had been published by Fitzmyer, "Contribution of Qumran Aramaic," 91–94.

> ## THE QUMRAN "SON OF GOD" TEXT
>
> [Then he said to the king, "Live,] O King, forever! You are vexed, and changed [is the complexion of your face; de]pressed is your gaze. (But) you shall rule over everything forever! [And your deeds will be g]reat. (Yet) distress shall come upon the earth; [there will be war among the peoples] and great carnage in the provinces, [which the bands of] the king of Assyria [will cause. And E]gypt [will be with them. But your son] shall be great upon the earth, [and all peoples sh]all make [peace with him], and they all shall serve [him.] (For) he shall be called [son of] the [gr]eat [God], and by his name shall he be named. He shall be hailed 'Son of God,' and they shall call him 'Son of (the) Most High.'"[a]
>
> a. 4Q426 1.2-2.1. Translation from Evans, *Jesus and His Contemporaries*, 107.

(1.7)—although here "son," or the subject of the verb, is reconstructed from the later line 2.1—and who "shall be called [son of] the [gr]eat [God]" (1.9).[31] Not only that, but "he shall be hailed 'Son of God,' and they shall call him 'Son of (the) Most High'" (2.1).

Several important observations can be made about this Qumran text, despite its fragmentary and disputed state. The first is that the text is apocalyptic or eschatological—that is, it looks forward to a future day of deliverance and restoration by the intervention of (probably) the "Son of God," or at the very least some figure acting on God's behalf in a powerful way to establish his kingdom. Second, the expressions "Son of God" and "Son of the Most High" are titular, as the verbs "hail" and "call" (2.1) make clear.[32] These are not mere names but titles that are used of a person and even of a function.

Some scholars have seen "Son of God" and "Son of the Most High" as referring to a wicked figure or possibly a historical figure such as a gentile ruler (or son of a king).[33] Most recent interpreters, however, take the titles as referring to a "son of God" figure who messianically comes as an eschatological figure in the line of the Davidic king.[34] The concept of messiah will be

---

31. But cf. Vermes, *Dead Sea Scrolls in English*, 332, who resists the reconstruction with God.
32. See Fitzmyer, "Contribution of Qumran Aramaic," 106.
33. See J. Collins, "'Son of God' Text from Qumran," esp. 67–69, for a survey of opinions.
34. See Brooke, "Luke–Acts and the Qumran Scrolls," 73–74; J. Collins, "'Son of God' Text from Qumran," 76–82; Evans, *Jesus and His Contemporaries*, 107–11. Fitzmyer's view can be called messianic as well, claims J. Collins, even though Fitzmyer distances himself from explicitly identifying the "Son of God" and "Son of the Most High" with the Messiah.

discussed further in chapter 7, but it is worth noting that the functions here probably attributed to the "Son of God" are those commonly attributed to God in the Old Testament, including judgment, being worshiped, and eternal rule. This single Qumran fragment, therefore, suggests a powerful conception of a messianic figure whose function is divine in nature.

Of greater significance, however, is how this Qumran text may illuminate the Gospel authors' depiction of Jesus. Parallels between Luke 1:32–35 and 4Q246 are especially worth noting. In Luke 1:28, Mary is visited by an angel, whose greeting greatly troubles her. The angel tells her not to be afraid, because she is going to give birth to a son, who is to be called Jesus. "He will be great, and will be called the Son of the Most High" (1:32). "The child to be born will be holy; he will be called Son of God" (1:35). "He will reign over the house of Jacob forever, and of his kingdom there will be no end" (1:33). The similarity in language is striking. Some think that "it is difficult to avoid the conclusion that Luke is dependent in some way, whether directly or indirectly, on this long lost text from Qumran."[35] Others employ Luke 1:32–35 as an aid for interpreting 4Q246, apparently because the New Testament text is clearer than the fragmentary Qumran text.[36] In any case, trying to establish dependence may be a fruitless exercise, since the "Son of God" tradition appears to have been a part of several Jewish movements within the Greco-Roman world, including establishment Judaism, the Qumran community, and early Christianity.

This summary of the evidence for "Son of God" language in the Greco-Roman and the Jewish religio-cultural milieu makes clear that there was wide-ranging acknowledgment that human figures could be seen as divine figures.[37]

Jesus as the Son of God in the New Testament

We now turn to the evidence regarding Jesus as the Son of God in the New Testament. The most frequent wording is ὁ υἱὸς τοῦ θεοῦ (the Son of God), but there are variations on it, such as expanding or changing the genitive qualifier ("of God"), or use of the anarthrous construction (without the article), υἱὸς θεοῦ. Ὁ υἱός, with variations, is used for Son. Before analyzing and trying to explain these uses, we first lay out the evidence to show how vast

---

35. J. Collins, "'Son of God' Text from Qumran," 66.
36. E.g., Evans, *Jesus and His Contemporaries*, 108–11.
37. Dunn, *Christology in the Making*, 16, 22, is one of the few recent scholars to recognize this, even if he distances Christianity from its surrounding environment by noting that the idea of a descending god was not to be found, except possibly in "popular pagan superstition." We are unclear what is meant by "pagan superstition" and why it would be excluded from recognition.

this usage is in the New Testament. Since Jesus plays a different role in the Gospels than in the other New Testament writings, we must examine them separately. First we will look at the Gospels to identify instances in which Jesus refers to himself as the Son of God or Son, in which he refers to God as his Father, and in which others refer to Jesus as the Son of God or Son. Then we will look at references to Jesus as the Son of God or Son in other New Testament texts.

The Gospels

We begin with the Gospels because of the role that Jesus plays in all four Gospels as a major participant and hence speaker. His words must be differentiated from what others say about him.

Jesus Refers to Himself as the Son of God or Son

In several places in the Gospels, Jesus refers to himself as the Son of God (or Son), sometimes in relationship to the Father. Most of these references in relationship to the Father occur in John's Gospel.[38]

- Matthew 11:27//Luke 10:22: Son and Father mentioned
- Matthew 24:36//Mark 13:32: Son and Father mentioned
- Matthew 28:19: Father, Son, and Holy Spirit mentioned, an arguably proto-trinitarian formulation
- John 5:19–26: Jesus appears to refer to himself as the Son (5:19, 20, 21, 22, 23, 26) and the Son of God (5:25) as well as to God as Father (5:19, 20, 21, 22, 23, 26)
- John 10:36: Jesus responds to accusations of blasphemy by questioning why, in light of Old Testament precedent, he is accused for saying, "I am Son of God" (υἱὸς τοῦ θεοῦ)
- John 11:4: Jesus appears to refer to himself as the Son of God (ὁ υἱὸς τοῦ θεοῦ)
- John 14:13: Father "glorified in the Son" (cf. 17:1, where Jesus addresses God as Father and himself as Son twice)

---

38. We could include Matt. 26:63–64//Mark 14:61–62//Luke 22:70 here, the passage in which the high priest asks Jesus whether he is the Messiah, the Son of the Blessed/God (Matthew and Mark) or, subsequently, the Son of God (Luke). We treat this passage in chap. 3 on the Son of Man but will note here that in his response, Jesus does not claim to be the Son of God but in some sense affirms its attribution to himself as a divine category. See the discussion in chap. 3.

Jesus Identifies God as His Father

There is an abundance of evidence in the Gospels of Jesus referring to God as his Father. In Matthew, he sometimes refers to God as "my Father in heaven" (or something equivalent). Matthew, Luke, and John use "my Father" relatively often. In John's Gospel, Jesus frequently refers to God as his Father in his extended discourses. We note that there are very few Synoptic parallels in this usage. We also note that in Mark the instances of Jesus identifying God as his Father are also relatively limited, but they are not unknown, as the examples below illustrate.

- Matthew 7:21: Jesus speaks of "my Father in heaven" (see also 10:32–33; 12:50; 15:30; 16:17; 18:10, 19, 35; cf. 20:23; 25:34; 26:29, 39, 42 [direct address]; 26:53)
- Matthew 11:25–27//Luke 10:21–22: Jesus thanks his "Father" directly and refers to him as "my Father"
- Matthew 16:27//Mark 8:38: Jesus states that the Son of Man will come "in the glory of his Father"
- Matthew 26:39 ("my Father")//Mark 14:36 ("Abba, Father")//Luke 22:42: Jesus at Gethsemane addresses God directly as "Father" (πάτερ μου)
- Luke's Gospel contains several instances of Jesus referring to his "Father" (2:49; 22:29; 23:34; 23:46 [direct address]; 24:49)
- John's Gospel contains several instances of Jesus referring to his "Father" (2:16; 5:19, 43; 6:32, 40; 8:19, 38, 49, 54; 10:17–18, 25, 29, 37; 12:26, 27 [direct address]; 14:2, 7, 13, 20–21, 23, 31; 15:1, 8, 10, 15, 23–24; 16:10, 23, 25, 32; 17:1, 5, 11, 21, 24–25 [direct address]; 18:11; 20:17; 20:21)

Others Refer to Jesus as the Son of God or Son

In a variety of passages in the Gospels, someone other than Jesus—including God, demoniac(s), a centurion, the devil, an angel, demons, and the Gospel authors—refers to Jesus as the Son of God or Son. The Synoptic Gospels tend to use similar wording, but John's Gospel elaborates on the christological title in various ways.

- Matthew 2:15: a quotation of Hosea 11:1 applies the title "Son" to Jesus
- Matthew 3:17//Mark 1:11//Luke 3:22: a voice from heaven declares, "This is my Son" at Jesus's baptism

- Matthew 4:3, 6//Luke 4:3, 9 (cf. 4:41): the devil calls Jesus "Son of God" (υἱὸς τοῦ θεοῦ)
- Matthew 8:29//Mark 5:7//Luke 8:28: demoniacs identify Jesus as "Son of God" (υἱὸς τοῦ θεοῦ)
- Matthew 14:33: Jesus's followers worship him as the "Son of God," and Peter repeats this declaration ("Son of the living God") in 16:16
- Matthew 17:5//Mark 9:7//Luke 9:35: a voice from the clouds declares, "This is my Son" at the transfiguration of Jesus
- Matthew 26:63//Luke 22:70: an inquiry by the high priest, a passage discussed below
- Matthew 27:40, 43: ridicule by one of the thieves on a cross, including stating that Jesus claimed, "I am the Son of God"
- Matthew 27:54//Mark 15:39: a centurion at the cross identifies Jesus as "God's Son"
- Mark 1:1: the Gospel author identifies Jesus as the "Son of God" (υἱὸς θεοῦ; but there are textual variants)
- Mark 3:11: unclean spirits call Jesus "Son of God" (ὁ υἱὸς τοῦ θεοῦ)
- Luke 1:32: an angel declares Jesus to be the "Son of the Most High" and "Son of God" (1:35)
- John's Gospel contains several instances in which the Gospel writer identifies Jesus as God's Son (1:14, 18; 3:16–18, 35–36; 20:31)
- John 1:34: John the Baptist identifies Jesus as the "Son of God" (ὁ υἱὸς τοῦ θεοῦ)
- John 1:49: Nathanael identifies Jesus as the "Son of God" (ὁ υἱὸς τοῦ θεοῦ)
- John 11:27: Martha addresses Jesus as Messiah and the "Son of God" (ὁ υἱὸς τοῦ θεοῦ)
- John 19:7: the Jewish leaders say that Jesus made himself "Son of God" (υἱὸς θεοῦ)

Other New Testament Writings

Although not as frequent as in the Gospels, there are also references to Jesus as the Son of God or Son in the rest of the New Testament. As might be expected in the writings outside the Gospels, most of the references to Jesus as Son are made by others about Jesus, not by Jesus himself (although there are a few of these instances). These books include Acts, Romans, 1–2 Corinthians,

Galatians, Ephesians, 1 Thessalonians, Hebrews, 1–2 Peter, 1–2 John, and Revelation.

Jesus Refers to Himself as the Son of God or Son or to God as His Father

As one might expect, examples of Jesus referring to himself as the Son of God or Son or to God as his Father are limited outside the Gospels because Jesus is not a direct participant in the other New Testament writings. However, on occasion he is represented as speaking and acting in books other than the Gospels, especially Revelation. There is one indirect statement in which Jesus refers to himself as the Son of God, and there are several passages in which Jesus is quoted as making such a claim. Revelation cites Jesus referring to "my Father."

- Acts 1:4 (indirect statement of what Jesus said)
- Revelation 2:18 (Son of God); 2:28; 3:5, 21 ("my Father")

Others Refer to Jesus as the Son of God or Son or Equivalent

In the other New Testament writings, others refer to Jesus in various ways as the Son of God or the equivalent. Most of these references are found in the Pauline Letters, but other letters use similar language. Some of these passages use a number of titles, especially in Paul. In some of the most important references, the New Testament authors refer to the "God and Father of our Lord Jesus Christ." This occurs most often in Paul but also once in 1 Peter (see below). In these passages, Jesus is referred to as Lord (see chap. 1 of this book) but also indirectly as the Son of God the Father.

- Acts 3:13 (Jesus his child); 3:26 (his child); 9:20 (Jesus proclaimed as "Son of God," ὁ υἱὸς τοῦ θεοῦ); 13:33 (Old Testament quotation of Ps. 2:7)
- Romans 1:3 (his Son); 1:4 ("Son of God," υἱὸς θεοῦ), a very important christological passage that we discuss further below; 1:9 (his Son); 5:10 (his Son); 8:3 (his own Son); 8:29 (his Son); 8:32 (one's own Son); 1 Corinthians 1:9 (his Son, Jesus Christ our Lord); 15:28; 2 Corinthians 1:19 ("the Son of God, Jesus Christ," ὁ τοῦ θεοῦ . . . υἱὸς Ἰησοῦς Χριστός); Galatians 1:16 (his Son); 2:20 (Son of God); 4:4 (his Son); 4:6 (the Spirit of his Son); Ephesians 4:13 (Son of God); Colossians 1:13 (his beloved Son); 1:15 (firstborn of all creation); 1 Thessalonians 1:10 (his Son); for an extended, compound title, see Romans 15:6 (God and Father of our Lord Jesus Christ); 2 Corinthians 1:3 (God and Father of our Lord Jesus Christ, the Father of mercies and the God of all comfort), a further

elaboration; 11:31 (God and Father of the Lord Jesus); Ephesians 1:3 (God and Father of our Lord Jesus Christ)
- Hebrews 1:2 ("in [his] Son," ἐν υἱῷ); 1:5 (Old Testament quotations of Ps. 2:7 and 2 Sam. 7:14); 1:8 (τὸν υἱόν); 3:6 (Son); 4:14 (Ἰησοῦν τὸν υἱὸν τοῦ θεοῦ); 5:5 (Old Testament quotation of Ps. 2:7); 5:8 (Son); 7:3 (Son of God); 7:28 (Son forever); 10:29 (Son of God)
- 1 Peter 1:3 (God and Father of our Lord Jesus Christ)
- 2 Peter 1:17 (citation of Matt. 17:5//Mark 9:7//Luke 9:35)
- 1 John 1:3 (his Son Jesus Christ); 1:7 (Jesus his Son); 2:22–24 (Father and Son); 3:8 (Son of God), 23 (his Son Jesus Christ); 4:9 (his Son the only begotten); 4:10 (his Son), 14 (Father sent his Son, "Savior of the world"); 4:15 (Ἰησοῦς ἐστιν ὁ υἱὸς τοῦ θεοῦ); 5:5 (Ἰησοῦς ἐστιν ὁ υἱὸς τοῦ θεοῦ), 9–13 (Son, Son of God, etc.), 20 (Son of God); 2 John 3 (Jesus Christ the Son of the Father); 2 John 9 (Father and Son)
- Revelation 1:6 (his God and Father)

This recounting of passages in the New Testament, both in and outside the Gospels, provides a comprehensive picture of references to Jesus as the Son of God by himself and by others, sometimes paired with other christological titles. The use of this christological title merits further explication.

"Son of God" as a Christological Title

The range of data cited above is highly instructive for formulating a christological understanding of Jesus as the Son of God in the New Testament. Several fundamental observations can be made.

The first is that the ancient world referred to individuals as "son of God" or "son." We see this in the Old Testament and in Greco-Roman literature from the time of the New Testament. The language was so ubiquitous in the Greco-Roman world that it invited ridicule by some philosophers and historians (which one might argue was because the people took it seriously). In that regard, the New Testament is consistent with its Jewish literary heritage and the Greco-Roman world from which it emerged.

A second observation is that both the ancient Israelite and the Greco-Roman cultures accepted a gradient scale between the divine and human realms. Genesis 6:2 speaks of the "sons of god" mating with the daughters of men, and the Psalms contain several instances in which the human and divine realms are merged. The New Testament authors were surrounded by cultures that worshiped divine men (and women). The ancient Greco-Roman pantheon integrated the human and the divine from the age of the Titans to the gods of Olympus to the deified Roman emperors. This is the world in which Christianity was birthed.

Third, the New Testament writers appear to have been aware of various ways that references to Jesus as the Son of God might be worded. Early Christianity used language that was similar to and expanded on the language found in the Greco-Roman world to describe its deified figures, especially emperors. They were described as "son of god" or "son." However, whereas the Greco-Roman wording tended to the anarthrous form, in early Christianity the wording tended to the articular, even though the anarthrous form was also used (as noted above). If the German classical scholar Ulrich von Wilamowitz-Moellendorff is correct that use of the article for the head term of the word group indicates divinity, then the New Testament authors often assert divinity by their use of the articular construction.

A fourth observation is that the term "Son of God" in the New Testament does not just share the language of its environment but reflects its contemporary culture, including the divinization within the Roman world (e.g., the emperor cult) and the similar language in the Jewish Scriptures (the Septuagint). This places the New Testament language firmly within its cultural context, making it accessible to its original audience.

With these observations in place, we now turn to the issue of what the New Testament writers meant by using the term "Son of God" with reference to Jesus. Some scholars, especially those influenced by the history of religions approach to the New Testament, have eagerly latched on to the Greco-Roman terminology, while others have rejected it and turned to the Old Testament. The result of looking to the Greco-Roman terminology has been the common acceptance of an adoptionist Christology in the New Testament. An adoptionist Christology claims that Jesus, the man, was "adopted" as a divine figure, in parallel with the way that Roman emperors (and others) were humans first and then ascended to divine status. Others have rejected this view and turned to the Old Testament language as the source of the New Testament understanding of "Son of God." This too is problematic, however, since the Old Testament language, as noted above, does not provide clear parallels for the wording of the New Testament. Further, the Old Testament does have some clear parallels with Greco-Roman deification language in which a human is in some way divinized. The Psalms, often turned to in New Testament Christology, present their views of "Son of God" in this light.

In other words, both Greco-Roman and Jewish sources point to an adoptionist Christology for the New Testament—if one simply accepts their presentation of "Son of God." Such an adoptionistic claim is dependent upon the New Testament reflecting a similar pattern by which Jesus was thought to be a man first and then made a God by his interpreters. We do not believe that the New Testament substantiates such a claim. In fact, we believe that the New Testament argues for a pattern in which, when the human and divine character of Jesus is addressed, the divine attributes are seen to be prior to—or at least contemporary with—his human status.

We may summarize the evidence above in several different ways to illustrate this. To begin with, we recognize that critical issues are raised by use of the Gospels in relation to the historical Jesus and the authenticity of his statements. However, the evidence of references to Jesus as the Son of God by others as well as by himself is so pervasive in the Gospel material—it is found both in John's Gospel and in parallel and independent passages in the Synoptic Gospels—that it is impossible to believe that all these statements were the later construction of the early church.[39] We may even go further and, on the basis of the usage in the New Testament, posit that Jesus himself was conscious of being in a special relationship with God, however that might be defined, which he and others described as sonship.[40] The language of the Greco-Roman sources was functional in that it provided a means of exalting human figures for political and religious purposes. However, the language regarding Jesus in the New Testament—in particular in Paul and the Gospels, supported by the book of Hebrews—indicates more than functionalism when it speaks of the unique filial relationship between God and Jesus Christ.[41] The earlier material in Paul's Letters provides a basis for interpreting the Gospel material as being consistent with Paul's writings, and therefore pointing to a continuity of understanding Jesus as the Son of God.

If we begin with the earliest writings of the New Testament that refer to Jesus as the Son of God, we must examine Paul's Letters. Some have observed that Paul's references to the Son of God or Son are relatively limited in number.[42] However, this prioritizes mere counting over examining the significance of the passages.[43] A common refrain throughout the New Testament, but

---

39. Longenecker, *Christology of Early Jewish Christianity*, 95; cf. Cullmann, *Christology of the New Testament*, 275, 278.

40. See Dunn, *Christology in the Making*, 32, but who retreats from the implications of Jesus's son-consciousness because of his explicit desire not to find preexistence in the earlier New Testament literature. See below. There is some confusion among scholars regarding jumping from Jesus's consciousness of being the Son of God to later dogmatic theological assertions. See, e.g., Grindheim, *God's Equal*, 169.

41. Contra Longenecker, *Studies in Hermeneutics, Christology, and Discipleship*, 136–37, who sees the New Testament language as functional, although he recognizes what he calls Jesus's "filial consciousness" in the Gospels.

42. Longenecker, *Christology of Early Jewish Christianity*, 98.

43. See Fee, *Pauline Christology*.

especially in Paul's Letters, is that God is "the Father of our Lord Jesus Christ" (Rom. 15:6; 2 Cor. 1:3; 13:31; Eph. 1:3; cf. 1 Pet. 1:3). There is no indication in such a statement that there was a time when the Lord Jesus Christ was not the Lord Jesus Christ or that his human birth preceded God being his Father. One might well argue that the phrase itself makes the claim that God as God and God as Father are parallel and coordinate statuses of the divine being and that the status of the Lord Jesus Christ as Son of the Father is what it means to be the Son. A similar pattern is found in the rest of Paul's Letters. In 1 Corinthians 1:9, Jesus is referred to as the "Son, Jesus Christ our Lord." Elsewhere Paul simply uses the term "Son," which appears to be an abbreviated form of his fuller expressions elsewhere.

Two passages might indicate a temporal sequence in which Jesus's humanity preceded his divinity. In the so-called Colossians hymn (Col. 1:15–20), Paul depicts Jesus Christ in language of divine function. At the outset, Paul refers to Christ as the image of the unseen God, the firstborn of all creation (1:15).[44] He proceeds to say that creation occurred in Christ, through Christ, and for Christ. This bestowed upon him certain privileges in the earthly sphere, such as head of the church, firstborn of the dead, and reconciler of humanity. However, all of this is predicated upon Jesus Christ being the image of the unseen God, the firstborn of all creation. Whatever it means to be "firstborn" in this context, it clearly precedes the earthly sphere and is predicated upon existing in the image of God. This pattern inverts the order of adoptionist language so that being the Son of God preceded becoming the earthly Jesus.

The second passage is Romans 1:3–4, already referred to above. Whether these verses come from an earlier Christian tradition, as some think, makes little difference to the argument. There is legitimate debate over whether this passage supports an adoptionist position.[45] This passage states that Christ Jesus (referred to in Rom. 1:1), subsequently designated as "his [God's] Son" (1:3), was designated "Son of God" on the basis of the "spirit of holiness" by or at the time of the "resurrection from the dead." He is thereby said to be "Jesus Christ our Lord" (1:4). This argument may appear to be adoptionistic since it retains the adoptionist chronology. However, this represents an arguably narrow and contextually insensitive reading of the text. Reading these two verses in context, we first note that Paul identifies himself as a slave and called apostle, designated by the good news of God, "concerning his Son" (1:3). Paul identifies Christ Jesus first as the divine son, then specifies that

---

44. See McDonough, *Christ as Creator*, 172–91.
45. The argument below follows Porter, *Letter to the Romans*, 45–47; cf. Bird, *Jesus the Eternal Son*, 11–24. For one recent adoptionist approach, see Kirk, *Unlocking Romans*, 42–44.

he "came about from the seed of David according to the flesh."⁴⁶ In other words, the divine son, when he became a human (the assumption is that he was already God's Son and divine), was from David's line, if one wishes to identify him in fleshly terms.⁴⁷

We note further that Paul makes several more statements about this Son. The first is that he is called "Son of God," a designation that indicates a kind of public or revealed sense. This is further supported by the second statement: he is called Son of God "in power." Jesus's revealed sonship, characterized by power, probably indicates that the Son of God has now revealed powers previously unmanifested.⁴⁸ The designation is clarified when Paul states that it is based on the work of the "spirit of holiness"—a unique phrasing for the Holy Spirit—and is said to have occurred either by means of, or at the time of, the resurrection. This can hardly be the initial indication of Jesus Christ as divine Son, according to the logic of Paul's argument (and the evidence from the Gospel accounts themselves). The Spirit's work results in the specification of that powerful Son's designation: Jesus Christ our Lord, a compound title that indicates that Jesus is the Messiah and God. As we will discuss in chapter 7, just as the notion of "one of God's anointed" came to indicate the *one* anointed by God, "Messiah" became a title of divinity for Jesus in the New Testament. The same is true of Jesus's designation as Lord. The word translated "Lord" (κύριος) came to be the Greek term used to translate the divine name in the Greek Old Testament (see chap. 1). This fuller designation of Jesus Christ is very similar to the statements found elsewhere in Paul (and the New Testament) indicating God as Father of the Lord Jesus Christ.

The Gospels contain a similar christological logic regarding Jesus as the Son of God. In those passages in which Jesus refers to himself as the Son of God or Son, several times he does so in the Synoptic Gospels in a context in which he also refers to God as his Father (Matt. 11:27//Luke 10:22; Matt. 24:36//Mark 13:32; Matt. 28:19). In John's Gospel, Jesus does not use the term "Son of God" very often, preferring instead simply to refer to himself as Son. Martin Hengel characterizes "Son of God" as dyadic and believes that the absolute use of "Son," that is, without modification, as opposed to the absolute use of "Father," indicates a higher level of intimacy between Jesus

---

46. Fee, *Pauline Christology*, 278; contra Longenecker, *Studies in Hermeneutics, Christology, and Discipleship*, 130, who takes the references to David and then Son of God as sequential.

47. See Bates, "Christology of Incarnation and Enthronement"; cf. Bates, *Hermeneutics of the Apostolic Proclamation*, 88–94.

48. See Cullmann, *Christology of the New Testament*, 292; Hengel, *Studies in Early Christology*, 3.

and God (and "Father" appears more than any divine title).⁴⁹ This may be true, but it is perhaps better to see "Son" not simply as conceptually absolute but as a shorthand for the more expressive "Son of God." As John records, Jesus does respond to the fact that others have called him "Son of God" (John 10:36; cf. 11:4). References by Jesus to God as his Father are abundant in all the Gospels, especially when he directly addresses God. Matthew uses Jesus's unique wording of "my Father in heaven."⁵⁰ There are also a number of instances in which others refer to Jesus as the Son of God or Son. The range of wordings used is surprisingly large, with terminology ranging from the usual "Son of God" to variations of this phrase (some of them resembling wider Greco-Roman usage) to "beloved/elect Son" to "Son of the Most High" to language linked to the Messiah.

Further, the adoptionist pattern of Jesus as human preceding Jesus Christ as divine is not found in the Gospels.⁵¹ The narrative pattern assumes from the outset that Jesus is the Son of God or Son, with Jesus and others using this terminology. Even before Jesus's birth, in the Lukan account when Mary is visited by an angel, the angel states that she will give birth to a son and that he will be great and called "Son of the Most High" (Luke 1:32). The angel explains that the Holy Spirit will come upon her and that the one she conceives will be called Son of God (υἱὸς θεοῦ) (1:35). Even the Priene inscription regarding Augustus does not have such a positive depiction, celebrating the "good news" of the birth of the god Augustus fifty-four years after his birth. In Luke's Gospel, there is no temporal priority of human before divine or divine resulting from human. Even in the episode of Jesus's baptism, there is no such priority. When Jesus emerges from the waters of baptism, the voice from heaven states, "This is / You are my Son, the Beloved" (Matt. 3:17//Mark 1:11//Luke 3:22). The verb used is the verb of being (εἰμί), not becoming. God appears to fully recognize Jesus as the divine Son before he has done anything to merit such recognition.

The most important passages for understanding Jesus as the Son of God may be Matthew 26:63–64//Mark 14:61–62//Luke 22:70, already discussed in the previous chapter. The high priest asks Jesus whether he is "the Messiah, the Son of God" / "the Son of the Blessed" (Matthew and Mark; cf. Luke 22:70). The question is posed to Jesus to get him to identify himself as the Messiah, thereby claiming to be the Son of God. Jesus declines to answer directly: "You say that I am" (Luke 22:70). This is not a denial, but it is also not

---

49. Hengel, *Studies in Early Christology*, 369.
50. See Longenecker, *Christology of Early Jewish Christianity*, 98. Cf. Myers, "Jesus the Son of God in John's Gospel."
51. Contra Dunn, *Christology in the Making*, 50, 254.

a strong affirmation. In Matthew's and Mark's accounts, Jesus instead states that he is the Son of Man and that his audience will see him seated at God's right hand (the right hand of power) and coming with the clouds of heaven (a combination of Dan. 7:13 and Ps. 110:1). In other words, Jesus defines what it means to be the Messiah and the Son of God as the Son of Man, thereby making clear that the Son of Man is a divine figure who accompanies God as God comes to judge the world, with both seated on God's chariot throne as he comes from heaven to judge the earth. This is a surprisingly strong statement about what it means to be the Son of God. The high priest concurs, as he tears his robes and declares that there is no need for additional witnesses to Jesus's blasphemy, since Jesus has condemned himself. Jesus has declared that being the Son of Man means being the Son of God—and being God himself.

This divine nature of Jesus is made theologically explicit in the book of Hebrews. There are various examinations of how this theological point is made by the biblical author. Amy Peeler notes that the author depends on a "familial theme" in which language of "Son" and two key references to "Father" (Heb. 1:5 and 12:9) provide the basis for the relationships among the book's readers (addressed as "sons," "children," household members, and "brothers," among other terms) and their relationship to God as Father.[52] Another way to interpret Hebrews is to examine the connection between God and the Son of God made clear through its direct appeal to the Old Testament. Jesus's identity as God's Son is introduced in Hebrews 1:2 when he is presented as the heir of all things and involved in the creation of the world. These verses go on to describe Jesus the Son as the "reflection of God's glory," "the exact imprint of God's very being," and seated by God on high (1:3). These descriptions depict not the human condition but rather something more heavenly or divine;[53] the verses contribute to a larger portrait of Jesus as the divine Son of God in Hebrews.[54] In the catena of citations in Hebrews 1:5–14, the author develops his understanding of Jesus as Son.[55] Particularly important is the pair of citations that God the Father speaks to the Son in Hebrews 1:8–12. The first is a quotation from Psalm 45:6 in which the Father says to the Son, "Your throne, O God, is forever and ever" (Heb. 1:8). If it seems shocking to us that here the Father refers to the Son as "God," then, as R. B. Jamieson has recently pointed out, we have failed to follow the author's argument up to

---

52. Peeler, *You Are My Son*, esp. 2–3 for summary.
53. On the christological language in Hebrews, see Bauckham, "Divinity of Jesus Christ in the Epistle to the Hebrews."
54. On Hebrews' high Christology, especially in relation to the language of sonship, see Brennan, *Divine Christology in the Epistle to the Hebrews*.
55. See Jamieson, *Paradox of Sonship*, 59–66.

this point.⁵⁶ The second citation begins in 1:10 with God speaking the words of Psalm 102:25–26: "In the beginning, Lord, you founded the earth, and the heavens are the work of your hands; they will perish, but you remain" (Heb. 1:10–11a). The Son is now given the title "Lord," and his eternal nature and activity in creation are emphasized.⁵⁷

Introduced with the words "But of the Son he says" (Heb. 1:8), these two citations are clearly descriptions of the Son. As Jamieson has argued, the exordium and catena of Hebrews 1 establish the term "Son" as a divine designation.⁵⁸ He writes, "Hebrews uses 'Son' to identify Jesus as the God confessed in Israel's Scriptures: what God does, Jesus does; what God is, Jesus is."⁵⁹

We recognize that many critical problems may be suggested regarding the "Son of God" language of the Gospels as well as of the other texts of the New Testament. However, rather than being adoptionistic, this language is built into the narrative structure of the various New Testament texts, which portray Jesus—as does Jesus himself—as the Son of God. The New Testament writers recognize that Jesus has a unique filial relationship in his spiritual being with God, and this relationship is manifested in various ways that merit the recognition as divine Son from before his becoming human.⁶⁰

Contribution to New Testament Christology

We have argued throughout this chapter that the "Son of God" language in the New Testament argues against an adoptionist view of Christology. The adoptionist view sees Jesus as a human that God elevated to divine status at some point in his life—commonly understood as occurring at his baptism but also possibly at the transfiguration, his resurrection, or the ascension. In the early centuries of the Christian movement, the Ebionites, for example, held that Jesus was the Messiah but was not a divine figure. God had chosen him because of his faithfulness and elevated him to a special status—that of the anointed one. In the second century, Theodotus of Byzantium articulated the view that Jesus was a righteous man who was adopted by God at his baptism and equipped to do miracles and other divine actions.⁶¹ Modern scholars, such as Bart Ehrman and others, have argued that some parts of the New Testament—especially those writings deemed to be among the earliest

---

56. Jamieson, *Paradox of Sonship*, 63.
57. Described in more detail in McDonough, *Christ as Creator*, 192–211.
58. Jamieson, *Paradox of Sonship*, esp. 51.
59. Jamieson, *Paradox of Sonship*, 74.
60. Cullmann, *Christology of the New Testament*, 270.
61. Hippolytus, *Philosophumena* 7.35.

> ### HIPPOLYTUS ON THE ADOPTIONIST HERESY
>
> In his *Refutation of All Heresies*, the third-century theologian Hippolytus describes an early adoptionist Christology that emerged in the late second century CE.
>
>> A certain Theodotos, a Byzantian, introduced a new heresy. . . . Drawing on the school of the gnostics, Kerinthos, and Ebion, he claims that Christ appeared in the following way. Jesus was born of a human being from a virgin according to the Father's will. He lived a life common to all people yet became the most pious. Later, at his baptism in the Jordan, he received the Christ, who descended from above in the form of a dove. Thus before the Spirit (which he calls "Christ") descended and was shown to be in Jesus, "the miracles were not activated in him." But they do not want him to have become a god when the Spirit descended. Others say that he became a god after he rose from the dead.[a]
>
> a. Hippolytus, *Philosophumena* 7.35.1–2. Translation from Litwa, *Refutation of All Heresies*, 571.

compositions—reflect such an adoptionistic Christology.[62] This is a view that has persistently recurred throughout the history of the church and one that continues to have a voice within biblical scholarship.

It may be that some writers of the New Testament held to some version of what was later called "adoptionism," and we will admit that some language used in the text lends itself to such an interpretation. But the overall witness of the New Testament moves in a different direction. Some scholars may consider this an evolution of christological thought—from an adoptionist stance to a more elevated or "high" Christology. Our task in this book is to examine the New Testament canon within its historical and cultural contexts. Taken as a whole, the New Testament paints a picture of Jesus that defies the standard adoptionist view. Jesus, as the Son of God, is an eternal figure who does many miraculous feats during his time on earth. He is identified as having a special relationship with God—even at his birth—and his resurrection and ascension into heaven are presented not as an elevation of his status but as an affirmation of and a return to his glorious position at God's right hand.

In the New Testament, Jesus is declared by others to be the Son of God. He also refers to himself as the Son of God and to God as his Father. New Testament authors do the same, as well as referring to God as the Father

---

62. See Ehrman, *How Jesus Became God*.

of Jesus. Even if one may wish to challenge some of these statements as to their authenticity, the evidence is overwhelming that Jesus and others believed from the outset that he was the Son of God. We also recognize that there are parallel conceptions of other figures within the Greco-Roman and Jewish worlds who were seen to be "sons of god." However, this does not mean that the writers of the New Testament, or even Jesus himself, simply unwittingly adopted this earlier "son of god" language. Nevertheless, nothing prevented those who followed Jesus from using the language of deification as an appropriate way to describe him. The Greco-Roman world was full of "son of god" language at least from the time of Augustus onward—the very world into which Jesus was born. Besides several important specific references in the Old Testament, the contemporary Jewish world was also familiar with similar kinds of language. Thus, it is not unreasonable that Jesus may have been referred to as the Son of God, especially if his followers saw him as the Messiah, to whom they looked to perform the acts of God such as judging, receiving worship, and ruling.

CHAPTER 5

JESUS THE SUFFERING SERVANT

Introduction

In Acts 8, an Ethiopian eunuch is traveling from Jerusalem back to Ethiopia. This eunuch is apparently a follower of Yahweh because he had been in Jerusalem to worship and is now returning home. A man of importance and responsibility, the Ethiopian is the treasurer for the queen of Ethiopia. As he rides in his chariot, he reads the following passage from the book of the prophet Isaiah:

> Like a sheep [πρόβατον] he was led to the slaughter,
>   and like a lamb [ἀμνός] silent before its shearer,
>   so he does not open his mouth.
> In his humiliation justice was denied him.
>   Who can describe his generation?
>   For his life is taken away from the earth. (Acts 8:32–33, quoting Isa. 53:7–8)

The apostle Philip, sent by an angel of the Lord, encounters the Ethiopian as he is traveling and reading and asks him whether he understands what he is reading. The man is candid in his response: "How can I, unless someone guides me?" (Acts 8:31). Despite his lack of knowledge, the Ethiopian senses that there is more to the passage than one at first might realize, so he asks whether the prophet Isaiah is speaking about himself or someone else. Philip responds by using this passage from Isaiah as an introduction to telling the Ethiopian about the good news of Jesus.

The book of Acts does not tell us what other passages Philip drew into the discussion; however, considering the Ethiopian's question and Philip's response, it is likely that Philip began to talk about passages that depict the Suffering Servant of Isaiah in relationship to Jesus. The use of the Suffering Servant in the New Testament is not a christological tradition that is as widely discussed as others. Some scholars even deny that Jesus is to be seen as the Isaianic Suffering Servant in the New Testament. Despite numerous discussions on the subject, no consensus has emerged regarding the Suffering Servant and its use in the New Testament.[1] Brevard Childs notes a possible reason for such difference of scholarly opinion: "Some of the difficulty obviously has arisen from the fact that Isaiah 53 appeared to offer the strongest biblical confirmation of Christ's atoning and vicarious death, yet was a passage without any prior tradition of a suffering messianic interpretation within Judaism."[2] Childs pinpoints the main issue in this discussion: while Isaiah 53 (and other chapters that we will look at) offers biblical support for Jesus's death and suffering, there apparently was no tradition before the time of Jesus for understanding these passages as describing a *suffering* messianic figure or person anointed by God for a divine purpose.[3] As a result, we must ask this question: Did Jesus or any New Testament writer think of Jesus as the Suffering Servant of God, and if so, what exactly did they think? We believe that the ministry of Jesus in the Gospels regularly and significantly displays qualities that mirror the Suffering Servant in Isaiah and that other New Testament writers, especially Paul, also saw Jesus in this light. The Gospels understand Jesus's ministry to involve vicarious suffering leading to his own death as a representative in place of others, and to indicate that he alludes to the Suffering Servant of Isaiah 53 when he makes such claims.

"Suffering Servant" in the Old Testament

With most discussions of the christological characteristics of Jesus, appeal is made to a range of passages spread throughout the Jewish Scriptures. The situation is different for the Suffering Servant, as the evidence is confined to four passages in Isaiah: Isaiah 42:1–4; 49:1–7; 50:4–11; and 52:13–53:12. It

---

1. See, e.g., Hooker, *Jesus and the Servant*; Bellinger and Farmer, *Jesus and the Suffering Servant*; Janowski and Stuhlmacher, *Suffering Servant*; and McKnight, *Jesus and His Death*, 207–24, with bibliography on 207–8n1.
2. Childs, *Biblical Theology of the Old and New Testaments*, 514.
3. In fact, there is not even a coherent view of vicarious suffering in the pre-Isaianic tradition. See Spieckermann, "Conception and Prehistory of the Idea of Vicarious Suffering."

is the last passage, Isaiah 52:13–53:12, that is likely the most familiar to the Christian reader since it fully articulates the vicarious suffering and death of the servant. However, before we turn to this passage, we will examine the other three passages since they bring a fuller articulation of the servant into view. These four passages make up the so-called Isaianic Servant Songs, yet that designation is somewhat misleading (they are less *songs* than they are *poems* or *prophetic words*). Taken together, these four passages present a distinguished tradition in Isaiah concerning the servant of God.[4]

The first Servant Song speaks of the servant as God's "chosen one" who will bring forth justice on earth.

> Here is my servant, whom I uphold,
>   my chosen, in whom my soul delights;
> I will put my spirit upon him;
>   he will bring forth justice to the nations.
> He will not cry or lift up his voice,
>   or make it heard in the street;
> a bruised reed he will not break,
>   and a dimly burning wick he will not quench;
>   he will faithfully bring forth justice.
> He will not grow faint or be crushed
>   until he has established justice in the earth;
>   and the coastlands wait for his teaching. (Isa. 42:1–4)

From this introduction, we can identify a few significant aspects of this figure. First, God has chosen him, and God's spirit is placed upon him (Isa. 42:1). Second, the servant is meek: he does not cry out or lift his voice or break a bruised reed. Third, the servant will "bring forth" justice. Thus, there is in this passage a sense that God has appointed and equipped the servant for a specific task.[5] The servant is presented as humble and meek, yet he has the task of establishing justice on earth. From this task he will neither "falter" nor "be discouraged" (42:3). Isaiah 42:1, with reference to the servant in whom God delights, is cited in various places in the Gospels, including the familiar account of Jesus's baptism (Matt. 3:17//Mark 1:11//Luke 3:22), the transfiguration (Matt. 17:5), and Jesus's healing episode in Matthew 12:17–21, among possibly other places.[6]

---

4. Some have argued that the four Servant Songs should not be regarded as distinct from the rest of so-called Deutero-Isaiah. See Mettinger, *Farewell to the Servant Songs*, esp. 45–46.

5. Westermann, *Isaiah 40–66*, 94.

6. This is not the place for a lengthy discussion on this topic, but see, e.g., Blomberg, "Matthew," 14; Myers, "Isaiah 42 and the Characterization of Jesus in Matthew 12:17–21."

The second passage, Isaiah 49:1–7, speaks of the servant having been called by God before birth for a specific task—to bring Israel back to God and to be a light to the gentiles.

> The LORD called me before I was born,
>   while I was in my mother's womb he named me. . . .
> And he said to me, "You are my servant,
>   Israel, in whom I will be glorified." . . .
> And now the LORD says,
>   who formed me in the womb to be his servant,
> to bring Jacob back to him,
>   and that Israel might be gathered to him,
> for I am honored in the sight of the LORD,
>   and my God has become my strength—
> he says:
> "It is too light a thing that you should be my servant
>   to raise up the tribes of Jacob
>   and to restore the survivors of Israel;
> I will give you as a light to the nations,
>   that my salvation may reach to the end of the earth."
> Thus says the LORD,
>   the Redeemer of Israel and his Holy One,
> to one deeply despised, abhorred by the nations,
>   the slave of rulers,
> "Kings shall see and stand up,
>   princes, and they shall prostrate themselves,
> because of the LORD, who is faithful,
>   the Holy One of Israel, who has chosen you." (Isa. 49:1, 3, 5–7)

This second Servant Song, taking the perspective of the servant himself, contains ideas similar to those in the first. That he is chosen by God is repeated (49:1), appealing to the fact that God formed him in his mother's womb to be Yahweh's servant (49:1, 5). A connection is made between the servant and the fortunes of Israel. The servant states that God's purpose in choosing him is to "bring Jacob back" to God so that "Israel might be gathered to him" (49:5). The passage points to the restoration of Israel but also states that the servant will be a "light to the nations" so that God's salvation "may reach to the end of the earth" (49:6), while being "despised" and "abhorred" (49:7) in the meantime. This passage is never used in reference to Jesus in the New Testament, although Isaiah 49:6, regarding God's eschatological salvation, is cited in Acts 13:47, as Paul defends his mission to the gentiles.

In the third passage, Isaiah 50:4–11, the servant affirms that he will continue to rely on God as his helper and vindicator in the face of adversity, despite the accusations brought against him.

> I gave my back to those who struck me,
>   and my cheeks to those who pulled out the beard;
> I did not hide my face
>   from insult and spitting.
>
> The Lord God helps me;
>   therefore I have not been disgraced;
> therefore I have set my face like flint,
>   and I know that I shall not be put to shame;
>   he who vindicates me is near.
> Who will contend with me?
>   Let us stand up together.
> Who are my adversaries?
>   Let them confront me. (Isa. 50:6–8)

The adversity that the servant suffers comes through strongly in this passage (50:6, 8). In verse 6 there is physical torment—he is beaten and mocked. Yet there is also an emphasis on the servant's dependence on God and the Lord's vindication (50:7–8). Further, adversaries confront and contend with the servant (50:8–9). In this situation, the servant relies on God and finds help in the Lord. So, with this Servant passage, there is a movement into conflict and dilemma. This will escalate as we move to the fourth and final passage.

> Surely he has borne our infirmities
>   and carried our diseases;
> yet we accounted him stricken,
>   struck down by God, and afflicted.
> But he was wounded for our transgressions,
>   crushed for our iniquities;
> upon him was the punishment that made us whole,
>   and by his bruises we are healed.
> All we like sheep have gone astray;
>   we have all turned to our own way,
> and the Lord has laid on him
>   the iniquity of us all. . . .
>   Out of his anguish he shall see light;
> he shall find satisfaction through his knowledge.
>   The righteous one, my servant, shall make many righteous,
>   and he shall bear their iniquities.

> Therefore I will allot him a portion with the great,
>   and he shall divide the spoil with the strong;
> because he poured out himself to death,
>   and was numbered with the transgressors;
> yet he bore the sin of many,
>   and made intercession for the transgressors. (Isa. 53:4–6, 11–12)

The fourth passage, Isaiah 52:13–53:12, contains the words of the prophet describing the servant rather than the words of the servant himself. This certainly makes sense given that the servant is beaten to the point of disfigurement. He is hated and rejected. It looks as though God has turned against him, and the servant is killed for our sinfulness. He does not protest, even though he is slaughtered like a lamb. He, as God's appointed righteous servant, will nevertheless prosper and justify others by bearing their sins. The suffering dimension of this servant of God comes into full force in Isaiah 52:13–53:12. In this passage the servant is said to be "despised and rejected by others" and "a man of suffering and acquainted with infirmity" (53:3). He is "oppressed" and "afflicted" like "a lamb that is led to the slaughter" (53:7). His death is described with vivid imagery: "he was cut off from the land of the living" (53:8) and "they made his grave with the wicked" (53:9).

An important feature of this passage is the servant's vicarious suffering for others. This is clear in Isaiah 53:4–6, which states, among other things, that the servant "has borne our infirmities and carried our diseases." Verse 5 says that he was "wounded for our transgressions, crushed for our iniquities"; and verse 6 states, "The LORD has laid on him the iniquity of us all." This passage stresses that the servant does not merit what he is receiving but suffers and dies for others. However, one must not miss the promise of vindication found in this passage. The prophet tells us that the servant's punishment has "made us whole" and that "by his bruises we are healed" (53:5). The closing verses affirm that God will vindicate the servant. Isaiah 53:11–12 promises that "out of his anguish he shall see light; he shall find satisfaction through his knowledge" and "I will allot him a portion with the great, and he shall divide the spoil with the strong." This Servant Song is cited several times in the New Testament, including in Romans 15:21, citing Isaiah 52:15; and in John 12:38 and Romans 10:10, citing Isaiah 53:1, but without reference to the Suffering Servant.

The above discussion offers an all-too-brief examination of the four Servant Songs of Isaiah. Nevertheless, it is worthwhile to examine these passages in at least some detail so that we are better positioned to judge the extent of their christological influence in the New Testament.

So Who Is This Servant (or Servants)?

Who is the servant of God in Isaiah? Early Jewish interpreters offered many different proposals regarding the identity of the servant, and interpretations have continued to this day.[7] Some see the servant as a future king of Israel who will possibly suffer and then have the kind of triumph described. Others take the figure as not just *a* king of Israel but *the* king—the Son of David, or the Messiah.[8] Others argue that the servant is an ideal or mythological figure, one that might fit several human beings.[9] Another interpretation is that the servant is a prophet, possibly Isaiah himself. This viewpoint is reflected in the eunuch's question in Acts 8:34 and could certainly be derived from the first-person speech used in the Isaiah passages. The identity of the servant in Isaiah continues to be debated within biblical scholarship.[10]

The variety of interpretations is no doubt a result of the relatively vague language found in these passages. For example, at certain points the figure looks like an individual person (Isa. 42:1–4), at other points he seems to be the nation Israel (49:3) or possibly a remnant within Israel (49:5–6). That said, we can ascertain several characteristics of the Suffering Servant—some of which are admittedly debatable—from the four passages. First, the servant is, at least, an individual, if not more than one person, but not likely a large group of people.[11] In several places in these passages, an individual person is being described: he is made by God (42:6; 49:5, 8); chosen in his mother's womb (49:5); elect, chosen, or called (42:1; 49:1); the focus of God's good pleasure (42:1); and prepared for his calling (49:2; 50:4–5). While it is possible that this language is being used collectively of a large group, it most likely refers to an individual.

The second characteristic—vicarious suffering—comes out most clearly in the fourth passage. The servant is characterized as one who surrenders to God while being obedient like a lamb led to slaughter (Isa. 53:7). The figure is assured of vindication from God (50:7–9), but he must first go through suffering and death (53:12). The servant's suffering is on behalf of other people, as a representative of a larger group. This is a form of corporate *representation*: a designated individual makes decisions with consequences for the whole group, such as a king for his people. This is significant for the Suffering Servant in

---

7. See Cullmann, *Christology of the New Testament*, 53–54.
8. See Hengel with Bailey, "Effective History of Isaiah 53 in the Pre-Christian Period."
9. North, *Suffering Servant in Deutero-Isaiah*, 218.
10. See also Lessing, "Isaiah's Servants in Chapters 40–55"; and Kaiser, "Identity and Mission of the Servant of the Lord," 92–94, for various views.
11. Rosenberg, "Jesus, Isaac, and the Suffering Servant," esp. 381.

> ### THE SERVANT AS ISRAEL IN THE ZOHAR
>
> The Zohar is a Jewish writing that first appeared in the thirteenth century but was held to be written in the second century. This passage quotes the Servant Song of Isaiah 53 and interprets the servant as Israel.
>
> > Come, consider the congregation of Israel, how it is called a *lamb*, as it is said, "Like a lamb that before her shearers is dumb." Why was it dumb? Because while the other nations ruled over it, it was deprived of speech and made dumb.[a]
>
> a. Zohar, section ואר‎א. Translation from Driver and Neubauer, *Fifty-Third Chapter of Isaiah*, 16.

Isaiah 53. The individual in this passage is intertwined in action and fortune with a group, though not confused with it. Nevertheless, in some ways what happens to him has consequences for this group. This is the vicarious self that is depicted, one who suffers on behalf of others. Although prophets and the servant of God are both called upon to suffer, prophets do not willingly take on suffering for others, and thus it is not vicarious suffering. Prophets suffer because it is the destiny of prophets to suffer; the servant, however, takes on this role for others.[12]

The final characteristic found in these passages relates to the covenantal restorative purpose behind the suffering that the servant endures. It does not appear to be random suffering or suffering that is just a part of one's lot in life. Therefore, this figure is probably not to be equated with a prophet or with the prophet Isaiah himself. Being a prophet was an unpopular vocation and often resulted in opposition and hardship. However, the Servant Songs present a figure who accomplishes a specific purpose through his suffering. Even more, this suffering restores the covenant relationship between God and his people (Isa. 42:4, 6; 49:5–6). In some ways, this suffering is a necessary part of getting to the point of restoration.

This discussion both summarizes the views of the Suffering Servant and highlights several of the major features of this figure. The enigmatic characteristics, however, prompt further thought when they are applied to Jesus. Even before we discuss Jesus, however, we must recognize some of the difficulties in seeing such a suffering figure in light of other Jewish expectations regarding deliverance figures.

12. Cullmann, *Christology of the New Testament*, 56.

Jesus the Suffering Servant

The Conundrum of a Suffering Messiah in Jewish Thought

In some respects, the Suffering Servant has characteristics of other Old Testament figures appointed by God to effect his will for his people Israel. People appointed for such tasks are often characterized as being messianic figures. (We deal specifically with Jesus the Messiah in chap. 7.) Messianic figures were expected to deliver God's people from their enemies. Problems emerge when we apply these servant characteristics to Jesus, especially that of being a vicarious sufferer, in light of the messianic expectations of deliverance surrounding the Suffering Servant. These problems begin in the Old Testament itself. There is a wide range of messianic expectation in the Old Testament and other Jewish literature, with anticipated messianic figures ranging from priestly to prophetic to royal figures of various types, invoking such figures as Moses, David, and even, on occasion, the Suffering Servant.[13] The concepts of messiah and servant of God are occasionally found in similar contexts. A few passages in which they appear to overlap include Ezekiel 34:23–24, where David is called servant and made prince over Israel; Ezekiel 37:24–25, where the servant David will be made king over God's one kingdom; and Zechariah 3:8, where the angel of the Lord speaks of the Branch, a messianic reference, as servant. These are not particularly strong messianic or servant passages, even if they do seem to bring the two ideas together. When the two concepts of God's chosen and God's servant do merge in the Old Testament (if, indeed, they do), the emphasis is typically on the restoration of the covenant relationship and a future kingdom, not on suffering or the suffering of the servant. Further, when expectations for messianic figures are expressed in the Old Testament or in Jewish literature, rarely is it part of a messiah's task to suffer. In extrabiblical apocalyptic works—such as *1 Enoch*, *4 Ezra*, and the apocalyptic Baruch traditions—characteristics of a servant are ascribed to a messiah, except for suffering. Even when the servant in Isaiah is interpreted as messianic, his triumph and exaltation are emphasized, not his suffering. The Messiah was supposed to be a deliverer, but he was not thought of as a deliverer who comes and is overwhelmed by the enemy. Rather, he was supposed to be a messiah who comes and strikes down his enemies.[14] Thus, Suffering Servant does not appear to be a messianic title, at least in the conventional sense, and we must look elsewhere to understand its origins and use.[15]

---

13. See Porter, "Introduction: The Messiah in the Old and New Testaments," esp. 1–4, with bibliography. See also the other essays in this edited volume on messianism.

14. Cullmann, *Christology of the New Testament*, 56; cf. V. Taylor, *Jesus and His Sacrifice*, 45–46. Longenecker (*Christology of Early Jewish Christianity*, 104–5) sees the suffering Messiah as a later development in Jewish thought.

15. Contra Longenecker, *Christology of Early Jewish Christianity*, 104, who sees the Suffering Servant as based on the Messiah.

This lack of reference to a suffering messiah creates a problem when we speak of the New Testament and Jesus's role as the Messiah. We are faced with a situation in which there is little precedent for someone to be thought of as a messiah who suffers. A messiah who says, "I am going to deliver you through suffering and death" does not fit into any identifiable messianic expectation. Christianity has so strongly identified with the concept of a suffering messiah that we must not lose sight of the novelty of such an idea in first-century Judaism. We must instead look elsewhere for understanding of the Suffering Servant, apart from messianic expectation.

Jesus as the Suffering Servant in the New Testament

There is little doubt that the writers of the New Testament understood Jesus in terms of the Suffering Servant from Isaiah. In order to navigate these texts, we will break down the evidence into three categories. The first category is the role that suffering plays in the ministry of Jesus. Here we will look at the emphasis that the Gospels place on Jesus's suffering and its function in his ministry. The second category consists of the various citations of Servant Songs in Isaiah used with reference to Jesus.[16] The third category is how the rest of the New Testament, in particular Paul's and Peter's Letters, views the Suffering Servant, especially with reference to Isaiah.

Suffering in the Ministry of Jesus

The Gospels present Jesus as teaching that his ministry on earth will involve suffering and ultimately death. The abundance of references in the Gospels indicates that this theme may have originated with Jesus himself. Whether or not that is the case, the Gospel portraits clearly present a Jesus who understands his vocation to include suffering and death—even as his disciples struggle to accept the notion.

Several passages in the Gospels present Jesus pointing to his suffering and death. In Matthew 9:14–15//Mark 2:18–20//Luke 5:33–36, for example, Jesus responds to the question of why his disciples do not fast by saying that when he is gone they will fast. Luke 13:31–35 contains a more direct reference to Jesus's death. In this passage Jesus responds to a threat from Herod by stating that he must finish his work (13:32)—while implying that his work as a prophet will lead to his death in Jerusalem (13:33). Similarly, Jesus states in Luke 12:50 that he has a "baptism" to undergo that will distress him until it

---

16. For what follows, see Cullmann, *Christology of the New Testament*, 61–69.

is complete. Another telling reference is when Jesus responds to a request by the scribes and Pharisees for a sign. In Matthew 12:39–40, Jesus states that no sign will be given except the sign of Jonah: "So for three days and three nights the Son of Man will be in the heart of the earth" (12:40).

The passages cited above are representative of Jesus's teaching regarding the role of suffering and death in his ministry. There are, however, even more explicit passages. These passages—as well as the previous ones—include some of the Son of Man sayings of Jesus.[17]

The first is Matthew 16:13–20//Mark 8:27–33//Luke 9:18–21, in which Jesus asks his disciples who people say he is—leading to Peter's confession that Jesus is the Messiah. Jesus's response is that they must not tell anyone about his identity. In all three Gospels, Jesus then teaches them that the Son of Man "must undergo great suffering, and be rejected by the elders, the chief priests, and the scribes, and be killed, and after three days rise again" (Mark 8:31). Jesus speaks quite plainly about these things, and Peter takes him aside and rebukes him. In response, Jesus turns and looks at his disciples and rebukes Peter: "Get behind me, Satan!" (Matt. 16:23//Mark 8:33). Here we see the tension brought on by the notion that the Messiah was not typically thought to be a suffering figure in, and before, the first century. This certainly seems to be the case for Peter, who is right in identifying Jesus as the Messiah but confronts Jesus when he talks about his upcoming suffering and death. In Peter's thinking, the anointed one is not supposed to suffer. Jesus's response, in Matthew 16:23, is that Peter has in mind not the things of God but the things of humans. In other words, Peter's exegesis of the Old Testament is wrong. That may be what humans are saying, but that is not the program of Jesus. Jesus essentially states that he is following God's program, and God's program involves his suffering, rejection, and death.

The second passage is Mark 9:31 (pars. Matt. 17:22–23; Luke 9:43b–45), in which Jesus tells his disciples, "The Son of Man is to be betrayed into human hands, and they will kill him, and three days after being killed, he will rise again." Mark makes clear in verse 32 that the disciples did not understand what Jesus was talking about but were afraid to ask him. Again, Jesus is connecting his ministry to suffering and death, and the disciples cannot make sense of it within their traditional categories of interpretation.

A similar pattern occurs for a third time in the Synoptic Gospels as Jesus and his disciples are on their way to Jerusalem. In Matthew 20:17–19 (Mark 10:32–34//Luke 18:31–34), Jesus pulls the disciples aside and tells them that they are going to Jerusalem but that the Son of Man will be handed over to

---

17. On the Son of Man, see chap. 3 of this book.

the Jewish authorities, condemned to die, and handed over to the gentiles for mockery, flogging, and crucifixion before he is raised after three days. The response of the disciples—in this case specifically James and John—calls into question what Jesus is teaching. The brothers approach Jesus to request that they sit at his right and left sides in his kingdom. For the third time the disciples are confused by Jesus's teaching on his suffering and death.

In an interesting example from John's Gospel, Jesus tells a crowd that he will be "lifted up from the earth" (John 12:32). The Gospel writer then comments, "He said this to indicate the kind of death he was to die" (12:33). The crowd is confused by Jesus's statement and responds, "We have heard from the law that the Messiah remains forever. How can you say that the Son of Man must be lifted up? Who is this Son of Man?" (12:34). Like the disciples in the previous passages, the crowd is confused by Jesus's teaching about his death because it does not cohere with their messianic expectations.

Numerous other passages could be cited that establish the Gospels' understanding of suffering and death as a part of Jesus's ministry. The parable of the vineyard and the evil tenants (Matt. 21:33–46 pars.), for example, foreshadows Jesus's own rejection and death. In another example, a woman anoints Jesus with ointment (Matt. 26:6–13//Mark 14:3–9//Luke 7:36–50). In response to others' condemnation, Jesus remarks, "She has anointed my body beforehand for its burial" (Mark 14:8). This event is immediately linked to Judas Iscariot's plans to betray Jesus (Matt. 26:14–16//Mark 14:10–11// Luke 22:3–6).

The Suffering Servant Passages and Jesus

The Gospels clearly present Jesus teaching that his ministry on earth will involve suffering and death. While this overlaps with the Suffering Servant from Isaiah, the connection is so far only a thematic one. In this section we will examine passages in which the New Testament writers explicitly link Jesus to the Suffering Servant.[18]

Matthew's Gospel includes an extended quotation of the first servant passage from Isaiah 42 (Matt. 12:18–21). After he defends healing people on the Sabbath, Jesus heals several others and warns them not to tell others about him. The Gospel writer states that "this was to fulfill what had been spoken through the prophet Isaiah" (12:17). Matthew also understands Jesus's healing of the sick as a fulfillment of the description of the servant as one who "took our infirmities and bore our diseases" (Matt. 8:17; cf. Isa. 53:4).

---

18. For a good examination of four relevant passages connecting Jesus's ministry to the Suffering Servant passages, see McKnight, *Jesus and His Death*, 207–24.

Jesus the Suffering Servant

Luke 22:37 provides the only formulaic quotation of a Suffering Servant passage spoken by Jesus. In the verse prior, Jesus indicates to his disciples that the time of peace has passed and the time of the sword or suffering is upon them. He then says, "For I say to you that it is necessary for this that is written to be fulfilled in me, 'And he was counted among the lawless'; for indeed what concerns me is being fulfilled" (Luke 22:37 AT). Here Jesus is linking himself directly with Isaiah 53:12, as being counted among the lawless. Luke's placement of this quotation comes at a critical point in his Gospel. It follows Jesus's explanation of his coming suffering and appears at the beginning of Luke's passion narrative. The quotation itself is emphatically stated, as Luke includes a lengthy introductory formula: "For I say to you that it is necessary for this that is written [using the perfect tense-form] to be fulfilled in me." David Pao and Eckhard Schnabel note these elements and conclude that "Luke wants his readers to understand Isaiah's fourth Servant Song as the hermeneutical key to the narrative of Jesus' suffering and death."[19]

Another important passage comes from the parallel accounts of the Lord's Supper. There are two separate traditions in the New Testament regarding the institution of the Lord's Supper (or Eucharist). One is reflected in Mark's and Matthew's accounts (Matt. 26:28–29//Mark 14:24–25), and the other in Luke (Luke 22:20–23) and Paul's First Letter to the Corinthians (1 Cor. 11:24–25). However, both traditions have much in common. The first common element is the emphasis that Jesus places on the vicarious aspect of his forthcoming sacrifice. In Mark (but not in Matthew),[20] this is expressed as Jesus presents the cup as his blood poured out "for many" (ὑπὲρ πολλῶν); Luke and Paul have "for you" (ὑπὲρ ὑμῶν). The preposition used here, ὑπέρ, translated "for," could be translated "for the benefit of many" or, in the Lukan and Pauline instances, "for you." This is not quite the same as saying "in the place of" or "as a substitute for" many. There is a great deal of theological discussion of this preposition and its meaning.[21] However, the substitutionary sense of the preposition ὑπέρ is well known in classical Greek and is regularly used in the Greco-Roman documentary papyri, especially when a scribe writes for (in place of—ὑπέρ) another (P.Teb. 104.39–40; P.Hamb. 4.14–15).[22] It is in this substitutionary sense—something being done in the place of another—that the preposition is being used here by Jesus. What Jesus does, he does not just

---

19. Pao and Schnabel, "Luke," 385.
20. Matthew has "concerning many," περὶ πολλῶν.
21. See Jeremias, *Eucharistic Words of Jesus*, 179–82; Riesenfeld, "ὑπέρ."
22. See A. T. Robertson, "Use of ΥΠΕΡ in Business Documents in the Papyri"; Porter, *Idioms of the Greek New Testament*, 176–77.

for the benefit of others but, as the crucifixion demonstrates, in the place of others—that is, vicariously.

The second common element of these parallel passages is the covenantal dimension. In each of the parallels of the Lord's Supper passage, Jesus points to the shedding of his blood, his death on the cross, as a way of establishing a covenant between God and humanity. Jesus displays a clear sense of what his suffering and death will accomplish in covenantal terms. Further, his language in these Gospel passages is very similar to that in the Servant Songs in Isaiah—especially Isaiah 53 (e.g., vv. 4–5, 11–12). The Markan language of Jesus's blood being poured out "for many" parallels the idea of the servant suffering for the many in Isaiah 53:11–12 ("many" appears three times in these final two verses). The one is doing something for the many. Further, what the one is doing for the many in the Lord's Supper passages is connected with the covenant—similar to the Suffering Servant who will be a covenant for the people (Isa. 49:8). The use of this allusive language in the Lord's Supper, along with the direct quotation from Luke 22:37, indicates that the Gospel writers understood Jesus in terms of the Suffering Servant.

Other passages support this connection, such as Jesus's baptism (Matt. 3:13–17//Mark 1:9–11//Luke 3:21–22). Mark states that "Jesus came from Nazareth of Galilee and was baptized by John. And immediately upon his coming up from the water, he saw the heavens dividing and the Spirit descending like a dove on him. And a voice came from heaven, 'You are my Son, the Beloved; in you I am well pleased'" (Mark 1:9–11 AT). There is a possible connection here with Isaiah 42:1, which speaks of the servant as one in whom God delights, especially if the word for "son" (υἱός) used in Mark is a translational variant of the word for "servant" in Hebrew (עֶבֶד) or Greek (παῖς) in the Old Testament.[23]

But why was Jesus baptized at all? This is a curious question that has been given much attention. In Matthew 3:15, Jesus tells John the Baptist that he should baptize him to "fulfill all righteousness." As Craig Keener points out, Jesus is probably expressing his obedience to God's plan as revealed in Scripture. Further, Keener notes that Matthew's readers have already been shown that Jesus fulfilled Scripture by "identifying with Israel's history and completing Israel's mission (2:15, 18)."[24] Jesus did not need to be baptized for his own sins but was being baptized as a stand-in for others. There is a vicarious aspect of his baptism—which itself points to his impending death. Elsewhere in the Gospels (Mark 10:38; Luke 12:50), Jesus equates his baptism

---

23. For connections of this passage and others (e.g., the transfiguration in Mark 9:7 and parallels and Luke 23:35), see McKnight, *Jesus and His Death*, 217–20.

24. Keener, *Commentary on the Gospel of Matthew*, 132.

with his death.[25] So at the beginning of his ministry, Jesus is seen as preparing for death and doing so on behalf of others.

Paul, Peter, and the Suffering Servant

Some passages in Paul's Letters show knowledge of Isaiah and a familiarity with the tradition of Christ as the Suffering Servant, but these are not overly explicit. For example, in Romans 4:25, Paul writes that Jesus "was handed over [παρεδόθη] on account of our transgressions and was raised on account of our justification" (AT). Significant here is the betrayal language (Isa. 53:6, 12) and the concept of the one suffering for the many (53:4–6, 11–12).[26] This notion appears again in Romans 5:19: "For just as by the one man's disobedience the many were made sinners, so by the one man's obedience the many will be made righteous." Another example is Philippians 2:7–8: "[Jesus] emptied himself, taking the form of a slave [δοῦλος], becoming in human likeness. And being found as a human, he humbled himself, becoming obedient to death, indeed, death on a cross" (AT). This connection to Jesus's death and role as a servant makes it probable that Isaianic Suffering Servant language is being used. As Gordon Fee states, "It is hard to imagine that early Christians . . . would not rather automatically have heard this passage [Phil. 2:6–8] with that background [Isa. 53:12] in view, especially since the passage in Isaiah begins (52:13) the way this one ends, with the Servant's exaltation by God."[27]

First Peter also presents Jesus's death as involving suffering on behalf of others as a reflection of the Isaianic servant. In 1 Peter 2:21–22, the author states that "Christ . . . suffered for [ὑπέρ] you. . . . 'He committed no sin, and no deceit was found in his mouth'" (cf. Isa. 53:9). The Suffering Servant is then further explicated in 1 Peter 2:23–25 with reference to Jesus. He is insulted, does not retaliate, and makes no threats but instead entrusts himself to God. He therefore bears human sins on the cross so that by his wounds we are healed. In this way, Christ's suffering on behalf of others serves as an example, in that Christians too are "like sheep hav[ing] gone astray" (Isa. 53:6).

The rest of the New Testament does not seem to consider the Suffering Servant concept, and only a few early church texts, such as *Didache* 9.2; 10.2 and *1 Clement* 59.3–61.3, present the idea. The two passages in the *Didache*

---

25. This is how John's Gospel sees it. John 1:29 states, "Here is the Lamb of God who takes away the sin of the world!" This passage in the light of Jesus as the Passover Lamb is discussed in chap. 6 below.

26. Hurtado, *Lord Jesus Christ*, 128, endorsing the opinion of C. E. B. Cranfield in his commentary on Romans.

27. Fee, *Pauline Christology*, 386.

are eucharistic passages in which Jesus is called "servant" (παῖς), while *1 Clement* is an extended prayer for help in time of suffering and distress.

Jesus as the Suffering Servant in Mark 10:45 and Isaiah 53:10–12

Mark 10:45, along with its parallel in Matthew 20:28, is a passage that weaves together many of the various threads that have been discussed so far in this chapter and is a focal point for discussion of the Isaianic Suffering Servant and Jesus.[28] This verse shows how the early church understood the death of Jesus as a self-sacrifice, and it enlightens us on several other important concepts.[29] For this reason, it is a heavily discussed and rigorously studied passage.

Mark 10:45 appears in Jesus's response to his disciples following the request by James and John to sit at his side in paradise (10:35–37).[30] Jesus's reply is that they misunderstand his mission. The rest of the disciples find out about this discussion and become angry with James and John. Jesus then gathers them and speaks on the need for humility and service in leadership. He closes with a Son of Man saying: "For the Son of Man came not to be served but to serve, and to give his life a ransom for many" (10:45).

Up until the mid-twentieth century, there was little debate that Mark 10:45 alluded to Isaiah 53. Since the work of Morna Hooker and C. K. Barrett, however, the evidence for this allusion is not so easily granted.[31] The critiques by Hooker and Barrett (and followed by many others) have limited the extent that this passage can be understood as appealing to Isaiah 53, but they have not completely foreclosed arguments for this connection. Yet if one is to connect Mark 10:45 to Isaiah 53, one must, so it seems, pass through Hooker and Barrett to get there.[32]

Several linguistic issues are often discussed regarding Mark 10:45 and Isaiah 53. A major challenge is that the word used by Mark for "serve" (διακονέω) is never used in the Septuagint to translate the verb עבד (serve) in Isaiah. However, the use of δοῦλος (slave/servant) in Mark 10:44 ("Whoever wishes

---

28. For discussions on the connection between Mark 10:45 and Isa. 53, see Barrett, "Background of Mark 10:45"; Cullmann, *Christology of the New Testament*, 60–69; Watts, "Jesus' Death, Isaiah 53, and Mark 10.45"; McKnight, *Jesus and His Death*, 159–71.

29. For the history of reception of this passage, see Edwards, *Ransom Logion in Mark and Matthew*. For comparison of the various relationships among the relevant passages, see Dunn, *Jesus Remembered*, 809–18.

30. This passage is paralleled in Matt. 20:28, within the similar episode found in Matt. 20:20–28.

31. Hooker, *Jesus and the Servant*; Barrett, "Background of Mark 10:45."

32. For a good overview of the debate, see Watts, "Jesus' Death, Isaiah 53, and Mark 10.45"; also Watts, "Mark," 203–6.

to be first among you must be slave of all"), a word that is used to translate the noun עֶבֶד in the Septuagint (e.g., Isa. 49:3, 5, 7), arguably establishes διακονέω as a contextually synonymous word for serving. Further, the verb used in Isaiah 53:11 LXX for "serve" (δουλεύω) is not found in the passive voice, so the formulation in Mark 10:45 would have needed to substitute another word, such as διακονέω, which is used in both active and passive voices.[33]

Another challenge put forth by Hooker is that the word "ransom" (λύτρον) in Mark 10:45 is never used in the Septuagint to translate אָשָׁם.[34] However, this challenge, like the first one, is dependent upon a direct quotation of the Septuagint on the part of Mark. If Mark is understood to be freely translating the Hebrew text of Isaiah, these concerns become far less significant.[35] So, while linguistically these words do not tie literally to Isaiah 53, they do connect thematically. A stronger tie between Mark 10:45 and Isaiah 53 makes the allusion clearer. The use of ἀντὶ πολλῶν (in the place of many) has direct correspondence to many places in the fourth Servant Song (Isa. 52:14–15; 53:11, 12). Particularly striking is the use of πολύς (many) in Isaiah 53:12 in reference to an atonement act for the "many."[36] The choice of ἀντί (in place of), instead of another preposition such as ὑπέρ (for),[37] makes clear the substitutionary aspect of Jesus's words. While other prepositions allow some possible ambiguity, ἀντί clearly indicates substitution or taking the place of one thing for another.[38] The use of this preposition also ties Mark 10:45 to Isaiah 53:12:

Mark 10:45b	Isaiah 53:12 LXX
καὶ δοῦναι τὴν ψυχὴν αὐτοῦ λύτρον ἀντὶ πολλῶν	ἀνθ' ὧν παρεδόθη εἰς θάνατον ἡ ψυχὴ αὐτοῦ
and to give his life as a ransom in place of many	in place of whom his life was given to death

Both passages connect the substitutionary aspect of the person's death using the preposition ἀντί: Mark's Gospel has "in place of many" (ἀντὶ πολλῶν); Isaiah has "in place of whom" (ἀνθ' ὧν, referring to "the strong" in the previous clause). More striking is the shared language referring to

---

33. Watts, "Mark," 203.
34. Hooker, *Jesus and the Servant*, 76–77; also Barrett, "Background of Mark 10:45," 5–7.
35. France, *Jesus and the Old Testament*, 118; McKnight, *Jesus and His Death*, 167; Watts, "Mark," 204.
36. McKnight, *Jesus and His Death*, 168.
37. Moulton, *Prolegomena*, 105, says that ὑπέρ is "colourless" compared to the rarer and more explicit ἀντί, especially in Mark 10:45, which logion of Jesus he sees quoted in 1 Tim. 2:6.
38. See Porter, *Idioms of the Greek New Testament*, 144–45.

the person "giving his life." The two verbs used (Isaiah: παραδίδωμι; Mark: δίδωμι) have a common semantic range, with the prefixed preposition on Isaiah's παραδίδωμι perhaps only intensifying the meaning of the verb or emphasizing its substitutionary sense, not indicating a divergent sense.[39] Together with ἡ ψυχή (the soul, here translated "life"), both verbs become idiomatic, referring to actively risking or laying down one's life.[40] Given how odd this language is both in the Old Testament and in Mark, there seems to be a strong case that Isaiah 53 is being alluded to in Mark 10:45.

Drawing together the thematic and linguistic connections between Mark and the fourth Servant Song—including the reference to the "many," the substitution of one suffering for others, and some loose references to suffering and ransom—Jesus's words invoke, to some degree, the Isaiah tradition. While some scholars want to point solely to Daniel 7 with the use of "Son of Man" in this passage, Mark seems to be creatively combining a number of traditions here to form a new one. In fact, he may be implicitly invoking the Suffering Servant to designate Jesus as the servant in the same way that he is the Son of Man.[41] To quote Oscar Cullmann, "It is as if Jesus said, 'The Son of Man came to fulfill the task of the *ebed Yahweh* [servant of God].' Jesus consciously united in his person the two central concepts of the Jewish faith, *barnasha* [son of man] and *ebed Yahweh*."[42]

Contribution to New Testament Christology

In this chapter we have argued that the Suffering Servant tradition found in Isaiah plays a significant role in New Testament Christology. In the Gospels, Jesus sees himself as the Suffering Servant of Isaiah, and other passages from the New Testament support this connection. The number of references is not large, but they are significant, especially Mark 10:45. Apart from a couple of references in Paul's Letters and 1 Peter, the connection between Jesus and the Suffering Servant is predominantly displayed in the Gospels. It may be that this was a feature of Jesus's teaching and so is reflected in the Gospels but not picked up much elsewhere in the New Testament. Whether or not this is the case, the Suffering Servant of Isaiah is clearly one of the traditions

---

39. See Louw and Nida, *Greek-English Lexicon*, esp. domains 37 and 57.
40. Παραδίδωμι τὴν ψυχήν is an idiom for "to risk one's life," while δίδωμι τὴν ψυχήν can be rendered "to give one's life." However, connected with the word for death (θάνατον) in Isa. 53:12, παραδίδωμι τὴν ψυχήν has a sense not of *risking* one's life but willingly dying. See Louw and Nida, *Greek-English Lexicon*, 23.100; 21.7.
41. We thank Bryan Fletcher for his insights on this point.
42. Cullmann, *Christology of the New Testament*, 65.

> ## THE *EPISTLE OF BARNABAS* ON THE SUFFERING SERVANT AND JESUS
>
> The *Epistle of Barnabas* is an early Christian writing (possibly from the late first century) that also applies the Servant Song of Isaiah 53 to Jesus.
>
> > It was for this reason that the Lord endured the deliverance of his flesh to corruption, so that we might be cleansed by the forgiveness of sins, that is, by his sprinkled blood. For the scripture concerning him relates partly to Israel and partly to us, and speaks as follows: "He was wounded because of our transgressions, and has been afflicted because of our sins; by his wounds we were healed. Like a sheep he was led to slaughter, and like a lamb he was silent before his shearer." We ought, therefore, to be exceedingly thankful to the Lord, because he has both made known to us the past and given us wisdom in the present circumstance, and with regard to future events we are not without understanding.[a]
>
> a. *Epistle of Barnabas* 5.1–3. Translation from Holmes, *Apostolic Fathers*, 391–93.

that the New Testament writers drew from when explaining and depicting Jesus's person and mission.

In light of chapter 3 above, on the Son of Man, it is interesting to see how the concepts of the Son of Man and the Suffering Servant overlap in Mark 10:45. While some scholars wish to move away from the Isaiah tradition and explain the thematic backdrop to this verse solely within Daniel 7 and the Son of Man, we have shown that connections to the Servant Songs are too strong to ignore. The choice is not between one christological depiction or the other. Instead, Mark's Gospel creatively combines Jewish sacred traditions in this passage. This is another example of how the New Testament writers draw from numerous traditions and christological concepts, sometimes even within the same passage, as they seek to understand who Jesus is.

A contribution of the New Testament's servant Christology is its focus on the sufferings of Christ. As the early church grappled with the reality of a messiah who suffered and died, it saw in the servant passages from Isaiah a lens through which to understand Christ. Understanding Jesus as the Suffering Servant makes sense of the innocent suffering that defines his earthly ministry. Further, the servant tradition describes how Jesus's sufferings are vicarious. Jesus suffered and died on behalf of others, and God has vindicated that suffering.

CHAPTER 6

JESUS THE PASSOVER LAMB

Introduction

In John 1, John the Baptist appears on the scene, proclaiming the coming of the Messiah. He denies, however, that he is the Messiah, which prompts those who are listening to ask him who he is. They ask whether he is instead Elijah or the prophet, and he denies this as well. He does say that he is preparing the way for another by his calling out to straighten the path in front of the Lord. He is merely preceding one more worthy than himself. When Jesus one day approaches John, John declares, "Here is the Lamb of God who takes away the sin of the world!" (John 1:29), indicating that Jesus is the one to whom he had previously referred. John had seen the Spirit descend upon Jesus, revealing him as God's chosen person. The identification of Jesus as the Passover Lamb, the Lamb who takes away the sin of the world, introduces a primarily, though not exclusively, Johannine christological title that is developed throughout the entirety of John's Gospel and beyond.

In some ways, this chapter marks a noticeable shift from previous chapters because it focuses not on the Synoptic Gospels, which are so important for establishing the christological identity of Jesus, but on John's Gospel, although we will also discuss other places in the New Testament where Jesus is possibly seen as the Passover Lamb. Further, the christological identity of the Passover Lamb moves away from Jesus's self-identifications, such as the Son of Man, the Messiah, or even the Son of God, to a christological title that is solely attributed to him by others on the basis of the Passover theme in the Old Testament. Despite this, Jesus as the Passover Lamb makes some profound statements about who Jesus is. Finally, this chapter employs elements of narrative Christology, whereby the narrative of John's Gospel establishes the significance of the christological title. This narrative approach will be evident in our presentation of how John's Gospel establishes Jesus as the Passover Lamb.

To explore Jesus as the Passover Lamb, we begin by discussing the Passover in the Old Testament. We then turn to the seven major passages in John's Gospel in which this christological title is developed, culminating in the death of Jesus in John 19. Turning to the book of Revelation, we will find that the Passover Lamb is the primary character within the drama of the book. Finally, we will briefly discuss several other places in the New Testament where the Passover Lamb theme is treated.

The Passover in the Old Testament

The Passover is arguably the most significant festival in the Jewish calendar because it marks the time when God delivered the people of Israel from their captivity in Egypt and led them to the promised land. Much must be said about the Passover within Jewish history and tradition because of both its inception and its neglect. Our focus in this section is on the institution of the Passover in Exodus 12 as well as on a few other passages in the Old Testament that refer to this event, by which it comes to represent a major Jewish tradition drawn upon in the New Testament.[1]

The Institution of the Passover and Exodus 12

The key Old Testament passage on the Passover is found in Exodus 12, where the Lord provides a way for the Israelites to be protected during the final plague against Pharaoh, who has kept them in captivity. This protection—the Passover—is a significant event in Israel's history. It has several important elements. First are God's instructions regarding the lamb:

> Tell the whole congregation of Israel that on the tenth of this month they are to take a lamb for each family, a lamb for each household. If a household is too small for a whole lamb, it shall join its closest neighbor in obtaining one; the lamb shall be divided in proportion to the number of people who eat of it. Your lamb shall be without blemish, a year-old male; you may take it from the sheep or from the goats. (Exod. 12:3–5)[2]

---

1. See Pitre, *Jesus and the Last Supper*, 375–89.
2. The Septuagint translation of Exod. 12:3–5 uses πρόβατον as the translation for "lamb." See also Exod. 12:21, 32. Πρόβατον is the usual term for sheep.

The Israelites are next instructed on how to slaughter and eat the lamb. This guidance is followed by instructions for protecting their families from the Lord's striking down the firstborn in each household:

> For I will pass through the land of Egypt that night, and I will strike down every firstborn in the land of Egypt, both human beings and animals; on all the gods of Egypt I will execute judgments: I am the LORD. The blood shall be a sign for you on the houses where you live: when I see the blood, I will pass over you, and no plague shall destroy you when I strike the land of Egypt. (Exod. 12:12–13)

Alongside instructions for the Passover itself, instructions for celebrating the event are also included. The Israelites are to celebrate the Lord's deliverance at the Passover as a festival. After this, Moses returns to the specific instructions regarding the performance of the first Passover. They are to "go, select lambs for your families, and slaughter the passover lamb" (12:21). Then they are to "touch the lintel and the two doorposts with the blood in the basin" (12:22). Moses tells the Israelites that "the LORD will pass through to strike down the Egyptians; when he sees the blood" he "will pass over that door" (12:23). Again, Moses describes the remembrance of this event and instructs the Israelites to teach their children its significance (12:24–27).

The next section (Exod. 12:29–42) describes the fulfillment of the final plague, resulting in Pharaoh driving the Israelites out of Egypt. Beginning at verse 43, the Lord again speaks about the Passover ceremony and remembrance. The Passover meal, the Lord tells Moses and Aaron, must be celebrated by the entire community. However, it is a celebration that should not be defiled, so the Lord instructs that no uncircumcised males or foreigners may take part. Further, the meal must be eaten inside the home, and not a bone of the animal should be broken (12:46).

The Passover in the Rest of the Old Testament

When reading through the account of the first Passover in Exodus, we notice that certain elements are often repeated. The need to remember and celebrate this event, for example, is emphasized again and again (Exod. 12:2, 14, 17, 24–27, 42, 43–50). We see similar repetition of the regulations of the Passover in other parts of the Old Testament. In Numbers 9:1–14, the Lord speaks to Moses in the wilderness and tells him to have the Israelites celebrate the Passover, giving instructions much like those found in Exodus. Similar commands are found in Deuteronomy 16:1–8 and Joshua 5:10–12. Given this repetition, it is evident that regularly commemorating this event was to be an important part of Israel's life.

The ceremony was forgotten, however, as 2 Kings 23:22 tells us: "No such passover had been kept since the days of the judges who judged Israel, even during all the days of the kings of Israel and of the kings of Judah." When Josiah discovers the law, he instructs the people to keep the Passover for the first time in centuries. The parallel account in 2 Chronicles 35 repeats many of the regulations that were given "according to the word of the LORD by Moses" (2 Chron. 35:6). Ezra 6, in a similar way, recounts the first Passover celebrated by Israel after returning from exile.

The Practice of the Passover

The Passover marks the time when Israel was freed from the Egyptians in a remarkable and memorable way. Before turning to the New Testament, we will examine some key features of the Passover tradition that will be helpful for our study.[3]

First, the Israelites had to follow a particular procedure when celebrating the Passover. They were to take a certain type of animal—a year-old lamb without defect—that represented the best in their flock. They were to take care of the lamb until the fourteenth day of the month and slaughter it at twilight that evening, then spread its blood over their doorframes and cook the meat over a fire (not boiling it or eating it raw). In addition, unleavened bread was to be eaten with the meat, and certain attire was to be worn while eating it. These detailed instructions are often repeated for emphasis; the effect of this repetition is to underscore their importance. Thus, the celebration of the Passover involved a carefully prescribed procedure.

Second, the biblical narrative stresses the Passover's memorial value. The repetition of this procedure in subsequent time periods encouraged the Israelites to remember the original Passover and the events surrounding it. This memorialization included, for example, their deliverance from the Egyptians—that they had been slaves in Egypt and that God had rescued them from their bondage. However, this was not only an ending; it was also to mark a beginning. It was a new start, the ushering in of a new time when they would be free from slavery. They were going to march out of Egypt, have new leaders, and become a group with its own identity. The Israelites were to move out and become God's people in a new land.

A third feature of the Passover, tied to the memorial value of the Passover celebration, is the symbolism attached to many of its elements, though only a few will be highlighted here. One important symbolic element is found in

---

3. For treatment of the Passover, among many examples, see Keil and Delitzsch, *Commentary on the Old Testament*, 1.2:9–32; Childs, *Exodus*, 178–214.

the concept of purity throughout the celebration. The animal chosen was to be without defect, and only a specific animal was appropriate for the sacrifice. The animal symbolized the kind of pure offering this was to be. Further, this purity is attached to the restrictions on who could participate and the conditions that had to be met. Another important aspect of the symbolism can be found in the propriety alluded to in the Passover procedure. For example, no bone of the animal was to be broken. This was to be a clean killing: the animal was not to be mauled or mutilated. The entire procedure was to be done with care and in a way that was respectful of the sacrifice given. There is also symbolism in the posture of eating. The Israelites were to eat in haste while wearing sandals and holding their staffs. Essentially, they were to be ready to leave, fitting the abruptness by which the Israelites fled Egypt.

While numerous features of the Passover have not been explored here, the following is a short summary of the Passover's meaning that will be of use in discussing the Passover, and more particularly, the Passover Lamb as a christological title. The sacrifice of the animal at Passover represented deliverance from the angel of death as well as redemption from the oppression of Egypt. There is deliverance from death but also an opening up of new possibilities. This event leads to the exodus from Egypt, crossing over the Jordan, and eventually entering the new land the Israelites had been promised. In a deliberate and formal way, the Passover marks the beginning of a new era for the people of God. The Passover Lamb is central to the sacrifice marking this beginning. These ideas lie behind the notion that Jesus is the Passover Lamb in the New Testament.

Jesus as the Passover Lamb in John's Gospel

The Passover tradition is a dominant motif in John's Gospel, and with it the theme that Jesus is the Passover Lamb who accomplishes for his followers what the lamb represented in the life and liberation of ancient Israel. This theme is stronger than many scholars recognize, even those who accept its presence.[4] Jesus as the Passover Lamb shows that Jesus is seen by the author of John's Gospel as the suitable—in fact, perfect—Passover victim and therefore a redemptive figure. Several other concepts support the Passover theme in John's Gospel. One of these is reference to Moses, the leader of the people during the Passover (John 1:17, 45; 3:14; 5:45, 46; 6:32; 7:19, 22, 23; 8:5; 9:28, 29).[5]

---

4. See Nielsen, "Lamb of God"; Hoskins, "Deliverance from Death by the True Passover Lamb"; Hoskins, "Freedom from Slavery to Sin and the Devil"; and Rainbow, *Johannine Theology*, 215–17.

5. See Glasson, *Moses in the Fourth Gospel*; Meeks, *Prophet-King*, esp. 228–30; and Rainbow, *Johannine Theology*, esp. 184–85.

More to the point are numerous references to the Passover either directly or as a "feast."[6] John's Gospel directly refers to the Passover ten times, which is more than any other New Testament book. These references prepare for the presentation of Jesus as the Passover Lamb.

The support for Jesus as the Passover Lamb in John's Gospel is found not just in a few passages, such as John 1 and 19. The theme is distributed throughout the Gospel, to the point that it constitutes a major christological title.[7] Seven major passages interspersed throughout the Gospel establish the significance of Jesus as the Passover Lamb. These span Jesus's life on earth. Their effect in establishing Jesus as the Passover Lamb is cumulative.

Jesus as the Lamb of God in John 1:29–36

The first episode that presents Jesus as the Passover Lamb coincides with Jesus's earliest earthly appearance in John's Gospel. John the Baptist sees Jesus approaching him and declares that Jesus is the Lamb of God who takes away the sin of the world, who is both after and before him, and to whom he bears witness. This passage contains two significant acclamations by John the Baptist (John 1:29, 36) in which he refers to Jesus as "the Lamb [ἀμνός] of God." These are the only two uses of ἀμνός in John's Gospel (out of a total of four in the entire New Testament; see also Acts 8:32; 1 Pet. 1:19). These two references appear in concentrated fashion at a crucial initiatory point in the Johannine narrative, marking the Gospel's as well as John the Baptist's introduction of Jesus and the commencement of Jesus's ministry (John 1:19–12:16).[8]

Scholars have debated the meaning of John the Baptist's words regarding Jesus being the Lamb of God.[9] For most interpreters, however, mention of the Lamb of God in this context includes at least some reference to the Passover. John's Gospel is often understood as using "lamb" here with reference to the Passover, even if John the Baptist's understanding was of some other meaning.[10] Although the word ἀμνός (lamb) is not used in Exodus 12 to refer to the Passover animal, in other places in the Septuagint, such as Numbers

---

6. The word translated "Passover," πάσχα, is used in John 2:13, 23; 6:4; 11:55 (2×); 12:1; 13:1; 18:28, 39; 19:14; and ἑορτή, "feast," used with reference to the Passover in John 2:23; 4:45; 5:1; 6:4; 11:56; 12:12, 20; 13:1, 29.

7. See Hoskins, "Deliverance from Death by the True Passover Lamb," 285–300; Lee, "Paschal Imagery in the Gospel of John"; and Rainbow, *Johannine Theology*, 215.

8. See Bernard, *Gospel according to St. John*, 1:43–47.

9. For summaries of the positions, see Carey, "Lamb of God and Atonement Theories"; Sandy, "John the Baptist's 'Lamb of God' Affirmation"; Skinner, "Another Look at 'The Lamb of God.'"

10. On this question, see Burrows, "Did John the Baptist Call Jesus 'The Lamb of God'?"

28:19, ἀμνός is used in the context of the Passover.¹¹ This verbal and conceptual correspondence, the association of the lamb with the sacrificial system, the significance of the Passover in this sacrificial system, and the function of both in John's Gospel and later Jewish thought (see below)—all point toward Jesus as the Passover Lamb. J. K. Howard says that this early episode serves as an introduction to the idea of Jesus as the Passover Lamb as a theme that is continued throughout the book.¹²

Perhaps more important in establishing Jesus as the Passover Lamb than the simple reference to his being the Lamb, however, is the additional comment attributed to John the Baptist that Jesus is the Lamb "who takes away the sin of the world" (John 1:29). At first glance, the author seems to be invoking the Suffering Servant motif of Isaiah 53 (esp. vv. 4–8, 10, 12; see chap. 5 of this book). John shows knowledge of Isaiah at several points in the Gospel, including formulaic quotations in John 1:23 of Isaiah 40:3, in John 12:38 of Isaiah 53:1, and in John 12:40 of Isaiah 6:10.¹³ However, the reference in John 1:29 is more specifically focused and moves beyond the Suffering Servant who bears the sins of Israel (Isa. 53:4). In Isaiah 53:7, the servant of the Lord is the ἀμνός who makes no noise and does not open its mouth before its shearers. Jesus is twice directly equated in this early episode of the Gospel with the Lamb of God. This equation builds upon the language of Isaiah 53:7, where the Suffering Servant is said to be like a lamb, to represent Jesus directly as the sacrificial victim who takes away sin.¹⁴ In his first appearance, Jesus is depicted as one whose life is sacrificial in nature, and the sacrifice is characterized as one that takes away the sin of all people (cf. Acts 8:32). Mark Stibbe rightly concludes that "the suggestion is that Jesus is the true passover Lamb, the Lamb of God who takes away the sin of the world."¹⁵

The Temple Episode and John 2:13–25

The second major passage that connects Jesus with the Passover lamb is the story of Jesus's cleansing the temple. John states at the outset that "the Passover of the Jews was near" (John 2:13) when Jesus enters Jerusalem and

---

11. See also Exod. 29:38–41; Lev. 9:3; 12:6; 14:10 with reference to other sacrifices. See M. Davies, *Rhetoric and Reference in the Fourth Gospel*, 234.
12. Howard, "Passover and Eucharist," 332. See also Koester, *Word of Life*, 112–13.
13. Daise, *Quotations in John*, 31–124.
14. Michaels argues that "takes away the sins of the world" resists an understanding of Jesus as a victim (*Gospel of John*, 108). While it may be appropriate to understand Jesus also as *victor* and not simply as passive victim, the metaphor of Jesus as Lamb certainly also brings with it the notion of a sacrificial victim.
15. Stibbe, *John's Gospel*, 35.

goes to the temple. This significant event, placed by the author at the outset of Jesus's ministry, is thus coordinated with the Passover. The Passover is mentioned not only in John 2:13 but also in 2:23 at the close of the incident. This inclusio usefully surrounds the intervening events of Jesus's temple cleansing with explicit reference to the Passover, so that Jesus's temple actions are understood as Passover activities.[16]

What Jesus does in the temple is depicted by the Gospel author as instituting a new Passover but with a major difference. Jesus is the focus rather than the old sacrificial institution. This shift of focus is indicated in several ways. In graphic fashion, Jesus drives those selling the animals, including sheep (πρόβατα) and cattle (βόας), out of the temple.[17] Then, through a series of verbal interchanges with the leaders who interrogate him, Jesus, by referring to his own body, puts himself forward as the substitute for the sacrificial system—that is, the temple system oriented toward the Passover sacrifice.[18] He tells them to destroy "this temple" (John 2:19) and he will raise it in three days. The author tells us that Jesus is speaking of "the temple of his body" (2:21), a clear reference to Jesus's death.[19] W. D. Davies goes so far as to use this new Passover as a means of accounting for the placement of the episode: "John places the Cleansing of the Temple very early in his Gospel, in 2:13–25, to signify that a New Order had arrived. The 'Holy Place' is to be displaced by a new reality, a rebuilt 'temple (*naos*),' which John refers to as 'the temple of his body.'"[20]

John is thus telling his readers that Jesus's death is the new temple institution, one that renders the old no longer serviceable because Jesus is the sacrificial Lamb of God.

The Feeding of the Five Thousand and John 6

The next episode that develops the Passover theme is John 6, especially verses 1–14 and 22–71. John's Gospel states that the events of the chapter, in particular Jesus's feeding of the five thousand, take place near the time of the Passover (John 6:4),[21] but there are other substantial reasons to see

---

16. Borchert, "Passover and the Narrative Cycles in John," 307–8. See also Borchert, *John*, 1:161.
17. Πρόβατον is the more usual term for sheep, and the one used in the Exod. 12 account of the institution of Passover. See Exod. 12:3, 4, 5, 21, 32, where cattle are also mentioned.
18. See Cirafesi, "Priestly Portrait of Jesus."
19. Cf. Stibbe, *John's Gospel*, 52.
20. W. Davies, *The Gospel and the Land*, 289–90. We set aside issues of historicity and chronology of the temple incident. See Porter, *Linguistic Analysis of the Greek New Testament*, 294–97.
21. See Lindars, *Gospel of John*, 240; cf. Keener, *Gospel of John*, 1:664.

this as a Passover episode. Many scholars agree that this chapter was a form of Christian Passover haggadah or retelling of the Passover, possibly read at Passover celebrations.[22] Further, several Moses-exodus allusions create a Passover milieu by referring to images often associated with the Passover.[23] In John 6:4–5,[24] after the author mentions that the time of the Passover is near, Jesus lifts up his eyes, sees a large, hungry crowd, and makes provision for them to eat bread. The eating of bread is linked to the Passover meal. In John 6:31–33, when asked for a sign, Jesus says that the Jewish people of a previous generation ate the manna from heaven in the desert and that it is not Moses but God the Father who gives the true bread from heaven, which is the one who comes down from heaven. Jesus is alluding here to himself as the bread.[25] In John 6:34–38, Jesus equates himself with the bread that comes down from heaven, after the people have apparently recognized his capability and asked him to give them this bread. Finally, in John 6:48–51, after reiterating more explicitly what he has just said, Jesus not only calls himself the living bread that comes down from heaven and guarantees life but also equates this bread with his flesh, which he says will be given for the life of the world (6:51). This is an invocation of sacrificial imagery in terms of the Passover theme.

We pointed out above, as have numerous interpreters of this passage, that John's Gospel emphasizes the role of Moses, the leader of the Israelite exodus and the instigator of the Passover, and so allusion to the manna of the exodus supports the Passover theme. But Jesus goes further and equates himself with this heavenly bread and sees this bread as sacrificial. Thus, Jesus himself makes his sacrificial death even more explicit in John 6:53–58, when he connects the idea of the bread coming down from heaven with eating his flesh and drinking his blood.[26] Not only does this language reflect exodus language (cf. 1 Cor. 10:3–4), but it is also sacrificial and makes direct appeal to Passover practices by means of Last Supper imagery. This imagery, maintained throughout John 6, is especially focused on the feeding miracle.[27]

---

22. Borgen, *Bread from Heaven*, esp. 1–27.
23. See Daise, *Feasts in John*, 138–42.
24. Schnackenburg (*Gospel according to St John*, 2:14) notes that this reference is "not chronological but theological," since John is the only one to mention the Passover being near.
25. Westcott (*Gospel according to St. John*, 1:228) notes that "bread from God" in John 6:33 is similar in phrasing to "Lamb of God" in 1:29, 36, indicating that it comes directly from God.
26. See Howard, "Passover and Eucharist," 334. Πίνειν τὸ αἷμα (drink the blood) is unique to John in the New Testament (6:54, 56); and τρώγειν τὴν σάρκα (eat the flesh), also unique to John, is used exclusively by him for the Last Supper (6:54, 56, 57, 58; 13:18).
27. See Exod. 12:7, 22; 1 Cor. 10:6–22. As Carson recognizes (*Gospel according to John*, 268–69), the reference to the Passover is complex. There may also be an allusion to the Suffering Servant ascent-descent motif. See Nicholson, *Death as Departure*.

Jesus, Freedom, and John 8:31–47

In John 8:31–47, Jesus addresses a group of believing Jews, saying, "If you remain in my word, truly you are my disciples, and you will know the truth, and the truth will set you free" (8:31–32 AT). This triggers a discussion of what they will be set free from. Jesus talks first of bondage to sin (8:34–38) and then of bondage to the devil (8:42–47). However, Jesus stresses the freedom that he provides: "If the Son makes you free, you will be free indeed" (8:36).

The connections of this episode to the Passover theme are not nearly as firmly established as are some others. One of the main reasons is that this exchange does not happen around the time of the Passover but rather around the Festival of Tabernacles (John 7:2). Paul Hoskins, however, has made a strong case that this section contributes to the Passover theme in John.[28] He first identifies that the Feast of Tabernacles and Passover are closely related—both look back to the events of the exodus (Passover) and the wandering of the Israelites before entering the promised land (Tabernacles). Hoskins rightly claims that the theme of freedom from slavery fits the context of the original Passover and correlates with the Passover theme in John's Gospel. In fact, the concepts of freedom and slavery may not be explicit but may invoke thematically related language.[29] Hoskins argues that this Johannine section "provides the redemptive picture that helps to fill out John's Passover typology. It clarifies both the nature of the slavery and the redemption that John has in view."[30] Hoskins may see more in this section than is there, but he is certainly right that John 8:31–47 is another important element in the overall development of John's Passover theme.

The Plot to Kill Jesus and John 11:47–12:8

John 11 describes an incident in which the intentions of the leaders of the Jewish people, captured by the words of Caiaphas the high priest, point specifically to Jesus as the sacrificial Passover victim. Considering the controversy caused by Jesus, Caiaphas states that he thinks it is better that "one man die for [ὑπέρ] the people" than that the whole nation be destroyed (John 11:50). The scene is full of dramatic and verbal irony. On the one hand, the author refers to Jesus in his sacrificial role as creating the unified children of God (11:51–52), while the high priest speaks with specific reference to the death of Jesus saving the Jewish people, in particular its leaders, from destruction

---

28. Hoskins, "Freedom from Slavery to Sin and the Devil," 47–63.
29. See Porter, *Sacred Tradition in the New Testament*, 43–46.
30. Hoskins, "Freedom from Slavery to Sin and the Devil," 62.

at the hands of the Romans. On the other hand, Caiaphas's words create an equation that captures (for John's Gospel) the function of the Passover sacrifice, in that the substitutionary death of the one victim (the "Lamb of God") prevents the destruction by sin of an entire people.[31] Although the preposition ὑπέρ (for) is used, the substitutionary idea is paramount.[32] The context itself is clearly substitutionary: Caiaphas sees the single individual as providing a substitute for the nation so that destruction will come only to one. This sense of the one taking the place of the whole is what is taken up by John in explaining the meaning of Caiaphas's statement.

There are two additional references to the approaching Passover in John 11:55 and 12:1. The first is a general reference to the Passover, and the second places the following events six days before the Passover. The effect of these two explicit time markers is to link Caiaphas's words to Jesus's anointing at Bethany by Mary (12:1–8), and then to link both these events to Jesus's impending death. John strengthens the connection when Jesus states that the purpose of Mary's action is to prepare his body for burial (12:7). Thus, Jesus is further depicted as the Passover victim being prepared for sacrifice.

Jesus's Passover Meal with His Disciples and John 13–17

Whereas John 1–12 covers several years in Jesus's life, chapters 13–19 depict a period of approximately twenty-four hours.[33] This latter series of events that culminate in Jesus's death begins with what is probably best seen as a Passover meal that Jesus partakes of with his disciples (John 13–17). Scholars have debated whether this is a Passover meal, largely because of the chronological difficulties between the Synoptic and Johannine accounts of the final days of Jesus's life. Brant Pitre has thoroughly addressed these and provided a plausible solution for their compatibility.[34] It is clear that, in light of the overwhelming similarities between the Synoptic and Johannine accounts, the meal depicted in John 13–17 is seen by John as a Passover meal, or at least as a meal that is infused with numerous Passover elements.[35]

What is often less widely recognized is Jesus's depiction as the Passover Lamb in several episodes within these five chapters. John 13:1 sets the scene by saying that just before the time of the Passover, Jesus realizes what will happen

---

31. Cf. Stibbe, *John's Gospel*, 130–31.
32. See the discussion of this preposition and substitution in chap. 5 on the Suffering Servant.
33. Culpepper, *Anatomy of the Fourth Gospel*, 72.
34. Pitre, *Jesus and the Last Supper*, 251–373.
35. An early, strong case for equating the meals in the Synoptic Gospels and John's Gospel was made by Jeremias (*Eucharistic Words of Jesus*, 41–84, esp. 81); now further supported by Pitre, *Jesus and the Last Supper*, 331–73.

to him.³⁶ This verse serves as a heading for John 13–17, in which Jesus's words and actions during the dinner (13:4) reveal his knowledge and compassion. Among other statements, Jesus identifies himself as the true vine (15:1–10). The vine image probably alludes to the wine consumed at the Passover celebration, which would have been consumed in the meal alluded to in the preceding narrative (see 13:2, 4, 26, 30).³⁷ More than that, however, the language used in John 15–17 is reminiscent of the "taking away" language of John 1:29 (see above) and the glory language (e.g., 12:23, 28; 13:31–32) that refers to Jesus's death on the cross (12:16).³⁸ In John 17, the entire scene is brought to a close by Jesus's prayer for himself and his followers. The concept of glorification (see 17:5) seems to have been inspired by the Suffering Servant passages of Isaiah, especially Isaiah 53 (see John 12:38, 41), which are used at the outset of Jesus's ministry to establish him as not only the one who suffers but also the one who dies as a sacrificial lamb (John 1:29; cf. 1:36). In Jesus's prayer, as the meal draws to a close, it is perhaps not too much to see Jesus offering a new prayer of blessing and consecration for the Passover feast—one that he himself is about to reenact as its victim.³⁹

The Sacrificial Death of Jesus and John 19:13–42

A number of elements in John 19:13–42 establish the importance of the Passover theme, all of which point to the double formulaic quotation in John 19:36–37—"A bone of his will not be broken" and "They will look at whom they pierced" (AT)—as the climactic statement regarding Jesus as the Passover Lamb. The first factor is the temporal references to the day on which Jesus dies. John 18:28 and 39 say that it is the evening of the day before the Passover; 19:14 says that it is the preparation for the Passover (παρασκευὴ τοῦ πάσχα); and 19:31 and 42 say that it is the day of preparation—for either the Passover or the Sabbath, since the two seem to have fallen on the same day so far as John is concerned.⁴⁰ Not only is the mention of the specific timing important, but the repetition also unites the account. The references in John 18:28 and

---

36. Harris, "Early Christian Interpretation of the Passover," cites the use of μεταβῇ (cross over) in John 13:1 as an allusion to the Passover since Philo describes the exodus using similar language, but this is thin evidence. See Glasson, *Moses in the Fourth Gospel*, 97–98.
37. Howard, "Passover and Eucharist," 335; Bernard, *Gospel according to St. John*, 2:478. Cf. Isa. 5:1–7; 27:2–11. Note also that this probably extends and applies to Jesus's language regarding Israel as the true vine (cf., e.g., Ps. 80:8–16; Jer. 2:21; 12:10–13; Ezek. 15:1–8; 19:10–14; Hosea 10:1). See Hoskyns, *Fourth Gospel*, 2:559–60.
38. Evans, *Word and Glory*, 180.
39. See Howard, "Passover and Eucharist," 336.
40. See Barrett, *Gospel according to St. John*, 555, who claims that there is a significant difference between v. 14 and vv. 31 and 42, on the basis of which day is being referred to.

39 prepare the reader for the specific chronology of events in John 19, and the crucial events surrounding Jesus's death are linked on three occasions to the day of preparation, once at the beginning, once in the middle, and once at the end (John 19:14, 31, 42). The significance of this linkage lies in the fact that the day of preparation was the day on which the Passover sacrifices were killed.[41] Thus, Jesus's death not only occurs on the day on which the Passover sacrifice was made but also is equated with that sacrifice itself by virtue of its contemporaneity.

The second factor is that Jesus is sentenced to death by Pilate at noon, or the eighth hour. According to Jewish chronography,[42] this is the hour at which the slaughter of the Passover lambs was to begin (John 19:14; cf. Exod. 12:6).[43] The presentation of Jesus by Pilate for death is accompanied both by the indication of the day, which is repeated twice more in the account, as noted above, and by the indication of the specific hour. This correlation points to Jesus's impending death as being interpreted in light of the Passover—the linkage having the same symbolic significance as the cleansing of the temple in bringing the previous ritual to a close and instigating a new one.[44] As Rudolf Bultmann states, "The end of the Jewish cultus, or the uselessness of its further observance, is thereby affirmed."[45]

A third factor involves specific elements associated with Jesus's death.[46] For example, both Exodus 12:22 and John 19:29 mention the hyssop branch. In light of the Passover theme already seen in John's Gospel, it is likely that John's mention of the hyssop branch is a reference to the Passover—especially since none of the Synoptic Gospels mention it. The hyssop was a small, weak plant, raising the problem of how it could be used to lift the sponge to Jesus's lips. This difficulty, along with the apparently conscious departure from the Synoptic reference to a "reed" (κάλαμος),[47] suggests that the author intentionally mentions it to refer to the Passover.[48] The branches are described in the Passover

---

41. Gray, *Sacrifice in the Old Testament*, 388.

42. There is some textual dispute regarding the time of Jesus's death, but readings for the sixth hour are almost certainly designed to bring John's Gospel into harmony with the Synoptic accounts.

43. Gray, *Sacrifice in the Old Testament*, 388–89; R. Brown, *Gospel according to John*, 2:833; Barrett, *Gospel according to St. John*, 545.

44. See Beasley-Murray, *John*, 341.

45. Bultmann, *Gospel of John*, 677.

46. On issues of chronology and Passover practice, see Grigsby, "Cross as an Expiatory Sacrifice," 54–56 and notes. He shows that the Passover theme is essentially unaltered by the various chronologies proposed.

47. See Matt. 27:49; Mark 15:33. Barrett, *Gospel according to St. John*, 553; Grigsby, "Cross as an Expiatory Sacrifice," 57.

48. Cf. Heb. 9:19, where blood, water, and hyssop are related.

and John 19 accounts as serving similar functions—that is, the hyssop branch is used to form a connection between the sacrificial victim and those for whom it or he is the sacrifice.[49] In John 19:34, the blood and water of Jesus that flow out when he is stabbed by the soldier may be reminiscent of the flow of blood and fluid out of the sacrificial animal (Exod. 12:7, 22). Several later rabbinic passages describe the flow of blood and water or fluid in a proper sacrifice. The idea appears to be that the blood was supposed to flow like water to prevent congealing. Furthermore, Jesus's body is not allowed to stay on the cross until the next morning (John 19:31, 38), just as the remains of the Passover meal were not to be left until the next day but were to be burned (Exod. 12:19). Thus, another parallel between Jesus's crucifixion and the Passover is evident.[50]

The fourth factor is that the scene is closed by the two formulaic quotations (or a double quotation) from the Old Testament in John 19:36–37: "A bone of his will not be broken" and "They will look at whom they pierced" (AT).[51] While most scholars believe that the author of John's Gospel cites Zechariah 12:10 in John 19:37, there has been much discussion regarding which text is being cited and from which version in John 19:36. Some scholars argue that Psalm 34:20 (33:21 LXX) lies behind this passage,[52] others that a passage from the Pentateuch (either Exod. 12:10, 46 LXX or Num. 9:12) is being cited,[53] and others that both sets are being drawn upon.[54] The evidence points to at least some reference to the pentateuchal quotations, although there may be secondary reference to Psalm 34:20. It is not necessary to establish whether the Hebrew Masoretic text or the Septuagint is being quoted here,[55] so long as it is agreed that John is quoting from the Old Testament. This is beyond doubt.[56] One of the pentateuchal passages is probably being cited, with the citation from Exodus 12:10 in the Passover account probable, although this cannot be proven beyond doubt.

---

49. See Lev. 14:6–7; Num. 19:6; Ps. 50:9, where hyssop is related to cultic sprinkling.

50. M. Davies, *Rhetoric and Reference in the Fourth Gospel*, 234, 305, 355.

51. For a recent discussion of the two passages, see Williams, "Composite Citations in the Gospel of John," esp. 115–24.

52. See, e.g., Dodd, *Interpretation of the Fourth Gospel*, 230–38; Bultmann, *Gospel of John*, 677n1. Usually mentioned in support of this proposal is the use of the passive voice of the verb and the use of Psalm quotations in John's Gospel.

53. See, e.g., Freed, *Old Testament Quotations in the Gospel of John*, 113.

54. See, e.g., Barrett, "Old Testament in the Fourth Gospel," 175; Lindars, *New Testament Apologetic*, 96; Schuchard, *Scripture within Scripture*, 138–40; Borchert, *John*, 2:278.

55. On the Hebrew Masoretic text, see Moo, *Old Testament in the Gospel Passion Narratives*, 315; on the Septuagint, see Schuchard, *Scripture within Scripture*, 133–40; Lindars, *Gospel of John*, 590.

56. Although see Freed, *Old Testament Quotations in the Gospel of John*, 109–14, who is undecided.

> ## HYSSOP AND THE PASSOVER LAMB
>
> Then Moses called all the elders of Israel and said to them, "Go, select lambs for your families, and slaughter the passover lamb. Take a bunch of hyssop, dip it in the blood that is in the basin, and touch the lintel and the two doorposts with the blood in the basin. None of you shall go outside the door of your house until morning."[a]
>
> Later, knowing that everything had now been finished, and so that Scripture would be fulfilled, Jesus said, "I am thirsty." A jar of wine vinegar was there, so they soaked a sponge in it, put the sponge on a stalk of the hyssop plant, and lifted it to Jesus' lips. When he had received the drink, Jesus said, "It is finished." With that, he bowed his head and gave up his spirit.[b]
>
> a. Exodus 12:21–22.
> b. John 19:28–30 NIV.

In conclusion to the discussion of John 19:36 and 37, these are two formulaic quotations, the first probably of Exodus 12:10, 46 LXX or possibly Numbers 9:12, both from Passover accounts, and the second from Zechariah 12:10. The first is introduced by John's fulfillment formula ("the Scripture might be fulfilled," with πληρωθῇ), which he uses frequently throughout the second half of the Gospel. Although the second quotation is introduced with "again another passage of scripture says," the two are meant to be taken together, with the second quotation an additional passage offered in support of the sacrificial imagery, here referring to the piercing of Jesus. This is the second double quotation (19:36–37) in John's Gospel, the first having begun the passion section of the Gospel (see John 12:38, citing Isa. 53:1; and John 12:40, citing Isa. 6:10).[57] The quotations in John 19 summarize a major christological theme that is developed throughout the Gospel. The numerous passages throughout John's Gospel indicate that John saw Jesus as the Passover Lamb, from the outset of his ministry to its earthly fulfillment and completion.

Jesus as the Passover Lamb in the Rest of the New Testament

There are several other places in the New Testament in which Jesus is referred to as a sheep or lamb or in which a sheep or lamb plays an important role in

---

57. On the quotation formulas used in John's Gospel, see Porter, *Sacred Tradition in the New Testament*, 146–48.

the context. This raises the question of whether these passages also support the notion of Jesus as the Passover Lamb. As we have noted above, many New Testament scholars believe that reference to a lamb indicates at least some reference to the Passover.[58] This is certainly true of John's Gospel, but we may also rightly wonder whether this is true of other places in the New Testament as well.

The Last Supper in the Synoptic Gospels

Like John's Gospel, each of the Synoptic Gospels describes Jesus and his disciples celebrating the Passover while in Jerusalem (Matt. 26:17–30; Mark 14:12–25; Luke 22:7–23). The New Testament seems to reflect two traditions of the Last Supper, one found in Matthew and Mark and the other in Luke and Paul (1 Cor. 11:25–27).[59] There are differences between these two major traditions, as noted in chapter 5 on the Suffering Servant. Nevertheless, several significant common features of these descriptions emphasize that the Last Supper is a Passover event. Even though the Passover lamb is not mentioned within the context of the meal itself,[60] the entire event strongly connects Jesus with the Passover and with it the Passover lamb. The first feature is that Jesus celebrates the meal while in Jerusalem, the place where the lamb was to be slaughtered in the temple.[61] Mark's and Luke's Gospels specify that Jesus sends his disciples out to prepare the meal on the day that the Passover lamb was sacrificed (Mark 14:12//Luke 22:7). When Jesus institutes the Lord's Supper, he reimagines the Passover meal in terms of himself. He says, "This is my body" (Matt. 26:26//Mark 14:22//Luke 22:19) and "This is my blood" (Matt. 26:38// Mark 14:24; cf. Luke 22:20: "This cup that is poured out for you is the new covenant in my blood"). The disciples are instructed to consume his flesh and drink his blood and enter into relationship with him through this act. As Pitre points out, in the Torah the sacrifice of the Passover lamb was not completed in its death but by the eating of its flesh (Exod. 12:8–11; Num. 9:11–13).[62] In the act of identifying himself with the elements and commending the eating

---

58. V. Taylor, *Jesus and His Sacrifice*, 226–27. See also Barrett, *Gospel according to St. John*, 176–77; R. Brown, *Gospel according to John*, 1:295n9; Lindars, *Gospel of John*, 109; Carey, "Lamb of God and Atonement Theories," 111; Moo, *Old Testament in the Gospel Passion Narratives*, 312–14; Carson, *Gospel according to John*, 150; Evans, *Word and Glory*, 181–82; M. Davies, *Rhetoric and Reference in the Fourth Gospel*; Keener, *Gospel of John*, 1:454.

59. See Jeremias, *Eucharistic Words of Jesus*, 138–203, for a detailed discussion of the issues.

60. Pitre, *Jesus and the Last Supper*, 283–84. This observation was made by a number of earlier scholars.

61. See Pitre, *Jesus and the Last Supper*, 391–94; cf. 394–98.

62. Pitre, *Jesus and the Last Supper*, 410.

and drinking—regardless of how one might conceive of the symbolism of the action—Jesus appears to appropriate the Passover meal, and with it the symbolism of the lamb, to himself. In this Passover meal with his disciples, Jesus defines himself as the eschatological Passover Lamb, anticipates his own sacrificial death in terms of the Passover sacrifice, and institutes a new cultic practice for the life of the community.

The Suffering Servant of Acts 8:32–33

We have already discussed the Suffering Servant as a christological title of Jesus in chapter 5. In Acts 8:32–33, the narrator tells us that the Ethiopian eunuch was reading from Isaiah 53:7–8 LXX: "Like a sheep [πρόβατον] he was led to the slaughter, and like a lamb [ἀμνός] silent before its shearer, so he does not open his mouth. In his humiliation justice was denied him. Who can describe his generation? For his life is taken away from the earth." There are many similarities between this passage and the depictions of the Passover lamb noted above. The two words used for sheep/lamb in Passover passages are used here. The two animals, especially the lamb, are seen as victims of unjust slaughter. The substitutionary sense of the role of the lamb is implied by the quotation within its larger Isaianic context. Finally, the lamb is seen to be sacrificial on behalf of humanity, especially for the forgiveness of sins. All these features of this Suffering Servant passage constitute basic requirements for a Passover passage as well. Although there are some indications that the Suffering Servant passages, and this passage in particular, are invoking the Passover, an explicit link to the Passover is missing. As we noted above when we discussed John 1:29–36, the Passover Lamb motif goes beyond the Suffering Servant to include equation of the Lamb with the lamb sacrificed at Passover. Such a direct equation is not made in the Suffering Servant passages, even if it may be hinted at.

The Passover Sacrifice of 1 Corinthians 5:7

In his discussion of how to handle a person in an immoral relationship, Paul draws an analogy with Jewish culinary practice: "Do you not know that a little yeast leavens the whole batch of dough? Clean out the old yeast so that you may be a new batch, as you really are unleavened. For our paschal lamb,[63] Christ, has been sacrificed. Therefore, let us celebrate the festival, not

---

63. The Greek has τὸ πάσχα ἡμῶν, which the NRSV renders as "our paschal lamb," as opposed to "our Passover." The Greek term may refer to the lamb (e.g., Mark 14:12; Luke 22:7, 15; John 18:28) or the meal (Mark 14:12; Luke 22:11). Cf. Pitre, *Jesus and the Last Supper*, 331.

with the old yeast, the yeast of malice and evil, but with the unleavened bread of sincerity and truth" (1 Cor. 5:6–8). As we noted above, unleavened bread was to be eaten at the Passover. Paul uses the distinction between leavened and unleavened dough as a means of offering moral judgment on the actions of the Corinthians. This provides a transition to the Passover festival itself, a move that not only constitutes an argument about morality but also indicates Paul's fundamental beliefs about the death of Jesus Christ.[64] Paul inverts the order of events by noting that, rather than cleanliness preparing for sacrifice (as in the Old Testament), Christ's sacrifice demands cleanliness. This is not the only rough approximation, as Paul seems to assume a Passover tradition regarding Christ[65] in which Christ is the Passover Lamb who was sacrificed (Exod. 12:21 LXX) on the cross as a means of purification (creating sincerity and truth).[66] All the major elements of the Passover lamb within the Jewish sacrificial system are exemplified in this depiction: Jesus is the victim who is substitutionarily sacrificed to enact purification for others. As Joseph Fitzmyer states, "Paul regards Jesus Christ who died on the cross ([1 Cor.] 1:18) at Passover, as the Passover lamb of a new dispensation."[67]

The Lamb of 1 Peter 1:18–19

In 1 Peter, Peter states, "You know that you were ransomed from the futile ways inherited from your ancestors, not with perishable things like silver or gold, but with the precious blood of Christ, like that of a lamb [ἀμνός] without defect or blemish" (1 Pet. 1:18–19). A mix of images exists within this passage, resulting in several different, occasionally overlapping proposals regarding how to understand its imagery. One proposal claims that this is a passage about redemption using language of slavery. In this case, the person(s) is bought or redeemed by paying a valuable price, probably with reference to the exodus from Egypt and perhaps with reference to Mark 10:45. This view is sometimes blended with the third option below.[68] A second proposal is that this represents any general sacrifice that required an unblemished lamb (e.g., Num. 6:14; 28:3, 9).[69] A third position invokes the Suffering Servant of Isaiah

---

64. Thiselton, *First Epistle to the Corinthians*, 403. Cf. Garland, *1 Corinthians*, 103.
65. See Barrett, *First Epistle to the Corinthians*, 128–29.
66. Robertson and Plummer, *First Epistle of St Paul to the Corinthians*, 103.
67. Fitzmyer, *First Corinthians*, 241; cf. 240 on the ordering in Paul vs. the Old Testament Passover procedure.
68. See Miller, *On This Rock*, 173, who also mentions the Suffering Servant; Jobes, *1 Peter*, 117–19, who is unclear at this point.
69. See Grudem, *1 Peter*, 84–85, although he goes on to equate this lamb with the "lamb of God who takes away the sin of the world" in John 1:31, cross-referencing 1 Cor. 5:7 and Isa.

53, especially verse 7, which speaks of the silent lamb being slaughtered. This passage came to be understood as a reference to the death of Christ, a view sometimes mentioned with the final option.[70] The final proposal is that this is a passage about the Passover Lamb, with Jesus equated with the lamb without defect of Exodus 12:5 (although Peter uses ἄμωμος rather than τέλειον as in the LXX) and having a sacrificial atoning function on the basis of equations in John 1:29, 36 and 19:36.[71] Some kind of sacrificial-lamb imagery appears to be used here. The question is whether it functions at the general level or at the deeper level of the Suffering Servant or the Passover Lamb. The equation of Christ's death with this specific sacrifice makes the equation more than simply representative of any sacrifice. The language that is typically equated with the Suffering Servant—being without blemish or defect, silence, suffering—is only partially present in 1 Peter. The language of the Passover Lamb is not much more specific, except we must note the link of the lamb with the valuable blood of Christ. This language indicates that Jesus is being equated with the Passover lamb whose death atones for sin.

The Lamb of Revelation

The book of Revelation makes constant reference to lamb imagery. In fact, the word translated as "lamb" throughout the book of Revelation occurs nearly thirty times. We noted above how the Greek Old Testament uses πρόβατον (lamb) to translate the Hebrew term. The New Testament uses πρόβατον in many places, but in the passages that establish Jesus as the Passover Lamb, it is used only in John 2:14–15, the temple-cleansing event.[72] The New Testament uses another word translated "lamb" (ἀμνός) in John 1:29, 36; Acts 8:32; and 1 Peter 1:19 (and only those places). However, the book of Revelation uses a third word translated "lamb" (ἀρνίον) (used elsewhere in the New Testament only in John 21:15).

The Lamb of Revelation is, for the most part, a symbol for Jesus Christ (the only exception is in Rev. 13:11). In Revelation 5, when the author despairs that

---

53:7, among other passages; Achtemeier, *1 Peter*, 128–29; Feldmeier, *First Letter of Peter*, 118, although he refers in a note (64) to Jeremias's work on atonement and Passover; Keener, *1 Peter*, 107–8, who is noncommittal.

70. See Goppelt, *1 Peter*, 115–17, linking Isa. 53 to Mark 10:45; Michaels, *1 Peter*, 65, who blends this with the redemption language.

71. Bigg, *Epistles of Peter and Jude*, 119–20; Selwyn, *First Epistle of St. Peter*, 144–45; Kelly, *Epistles of Peter and Jude*, 75, who also makes a case for the Suffering Servant; Best, *1 Peter*, 90, who also makes the case for the Suffering Servant; Davids, *First Epistle of Peter*, 72–73, who sees the Suffering Servant introduced later in the letter.

72. The word is used many times elsewhere in John's Gospel, especially John 10.

the scroll cannot be opened, an elder tells him, "See, the Lion of the tribe of Judah, the Root of David, has conquered, so that he can open the scroll and its seven seals" (Rev. 5:5). The Lamb, "standing as if it had been slaughtered" (5:6; cf. 5:8), steps forward—the Lion now become a Lamb. The Lamb is proclaimed: "Worthy is the Lamb that was slaughtered to receive power and wealth and wisdom and might and honor and glory and blessing!" (5:12). The Lamb is heralded further in imagery reminiscent of the Son of Man sitting on the throne next to God: "To the one seated on the throne and to the Lamb be blessing and honor and glory and might, forever and ever!" (5:13). The Lamb then opens the seven seals (6:1, 16). Similar imagery of the Lamb standing near the throne of God and being praised is found in Revelation 7:9–10. The author of Revelation also sees a multitude who endure tribulation and whose robes are washed "in the blood of the Lamb" (7:14; see also 12:11). In the presence of the throne of God is the Lamb who will lead them (7:17). The Lamb "that was slaughtered from the foundation of the world" (13:8 [NRSV marginal note]) also keeps the book of life. The Lamb stands on Mount Zion with the 144,000 (14:1); the 144,000 are redeemed, and they follow the Lamb because they were purchased from humanity as the first fruits to God and to the Lamb (14:4; cf. 14:10). The Lamb is praised along with God (15:3). The Lamb will be attacked by others, but he "will conquer them, for he is Lord of lords and King of kings" (17:14). Finally, there will be the wedding of the Lamb to its bride dressed in white (19:7, 9). In the new heaven and the new earth, the Lamb takes its bride, the new Jerusalem (21:9). The new Jerusalem is inscribed with the names of the Lamb's twelve apostles (21:14). This city does not require a temple, because God and the Lamb constitute the temple (21:22), and its light is provided by God and the Lamb (21:23). No one will enter the city unless their name is in the Lamb's book of life (21:27). The book ends with a return to the image of the throne of God and the Lamb (22:1, 3).

The Lamb clearly occupies a central role in the book of Revelation, as it does elsewhere in the New Testament, as noted above.[73] A number of passages contain echoes of various other christological themes, such as the sacrificial lamb of ancient Israelite religion, the Suffering Servant, the Passover Lamb, and even Jesus the Lord.[74] Several of the characteristics of the Lamb—being slain, the association with blood, its death being purificatory, and its redemptive capacity—draw strong lines of correlation with some of the themes we

---

73. For a lengthy, if ultimately inconclusive, survey of the New Testament treatment of "Christ as the Lamb," see Aune, *Revelation*, 1:367–73.

74. Many commentators debate the significance of the Lamb. See, e.g., Ladd, *Revelation of John*, 85–87, who surveys various opinions; and Osborne, *Revelation*, 255–56, who opts for both the Suffering Servant and Passover Lamb.

have discussed in this chapter and others (e.g., chap. 5 on the Suffering Servant). However, none of these is entirely satisfactory. There is no indication of this Lamb being the Suffering Servant, and there is no reference to the Passover in Revelation. The function of the Lamb seems to move beyond the ancient Israelite sacrificial system, or even any more specific christological imagery such as the Suffering Servant[75] or the Passover Lamb,[76] to become the eschatological and even apocalyptic Divine Lamb who sits on the divine throne with God and together with God defeats God's enemies and redeems his people and creates the new heaven and the new earth, where the Lamb continues to reign with God.[77] This constitutes a powerful christological statement about the Lamb as God's divine coequal, one that encompasses the Suffering Servant and the Passover Lamb and expands them into the Divine Lamb.

Contribution to New Testament Christology

Two similar, even overlapping, christological titles of Jesus are the Suffering Servant and the Passover Lamb. We have seen in this chapter and in chapter 5 how a number of passages engage both traditions. However, some passages make clear that one of the unique christological identifications of Jesus is as the Passover Lamb. Jesus is most clearly and expansively described as the Passover Lamb in John's Gospel. One might well argue that the narrative backbone or frame of John's Gospel is Jesus as the Passover Lamb who takes away the sin of the world. The Passover Lamb in John's Gospel is a sacrificial victim who, in keeping with the ancient Israelite Passover tradition, is slaughtered on behalf of (substitutionarily) the people and by whose death the people are saved. At the outset of Jesus's ministry, he is revealed and proclaimed as the sacrificial Lamb of God (John 1:29, 36), introducing a christological title that is developed throughout the Gospel. At several significant junctures in the ministry of Jesus, John reaffirms Jesus's role as Passover victim, including in the temple cleansing (2:13–25), the feeding episode (6:1–14), Jesus's discourse with believers (8:31–47), the discussion with Caiaphas (11:47–12:8), and Jesus's celebration of a last Passover with his disciples (13:1–17:26). Then in the climactic events leading up to and including Jesus's death (19:13–42), John brings the passion story to a close by citing in double, emphatic fashion

---

75. Contra Beale, *Book of Revelation*, 353.
76. Contra Mounce, *Book of Revelation*, 132; Beasley-Murray, *Book of Revelation*, 125, who equates this image of the Lamb with John 1:29 and 19:14, 31–36; Smalley, *Revelation to John*, 135; Boxall, *Revelation of Saint John*, 98–99.
77. For a much fuller development of some of these ideas regarding the Lamb in Revelation, see Middleton, *Violence of the Lamb*.

Old Testament quotations that make the sacrificial Passover death not only specific but also virtually undeniable. The quotations in John 19:36 and 37 are therefore final fulfillment statements that bring the plot development to a close. A primary motivation for the action of the story is Jesus's death as a substitute and replacement for the Passover sacrifice, seen in his fulfilling various features of that sacrifice. Such a congeries of events cannot be ignored.

In several other places in the New Testament, however, Jesus is not necessarily depicted as the Passover Lamb, as he is in John's Gospel, but is described in similar language that assumes such an identification. In 1 Corinthians 5:7, Paul supports his moral judgment by using the analogy of leaven, which immediately links with the Passover. He states that Christ is our Passover or Passover Lamb, who was sacrificed. Paul is not arguing for this depiction but seems to assume that it was already recognized that Jesus was the sacrificial Passover Lamb. We may well wonder where Paul got this idea, unless this was one of the early ways in which Christians thought of Jesus.[78] The fact that 1 Peter 1:18–19 has a similar depiction of Jesus points to the possibility of the earliest followers of Jesus seeing him in this light. John's Gospel may simply be depicting in narrative form what the early church believed it saw in the events depicted in the Gospel—that Jesus was the Passover Lamb who replaced the Jewish institution by means of his own being and body and died a sacrificial death for those who follow him. The book of Revelation seems to assume this understanding of Jesus as the Suffering Servant but also the Passover Lamb as the basis of its depiction of Jesus not just as victim but as ultimate victor. Jesus is not just a sufferer and slaughtered lamb; he is the Divine Lamb who sits at the side of God and comes in ultimate triumph and judgment.

The Passover Lamb is an important christological title in the New Testament. Just like the lamb in the Old Testament Passover festival, Jesus was sacrificed on behalf of and in the place of his people as a means of forgiveness of sins. This christological title is often associated primarily with John's Gospel, and for good reason, as it provides a fundamental means of examining John's Gospel. However, the notion of Jesus as the Passover Lamb is found in a variety of other places in the New Testament, with some of these instances revealing an early depiction of Jesus in this way. Nevertheless, John's Gospel develops this idea to its fullest extent, to the point that in the crucifixion account individual elements of the Passover are depicted in the death of Jesus so that he is interpreted in this light. The author of the book of Revelation assumes such a depiction of Jesus, along with Jesus as the Suffering Servant,

---

78. Cf. Fee, *First Epistle to the Corinthians*, 238–39, who thinks that we are limited in knowing the full extent of Paul's thought in this regard.

> **MELITO OF SARDIS'S "ON THE PASSOVER"**
>
> The following excerpt appears in a sermon commonly dated to the second half of the second century CE. Speaking from the perspective of Jesus, the sermon incorporates various elements of the Passover Lamb tradition and applies them to Christ.
>
>> Therefore, come, all human families,
>> you who have been befouled with sins,
>> and receive forgiveness for your sins.
>> I am your forgiveness,
>> I am the passover of your salvation,
>> I am the lamb which was sacrificed for you,
>> I am your ransom,
>> I am your light,
>> I am your savior,
>> I am your resurrection,
>> I am your king,
>> I am leading you up to the heights of heaven,
>> I will show you the eternal Father,
>> I will raise you up by my right hand.[a]
>
> a. Translation from Hawthorne, "New English Translation of Melito's Paschal Homily," 174.

and portrays the sacrificed lamb as the Divine Lamb who not only dies for his people but also becomes the divine victor and, along with God, ushers in the new heaven and the new earth. This often overlooked christological title has much to offer New Testament Christology, as it touches on major themes regarding covenantal continuity, sacrifice, substitution, and atonement.

CHAPTER 7

JESUS THE MESSIAH

Introduction

In parallel passages in Matthew 11:2–6 and Luke 7:18–23, John the Baptist's disciples come to Jesus and ask him a question based on what they and others have witnessed regarding his developing ministry. They ask him, "Are you the one who is to come, or are we to wait for another?" (Matt. 11:3//Luke 7:20).[1] Jesus replies, "Go and tell John what you hear and see [Luke: "what you have seen and heard"]: the blind receive their sight, the lame walk, the lepers are cleansed, the deaf hear, the dead are raised, and the poor have good news brought to them. And blessed is anyone who takes no offense at me" (Matt. 11:4–6//Luke 7:22–23). These parallel passages set the stage for discussion of Jesus as the Messiah because they contain several of the most important components related to this identification. At the time of the New Testament, there was widespread expectation among the Jews that there would be one who was sent from God to rescue his people. This expectation of a coming deliverer, whatever form that deliverer might take, came to be known as messianic expectation, and the coming deliverer was known as the Messiah. This is because the Old Testament often uses language of anointing (Hebrew משח, "anoint") to indicate one chosen by God for divine purposes. In the New Testament, Jesus is often addressed as or referred to as Messiah with the Greek word "Christ" (χριστός, from a Greek verb, "anoint"). Hence, in

---

1. The Matthean and Lukan wordings are identical except for one word, translated "someone else" in each place.

the New Testament, Jesus is often depicted as or said to be the Messiah, or even addressed as Jesus Messiah.

This chapter explores the scriptural basis for seeing Jesus not just as a messiah but as *the* Messiah and what that would have meant to a first-century audience. The traditional Christian answer has been that, indeed, Jesus saw himself as the Messiah, God's anointed one, chosen for a divine purpose, and that he was crucified for this reason. Much of modern biblical criticism views this traditional position with great skepticism. This is either because Jesus made no overt or direct messianic claim or because messianic claims, being common, did not distinguish him from others making similar claims. It is sometimes argued that there was no well-defined messianic expectation in Judaism at the time of Jesus because there was not a clearly defined notion of messiah in ancient Israelite religion. As a result of these and other reasons, the concept of messiah is sometimes played down in scholarly discussion. We believe, and will attempt to show below, that there was a broadly (even if not precisely) defined concept of messiah grounded in Old Testament tradition and recognized within the varied Judaism of Jesus's time. As a result, around the time of Jesus, several people in the Greco-Roman world saw themselves as God's anointed one. Although messianic claimants in the Greco-Roman world of the first century did not fare too well at the hands of the Romans, it is not clear that they were executed simply because they had messianic pretensions. The relation of Jesus to messianic expectation as found in a variety of Jewish and related texts thus warrants examination.[2]

Thinking of Jesus as the Messiah is a common way to refer to him in the New Testament.[3] However, as common as it is, it is difficult to understand what exactly the term "messiah" conveyed in ancient times due to the diversity of previous and contemporary usage. As Matthew Novenson has pointed out, there have been several stages in recent scholarly thought regarding the definition of the Jewish Messiah. The conception of a "messianic idea" from the nineteenth century to the Second World War was tied more closely to philosophical categories than to ancient texts; this was followed by the idea of minimalist or imprecise meaning from World War II to fairly recently. Novenson rejects both views and argues that what he calls "messiah

---

2. See the essays in Porter, *Messiah in the Old and New Testaments*; and Bird, *Are You the One Who Is to Come?*, although Bird, despite recognizing the diversity of "messiah" language, tends to endorse a more idealized or essentialist view than we take here. Cf. Satterthwaite, Hess, and Wenham, *The Lord's Anointed*; and Evans, "Messianic Hopes and Messianic Figures in Late Antiquity."

3. The recent study by Joshua Jipp has as its central thesis that "Jesus's messianic kingship is something of a root metaphor, a primary designation and driving image for making sense of NT Christology" (Jipp, *Messianic Theology of the New Testament*, 13).

language" within Judaism was meaningful, even if it was not meaningful in ways that fulfilled a prescribed messianic idealization.[4] We agree with Novenson that "messiah" language in the Old Testament, as well as in the New, has meaning, even if it does not fulfill idealized views or even theological expectations. Novenson is part of a wider set of discussions within recent New Testament scholarship that tends to argue that messianic expectation focused on a Davidic or kingly or royal messiah, sometimes referred to as Son of David (a title we do not treat separately, because we see it as part of the larger concept of messiah). This view has sometimes utilized forms of narrative Christology to the point of seeing Jesus as Messiah as encompassing much, if not most, of New Testament Christology. This move toward greater prescription of messianic conception to Jesus, and the tendency to enfold other christological formulations within the concept of messiah, represents a trend in scholarly discussion of messianism in the New Testament that began in the 1990s and has picked up pace in the twenty-first century. Richard Bauckham has argued for a Davidic messiah in Revelation.[5] Others have argued similarly for other parts of the New Testament. Besides Novenson, some of the other scholars engaged in the discussion, much of it focusing on Paul's view of Jesus as the Messiah, include N. T. Wright, Adela Collins, John Collins, Sean McDonough, Michael Bird, Joshua Jipp, Matthew Thiessen, Paula Fredriksen, Matthew Bates, and Esau McCaulley.[6] The culmination of such recent work appears in Joshua Jipp's *The Messianic Theology of the New Testament*.[7] As Jipp explains in his opening chapter, reflecting the trend among other scholars, he uses the notion of Jesus as Messiah as the encompassing or root metaphor to explain the Christology of the New Testament.

This recently accentuated position emphasizes the importance of Jesus as Messiah in the New Testament, whether one is considering the Gospels, the Letters, or even Revelation. However, we do not take that position in this volume. We believe that this recent approach is both too broad and too narrow. It is too broad in that it tends to subordinate much if not most

---

4. Novenson, *Christ among the Messiahs*, 34–63. Novenson expands on his analysis of previous scholarship in *The Grammar of Messianism*.

5. Bauckham, *Climax of Prophecy*.

6. See Wright, *Jesus and the Victory of God*, 477–539; A. Collins and J. Collins, *King and Messiah as Son of God*; McDonough, *Christ as Creator*, 65–97; Bird, *Jesus Is the Christ*; Jipp, *Christ Is King*, esp. 1–42; Thiessen, *Paul and the Gentile Problem*; Fredriksen, *Paul*; Bates, *Salvation by Allegiance Alone*, esp. 47–66; and McCaulley, *Sharing in the Son's Inheritance*.

7. Jipp, *Messianic Theology of the New Testament*, 12–25, esp. 19–20, where most of the major contributors to this movement, as well as others, are at least briefly mentioned (and drawn upon above).

Christology to messianism. We wholeheartedly embrace that the New Testament sees Jesus as Messiah, including seeing him as Son of David, royal, and kingly. But we also believe that other christological titles are also very important, some perhaps equally so (such as Son of Man), and are often used together with Messiah. The other christological titles deserve their place in the discussion, and we have attempted to give them their due by devoting separate chapters to them. We also recognize that there is strong interaction among the various christological titles of Jesus in the New Testament, and we attempt to highlight these where we can. However, we do not believe that they are subordinate to Jesus as Messiah, as important as Jesus as Messiah is in the New Testament. The messianic position is too narrow in that it sees messianism as focusing on one of several streams of messianic thought within Judaism, the one that emphasizes Jesus as Messiah in light of the Davidic line of kingship and rule. We believe, as we will show below, that the concept of an anointed deliverer certainly included a Davidic messiah, but it was not confined to this concept and extended much further within contemporary Jewish thought.[8]

In this chapter we will examine the Old Testament "messiah" language and then describe the range of depictions of Jesus as Messiah in the New Testament and its various authors. We concentrate on those passages that use explicit χριστός language but recognize that we must go beyond such language to understand the Messiah in the New Testament.[9]

Messianic Expectation in Jewish Literature

Jewish history has known a variety of figures who could be called messiahs or who even went so far as to think of themselves as God's divinely appointed figure.

The Old Testament is full of various messianic figures, if by that we mean people who saw themselves or were seen by others simply as God's appointed or anointed ruler or leader.[10] Richard Hess observes that, in the Septuagint, the Greek word χριστός always translates a form of the Hebrew word משח,

---

8. See Horbury, *Jewish Messianism and the Cult of Christ*, for a view of Jewish messianism as a rich and diverse tradition growing out of the Old Testament.
9. See Grindheim, *Christology in the Synoptic Gospels*, 13, who notes that scholars cannot agree on messianic passages to discuss and how closely these are tied to the use of χριστός language.
10. See Hess, "Image of the Messiah"; and Evans, *Jesus and His Contemporaries*, 58–61, who are followed below. The diversity of messianic language is summarized in Porter, "Introduction," 1–9, esp. 1–2; cf. Kreider, "Jesus the Messiah as Prophet, Priest, and King." See also R. Rowe, *God's Kingdom and God's Son*, 165–306.

while מָשִׁיחַ is not always translated as χριστός or a related word.[11] Both words are glossed as "anoint," indicating that they represent someone who was anointed, usually with oil, as a sign that they were being chosen to fulfill a particular task. As a result, there are many times in the Hebrew Bible when forms of מָשִׁיחַ are used to indicate people and things that are anointed for a particular purpose. However, many of these are not messianic passages, at least as we are using the term in this chapter, because the person is not being chosen for a special divine purpose, especially in the life of God's people.

There are, nevertheless, instances in which people are anointed to positions or for functions of significance within the life of Israel. These may not always be messianic in the full sense of the word, but they certainly are suggestive of the messianic role as one who is selected by God and anointed for an important task in God's economy. Kings in particular are messianic in that sense. Thus, Samuel anoints both Saul (1 Sam. 9:16; 10:1; 15:1, 17) and David (1 Sam. 16:3, 12, 13; 2 Sam. 2:4//1 Chron. 11:3; 2 Sam. 2:7; 3:39; 5:3, 17//1 Chron. 14:8; 2 Sam. 12:7) as king, and they are identified as God's anointed (1 Sam. 24:6, 10; 26:9, 11, 16, 23; 2 Sam. 1:14, 16; 19:21; 23:1), along with all David's descendants (e.g., 2 Sam. 22:51; cf. Ps. 18:50). Zadok the priest anoints Solomon (1 Kings 1:34, 39, 45; 5:1; 1 Chron. 29:22) as king. Subsequent kings of Israel were also anointed, such as Absalom (2 Sam. 19:11 [19:10 LXX]), Hazael (1 Kings 19:15), Jehu (1 Kings 19:16; 2 Kings 9:3, 6, 12; 2 Chron. 22:7), Joash (2 Kings 11:12//2 Chron. 23:11), and Jehoahaz (2 Kings 23:30). The anointing of kings in the life of the Jewish nation had a large impact on the equation of the Messiah with a divinely appointed ruler, to the point that David was seen as the archetypal king (2 Sam. 7:11–16). Even Cyrus the Persian, though he was not appointed to rule the Jewish people, is depicted in messianic terms because he is anointed for a specific purpose within God's work with his people Israel (Isa. 45:1). Although these anointings of kings are distinctly political acts, in other Old Testament literature the anointing of the king had a distinctly religious sense. Psalm 45:8 (45:7 LXX) mentions the anointing of a king of Jerusalem, and Psalm 89:21 (89:20 LXX) refers to the anointing of David by God. Later Jewish literature continued this depiction, as is noted below.

In addition to kings, some ancient Israelite prophets were anointed or messianic figures. In 1 Kings 19:15–16, Elijah is told to anoint two kings, Hazael of Aram and Jehu of Israel, but also Elisha as his successor as prophet. Moses is presented as a prophet in both the Old Testament and especially later Jewish literature (see chap. 2 for discussion). In the later rabbinic literature, Moses

---

11. Hess, "Image of the Messiah," 22–23.

is said to possess many of the Messiah's characteristics, such as existence before creation (*Testament of Moses* 1.14). He is also compared to David, to the point that they are depicted as occupying the same roles in the life of Israel (e.g., *Midrash on Psalms* 1.2 [on Ps. 1:1]; *Sifre on Deuteronomy* 344 [on Deut. 33:3]). These traditions are late but are consistent with how the New Testament depicts Moses (John 1:14–18; Acts 3:22–23; 7:37; Heb. 3:1–6; 8:5–6).[12] We may also mention here the Messiah as Suffering Servant. In Isaiah 61:1, Isaiah states, "The spirit of the Lord GOD is upon me, because the LORD has anointed me; he has sent me to bring good news to the oppressed." The Suffering Servant has been identified with a variety of figures, including the prophet Isaiah himself (Targum on Isa. 61:1) and Moses (*Mekilta* on Exod. 20:21).

Ancient Israelite priests were also seen as anointed or messianic figures. Although Moses was understood as a prophetic messianic or Davidic figure in later literature, it is Aaron the high priest and his sons who are anointed by Moses in the Old Testament (Exod. 29:6–7; 30:30). Melchizedek (Gen. 14:18) is depicted as a priest by receiving a tithe, even though he is said to be king of Salem, thus linking priesthood with kingship and hence with messianism (see chap. 11 for further discussion). Those who entered the priestly office were anointed (Lev. 16:32) with a major task to offer sacrifices on behalf of the people (4:3, 5, 16; 6:22). Even though Zadok anointed a king (see above), he was himself anointed (1 Chron. 29:22). This practice continued in later times, when priests came to exercise much political control, even seeing themselves as kings after the Maccabean revolt. As a result, Onias III and Jason his son, the high priests, ruled over Jerusalem (2 Macc. 3–4). Under the Hasmoneans, the kingly and priestly roles were combined by the Hasmonean rulers into one (Josephus, *J.W.* 1.70; *Ant.* 13.301, 320). Later writers continued to anticipate a combined figure.[13] In *Testament of Levi* 8.11–19, in fact, in the only passage like this in Jewish literature, prophet, priest, and king are apparently combined into one messianic figure.[14]

Since the sacrilege of Antiochus IV Epiphanes in 167 BCE, when he decimated Jerusalem and profaned the temple, there had been a growing tide of Jewish belief in some form of messianic deliverer or deliverers. Characteristics of messianic figures of the time vary, but several are worth noting to understand messianism in the New Testament, and especially the messianism of Jesus. It is surprising how many characteristics of God are attributed to this

---

12. See Longenecker, *Christology of Early Jewish Christianity*, 34–35.
13. *Testament of Simeon* 72; *Testament of Judah* 21.2; *Testament of Joseph* 19.6.
14. We thank Brook W. R. Pearson for reference to this passage.

> ## THE MESSIAH IN *4 EZRA*
>
> This Jewish apocalyptic work, usually dated to the first or second century, portrays the coming Messiah as sitting on the judgment seat and overseeing the day of judgment.
>
> > And as for the lion whom you saw rousing up out of the forest and roaring and speaking to the eagle and reproving him for his unrighteousness, and as for all his words that you have heard, this is the Messiah whom the Most High has kept until the end of days, who will arise from the offspring of David, and will come and speak with them. He will denounce them for their ungodliness and for their wickedness, and will display before them their contemptuous dealings. For first he will bring them alive before his judgment seat, and when he has reproved them, then he will destroy them. But in mercy he will set free the remnant of my people, those who have been saved throughout my borders, and he will make them joyful until the end comes, the day of judgment, of which I spoke to you at the beginning.[a]
>
> a. *4 Ezra* 12.31–34. The translation is from the NRSV, which uses the alternative title "2 Esdras" for this text.

anointed figure. Those who will continue the Davidic kingship, a messianic characteristic found in several texts, are spoken of in a variety of ways. For example, 4QFlorilegium 1.10–13 interprets the anointed king of 2 Samuel 7:11–14 in terms of his reigning forever:

> "[And] Yahweh [de]clares to you that He will build you a house; and I will raise up your seed after you, and I will establish his royal throne [forev]er. I wi[ll be] a father to him and he shall be My son" [2 Sam. 7:11c, 12bc, 13, 14a]. This is the "branch of David" who will stand with the Interpreter of the Law, who will sit on the throne in Zion at the end of days; as it is written, "I will raise up the tent, of David which is fallen" [Amos 9:11]. This is the "fallen tent of David" who will stand to save Israel.[15]

Another text, 1QSa 2.1–12, probably alludes to the begetting of the Messiah in Psalm 2:2, 7 in lines 11–12: "when [God] will have be[got]ten the Messiah among them (the community)." Other major characteristics of this figure are that the Messiah will fulfill promises made to the house of David (*Pss. Sol.*

---

15. See Evans, *Jesus and His Contemporaries*, 104.

17.4, 21), ruling over Israel and judging the tribes (*Pss. Sol.* 17.26, 28); that heaven and earth will obey him (4Q521 1 ii 1); and that the rulers of the earth will worship at the feet (*1 En.* 62.9) of one who existed before time (*1 En.* 48.2) and who is called Messiah (*1 En.* 48.10; 52.4) and "Elect One" (*1 En.* 48.6; 49.2; 51.4; 52.6; 53.6; 55.4; 61.8; 62.1).

There is also at Qumran evidence for what has been called a diarchic messianism, consisting of two messiahs, one a ruler and the other a priest. In other words, Qumran messianism appears to have believed that the kingly and priestly messianic roles would be fulfilled by two separate people. These are often summarized in terms of Aaron and Israel, the first representing the priestly line and the other the ruling line (see CD 12.23–13.1; 14.19 = 4Q266 10 i 12; 19.10–11; 20.1; 1QS 9.11). There are, besides these passages, many other messianic passages referring to an anointed figure.[16]

In ancient Jewish tradition, a messiah was a figure chosen for a purpose who fulfilled that purpose in a variety of ways. Three of the most commonly cited functions were that of ruler, priest, and prophet, with a variety of implications created by each of these, depending on the circumstances in which the messiah figure is called to function.

Messiahs in the Greco-Roman World

In the Greco-Roman world of the first century, various people proclaimed their messiahship or were proclaimed a messiah by others. These messianic upstarts were often represented in terms of the functions identified above, especially as one who militaristically takes up arms against the oppressive Romans. Such figures include the anonymous Samaritan who went to Mount Gerizim but was routed by Pilate's troops; Theudas, who was beheaded by the Roman governor; and the anonymous Egyptian who went to Jerusalem to bring the walls down but was routed by the governor Felix.[17] From the evidence that we have, it was not the aspiration to messiahship or even the declaration of messiahship (when made) that led to trouble. Rather, when the person, usually as a kingly claimant or prophet, took confrontational measures against fellow Jews or, more particularly, against the Romans, the virtually inevitable result was bloodshed—and another failed messianic pretender.

---

16. E.g., 1QM 11.7–8; 1Q39 1 21; 4Q252 5,3–4; 4Q270 2 ii 13–14; 4Q375 1 i 9; 4Q376 1 i 1; 4Q458 2 ii 6; 4Q521 1 ii 1; 4Q521 7 3; 4Q521 8 9; 11QMelch 2.18. These references are cited in Abegg and Evans, "Messianic Passages in the Dead Sea Scrolls," esp. 192–94. Cf. Oegema, *The Anointed and His People*, 86–97.

17. See Evans, *Jesus and His Contemporaries*, 73–77.

One figure stands out among those who had messianic pretensions: the second-century rebel/patriot Simon ben Kosiba.[18] Simon was the major leader of the Jewish rebellion against Rome in 132–35 CE. After early success in the battle against the Romans (so far as we can tell from the limited sources), according to one tradition, he apparently declared himself to be the Messiah and was then subjected to a test by the rabbis to determine whether he was in fact the Messiah. The test was based on Isaiah 11:3–5. This passage states, "He shall not judge by what his eyes see, or decide by what his ears hear; but with righteousness he shall judge the poor, and decide with equity for the meek of the earth; he shall strike the earth with the rod of his mouth, and with the breath of his lips he shall kill the wicked. Righteousness shall be the belt around his waist, and faithfulness the belt around his loins." This passage was construed to mean that the Messiah had to pass a test of smell, according to which the Messiah was supposed to be able to judge by smell over sight (*b. Sanh.* 93b). Either Simon ben Kosiba failed the test and was killed (so *b. Sanh.* 93b, although this is unlikely) or, more probably, he was killed in battle (so *y. Ta'an.* 4:5).

Messianic expectation grew in accordance with the development of the Jewish people. The tradition was complex, and there were various conceptions of the Messiah, focusing on the leading religious authority figures within the culture: the king, the prophets, and the priests. By the time of the New Testament, there was widespread textual discussion of a messiah as a figure who would serve the people in a variety of ways. It is understandable that this figure came to be equated with one who would deliver the Jewish people from the oppression of the Romans.

The New Testament and the Messiah

The New Testament was written during a time of messianic expectation within Judaism. This expectation was heightened by interpretation of the Old Testament that indicated that God used selected or anointed individuals for his purposes regarding Israel. For many, this was primarily focused on resistance to Roman imperial control of the nation. As a result, various groups such as the zealots sought to overthrow Roman tyranny. The result of such factors was expectation of a messiah, even a political messiah. A critical distinction is sometimes made by scholars who argue that Jesus did not see himself as the Messiah and that, without the efforts of his later followers to establish

---

18. See Evans, *Jesus and His Contemporaries*, 70–73, 183–211; and Pearson, "Book of the Twelve"; cf. Porter, "Greek Papyri of the Judaean Desert."

him as the Messiah, he may well have been forgotten as another messianic pretender.[19] Such a view is overly pessimistic regarding the New Testament evidence, and even the evidence of Jesus himself. Further confusion is caused by the tendency to conflate various christological titles, such as the Son of Man, when discussing messianism.[20] We have already seen that there are places where Messiah, Son of God, and Son of Man—and even other titles—may be brought together. For the sake of clarity here, we will try to keep these as separate as we are able, with consideration of other titles given in other chapters as much as this is possible. However, we acknowledge that there is often conceptual overlap, especially because various titles seem to have been used of Jesus by his followers, and even by himself, within the same context.[21] In the New Testament, descriptions of the Messiah vary within the subcorpora, although there is an underlying belief that the Messiah was in some sense a Davidic figure.[22] The use of the language of "Messiah," especially use of the word χριστός as a messianic designation, is plentiful in the New Testament.

Jesus as the Messiah in the Gospels and Acts

The evidence regarding Jesus as the Messiah in the Gospels and Acts is great, to the point that it becomes hard not to see that the Gospels depict an inter-Jewish debate surrounding Jesus regarding the question of his being the Messiah.[23]

Mark and Matthew frame their narratives around Jesus Christ ('Ιησοῦς Χριστός). Mark recounts "the beginning of the good news of Jesus Messiah" (Mark 1:1 AT), and Matthew is a "book of the origin of Jesus Messiah" (Matt. 1:1 AT). Matthew closes his genealogy of Jesus by listing his mother Mary, "from whom Jesus the one called Messiah was begotten" (1:16 AT), summarized in the following verse (1:17). Jesus as the Messiah is then assumed when the birth of Jesus is recounted (1:18).

Throughout the Gospels, questions regarding the Messiah are raised on numerous occasions. In Matthew's Gospel, Herod asks the magi where the Messiah was to be born (Matt. 2:4). In Luke's Gospel, John the Baptist provokes questions about whether he himself is the Messiah (Luke 3:15), and in

---

19. Oegema, *The Anointed and His People*, 149.
20. Cf. Bird, *Are You the One Who Is to Come?*, 77–98, who attempts to define a Son of Man Messiah.
21. See Hengel, *Studies in Early Christology*, 69, who claims that some of the designations, such as Son of Man and Messiah, cannot be differentiated.
22. Cf. Byrne, "Jesus as Messiah in the Gospel of Luke," esp. 81.
23. For a survey of the evidence in the Gospels, see Grindheim, *Christology in the Synoptic Gospels*; cf. Hurtado, *Lord Jesus Christ*.

John's Gospel he explicitly denies that this is the case (John 1:20, 25; 3:28). Later, when in prison, John the Baptist hears about the "works of the Messiah" (Matt. 11:2 AT) and sends his disciples to ask Jesus whether he is the coming one or whether they should expect another (Luke contains the same episode and inquiry but not reference to "works of the Messiah"; Luke 7:19). Jesus identifies John as a prophet (Matt. 11:7–10)—indeed, as greater than a prophet; however, John himself is not the Messiah but the one who anticipates the Messiah.[24] When Jesus is teaching in the temple, according to John, the question is raised whether Jesus is the Messiah (John 7:26, 27, 41), and this leads to debate among the people (7:42). Jesus enters into the discussion in Matthew 22:42 when he asks the Pharisees for their opinion on the identity of the Messiah. He even observes in Matthew 24:5 that some will come claiming to be the Messiah, and in Matthew 24:23 and Mark 13:21 that one should be skeptical of such claims.

When some Greeks interrogate Jesus, he says that it is time for the Son of Man to be glorified. They reply that the law says the Messiah remains forever and so question how Jesus can say the Son of Man will be lifted up (John 12:34). Their reply implies that the Son of Man is related to the Messiah, although the interrogators raise questions about that relationship. The culminating inquiry occurs at Jesus's interrogation by the high priest when, in all three Synoptic Gospels, Jesus is asked whether he is the Messiah (Matt. 26:63//Mark 14:61//Luke 22:67). In Matthew he is asked if he is the Messiah, the Son of God; in Mark whether he is the Messiah, the Son of the Blessed (God); and in Luke simply whether he is the Messiah (then he is asked later in Luke whether he is the Son of God). In this episode the high priest attempts to trick Jesus. A positive answer will expose him as a potential political rival to the Roman establishment, and a negative answer will discredit him in the eyes of others.[25] Jesus answers by defining himself as the Son of Man, but with implications for being the Son of God and the Messiah (see chaps. 3–4).

Other passages in the Gospels reflect the prophetic and kingly functions often associated with the Messiah. The view that the Messiah would be a prophet seems to be reflected in Matthew 26:68 when the high priest and others strike Jesus and demand, "Prophesy for us, Messiah, who is the one striking you?" (AT). When before Pilate, according to Luke, Jesus is accused of saying that he is the Messiah (Luke 23:2). All four Gospels then have Pilate ask Jesus the question, "Are you the King of the Jews?" (Matt. 27:11//Mark 15:2//Luke 23:3//John 18:33), thus linking the Messiah to a kingly function.

---

24. Cullmann, *Christology of the New Testament*, 23.
25. Cullmann, *Christology of the New Testament*, 117–18.

That Jesus was seen as at least a messianic pretender, if not the Messiah, is further endorsed by Pilate, who asks the people whether they want Barabbas or Jesus the one called Messiah to be released and what should happen to Jesus (Matt. 27:17, 22). While Jesus is on the cross, Mark records that one of those mocking him says, "Let the Messiah, the King of Israel, come down from the cross now" (Mark 15:32), with Luke 23:35 containing the statement "Let him save himself if he is the Messiah of God, his chosen one!" One of the thieves crucified with him asks, "Are you not the Messiah? Save yourself and us!" (Luke 23:39). The Gospels make much of Jesus being mocked as king of the Jews (Matt. 27:29//Mark 15:18//John 19:3; cf. John 19:14–15), and the *titulus* placed over the cross most likely reflects the mockers' implication that Jesus is another failed messianic pretender (Matt. 27:37//Mark 15:26; John 19:19).

Some in the Gospel narratives make positive proclamations regarding the Messiah. In Luke's Gospel, the angels tell the shepherds, "To you is born this day in the city of David a Savior, who is the Messiah, the Lord" (Luke 2:11). Later, at Jesus's presentation in the temple, Simeon says that he has been promised that he will not die before seeing the Lord's Messiah (Luke 2:26). Both these Lukan references reflect the royal Davidic messianic conception. When Jesus calls his disciples, according to John, Andrew tells Simon Peter that "we have found the Messiah [Μεσσίας]," which John adds is translated "Christ" (John 1:41 AT).[26] When Jesus discusses matters with the woman from Samaria, she knows that the Messiah (Μεσσίας) who is the Christ is coming (4:25) and then tells others of Jesus and raises the question whether he is the Messiah (4:29). The reader is left to infer that Jesus is the Messiah of whom she speaks when he answers, "I am, the one who is speaking to you" (4:26 AT).[27]

When some who are ill are brought to Jesus and he heals them, the people exclaim, "You are the Son of God," but Jesus tells them not to repeat this because "they knew him to be the Messiah" (Luke 4:41 AT). Matthew and Mark do not have the same admonition as in Luke, but Matthew (8:17) says the healings are to fulfill the words of the prophet in Isaiah 53:4, one of the Suffering Servant passages. In Mark 8:29, Matthew 16:16, and Luke 9:20, Peter declares that "you [Jesus] are the Messiah" (Luke simply states "the Messiah of God," and Matthew adds "the Son of the living God," another instance in which "Messiah" and "Son of God" language are brought together). Matthew continues with the statement that Jesus tells his disciples not to tell anyone

---

26. See Rainbow, *Johannine Theology*, 185, who notes the unique translation of John's Gospel of the word Μεσσίας by Χριστός.

27. Longenecker, *Christology of Early Jewish Christianity*, 70.

that he is the Messiah (Matt. 16:20), with Mark including a similar statement that specifically mentions Jesus as Messiah (Mark 8:30).[28] When Jesus heals the blind man in John's Gospel, the man's parents fear because the Jewish leaders had declared that anyone confessing Jesus as the Messiah was to be expelled from the synagogue (John 9:22). At the incident in Bethany with Lazarus's sisters, Jesus asks Martha whether she believes what Jesus has said, and she declares, "I believe that you are the Messiah, the Son of God" (John 11:27). Here the Son of God is again linked to the Messiah. John says that his Gospel was written so that readers may believe that "Jesus is the Messiah, the Son of God" (John 20:31),[29] with the Messiah and the Son of God brought together. This is a clear case in which the Messiah is identified with the man Jesus as well as with the Son of God.

Jesus refers to himself, even if indirectly, as the Messiah. In John 4:26, as noted above, after the Samaritan woman states that she knows that the Messiah called Christ is coming and that he will proclaim all things, Jesus says, "I am, the one who is speaking to you" (AT). In John's Gospel, on the basis of the use of "I am" statements (cf. John 8:58), this might indicate a subtle claim not just to being the Messiah but to divine identity.[30] In Mark 9:41, in third-person language reminiscent of "the Son of Man," Jesus says that "whoever gives you a cup of water to drink because you bear the name of Christ will by no means lose the reward." When Jesus is in Jerusalem for one of the festivals, the Jewish leaders ask Jesus to tell them if he is the Messiah (John 10:24), and Jesus answers that he has told them and they do not believe him. Mark 12:35, Matthew 22:42, and Luke 20:41 may constitute another such indirect reference. While teaching, Jesus asks about the identity of the Messiah, especially his relationship to David, and he cites Psalm 110:1. Although Jesus does not directly state that he is the Messiah who is the Lord of the psalm, the implication is that he is the Messiah who is the Son of David. This Gospel pericope reflects the view of the Messiah as in the royal line of David, such that the king of the psalm is the Messiah.[31] After the resurrection, on the road to Emmaus, Jesus speaks with the travelers and asks them whether the Messiah had to suffer as he did (Luke 24:26). When Jesus then appears to the disciples before his ascension, he essentially answers the

---

28. Such statements give some evidence for the so-called messianic secret, a notion made popular by Wrede, *Messianic Secret*. Cf. Manson, *Teaching of Jesus*, 202–3, who answers such claims by pointing out that the acclamation is made on the basis of Peter's own personal experience, as it is for every person.

29. Porter, *Idioms of the Greek New Testament*, 109–10.

30. See Porter, *John, His Gospel, and Jesus*, 128, 131–33, 135.

31. See Cullmann, *Christology of the New Testament*, 84. Cf. 131, where Cullmann contends that "Jesus argues against the idea that the Messiah must be of the physical lineage of David."

question by affirming that the Scriptures said that the Messiah would suffer and rise from the dead (24:40).

John's Gospel includes references to Jesus as Jesus Christ (or Jesus Messiah), unlike the Synoptic Gospels (see John 1:17; 17:3). The book of Acts also uses "Jesus Christ" (or "Christ Jesus") about fifteen times, much more than in the Gospels.[32] In many other passages, Jesus, whose name is not mentioned, is equated with being the Messiah (e.g., Acts 2:31, 36; 3:18; 4:6; 8:5; 17:3; 26:23). There are, nevertheless, several major passages regarding Jesus as the Messiah in Acts.[33] The first occurs in Peter's speech at Pentecost (Acts 2:14–36). This is a programmatic statement for the entire book. Peter stands to address the crowd to explain his fellow disciples' behavior and explicates Joel 2:28–32 (3:1–5 LXX) in Acts 2:17–21; Psalm 16:8–11, a royal psalm, in Acts 2:25–28; and Psalm 110:1, a royal Davidic psalm, in Acts 2:34–35. On the basis of Jesus as the prophesied crucified and resurrected one, Peter proclaims Jesus as the Messiah. Because David was a prophet, Peter says (Acts 2:30–31), he could look forward to the resurrection of the Messiah. After his citation of Psalm 110:1 in Acts 2:34–35, Peter says that all Israel should know that God has made Jesus both Lord and Messiah. Finally, in Acts 2:38, Peter tells the respondent crowd to repent and be baptized in the name of Jesus the Christ. This passage further develops the prophetic and royal or Davidic messianic conception found in Luke's Gospel and puts it at the forefront of Acts as a theme developed throughout. Peter gives his second major sermon in Acts 3:12–26; in 3:18, he refers to what God announced beforehand by the prophets, that the Messiah should suffer. He thus calls for the people to repent of their sins in anticipation of the sending of Christ Jesus (Acts 3:20). This passage focuses on the Messiah as fulfilling prophecy, especially the necessity of the Messiah suffering.[34] In Acts 9, Paul preaches in synagogues that Jesus was the Son of God (9:20); emboldened, he spends time in Damascus "proving that Jesus was the Messiah" (9:22). Jesus is depicted as the Son of David in Paul's extended exposition in his speech in Pisidian Antioch (Acts 13:21–41, citing Ps. 2:7; Isa. 55:3, a Suffering Servant passage; Ps. 16:10 LXX; Hab. 1:5; Isa. 49:6) and in the Davidic line in James's speech in Jerusalem (Acts 15:13–21, citing Amos 9:11–12 LXX). Although neither passage specifically mentions Jesus as the Messiah, the clear implication is that Jesus is the Davidic Messiah. This is not the same in Thessalonica, where Paul addresses the synagogue

---

32. Acts 2:38; 3:6, 20; 4:10, 33; 5:42; 8:12, 37; 9:34; 10:36, 48; 11:17; 15:26; 16:18; 18:5, 28; 20:21; 24:24; 28:31.
33. See Porter, "Messiah in Luke and Acts," esp. 159–63, which we depend on, although we have changed our view on the honorific view of Christ as indicating Messiah.
34. See L. Johnson, *Acts of the Apostles*, 68.

and opens the Scriptures (Acts 17:2). He explains to them that Jesus as the Messiah had to suffer and rise from the dead (17:3). Paul here views Jesus as a prophetic messiah fulfilling the Scriptures; it's also possible that he sees Jesus as the Suffering Servant of Isaiah 53. Finally, in Paul's speech before Agrippa, Festus cuts off the speech after Paul appeals to the prophets and Moses in stating that the Messiah would suffer and rise from the dead (Acts 26:22–23). Luke emphasizes that the suffering of the Messiah is a fulfillment of prophecy, and the Messiah fulfills prophetic expectations.

Jesus as the Messiah in Paul's Letters

Paul makes frequent mention of Jesus Christ or Jesus Messiah. A few times in his letters, Paul refers simply to the Messiah without designating the Messiah as Jesus, but in most of them he is referring to the figure Jesus from the Gospels in messianic terms (e.g., Rom. 5:6, 8; 6:4, 8, 9).[35] The more contentious idea, at least within recent study, is what Paul means when he refers to "Jesus Christ" or "Christ Jesus." Paul uses the two configurations in roughly equal numbers. As with many issues in New Testament studies, the history of interpretation has been influenced by Ferdinand Christian Baur. In his attempt to distance Pauline Christianity from Jewish Christianity, Baur also attempted to distance any estimation of Paul's view of the Messiah from Jewish thought. This view influenced much subsequent Pauline interpretation and resulted in a spiritualized and eventually a vacant view of the Messiah. The result was an emphasis on Jesus as Lord, promoted by the history of religions school, rather than Jesus as Messiah. This stream of thought culminated in an essay in 1953 by Nils Dahl in which he argued that Paul uses "Christ" along with Jesus as a name rather than as a title,[36] a view that has generally held sway, apart from a few occasional interpreters.[37]

Recently, however, it has rightly been argued that Paul uses "messiah" language, even if he does not formulate his messianism in the same way as other New Testament authors. Contrary to Dahl's position, Paul is a messianic thinker regarding Jesus. However, that does not mean that every time Paul uses "Christ" he implies a singular, fully developed concept of messianism,

---

35. For other surveys of the evidence, see Fee, *Pauline Christology*; cf. Hurtado, *Lord Jesus Christ*.

36. See Dahl, "Messiahship of Jesus in Paul." He has been followed by many. However, some retained a sense in which "Christ" still indicated "Messiah." See Cullmann, *Christology of the New Testament*, 112.

37. See Novenson, *Christ among the Messiahs*, 12–32, for a history of this discussion. His volume is a defense of Paul using "messiah" language, and he discusses some of those who have dissented and argued that "Christ" indicates "messiah" language.

since it is doubtful that there was such a thing. It does indicate at the least that Paul thought of Jesus as the Messiah and so used "Christ" as an honorific.[38] This also helps to explain the variation in word order between "Jesus Christ" and "Christ Jesus"; the wording of a name and an honorific was variable in the ancient Greco-Roman world.[39]

Novenson believes, on the basis of the equations Paul makes and the scriptural passages he invokes, that Paul generally accepts a Davidic view of Jesus's messiahship.[40] Jesus as Messiah is the fulfillment of the Davidic rule over God's people. Novenson's proposal is helpful but does not go far enough in integrating the honorific "Christ" with the man Jesus. One of the subtle but consistent ways that Paul expresses his belief in Jesus as the Messiah is through the actions that he attributes to Christ in relation to the earthly Jesus. These are not simply post-Easter actions; Paul seems to conceive of Jesus as the Messiah who was crucified, offered himself as a blood sacrifice through his death, and was raised, among other possible actions. There is certainly more to Paul's messianism than these few events—as will become clear in the following paragraphs—but Paul's referring to Christ and his actions in the context of his description of Jesus the man reinforces his conception of Jesus as the Messiah.

Paul does not apparently see—or at least does not attempt to exploit—a difference between the earthly Jesus and the risen Christ so far as his messiahship is concerned. For Paul, Jesus as Messiah encompasses his earthly and his postresurrection activities, so that what is said of Jesus is said of Jesus the Messiah. In one of the most important passages regarding Paul's knowledge of the earthly Jesus (1 Cor. 15:3–7), Paul begins by stating that "I passed on to you in the first place what I also received" (AT). Most scholars think that Paul is referring here to tradition that he had received from other Christians, perhaps those who had known or seen the earthly Jesus.[41] However, Paul also insists in his Letter to the Galatians (1:11–24) that he received the gospel directly from God. There is also a possibility that Paul was a witness to the earthly ministry of Jesus, in which case he may even have had some firsthand knowledge of his own.[42] In other words, we do not know from 1 Corinthians alone how Paul received this knowledge, although he clearly has it. Never-

---

38. Novenson, *Christ among the Messiahs*, 138.
39. Novenson, *Christ among the Messiahs*, 99–102. Novenson gives the example of "Herod the king" having variable word order, among other examples (101n16).
40. Novenson, *Christ among the Messiahs*, 173.
41. See, e.g., Fee, *First Epistle to the Corinthians*, 798.
42. See Porter, *When Paul Met Jesus*, who argues that there is evidence, including biblical evidence (1 Cor. 9:1; 2 Cor. 5:16), that Paul had encountered the earthly Jesus.

theless, he then states that "Christ died for our sins in accordance with the scriptures, and that he was buried, and that he was raised on the third day in accordance with the scriptures, and that he appeared to Cephas, then to the twelve" (1 Cor. 15:3–5). The images are clear: death, burial, resurrection, and appearances of Christ. A similar pattern is found in Romans 8:34, where Paul says that Christ Jesus died, was raised to life, and is at the right hand of God interceding for us. Notice that in these passages Paul refers not merely to "Jesus" but to "Christ" or "Christ Jesus" and that he moves from earthly events such as death and burial to resurrection, postresurrection appearance, and heavenly installation all in one chronological (and to him, at least, logical) narrative motion.

Other examples may help to illustrate this more fully. In more than a few instances, events that are clearly ascribable to the earthly life of Jesus are described with reference to "Christ," "Christ Jesus," or "Jesus Christ," besides the simple use of "Jesus." For example, Romans 3:24–25 speaks of the redemption that came by Christ Jesus as a sacrifice involving blood, a clear reference to his death on the cross. Romans 6:3 speaks of Christians being baptized into the death of Christ Jesus, with the baptismal downward motion mirroring his descent into death and the grave. Romans 5:6–8 says twice that while humanity was sinful or powerless, Christ died for the ungodly. Romans 9:5 refers to the earthly or fleshly ancestry of Christ from the patriarchs. However, this passage is important because it also indicates that the Messiah, according to Paul, is "the God who is over all, blessed into the ages" (AT). This is a highly contentious verse because the Greek wording quoted above may be an independent statement about God, not about the Messiah. There are many good reasons, however, to take this as a statement about who the Messiah is in his fleshly or earthly nature: he is over all things, he is God with the same divine nature, and he is blessed forever.[43] This is a major claim to make about the earthly Messiah, Jesus, attributing divinity to him. Romans 14:9 says Christ died and came back to life, and 14:15 speaks of concern for the brother for whom Christ died. In 1 Corinthians 1:17, 23, as well as in 8:11, Paul says that he preaches the cross of Christ or Christ crucified (not Jesus crucified), which he labels a stumbling block to Jews and foolishness to gentiles. Galatians 6:12 and Philippians 3:18 refer to the cross not of Jesus but of Christ. Ephesians 1:1 refers to Christ Jesus, and 2:13–16 speaks of the blood of Christ (not of Jesus), his abolishing the law in his flesh, and the cross.

---

43. See Porter, *Letter to the Romans*, 182–84, for discussion. Cf. Fee, *Pauline Christology*, 253, who takes reference to Messiah as "climactic" and showing that Paul's Son of God Christology is "rooted deeply in Jewish messianism: Christ is the long-awaited Davidic scion from the root of Jesse and thus of Judah."

While in this large list of passages Paul uses "Christ" or "messiah" language to speak of Jesus's earthly being, life, and events, Paul also uses the name Jesus when referring to the events and activities of the resurrected and exalted figure, thus further depicting Jesus as the Messiah. For example, 1 Thessalonians 1:10 speaks of waiting for God's Son from heaven, whom God raised from the dead: "Jesus, who rescues us from the wrath that is coming." Later, 4:14 says that Jesus died and rose again and that Paul believes God will bring with Jesus—referring to his parousia (return)—those who are sleeping (already dead). Paul seems to believe in not just a kingly or Davidic messiah, or even a priestly or prophetic messiah, but a dying and rising messiah, one who sacrificially died and was resurrected for humanity. More than that, not only does he ascribe a range of redemptive and salvific functions to the Messiah, Jesus, but he also seems to indicate that Jesus the Messiah was himself a divine being, functioning in both earthly and heavenly realms.

Jesus as the Messiah in the Rest of the New Testament

The other books of the New Testament, including Hebrews, the General Epistles, and Revelation, contain an abundance of "messiah" language.[44] As in Paul's Letters, one of the common phrases is "Jesus Christ" or "Christ Jesus." Of the approximately seventy instances of χριστός in these writings, at least forty of them appear in the phrase "Jesus Christ," with only one questionable example of "Christ Jesus."[45] This evidence might indicate that "Jesus Christ" has become a proper name within these writings. However, the way that "Christ" is used in most of them indicates that the term is used to portray Jesus as the Messiah.[46]

The book of Hebrews, as one might expect, utilizes "messiah" language in a priestly fashion. However, that is not its only use. In Hebrews 3:6, Christ is the faithful Son over God's house, but this is in the context of Moses hav-

---

44. For a concise summary of the evidence (except for Revelation), see Westfall, "Messianic Themes." One need not accept her eschatological definition of "Messiah"—which appears to be far too narrow a definition on the basis of the evidence we have examined in this chapter—to appreciate her summary.

45. This example occurs in 1 Pet. 5:10, where UBS⁵ and NA²⁸ have traditionally included Ἰησοῦ in square brackets. Codexes Sinaiticus and Vaticanus do not include Ἰησοῦ. NA²⁸ and UBS⁵, reflecting the Editio Critica Maior, do not include it. It is unlikely that it should be included.

46. The issue of authorship for each of these works may come into play in determining their messiah consciousness. Each of these writings has had questions raised about authorship, and the later they are placed by means of later (and often pseudepigraphal) authorship, the more likely it is that they will reflect language that is not messianic.

ing also been faithful in God's house (3:5; cf. 11:26). Subsequent reference to Christ (3:14) also occurs within the context of Moses holding to these convictions (3:16). In Hebrews 5:5, Christ is depicted in relationship to the high priest, with Aaron as the first example. Christ is a greater priest after the order of Melchizedek (5:6). This depiction is reinforced in Hebrews 9, where Christ comes as the high priest (9:11) who enters the sanctuary (9:24). He also becomes the sacrifice in the temple to take away sins and bring salvation (9:28), with specific reference to his blood (9:14). This sacrifice of Jesus Christ's body makes us holy (10:10).

The Letter of James uses "Jesus Christ" twice (James 1:1; 2:1) in ways that do not reveal his messianic conceptions. However, 1 Peter contains language that is redolent of the sacrificial language of Hebrews (and Paul?). Peter speaks of being sprinkled with the blood of Jesus Christ (1 Pet. 1:2), further elucidated as "the precious blood of Christ, like that of a lamb without defect or blemish" (1:19). He also mentions the resurrection of Jesus Christ from the dead (1:3) and the revelation of Jesus Christ (1:7). Peter explicitly speaks of the prophets seeking to determine by means of the Spirit of Christ when the "sufferings destined for Christ and the subsequent glory" might occur (1:11) so that we might be ready for when Jesus Christ "is revealed" (1:13). Peter speaks of Christians being built into a "spiritual house, to be a holy priesthood, to offer spiritual sacrifices acceptable to God through Jesus Christ" (2:5). Christ had to suffer to do this (2:21). The call to good behavior is predicated upon Christ suffering for sins (3:18; cf. 3:15, 16). In language again reminiscent of Paul, Peter speaks of baptism that saves by means of the resurrection of Jesus Christ (3:21). Christ "suffered in the flesh" of his earthly body (4:1) for his followers, and they should share in Christ's sufferings (4:13; 5:10; cf. 4:14) and be witnesses to them (5:1).

Every instance of "Christ" is found in the phrase "Jesus Christ" in 2 Peter and Jude. Nevertheless, the Petrine passages contribute to our understanding of "messiah" language. Several of the passages link Jesus Christ with being the Savior (2 Pet. 1:1, 11; 2:20; 3:18), which probably invokes the notion of the royal messianic figure, along with images of eschatological victory (see also 2 Pet. 1:8). Cynthia Westfall sees a probable link between the transfiguration account in 2 Peter 1:16–19 and the ultimate triumph of the Messiah (2 Pet. 1:16).[47] Jude also connects Jesus Christ with "our Savior" (Jude 25), but more important is Jesus Christ being called Sovereign and Lord (Jude 4), invoking the kingly messianic conception. Jesus Christ is linked with "Lord" in four instances in Jude (4, 17, 21, 25).

---

47. Westfall, "Messianic Themes," 225.

The Johannine Letters (1 John and 2 John, but not 3 John) contain twelve references to Christ, with nine of them to Jesus Christ. Clear instances of "messiah" language are found in 1 John 2:22 (cf. John 20:31), where John says that a liar is one who denies that "the Christ is Jesus," and 1 John 5:1, where John says that everyone who believes "the Christ is Jesus" is begotten from God.[48] This predicate construction is clearly not nominal but identifies the Messiah as the person Jesus. In 1 John 1:3, John attributes Christian fellowship to the Father and to the Son Jesus Christ, which makes sonship a feature of the Messiah. This relationship is continued in the book, which Westfall sees as indicating enthronement language and hence royal messiah language (cf. also mention of "seed" in 1 John 3:9; cf. 4:7; 5:4).[49] First John 2:1 states that when we sin, we have a representative with the Father who is the righteous Jesus Christ. The attribution of the adjective "righteous," δίκαιον, may be to either Χριστόν Ἰησοῦν or Χριστόν. It is more likely an attribute of the latter, and hence a definer of who the Messiah is: he is the righteous Messiah. This is based on the next verse, which says that he is the atonement for our sins and for the sins of the entire world (1 John 2:2). The equation of Jesus Christ with the Son is continued in 1 John 3:23 and 4:15. First John 3:23 is often translated in a way that may be confusing. The NIV translates the verse as "to believe in the name of his Son, Jesus Christ . . . ," where "Jesus Christ" is distinguished from the Son as his name. However, the verse may better indicate that we are to believe "in the name of his Son Jesus Christ" (as in the NRSV), in which the messianic feature of sonship is maintained, as elsewhere in 1 John. The connection of Jesus Christ to the Son is continued in 1 John 5:6, where John speaks of Jesus Christ as coming through water and blood. There are three witnesses to the identity of Jesus Christ, the Spirit, water, and blood. This probably refers to the birthing process, although this is potentially sacrificial priestly "messiah" language. The last reference to the Son as Jesus Christ is found in 1 John 5:20. Second John continues the equation of the Son with Jesus Christ (2 John 3, 9), said to come in the flesh (2 John 7).

The book of Revelation uses "messiah" language that seems to reflect both a prophetic and a royal function. Revelation 1:1–2 says that it is a revelation of Jesus Christ given to John, who witnesses to the word of God and the testimony of Jesus Christ. In Revelation 11:15, at the seventh trumpet, language reminiscent of a variety of Old Testament passages is used (Exod. 15:18; Pss. 10:16; 22:28; Dan. 2:44; 7:14; Obad. 21; Zech. 14:9) that speaks

---

48. Rather than "Jesus is the Christ," a matter of understanding the Greek wording. See Porter, *Idioms of the Greek New Testament*, 109–10.
49. Westfall, "Messianic Themes," 228.

of the coming of our Lord and of his Messiah and in which a distinction is made between God and the Messiah. A similar understanding is reflected in Revelation 12:10, where a heavenly voice declares the coming of the salvation and the power and the kingdom of our God and the authority of his Christ. In Revelation 20:4, John distinguishes between testimony by martyrs about Jesus and their reigning with the Messiah for a thousand years. Revelation 20:6 says that these martyrs are to become priests of God and of Christ and will rule with him for a thousand years.

There is a mix of "messiah" language in Hebrews, the General Epistles, and Revelation. Although questions can be raised regarding some of the passages and their messianic assertions, the invocation of royal, priestly, and prophetic images in a variety of contexts indicates that language of the Messiah is being used, and the association of Jesus Christ with the Son and Lord adds to the understanding of "messiah" language by invoking other christological titles.

Contribution to New Testament Christology

The concept of the Messiah in the ancient Jewish world constituted a complex tradition or set of traditions. The history of its discussion has been equally complex. There has been an overriding tendency to attempt to find a singular definition of what it meant to be the Messiah. As a result, much scholarship has been concerned to provide a reified or unified picture of the Messiah. As we have seen in our brief survey of the evidence, such an idealized tradition was bound to be problematic, because there is no easy way to condense this evidence in a single picture. Such complexity led to a general vacating of the notion of the Messiah in much scholarly discussion. However, there have been recent resurgences of interest in such a figure, often extending the definition so that it impinges upon other christological designations that are treated elsewhere in this volume, such as Lord, prophet, Son of God, and possibly others. Rather than attempting to define this kernel of messianic thought—whether it is a military ruler or an eschatological figure, among others—we believe that the evidence points in a variety of ways. Ancient Jewish "messiah" language revolved around various figures who were identified as having been chosen by God—and hence often anointed—to intervene in the life of God's people. Some of these figures were rulers, others prophets, and still others priests—and sometimes they combined functions of two or more of these. Most of the time these figures were followers of the God of the Old Testament, but God was not bound to use his followers, just as he was not bound to use only certain actions that he called on these various messiahs to perform.

> **IGNATIUS ON "OUR GOD, JESUS THE CHRIST"**
>
> For our God, Jesus the Christ, was conceived by Mary according to God's plan, both from the seed of David and of the Holy Spirit. He was born and was baptized in order that by his suffering he might cleanse the water.[a]
>
> a. Ignatius, *To the Ephesians* 18.2. Translation from Holmes, *Apostolic Fathers*, 197.

As a result, in the time of the New Testament there were widely varied messianic expectations revolving around God appointing a figure to rescue his people from Roman oppression. Some attempted to fulfill this messianic role. The christological question focuses on the relationship of Jesus to this messianic expectation and how the "messiah" language used in the New Testament describes his functions in relation to his followers. Rejecting views that see Jesus as *later* identified as the Messiah by his followers, we believe that the New Testament presents *early* attestation of Jesus as the Messiah, possibly upholding a view that Jesus himself held. Paul is probably the most significant writer in expanding the role of the Messiah in how he characterizes the work of Jesus Christ in his letters. As a result, in the New Testament, Jesus Christ is not just in the line of David and hence a royal messiah, or a priest replacing the Jewish cult, or a prophet in the line of Isaiah; he is the Messiah who encapsulates these functions and goes further by offering himself as the crucified and resurrected Messiah who saves his people, possibly doing so as God himself.

CHAPTER 8

JESUS THE SAVIOR

Introduction

In his Letter to the Philippians, Paul uses a variety of titles to refer to Jesus Christ. He frequently uses the term Χριστός simply by itself as "Christ" or "Messiah" (Phil. 1:15, 18; 2:1; 3:8–10) but also in the phrases "Christ Jesus" (1:1, 8, 26; 2:5; 3:3; 4:7, 19, 21) and "Jesus Christ" (1:2, 6, 11; 2:21).[1] Paul also uses κύριος throughout the epistle, referring simply to "Lord" (1:14; 2:11, 24, 29; 3:1, 4:1, 2, 4, 10) but also to "Lord Jesus" (2:19), "Lord Jesus Christ" (1:2; 3:20; 4:23), and "my Lord" (3:8). These designations are all typical for Paul, as they can be found throughout his letters, and we discuss them elsewhere in this volume.

However, Paul uses a term for Jesus in Philippians 3:20 that is found far less frequently: σωτήρ, or "Savior." This is the only use of σωτήρ in Paul's undisputed letters, but the term also appears in reference to Jesus in Ephesians (5:23), 2 Timothy (1:10), and Titus (1:4; 2:13; 3:6). Paul's use of σωτήρ in Philippians, which is usually dated to the late 50s or early 60s CE,[2] is the earliest Christian use of the term in reference to Jesus that we know of. It appears in a section in which Paul encourages his audience to imitate those who live for Christ (Phil. 3:17–21). In contrast to those who live as enemies of the cross of Jesus and have their minds set on earthly things, "our citizenship is in heaven, and it is from there that we are expecting a Savior, the Lord Jesus Christ" (3:20). These few references to Jesus as Savior—a terminology

---

1. There is scholarly discussion about whether Paul uses "Christ" as a name or as a title, and why he sometimes places "Jesus" first and sometimes "Christ." We discuss these issues in more detail in chap. 7.
2. See Porter, *Apostle Paul*, 347.

157

that we are very familiar with in contemporary Christianity—may come as a surprise, as we might have expected Paul, of all people, to refer often to Jesus as Savior, as contemporary Christians often do.

What is behind Paul's choice here, and what is he hoping to communicate to his audience by introducing this title for Jesus? There is clearly a notion of anticipation since Paul defines the people of God as *expecting* a savior. This concept of God's people waiting for a savior draws from a rich tradition found in Israel's Scriptures. As we will see, the biblical writers often identified Yahweh as Israel's Savior. What is remarkable is that Paul identifies the people's savior as Jesus. Other New Testament writers pick up on this idea—Jesus as Savior—and extend it beyond God's people to the entire world. In addition, the New Testament writers lived in a culture in which the designation "savior" was commonly reserved for the Roman emperor. Within this context, what does it mean that Jesus—and implicitly, not Caesar—is Savior? The notion of Jesus as Savior makes a significant contribution to the developing understanding of Jesus in early Christianity and to the Christology of the New Testament.

"Savior" in Ancient Jewish and Greco-Roman Writings

An abundance of evidence shows that the title "Savior" was a common designation within the first-century world. This is true for both Jewish and Hellenistic literature and culture. Greco-Roman literature applies the title to gods and heroes, and archaeological evidence includes shrines dedicated to individual gods as saviors. First-century Jewish writers such as Philo regularly used the designation for the God of Israel.[3] Yet the notion of Israel's God as Savior is present in the Hebrew Bible as well. When translating the Hebrew Scriptures into Greek, the translators of the Septuagint used the popular word σωτήρ to convey this concept. More than with some other sacred traditions explored in this study, both the Jewish and the Hellenistic backgrounds of σωτήρ are of vital importance for understanding how the New Testament writers applied the title to Jesus.

Ancient Jewish Writings

In the Old Testament, the designation "savior" or, sometimes, "deliverer" (ישׁע) is most frequently used of God, although it sometimes refers to a human. When used for humans, these saviors are instruments of God's salvation, sent by him for this purpose (2 Kings 13:5; Isa. 19:20; Neh. 9:27).

---

3. Philo, *Allegorical Interpretation* 2.56; 3.27; *On the Sacrifices of Cain and Abel* 70–71; *On the Migration of Abraham* 25; 124; *On Flight and Finding* 162.

Often harking back to previous experiences of deliverance, the biblical writers overwhelmingly identify Yahweh as Israel's Savior (Isa. 43:3; Ps. 106:21; cf. Hosea 13:4). In the book of Isaiah, the Lord declares to the prophet, "I am the LORD your Savior, and your Redeemer, the Mighty One of Jacob" (Isa. 49:26). In 2 Samuel, David cries out,

> The LORD is my rock, my fortress, and my deliverer,
>   my God, my rock, in whom I take refuge,
> my shield and the horn of my salvation,
>   my stronghold and my refuge,
>   my savior; you save me from violence. (2 Sam. 22:2–3)

A defining characteristic of God in the Old Testament is that he is the one who saves. Just as Yahweh saved his people in the past, the Israelites could count on their salvation at God's hands in the future (Isa. 35:4).

The most significant moment of deliverance for Israel was when Yahweh saved them from bondage in Egypt. This event is recounted throughout Israel's Scriptures and became a defining moment not only for Israel but also for Yahweh, who is established as Israel's Savior. In the retelling of the exodus in the Pentateuch, Moses tells the Israelites, "Remember this day on which you came out of Egypt, out of the house of slavery, because the LORD brought you out from there by strength of hand" (Exod. 13:3). They are to retell the story to their children so that they may know God (Exod. 13:14; Deut. 6:21). After the exodus, Yahweh identifies himself as the one "who brought you out of the land of Egypt" (Exod. 20:2; Lev. 18:3; Num. 15:41; Deut. 5:6; Judg. 6:8; 1 Sam. 10:18; Neh. 9:18; Ps. 81:10; Jer. 34:13). More than any other event in their history, the Israelites are called to remember their deliverance from Egypt by God. Other Jewish literature from the Second Temple period refers to the exodus as the key event in Israel's history and offers insight into Yahweh's saving character (4 *Ezra* 1.7; 15.10; cf. Bar. 2:11).

Yahweh not only saves his people from peril and oppressors but also is the source of salvation from sin and judgment. Only Yahweh offers eternal salvation. In Isaiah 45, the prophet declares, "Israel is saved by the LORD with everlasting salvation; you shall not be put to shame or confounded to all eternity" (45:17). This salvation is available to all the earth (45:22). Significant also is the expectation of a coming one of God who will be the people's savior (19:20). As Oscar Cullmann points out, the designation "savior" corresponds well to certain expectations of the Messiah in Jewish tradition—even though the title "Savior" is not often used.[4]

---

4. Cullmann, *Christology of the New Testament*, 239.

> ## "SAVIOR OF THOSE WITHOUT HOPE"
>
> The description of God as "savior of those without hope" is found in the book of Judith, an apocryphal book that was included in the Septuagint and contains many titles for God. God as "savior" is connected to his protection of the weak, lowly, and forsaken.
>
>> For your strength does not depend on numbers, nor your might on the powerful. But you are the God of the lowly, helper of the oppressed, upholder of the weak, protector of the forsaken, savior of those without hope. Please, please, God of my father, God of the heritage of Israel, Lord of heaven and earth, Creator of the waters, King of all your creation, hear my prayer![a]
>
> a. Judith 9:11–12.

The Septuagint translates the Hebrew יָשַׁע and similar terms as σωτήρ (i.e., Judg. 3:9; Isa. 12:2).[5] In Second Temple Jewish literature, God alone is σωτήρ (1 Macc. 4:30; *Pss. Sol.* 8.33; Bar. 4:22; Sir. 51:8; *Sib. Or.* 3.35), as the term "savior" rarely appears in reference to a human savior (cf. Sir. 46:1, an exception to the general rule). There is also no connection between the Messiah and σωτήρ in Second Temple Jewish literature. The designation is a significant one for the author of 3 Maccabees. After God saves the Israelites from annihilation at the hands of the evil king Philopator, they sing praises to "their holy God and Savior" (3 Macc. 6:29; cf. 6:32). Later, the Israelites are "joyfully and loudly giving thanks to the one God of their ancestors, the eternal Savior of Israel" (7:16). Here, as elsewhere, the title "Savior" is appropriate, as it is used within a context in which God physically saves his people from destruction. Further, God is called Savior because of his previous saving activity and protection of his people (Jud. 9:11; 1 Macc. 4:30).

Philo uses σωτήρ frequently in reference to God,[6] regularly giving God the title "only Savior."[7] He also uses the title "Savior of the world,"[8] which was

---

5. Schelkle, "σωτήρ, ἦρος, ὁ," 3:326.
6. Philo, *On the Sacrifices of Cain and Abel* 70; *On the Migration of Abraham* 25; *On the Preliminary Studies* 171.
7. Philo, *That God Is Unchangeable* 137; *On Agriculture* 80; *On the Confusion of Tongues* 93; *Who Is the Heir?* 60.
8. Philo, *On the Special Laws* 2.198; cf. *That God Is Unchangeable* 156; *On Flight and Finding* 162.

commonly used within the context of emperor worship. Josephus never uses σωτήρ in reference to God but does use it for humans (*Ant.* 2.94; 11.278). Josephus's writings offer evidence that rulers were commonly given the title (*Ant.* 12.223; 13.222; 13.271). An example of this is found in *Jewish Antiquities*: after Herod defeated his enemies in battle "and thereby rendered the way safe for those that came after, . . . these called Herod their savior [σωτήρ] and protector" (*Ant.* 14.444).[9]

Greco-Roman Literature

Significant also is the use of σωτήρ in Greco-Roman writings and traditions.[10] Gods, great heroes, and rulers are all described as saviors if they saved others from peril.[11] Zeus was worshiped as Zeus Savior (σωτήρ), and kings were often surnamed Savior (σωτήρ).[12] Herodotus tells of the Greeks praying "to Poseidon as their savior" after several hundred Persian ships were destroyed in a storm and that "from that time on they call Poseidon their savior [σωτῆρος]" (*Histories* 7.192–93).[13] A temple dedicated to Zeus, built in the fourth century BCE, is described by Pausanias as "a sanctuary of Zeus, surnamed Saviour [Σωτῆρος]. It is adorned with pillars round it. Zeus is seated on a throne, and by his side stand Megalopolis on the right and an image of Artemis Saviour [Σωτείρας] on the left."[14]

Great men were also designated as saviors within Greek literature. In Aeschylus's *The Suppliant Maidens*, Danaus declares that it is right to praise the people of Argos as one does the gods since they are "our saviors" (lines 980–82).[15] Dion of Syracuse was praised as "Savior" after restoring the city (Diodorus, *Library of History* 16.20); Plutarch even notes that the Syracusians considered him a god (*Life of Dion* 46.1). Dio Chrysostom used the title σωτήρ for philosophers, who "have the power through persuasion and reason to calm and soften the soul" (*To the People of Alexandria* 32.18).[16]

In addition, it was common for Roman emperors to be given the title and characteristics of a savior.[17] Titus, for example, is praised by the Chalcidians

---

9. Translation from Whiston, *Works of Flavius Josephus*, 394.
10. See Gilbert, "Roman Propaganda and Christian Identity," esp. 237–42.
11. See Wendland, "Σωτήρ."
12. Wills, "Wisdom and Word among the Hellenistic Saviors," 122.
13. Translation by A. D. Godley (LCL).
14. Pausanias, *Description of Greece* 8.30.10. Translation by W. H. S. Jones (LCL).
15. Translation by A. H. Sommerstein (LCL).
16. Translation by J. W. Cohoon and H. L. Crosby (LCL).
17. Cullmann, *Christology of the New Testament*, 240; Bousset, *Kyrios Christos*, 311.

after he intercedes on their behalf, protecting them against the Romans. They dedicate numerous buildings to him, offer sacrifices in his honor, and sing a hymn to him that includes the phrase "Hail, Titus our savior!"[18] In 9 BCE, Augustus was given the title in an official decree by Greek cities in Asia, establishing his birthday as their New Year's Day:

> Whereas the providence which divinely ordered our lives created with zeal and munificence the most perfect good for our lives by producing Augustus . . . , blessing us and those after us with a savior who put an end to war and established peace. (*OGIS* 458)[19]

As is clear from this decree, a major reason for the emperor's status as savior was his ability to establish and maintain peace.[20] In his history of Rome, Velleius describes the justification for the deification of Augustus in large measure because of his establishing peace. "When were the blessings of peace greater?" he asks. "The *pax augusta* . . . preserves every corner of the world safe."[21] The phrase "savior of the world" was used, with some variation, to describe Julius Caesar, Augustus, Claudius, Nero, Vespasian, Titus, Trajan, Hadrian, and other emperors.[22]

There are also examples of the title "Savior" being used of the emperor alongside other designations. One inscription calls Augustus "son of god, Caesar, ruler of the earth and sea, benefactor and savior of the whole world" (*IGR* III.719). Elsewhere he is called "Caesar, son of god, savior" (*IG* VII.1836). An inscription in the city of Eleusis called Augustus "Imperator Caesar, son of god, Julius, his saviour and benefactor."[23]

The designation σωτήρ was well established in both Jewish and Hellenistic writings by the first century BCE. It is likely that both the Jewish and the Hellenistic usage informed the application to Jesus. Jewish literature primarily used the title for God, who is Israel's Savior—both in the past and in the present. God is characterized by his saving activity, and this is a source of comfort in times of peril. Greco-Roman literature used the term frequently with an abundance of referents—both divine and human. Significant is that the phrase "savior of the world" was commonly used in emperor veneration.

---

18. Plutarch, *Life of Titus Flamininus* 16.4. Translation by B. Perrin (LCL).
19. Translation from Lewis and Reinhold, *Roman Civilization*, 64.
20. Gilbert, "Roman Propaganda and Christian Identity," 239–40.
21. Velleius Paterculus 2.126. Translation by F. W. Shipley (LCL).
22. Deissmann, *Light from the Ancient East*, 368; Gregorovius, *Emperor Hadrian*, 51. See the chart in Koester, "'Savior of the World,'" 667.
23. Cited in Winter, *Divine Honours for the Caesars*, 63.

Jesus the Savior in the New Testament

The New Testament writers continued to use σωτήρ in reference to God (Luke 1:47; 1 Tim. 1:1; 2:3; Titus 1:3; Jude 25) but more frequently applied the title to Jesus. That said, Jesus is called Savior more selectively than many of the other titles examined in this study. Of the Synoptic Gospels, only Luke's Gospel uses the title, while John's Gospel uses it only once. Aside from the use in Philippians, all the occurrences in the Pauline writings appear in the Pastoral Letters (and once in Ephesians). We also find the title being used of Jesus in 2 Peter and 1 John.

The Gospels and Acts

The title σωτήρ is rarely used in the Gospels. Nowhere does Jesus refer to himself as Savior, and only once does anyone in a Gospel narrative refer to Jesus using this title (John 4:42). However, the notion that Jesus brings salvation is ingrained in each of the Gospels. Matthew's Gospel plays on the name Jesus (the Hebrew *Yeshua* means "Yahweh is salvation") through the angel's declaration that Joseph should name Mary's baby Jesus, "for he will save his people from their sins" (Matt. 1:21). Luke's Gospel includes the account of Zacchaeus, the tax collector, repenting before Jesus, at which point Jesus replies, "Today salvation has come to this house" (Luke 19:9). In each of the Gospels, the disciples inquire about one's final salvation (Matt. 19:25; Mark 10:26; Luke 18:26).

Of the Gospel writers, Luke is particularly fond of the title σωτήρ. Mary refers to God as "Savior" in Luke 1:47, likely drawing from Habakkuk 3:18 and other Old Testament uses (e.g., 1 Sam. 2:1; Pss. 25:5; 35:9).[24] In Luke's infancy narrative, an angel tells nearby shepherds, "I am bringing you good news of great joy for all the people: to you is born this day in the city of David a Savior, who is the Messiah, the Lord" (Luke 2:10–11; cf. 1:69). Here Luke uses a variety of titles and traditions when identifying Jesus: Savior, Messiah, Lord, and David and his kingship. These titles overlap, but it seems as though Luke is coordinating them to expound upon Jesus's messianic identity. The long-awaited Messiah has arrived, and he will save his people. The interpretive context of this usage is from the Old Testament, especially Isaiah 9:1–7,[25] but there is a political dimension as well. By calling Jesus σωτήρ and connecting his arrival to peace on earth (2:14), Luke challenges the

---

24. See Marshall, *Gospel of Luke*, 82; Fitzmyer, *Gospel according to Luke*, 367; Green, *Gospel of Luke*, 102.
25. Green, *Gospel of Luke*, 134.

status of Emperor Augustus (mentioned in Luke 2:1) as savior and bringer of peace.[26]

In Luke's Gospel σωτήρ is clearly used in reference to Jesus's incarnation, but in Acts the title is used of Jesus's risen status. In Acts 5, Peter and the apostles declare, "God exalted [Jesus] at his right hand as Leader and Savior that he might give repentance to Israel and forgiveness of sins" (5:31). For Peter, the title "Savior" is appropriate, as Jesus is the only source of salvation (4:12). Similarly, Luke portrays Paul as preaching, "Of [David's] posterity God has brought to Israel a Savior, Jesus, as he promised" (Acts 13:23). In these uses, the history of Israel is an immediate interpretive context. As a result, Luke is continuing the tradition of God as Israel's Savior but applying that title to Jesus.

The single occurrence of σωτήρ in the Fourth Gospel likely has a similar backdrop to Luke's usage. After a life-changing encounter with Jesus, a Samaritan woman tells her community about her experience. They invite Jesus to stay with them, and after two days of being with Jesus they tell the woman, "It is no longer because of what you said that we believe, for we have heard for ourselves, and we know that this is truly the Savior of the world" (John 4:42). This statement is in keeping with what was said earlier in the Gospel—that Jesus was sent into the world "in order that the world might be saved through him" (3:17). This phrase, "Savior of the world," was applied to Roman emperors, and its use in John 4:42 has obvious imperial associations.[27] While acknowledging that salvation is from the Jews (4:22), the Samaritans correctly recognize that this has universal significance. As Craig Koester points out, the Samaritans here realize that while the title "Savior of the world" is used by Caesar, it is correctly applied to Jesus Christ.[28]

Paul's Letters

The title σωτήρ occurs twelve times in the letters attributed to Paul and contributes to a larger Pauline theme of the deliverance from sin by God through Jesus Christ.[29] The purpose of Jesus's incarnation is to offer salvation to sinners (1 Tim. 1:15), and the gospel message is one of salvation (1 Cor. 15:1–2). This salvation is frequently described as being saved from God's wrath due to sin (Rom. 5:9; 1 Thess. 1:10). This salvation is brought

---

26. Green, *Gospel of Luke*, 135; Carroll, *Luke*, 69; Gilbert, "Roman Propaganda and Christian Identity," 242.
27. Koester, "'Savior of the World,'" 667.
28. Koester, "'Savior of the World,'" 680.
29. See Morris, "Salvation."

about through Jesus Christ (Rom. 10:9–13) and is available to all people (1 Tim. 2:4).

For many scholars, the only authentic Pauline use of σωτήρ appears in Philippians 3:20, which was introduced at the beginning of this chapter.[30] Although the passage is brief, the use of σωτήρ here is significant. Paul states that "we are expecting a Savior, the Lord Jesus Christ." The statement is eschatological; Paul awaits Christ's saving work at the end of time. At that time, "he will transform the body of our humiliation that it may be conformed to the body of his glory" (3:21). Jesus's work as Savior, then, is to deliver his people from their toil in the flesh. This expectation of Jesus as Savior offers Paul hope and serves as encouragement for the Philippians to "stand firm in the Lord" (4:1). Paul's use here mirrors the use found in the Old Testament of Yahweh as Savior. Essentially, Paul has taken a common title for God in Israel's Scriptures and applied it to Jesus.[31]

Yet like the use of σωτήρ in the Gospels, this passage in Philippians is also political—Paul is subverting the notion of the Roman emperor as savior. That the title appears within a discussion of the recipients' citizenship makes this political meaning clear.[32] Unlike the enemies of the cross of Christ (Phil. 3:18), the Philippian Christians' true citizenship is in heaven. By naming Jesus "Savior" in conjunction with the title "Lord," Paul sets him apart from Caesar, who was commonly given those designations.[33] As a result, there is a subversive element to Paul's use of σωτήρ in Philippians 3:20: Jesus, not Caesar, is the true Savior.

Jesus is called Savior five times in the other letters attributed to Paul. In Ephesians the reference comes amid a discussion of headship (Eph. 5:23). Jesus is the head of the church, and he is the Savior of the body (of the church). However one understands Jesus as the "head" of the church, it is defined by his saving activity on the church's behalf. In 2 Timothy the author states that God's salvific grace "has now been revealed through the appearing of our Savior Christ Jesus, who abolished death and brought life and immortality to light through the gospel" (2 Tim. 1:10). Unlike in Philippians 3:20, in which Paul awaits Jesus's activity as Savior, here that activity has been accomplished.[34] The book of Titus uses σωτήρ six times in reference to

---

30. For an overview of σωτήρ in the Pauline writings, see Luter, "Savior." On this instance, see Cohick, "Philippians and Empire."
31. Fee, *Paul's Letter to the Philippians*, 381.
32. See Oakes, *Philippians*, 138–47.
33. Cousar, *Philippians and Philemon*, 80–81; Fee, *Paul's Letter to the Philippians*, 381; Oakes, *Philippians*, 138–47.
34. Cullmann, *Christology of the New Testament*, 244.

both God and Jesus (1:3, 4; 2:10, 13; 3:4, 6). In each of these occurrences, the author identifies God or Jesus as "our" Savior. As with all the other Pauline uses, σωτήρ more closely resembles Old Testament usage than Greco-Roman. The New Testament author is taking a common title for God and using it for Jesus.

The General Epistles

The author of 2 Peter uses σωτήρ five times in reference to Jesus. In the opening salutation, the author describes the recipients as "those who have received a faith as precious as ours through the righteousness of our God and Savior Jesus Christ" (2 Pet. 1:1). In the remaining four instances, the author combines κύριος with σωτήρ ("Lord and Savior"; 1:11; 2:20; 3:2, 18). In 2 Peter, knowledge is of vital importance. Believers are to grow in their knowledge of the Lord and Savior Jesus Christ (2:20; 3:18; cf. 1:2, 3, 5, 6, 8), while ignorance is to be avoided (3:16). Knowledge of the Lord and Savior can purify the defilements of the world (2:20) and keep one from being led astray (3:17). The concept of Jesus as Savior is never elaborated on in 2 Peter. Rather, it appears to be an established and appropriate title for Jesus—especially in conjunction with κύριος.

The use in 1 John 4:14 is like that of John 4:42 in that Jesus is called the "Savior of the world." Not unlike the context in the Fourth Gospel, in 1 John the context of this phrase is God's sending Jesus into the world. God sent Jesus into the world so that he might save it (cf. John 3:17). There is a similar emphasis that the salvation Jesus offers is not limited to a particular group but is boundless. Caesar may claim the title "Savior of the world," but it is correctly applied only to Jesus.

The Significance of Both Greco-Roman and Jewish Influence

Commentators often identify both the Jewish and the Greco-Roman backgrounds of the title σωτήρ in the New Testament and choose one context over the other. For example, in his commentary on the Gospel of John, Rudolf Bultmann acknowledges the Jewish parallels to "Savior of the world" but states that the title is taken from Hellenistic eschatology.[35] It may be that in each individual appearance a case must be presented concerning the interpretive framework behind the use of σωτήρ. Looking at the entire New Testament witness, we see that both the Jewish and the Hellenistic traditions behind the title are crucial for understanding its application to Jesus.

---

35. Bultmann, *Gospel of John*, 201n4.

In many cases, parallels to the Old Testament, where God is identified as Savior, are obvious. The New Testament writers continue this tradition of describing God as Savior (Luke 1:47; Jude 25). However, when they apply the title to Jesus, they are making a profound christological association. This title that was used of Yahweh as the one who offers salvation from despair and sin now applies to Jesus. While an emphasis on the Savior's ability to bring salvation from sin is not absent in the Old Testament, the New Testament writers bring this into focus. This may signify a shift in messianic expectation away from a Savior who will defeat Israel's enemies toward one who will offer salvation to the entire world.

The political dimensions of this designation within the Roman world are critical as well. Similar to the political weight implied by the declaration "Jesus is Lord," to say that Jesus is "Savior" is to simultaneously say that Caesar is not. Jesus alone offers salvation and peace (Luke 2) and is the true "Savior of the world" (John 4:42; 1 John 4:14).

Contribution to New Testament Christology

Compared to other titles and sacred traditions used by the New Testament writers, Jesus as Savior is relatively infrequent. However, it has a profound impact on our understanding of Christology. The designation became popular in the early church, as it appears in the letters of Ignatius, *The Martyrdom of Polycarp*, and other early Christian writings.[36] The title "Savior" is closely connected not only to the *person* of Jesus but also to the *work* of Jesus. He is called "Savior" because of what he has done: atoning for the sins of his people.

As Savior, Jesus is the one who delivers his people from peril. He alone brings peace and is worthy of worship and devotion. Christ has been exalted to the heavenly realm and is seated in divine rule. The combination of σωτήρ and κύριος in the New Testament suggests that Jesus's role as Savior is connected to his lordship. He is the true ruler and Lord. This salvation includes concern for the physical needs of his people. While on earth, Jesus regularly healed and performed miracles for the sick and needy. These encounters are often described using "salvation" language (Matt. 9:2; Luke 7:50). Jesus, therefore, remains a source of salvation for believers in peril.

Beyond being a source of deliverance in times of trial, Jesus is the one who saves his people from sin and death (Acts 5:31), a major theme for the New Testament writers. Jesus's salvation includes forgiveness of sins but

---

36. Ignatius, *To the Ephesians* 1.1; *Martyrdom of Polycarp* 19.2; Athanasius, *On the Incarnation* 10.

> ## "SAVIOR" IN *2 CLEMENT*
>
> *Second Clement* is an early Christian homily that was likely written in the early second century. It closes with this doxology praising God and identifying Jesus with the title "Savior."
>
> > To the only God, invisible, the Father of truth, who sent to us the Savior and Founder of immortality, through whom he also revealed to us the truth and the heavenly life, to him be the glory forever and ever. Amen.[a]
>
> a. *2 Clement* 20.5. Translation from Holmes, *Apostolic Fathers*, 165.

also participation in the kingdom of God. It moves beyond the realm of any emperor by attributing to Jesus the work of Yahweh. For the early Christians, Jesus's role as Savior was intimately tied to his defeat of death (2 Tim. 1:10) and atoning work (Titus 2:13–14). It is eschatological in nature. While Luke can declare that the Savior has come (Luke 2:11), the salvation that Jesus brings has yet to be fully realized on earth. Therefore Paul declares that believers wait for their Savior (Phil. 3:20), and the biblical writers describe a future day when the final salvation of God will arrive (Matt. 28:19–20; Eph. 1:9–10; Rev. 21–22).

That Jesus is the Savior of the world communicates the universal nature of God's deliverance. The salvation that Jesus offers is not limited to Israel but is available to all. Jesus's encounter with the Samaritans is a powerful illustration of this. The Savior's work is not limited to a specific people group or location—it is for all who come to him. In this way, Jesus fulfills the Old Testament vision of Yahweh's salvation being offered to the entire world (Isa. 49:6; cf. Gen. 12:3; Ezek. 29:9; Zech. 2:11).

CHAPTER 9

JESUS THE LAST ADAM

Introduction

Romans 5 is crucial for understanding Paul's argument in the epistle. The opening verses summarize the earlier chapters of Romans by affirming that believers are "justified by faith," but then they turn to a new concept: what it means to "have peace with God through our Lord Jesus Christ" (Rom. 5:1). More than that, Paul exhorts those who have been justified to have this peace with God ("Let us have peace with God"—using a subjunctive verb). Peace with God is another way of speaking of reconciliation, which Romans 5:1–11 defines as that personal relationship of being at peace with God. Paul explains humanity's new relationship with God as the foundation for hope and assurance of salvation (5:6–11). This salvation from wrath (5:9) means that those who were once enemies of God can now be at peace with or reconciled to him, and thereby experience salvation (5:10). The next section elucidates what it means to be reconciled to God and no longer at enmity with him. This is done on the basis of two contrasting figures, Jesus and Adam. Whereas Adam severed the relationship between God and humanity, Jesus provides the means for restoring it. Paul then goes on to explore the implications of this new relationship in chapters 6–8, culminating in life in the Spirit.

According to Paul, "one man" is responsible for sin entering the world (Rom. 5:12). Since death came through sin, it therefore came for everyone since everyone sins. This was prior to the giving of the law at Sinai, so Paul can declare that "death exercised dominion from Adam to Moses" (5:14). Yet Paul is quick to point out that while sin ruled over humanity prior to the law, it was not until the law was given that sin was identified as sin. In this way, those prior to Moses did in fact sin, but their sins were "not like the transgression of Adam"—that is, they did not disobey a specific command from God.

Paul then makes a striking claim by calling Adam "a type of the one who was to come" (Rom. 5:14). As is clear from the following verses, "the one who was to come" is Jesus. But how are we to understand Adam as a "type" for Jesus? When Paul uses this term (τύπος) elsewhere in his writings, he is presenting an example that he wants his audience to emulate (1 Cor. 10:6; Phil. 3:17; 1 Thess. 1:7; 2 Thess. 3:9). Even in Romans, Paul praises his audience because they are obedient to this "type" of teaching (Rom. 6:17). This clearly cannot be how Paul is using the term in Romans 5:14, since Jesus can hardly be understood as following Adam's example.

Realizing that his statement about Adam being a type for Jesus could be easily misunderstood, Paul sets out a series of qualifications in Romans 5:15–17. Everything that Adam did to sever the relationship between humanity and God through sin and disobedience, Jesus undid through his obedience. Put simply, Adam's trespass is in no way like the "free gift" offered through Christ. Adam's transgressions brought death to all, while Jesus's actions are the source of righteousness and new life. Yet to get to the bottom of how Paul understands Adam as a type for Jesus, we must understand how the figure of Adam was interpreted by the New Testament writers and their contemporaries. In the New Testament, a notion emerges of Jesus as a "second Adam" who, unlike the first, remains completely obedient to God and so restores creation to its original purpose.

Adam in Israel's Sacred Scriptures

The word translated "Adam" in Hebrew is אדם, which could be used of "humanity" generally or of an individual "human" specifically. The text of Genesis plays with these different uses; אדם has a variety of meanings in various contexts. Genesis 1:26–27 states that God created "humankind" (אדם) in his image, specifying that אדם was created as both "male" (זכר) and "female" (נקבה). The commands to אדם in Genesis 1 are given to humanity generally. In Genesis 2, God creates אדם—that is, an individual human—yet this first human also represents humanity generally. It is not until Eve is created in Genesis 2:22 that אדם is distinguishable as a male human. In addition to meaning "humanity," "a human," and "a male human," the term is also used as a proper name—"Adam." This use does not appear in the Hebrew text of Genesis until 4:25.[1] Therefore, "Adam" in Genesis 1–3 most directly refers to the first human, distinguishable from Eve, who can

---

1. The Septuagint uses ἄνθρωπον in its translation up until Gen. 2:16, where it replaces the general term with the proper name Ἀδάμ. See Brayford, *Genesis*, 230.

simultaneously also represent humanity generally. This ambiguity inherent in the term is significant for understanding how the creation, temptation, and shortcomings of the first humans correspond to the experience of all humans.

In these early chapters of Genesis, Adam is created in God's image (Gen. 1:27), from the dust of the earth, and through God's breath of life (2:7). He and Eve are given authority over the animals (1:28), while Adam is charged with caring for the garden in which he is placed (2:15). The first human is tasked with naming the animals (2:19), and he is also given the direct commandment to never eat from the tree of the knowledge of good and evil (2:17). God creates a woman (אשה) from Adam's rib, and Adam rejoices at finding the ideal companion (2:22–23).

The first humans are deceived by the snake and disobey the command to not eat from the tree of the knowledge of good and evil (Gen. 3:1–7). This act of disobedience disrupts the peaceful existence that the humans enjoyed with God and with each other. There is no mention of sin in this episode, but it is clear that the humans' actions radically affect God's creation. Adam and Eve are presented as mature adults who have acquired knowledge reserved for God—the difference between good and evil. They are separated from the animals by their awareness of their nakedness and are banished from the garden. The effects of Adam's and Eve's actions are fully felt in the following episode when their children quarrel, resulting in murder (4:1–16). Before killing his brother Abel, Cain is told by God that he has a choice not to surrender to sin (4:7).

Adam appears infrequently in the rest of the Old Testament. Genesis states that he had many children with Eve and lived to be 930 (Gen. 5:5). The appearance of אדם outside the opening chapters of Genesis is often a matter of interpretation as to whether it is "humanity" that is in mind or Adam, the first human. In Psalm 82:7, for example, the psalmist writes, "You shall die like אדם." This could be a reference to Adam but is often translated as "mortals" despite appearing in the singular form. In Hosea 6:7, אדם may refer to the first human ("like": per the older rendering) or a small town in the Transjordan ("at"): "But at/like Adam they transgressed the covenant." Adam seems to be invoked in Job 15 when Eliphaz asks Job, "Are you the firstborn of the human race [אדם]?" (15:7).

The figure of Adam appears with some frequency in Jewish literature from the Second Temple period. Different retellings of the Genesis creation account fill in certain details and present the major figures—including Adam—in new ways. A prevalent feature of several studies in the mid-twentieth century is an argument for a unified Adam motif or myth in Jewish literature leading up to the letters of Paul.² However, the literature of Second Temple Judaism demonstrates a surprising array of diverse views and portraits of Adam.³ Indeed, there is no straight line from Genesis to Paul, as the figure of Adam was understood in a variety of ways. Just as Paul should be read on his own terms, so also these Jewish texts should not be read through the lens of Paul's writings.

The creation narrative in Genesis dominates subsequent retellings of the story of Adam and Eve. A Jewish sibyl, for instance, summarizes the creation narrative (*Sib. Or.* 1.22–64). In this retelling, the first couple's sin introduces death (1.41, 63) but also disrupts the unity of their relationship (cf. 1.33–34). This account places an emphasis on the luxurious setting that they are forced to leave. Wisdom of Solomon connects the serpent from Genesis to the devil and places him at fault for death entering the world (Wis. 2:24; cf. *2 En.* 31.3–6). Other texts place the burden on Eve (Sir. 25:24; *L.A.E.* 21.1–6).

Some texts portray Adam in a positive light, seeing him as an exemplar and honorable forefather to the Israelites (*Jub.* 2.23; Wis. 10:1–2; Sir. 49:16). The book of *Jubilees*, for example, retells the Genesis narrative in a way that absolves Adam from fault for introducing sin into the creation.⁴ Adam is presented as the first patriarch (2.23) and as the first in a line of priests (3.27).⁵ In *Jubilees*' account of the first sin, God's anger is aimed at the serpent and then at Eve and then at Adam (3.23–25). When leaving Eden, Adam lights incense as a sacrifice to God (3.27). This act aligns Adam with the patriarchs, who similarly light incense (cf. 4.25; 6.1–3; 16.24). However, it is Adam who sacrifices beside Eden, a symbolic holy of holies.⁶ In Wisdom of Solomon, Adam is an illustration of the necessity for wisdom: "Wisdom protected the first-formed father of the world, when he alone had been created; she delivered him from his transgression, and gave him strength to rule all things" (Wis. 10:1–2). It is Cain, not Adam, who is blamed for sin and the flood (10:3–4; cf. 2:24). The book of Tobit offers Adam and Eve as exemplars in marriage (Tob. 8:6).

Other texts portray Adam in a much more negative light. In two important apocalyptic texts, *4 Ezra* and *2 Baruch*, Adam is depicted as a figure of the current evil age, and his transgression is what brought it into being. *Fourth Ezra* is particularly pessimistic in its outlook, and Adam is portrayed almost entirely in a negative light.⁷ In the discussion between Ezra and Uriel, Adam

---

2. Barrett, *From First Adam to Last*; Scroggs, *Last Adam*.
3. Levison, *Portraits of Adam*.
4. See especially Levison, *Portraits of Adam*, 89–98.
5. VanderKam, *Book of Jubilees*, 32.
6. Levison, *Portraits of Adam*, 94.
7. Levison, *Portraits of Adam*, 113–28. He notes that the positive statement in *4 Ezra* 6.45–59 is almost immediately negated in 7.11–14.

> ## SIRACH 15:13-15
>
> The Lord hates all abominations;
>   such things are not loved by those who fear him.
> It was he who created humankind in the beginning,
>   and he left them in the power of their own free choice.
> If you choose, you can keep the commandments,
>   and to act faithfully is a matter of your own choice.

is sometimes understood as simply the first to sin (*4 Ezra* 3.4–11) and other times as responsible for universal sinfulness (7.118). *Second Baruch* offers a more optimistic portrait of Adam. He is clearly seen as the one who brought death to all by his transgression (*2 Bar.* 17.3; 23.4; 56.6), but Adam is also an example of personal choice. *Second Baruch* 54.19 says, "Adam is therefore not the cause, except only for himself, but each of us has become our own Adam."[8] The individual must choose faithfulness over wickedness and is not condemned because of Adam's action. Adam's sin brought about the current evil age, but the future righteous age will be marked by a reversal of the curses of Genesis 3 (73.3–74.3).

Wisdom texts like Wisdom of Solomon and Sirach tend to present Adam less as an individual and more as a representative of humanity.[9] Ben Sira returns to Genesis 1–3 frequently but is concerned not so much with the figure of Adam as with how that text depicts the human condition (cf. Sir. 33:7–15; 40:1–11). Like Adam, all humans have the free choice to follow wisdom or destruction (15:13–20; see sidebar).

Wisdom of Solomon similarly uses imagery from Genesis to discuss the human condition: "for God created us for incorruption, and made us in the image of his own eternity, but through the devil's envy death entered the world" (Wis. 2:23–24a).

Adam in the New Testament

The figure of Adam is invoked with greater frequency in the New Testament than in the Old Testament, as Jesus is understood as the means through

---

8. Translation from Stone and Henze, *4 Ezra and 2 Baruch*, 121.
9. See Levison, "Adam and Eve," 300.

which God begins to undo the effects of the fall on creation. The Gospels do not mention Adam much, but we do witness an Adam typology in the way that Jesus is portrayed. At key moments—including Jesus's temptation in the wilderness and his passion—the Gospel writers tell their stories in ways that recall the creation stories and specifically the narrative about Adam. It is in Paul's Letters that Adam is directly compared to Jesus, who is depicted as a "second" or "last" Adam. According to Paul, Adam's sin is responsible for the tenuous situation of humanity, but Jesus's gift of grace restores creation and brings eternal life.

Jesus as the New Adam in the Gospels

There is no direct connection between Jesus and Adam in the Gospels. However, the Gospel writers demonstrate an Adam typology at certain places in their biographies of Jesus. Further, as Brandon Crowe has argued, "Jesus establishes the kingdom of righteousness through his mission as a whole, manifesting an obedience that overcomes the disobedience of Adam and the effects of Adam's sin."[10] In their portrayals of Jesus's incarnation, faithful obedience, initiation of a new kingdom, and salvific death and resurrection, the Gospel writers implicitly compare Jesus with Adam. Jesus succeeds where Adam failed and begins the work of undoing the effects of sin in the world.

Several features of the Gospels' portrayals demonstrate how Jesus restores creation and undoes the effects of Adam's sin. The Gospels present a clash of kingdoms between that of Jesus and that of Satan, with Jesus ultimately victorious. Satan's temptation of Christ in the wilderness is rich with Adamic imagery—as we will see—and marks the beginning of Jesus's defeat of Satan.[11] Jesus's miracles demonstrate his power over creation; "even the wind and the sea obey him" (Mark 4:41; cf. Matt. 8:27; Luke 8:25). If Adam's disobedience brought about disorder in God's creation, then Christ's command over that creation points to its redemption and restoration. Jesus offers relief and rest from one's burdens or the toil associated with Adam's curse (Matt. 11:28). Further, Jesus offers forgiveness of sins as he actively counters the effects of Adam (cf. Matt. 9:2–8).

We will highlight a few places in the Gospels where Adamic imagery is used to draw this parallel between Jesus and Adam: the genealogies of Jesus in Matthew and Luke, Jesus's temptation by Satan, and Jesus's passion and resurrection.

10. Crowe, *Last Adam*, 170.
11. Crowe, *Last Adam*, 156–57.

The Genealogies of Jesus

Only Matthew and Luke include genealogies of Jesus in their Gospels. Matthew does not mention Adam in his genealogy but begins with Abraham and moves through David to Jesus (Matt. 1:1–17). Yet the opening words of Matthew's Gospel, Βίβλος γενέσεως (an account of the genealogy), evoke the early chapters of the Genesis narrative and appear in Genesis 2:4 and 5:1 (the only places the phrase appears in the Septuagint). As Dale Allison points out, these two words at the beginning of Matthew's Gospel are intended to recall the two uses in the Septuagint and possibly the entire book of Genesis, which was known simply as *genesis* (γένεσις) by the first century.[12] As a result, Matthew's opening verse introduces not just the genealogy but the entire Gospel and conveys the notion of Jesus as a new beginning of creation.[13]

The genealogy in Luke is unique in a variety of ways: it moves backward from Jesus rather than chronologically toward Jesus, it traces Jesus's genealogy all the way back to Adam, and it is placed not at the beginning of the Gospel but immediately after Jesus's baptism (Luke 3:23–28).[14] Luke's decision to construct Jesus's genealogy not chronologically but rather moving backward from Jesus is significant, since it was much more common for genealogies to move forward in time from the past.[15] While genealogies in the Old Testament frequently list the "sons of" various figures, they most often move forward chronologically.[16] By moving backward—using the literary pattern "son of"—Luke places special emphasis on where the list ends.

Moving from Jesus to Adam, Luke lists seventy-seven names. He ends the genealogy with God, since Adam, as the first human, is the "son of God." There may be a theological point for tracing Jesus's lineage back to God himself to establish him as the Son of God, an idea introduced immediately before this genealogy at Jesus's baptism (Luke 3:22). Yet the point of the genealogy gets lost if the names between Jesus and God become irrelevant. Further, there is a possible conflict with Luke's birth story if Jesus's divine sonship is seen as facilitated through his ancestors and not directly from God.[17] Instead, Jesus's lineage, which traces back to Adam, is intended to place him within

---

12. Allison, "Matthew's First Two Words."
13. Hays, *Echoes of Scripture in the Gospels*, 110. Against this reading, see Nolland, "What Kind of Genesis Do We Have in Matt. 1.1?"
14. On differences between Luke's and Matthew's genealogies, see Marshall, *Gospel of Luke*, 157–62.
15. However, it is not without precedent. Josephus used this type of backward genealogy to emphasize the person one was descended from (*Ant.* 1.79; 2.229; 12.265).
16. See Gen. 5:1–32; Exod. 6:14–25; 1 Chron. 3:10–24; 6:16–30. Exceptions to this include the much shorter lists found in 1 Sam. 9:1; Zeph. 1:1; Tob. 1:1.
17. Marshall, *Gospel of Luke*, 161.

the history of humanity. Whereas Matthew connects Jesus to Abraham, the major figure of Israel's history, Luke traces Jesus's lineage further back to the first human. In this way, Luke stresses the universal impact of Jesus on the entire human race, not just on Abraham's descendants.[18]

By linking Jesus's lineage to Adam, the author may be offering a contrast between the two figures.[19] Seen this way, Luke presents Jesus as a "second Adam" who demonstrates obedience where the first failed. This contrast helps us understand why Luke places the genealogy after Jesus's baptism and right before the account of Jesus's temptation in the wilderness (Luke 4:1–12). As we will see, the temptation narrative offers a striking example of Jesus's obedience when tempted directly by Satan. By placing his genealogy here and by ending it with Adam, Luke leads into this temptation account by establishing Jesus as a new Adam. In his arrangement of material, Luke demonstrates not only that Jesus is descended from Adam but also that Jesus will succeed where the first human failed.[20]

Jesus's Temptation by Satan

In the opening chapter of Mark's Gospel, Jesus is led by the Spirit into the wilderness immediately after his baptism. The author writes, "And the Spirit immediately drove him out into the wilderness. He was in the wilderness forty days, tempted by Satan; and he was with the wild beasts; and the angels waited on him" (Mark 1:12–13). This passage invokes several traditions from the Old Testament, including Abraham's testing (Gen. 22:1–19), Elijah spending forty days in the wilderness (1 Kings 19:4–8), and Israel's testing in the wilderness (Num. 10:11–22:1). More pronounced, however, is Adamic imagery.[21] Like Adam, Jesus is presented as going into an Eden-like setting to be tested. Unlike Adam, however, Jesus succeeds in resisting Satan's temptations. The term "wilderness" (ἔρημον) frequently refers to a barren or deserted place (cf. Mark 1:35; 6:31) but can also have the sense of a nonhuman space.[22] Jesus is led into the wilderness by the Spirit and engages with nonhuman agents: Satan, wild beasts, and angels. Jesus being led by the Spirit into this nonhuman space is a reversal of the narrative of Adam being led by Yahweh out of Eden (Gen. 3:24). Any connection of Adam to forty days

---

18. Green, *Gospel of Luke*, 189.
19. This was famously argued by Jeremias, "Ἀδάμ," and just as famously critiqued by M. Johnson, *Purpose of the Biblical Genealogies*, 234–35.
20. Crowe, *Last Adam*, 27–28.
21. See esp. Marcus, *Mark 1–8*, 169–71; Crowe, *Last Adam*, 24–28. For arguments against such an interpretation, see Stein, *Mark*, 64–65.
22. Bauckham, "Jesus and the Wild Animals," 8.

in Eden is missing from the Genesis account, although according to a later tradition, Adam spent forty days fasting in an act of repentance upon leaving Eden (*L.A.E.* 6.1–3; cf. *Jub.* 3.9).

The tempter in Genesis, of course, is a serpent (LXX: ὄφις) and is not given the name "Satan" (Σατανᾶς). The figure of Satan or the devil is a later development (cf. Job 1:6) and was later connected to the serpent in Eden in literature that is, at best, contemporary to Mark's Gospel (Wis. 2:24; cf. *Apoc. Mos.* 17.4). Regardless, the connection of the serpent and Satan in Mark's Gospel is clear in that they serve as agents of temptation in nonhuman space.

The references to wild beasts and angels, which may seem like unimportant details, further connects this story to that of Adam. In Genesis, Adam lived at peace among the wild animals in Eden (Gen. 2:19–20). In some Jewish traditions, enmity between humans and the wild animals was understood as a result of the distortion of the created order.[23] The restoration of human and animal relationships was identified as a sign of the messianic age.[24] Further, later Jewish legend presented angels caring for and feeding Adam (*b. Sanh.* 59b), so the reference to angels caring for Jesus in this episode is not without precedent in traditions about Adam.[25]

Mark's version of Jesus's temptation by Satan is relatively brief in comparison with the detailed accounts in the Gospels of Matthew and Luke (Matt. 4:1–11; Luke 4:1–13). Yet each account includes the key details of Jesus being tempted by Satan in the wilderness and attended to by angels. Luke's insertion of the genealogy just prior to his temptation account further links Jesus to Adam. As we saw, the genealogy in Luke 3 traces Jesus's lineage to "Adam, son of God" (3:38) and connects to the title of Jesus spoken by Satan in the wilderness temptation (4:2, 9). "Thus Jesus not only is descended from Adam but also overcomes temptation in contrast to Adam."[26]

Jesus's Passion and Resurrection

The significance of Jesus's obedience is seen most profoundly in the Gospels' descriptions of his passion, death, and resurrection. Jesus is both actively and passively obedient as he surrenders to the Father's will and overcomes death. Seen through the lens of an Adamic Christology, Jesus's salvific work stands in stark contrast to the first human, whose disobedience brought about

---

23. Sir. 17:2–4; *Apoc. Mos.* 10.1–11.1; Wis. 9:2–3; *Jub.* 1.14; *2 En.* 58.3; *4 Ezra* 6.54. See Bauckham, "Jesus and the Wild Animals," 10–11.

24. Isa. 11:6–9; *Sib. Or.* 3.788–95; *2 Bar.* 73.6. See Bauckham, "Jesus and the Wild Animals," 14–17.

25. Marcus, *Mark 1–8*, 168.

26. Crowe, *Last Adam*, 29.

sin and death. Of the four Gospels, John's Gospel most clearly brings out this theme, as his entire passion narrative draws from images from Genesis 1–3.[27]

John's Gospel is full of allusions to creation and the Genesis narrative, even in its opening words: "In the beginning" (John 1:1).[28] This is most pronounced in the Fourth Gospel's passion and resurrection narrative, especially chapters 19–20. This can be illustrated by the author's emphasis on putting the major events in the narrative in a "garden" (κῆπος).[29] The passion account begins in a garden (18:1), Peter is confronted about being seen with Jesus in the garden (18:26), and Jesus is said to have been crucified, buried, and raised in a garden (19:41). The raised Jesus is even mistaken for a gardener (κηπουρός) by Mary at the empty tomb (20:15). This account of mistaken identity may be intended to provoke the reader to compare the risen Christ to the first gardener, Adam.[30]

The author of the Fourth Gospel connects Jesus to Adam at other places in the passion narrative as well. Pilate's pronouncement "Here is the man!" (John 19:5; Ἰδοὺ ὁ ἄνθρωπος) echoes Genesis 3:22, "Behold, Adam" (Ἰδοὺ Ἀδάμ).[31] The phrase is ironic: Pilate is mocking the frail humanity of a prisoner who is believed to be divine. In Genesis, the phrase is also ironic but for the opposite reason. God's pronouncement "Behold, Adam" comes after Adam's sin, by which he has acquired divine knowledge of good and evil. Of course, even as Pilate uses the phrase ironically, John's readers know that Jesus is the true Son of God. Another important allusion appears in John 20:22, where Jesus "breathes" (ἐμφυσάω) on his disciples and tells them to receive the Holy Spirit (πνεῦμα ἅγιον). This recalls God breathing (ἐμφυσάω) "new life" (πνοὴν ζωῆς) into Adam upon his creation in Genesis 2:7 LXX. This is the only use of ἐμφυσάω in the New Testament, and it appears only seven other times in the Septuagint. Given the infrequency of the term, it is even more likely that John's Gospel is intentionally recalling the creation account.

Finally, John's Gospel twice iterates that Jesus's resurrection occurs on "the first day of the week" (μιᾷ τῶν σαββάτων; John 20:1, 19). The reference to it still being "dark" (σκοτία) when Mary Magdalene visits Jesus's tomb recalls the "darkness" (σκότος) that filled the earth prior to God's work on the first day of creation (Gen. 1:2).[32] However, the start of a new week points to the

---

27. For a survey of scholarship on this topic, see Schaser, "Inverting Eden," esp. 264–66.
28. J. Brown, "Creation's Renewal."
29. Note that the Septuagint uses παράδεισος, and not κῆπος, in the Genesis narrative.
30. J. Brown, "Creation's Renewal," 281.
31. Litwa, "Behold Adam." The phrase "Behold, Adam" is also used in the Latin *The Life of Adam and Eve* 13.3.
32. Schaser, "Inverting Eden," 269.

beginning of creation's renewal through Christ's resurrection. "John turns the clock ahead in his dual reference to ["the first day of the week"], thereby signaling that re-creation begins at the resurrection of Jesus Christ."[33] Jesus's resurrection in a garden on the first day of the week serves the theological function of renewing creation, which was spoiled in a garden by Adam. The resurrected Jesus emerges as the last Adam, defeating death and undoing the effects of sin. What started in a garden only to be tarnished by the first Adam is restored in a garden by Jesus, the obedient last Adam.

Jesus as the Last Adam in Paul's Letters

If Adam plays a relatively minor role in the Gospel portrayals of Jesus, he is much more pronounced in Paul's Letters.[34] He appears by name four times in the Pauline corpus (Rom. 5:4; 1 Cor. 15:22, 45; 1 Tim. 2:13–14) and is a feature of other key passages even when his name does not appear (cf. Rom. 5:12–21; 1 Cor. 11:8–9; 2 Cor. 5:21; Eph. 5:20–22; Phil. 2:5–11). The key passages for our purposes are Romans 5:12–21 and 1 Corinthians 15:20–22, 45–49, in which Paul explicitly draws from Adam in his understanding of Jesus. In these passages, Adam functions as a figurative person or type (τύπος, used in Rom. 5:14) of Jesus. Before we turn to those passages, we will first examine how the creation narrative of Genesis 1–3 serves as an important backdrop for Pauline thought.

Adam and the State of Humanity

The focus of our study is Paul's Christology, but it is necessary to briefly explore how Adam and the creation narrative shape Paul's thinking—especially his soteriology.[35] For Paul, the current sinful state of humanity is a direct result of Adam's sin. The description of fallen humankind in Romans 1:18–25 takes its cues from Genesis 1–3 in that the divine nature was made plain to them at creation (1:20) yet they did not honor or give thanks to God (1:21) but "exchanged the truth about God for a lie and worshiped and served the creature rather than the Creator" (1:25). Like Adam in Genesis, sinful humanity became foolish despite attempting to become wise (1:22) and exchanged the glory of the immortal God for images of humans or animals (1:23).[36]

---

33. J. Brown, "Creation's Renewal," 283.
34. See Fee, *Pauline Christology*, 513–29; Kreitzer, "Adam and Christ."
35. See Dunn, *Christology in the Making*, 101–7.
36. It is worth noting that the Genesis narrative is not the only tradition that Paul appeals to here. The reference to idols or images of humans/animals clearly draws on the tradition of the Israelites and the golden calf (Exod. 32; even using the language of Ps. 106:20).

This parallel is made clear as Paul goes on to portray Adam as the representative of all who sin and therefore die (Rom. 5:12). Sin and death came into the world through Adam and spread to all humanity. Adam's sin affected not just humanity but the whole creation, which is "subjected to futility" and in "bondage to decay" (8:20–21). As a result, both humanity and creation cry out for redemption (8:22–23). All of creation—including all of humanity—is completely corrupted by sin and destined for death. Adam serves as a representative of humanity in Paul's thinking but also is presented as the one responsible for humanity's situation. The fall of Adam is repeated over and over throughout history as the human race continually falls victim to sin and to death.

It is through Jesus, especially by his death and resurrection, that God addresses the problem set in motion by Adam. Indeed, God has inaugurated a "new creation" through Christ—as was promised in Isaiah 65.[37] In Christ, one is a "new creation" and should no longer look at things "from a human point of view" (2 Cor. 5:16–17). The old ways are on their way out as the new creation takes hold. In Galatians, Paul declares, "Neither circumcision nor uncircumcision is anything; but a new creation is everything!" (Gal. 6:15). This is repeated in Colossians 3 as the author reminds his audience that they have "stripped off" their old self and "clothed" themselves with a new self— one in the εἰκών (image) of the Creator (Col. 3:9–10).

Romans 5:12–21

Paul offers an Adam-Christ parallel in Romans 5:12–21 that illustrates the peace and reconciliation offered through Christ discussed in 5:1–11.[38] Romans 5:12 states succinctly Adam's role in the present state of humanity: "Therefore, just as sin came into the world through one man, and death came through sin, and so death spread to all because all have sinned." Paul does not complete his thought here but picks it back up later (in 5:19). Instead, he speaks briefly on the law, since, prior to Moses, sin and death held dominion (5:13). In 5:14, Paul describes Adam as a type of the one to come.[39] This sets up the parallel that follows in 5:15–18.

The parallelism in the next section contrasts the "free gift"—that is, God's gift of Jesus Christ—and the "trespass" of Adam. Using a series of questions,

---

37. Fee, *Pauline Christology*, 514–15.
38. Porter, *Letter to the Romans*, 124; for a more fulsome interpretation of this passage, see 123–29.
39. There is a good amount of discussion on whether Adam is a historical figure. For Paul's argument to hold together, Adam must be considered a historical figure—at least in Paul's thinking. See Dunn, "Adam and Christ," 126.

Paul first introduces an element associated with Adam and then follows it with an even greater benefit of Christ.

Adam's Trespass	Gift of Christ
caused many to die	causes God's grace to abound to many
brought condemnation	brings justification
death dominated	righteousness dominates

Paul summarizes this contrast in 5:18 by restating that as one man's (Adam's) trespass led to condemnation for all humanity, so one man's (Jesus's) righteousness brings life-giving righteousness to all humanity.

It is important to note here that while Genesis 1–3 is clearly in view in this passage, Paul does not rehearse the creation story or include many of its elements. There is no mention of the garden or the serpent or Adam's temptation. Instead, Paul universalizes Adam so that he represents all of humanity and its current fallen state. The effect of Adam's trespass is similarly universalized so that all sin and die through Adam.

In Romans 5:19, Paul picks up the clause he left open in 5:12 by restating the point of 5:13–18 with a new set of contrasts. In this verse he writes that just as the "disobedience" (παρακοή) of one man "established" (κατεστάθησαν) many as "sinners" (ἁμαρτωλοί), so the "obedience" (ὑπακοή) of one man "will make" (κατασταθήσονται) many "righteous" (δίκαιοι). Here again Paul inserts a comment on the law that builds on his earlier comment in 5:13. In the period between Adam and Moses, sin existed, but it was not counted against people in the same way as when the law was introduced. Once the law was given and God's righteous requirements were made known, the sin that began with Adam's transgression only multiplied. Paul's point seems to be that the human condition under Adam was not God's intention and indeed warrants God's wrath. Yet God instead provided a way for sinners to be reconciled to him through Jesus Christ. This being the case, Paul can state that "where sin increased, grace abounded all the more" (Rom. 5:20).[40]

Paul offers a third and final "just as" contrast in Romans 5:21, which brings Paul's argument regarding sin and grace within the context of eternal life. Sin, Paul writes, dominated in death—which indeed has been the common existence of all humanity since Adam. Yet grace might dominate through righteousness—which leads to eternal life. This is done "through Jesus Christ our Lord"—recalling Paul's earlier statements in 5:1 and 5:11. Through Jesus

---

40. Porter, *Letter to the Romans*, 129.

> ## ORIGEN ON ROMANS 5
>
> In his commentary on Paul's Epistle to the Romans, the third-century theologian Origen reflects on the comparison between Jesus and Adam.
>
> > It was therefore not without profound skill in speaking that the Apostle calls Adam a type of Christ. The type is similar in genus but contrary in species. For the type is similar in genus in that, just as something is diffused to very many men from the one Adam, so also something is diffused to very many men from the one Christ. But the species is contrary because the transgression which began with Adam "made the many sinners," whereas by Christ's obedience "many will be made righteous."[a]
>
> a. Origen, *Commentary on the Epistle to the Romans* 5.2.2. Translation from Scheck, *Origen*, 329.

Christ, God has overcome the chasm created by Adam's transgression and offers reconciliation.

The parallel between Adam and Christ in Romans 5:12–21 focuses on the topic of sin and righteousness and attempts to explain the role of the law. The universal nature of both the sin that Adam brought and the righteousness made available to all through Christ is essential to understanding Paul's argument.[41] Both Adam and Jesus are representatives of humanity, and the passage indicates that one finds oneself either "in Adam" or "in Christ." Yet it should not be overlooked that Paul, through this contrast, demonstrates how Jesus fully meets the negative effects of Adam's sin: death is met by life, condemnation by righteousness, disobedience by obedience.[42] In the one man, Christ, righteousness is offered to all who have sinned—both Jew and gentile. The law serves an important role in Paul's thinking, but it is through God's gift of his Son Jesus that righteousness and reconciliation are made fully available to all.

1 Corinthians 15:20–22

The two passages that invoke Adam in 1 Corinthians 15 (vv. 20–22, 45–49) appear in a discussion of the resurrection. In 1 Corinthians 15:1–19 Paul offers an argument for the resurrection of the dead as foundational to the Christian

---

41. Fee, *Pauline Christology*, 272.
42. Kreitzer, "Adam and Christ," 13.

faith. As verse 12 states, some among the Corinthians had been stating that there was no resurrection of the dead. Paul responds by forcefully asserting that the reality of resurrection is critical or else the believer's hope and faith are in vain (15:14). If there is no raising of the dead, Paul reasons, then Jesus has not been raised and believers are still in their sin and doomed to die physically and spiritually. When Paul first invokes an Adam-Christ typology in 15:20–22, it is to affirm the reality of the resurrection. (The second appearance of Adam-Christ typology in 15:45–49 addresses the question raised in 15:35 concerning the resurrected body.)

In 1 Corinthians 15:20–22 Paul sets out to confirm the reality of Christ's resurrection and to demonstrate its implications for those who are "in Christ" (15:18–19). In 15:20, Paul affirms the truth of Christ's resurrection and calls him the "first fruits" of those who have died. The term "first fruits" (ἀπαρχή) can invoke biblical traditions of setting aside the first part of the harvest for God (Lev. 19:23–25; 23:9–14), but here the metaphor of Jesus as ἀπαρχή functions as a guarantee of God's promise to resurrect believers. Acting as a sort of down payment, Jesus's resurrection guarantees the full harvest of the dead in Christ being raised.[43] Paul elaborates on this in 15:21–22 by offering a comparison between Adam and Christ in a parallel manner:

> Since death came through a human being [15:21a],
> > the resurrection of the dead has also come through a human being [15:21b];
> for as all die in Adam [15:22a],
> > so all will be made alive in Christ [15:22b].

The logic of Paul's argument is easy to follow: sin and death came from one man; resurrection and life came through another man.

Paul utilizes the Adam-Christ parallel here in a way similar to what he uses in Romans. Paul works under the assumption, which he shares with his audience, that Adam's transgression brought about sin for all of humanity. Everyone since Adam has shared in this sin and therefore all have died. As in Romans, Jesus stands as the human being through whom life is offered as an antidote to the death brought by Adam. However, in this passage Paul emphasizes Jesus's resurrection as the means through which the curse of death is broken.

---

43. "By calling Christ the 'firstfruits,' Paul is asserting by way of metaphor that the resurrection of the believing dead is absolutely inevitable; it has been guaranteed by the eternal God, the *living* God, who in Christ's life, death, and resurrection has set that future in motion" (Fee, *First Epistle to the Corinthians*, 830 [emphasis original]).

There is also an emphasis on Christ's full humanity in this comparison to the first "human being" (ἄνθρωπος). In order for the logic of Paul's parallel to work, Jesus must be understood as fully human. Just as death came into the creation through the first ἄνθρωπος, so now resurrection and life will be brought to God's people in the new creation through the second ἄνθρωπος.

1 Corinthians 15:45–49

Later in 1 Corinthians 15, Paul addresses an objection to the resurrection of the dead. Whereas in 15:20–22 Paul contrasts Jesus and Adam to demonstrate the truth of resurrection by establishing Christ as the first to be resurrected among humanity, in 15:45–49 the topic shifts to the bodily nature of the resurrection. The question that prompts this discussion is recounted in 15:35: "But someone will ask, 'How are the dead raised? With what kind of body do they come?'" Paul then establishes two types of bodies—heavenly (ἐποθράνιος) and earthly (ἐπίγειος). This informs his comparison between Adam and Jesus:

> Thus it is written, "The first man, Adam, became a living being"; the last Adam became a life-giving spirit. But it is not the spiritual that is first, but the physical, and then the spiritual. The first man was from the earth, a man of dust; the second man is from heaven. As was the man of dust, so are those who are of the dust; and as is the man of heaven, so are those who are of heaven. Just as we have borne the image of the man of dust, we will also bear the image of the man of heaven. (1 Cor. 15:45–49)

Several important elements of this passage are worth exploring. First, this is the only place in Paul's writings where Jesus is explicitly given the title "last Adam" (1 Cor. 15:45). Adam is described as the "first human" (πρῶτος ἄνθρωπος), while Jesus is described as ὁ ἔσχατος Ἀδάμ (the last Adam). Second, Paul here quotes from Genesis 2:7 but adds two words to the Septuagint rendering: "The *first* man, *Adam*, became a living being." These additions set up the comparison to Jesus, the last Adam, in the second part of the verse. They further establish the main point of contrast: Adam became a "living being" (ψυχὴν ζῶσαν), and Christ a "life-giving spirit" (πνεῦμα ζῳοποιοῦν). Adam therefore was given a ψυχικός (physical) body, whereas Christ was raised in a πνευματικός (spiritual) body (1 Cor. 15:44). Not only does Jesus serve here as a representative for all who will be raised in spiritual bodies, but he is also the one who is "life-giving."

Third, Paul picks up the language of "earthly" and "heavenly" (1 Cor. 15:40) to further contrast Adam and Jesus in 15:47–49. The "first human" is described as "from the earth" and given the title "a man of dust" (15:47).

Jesus, the "second human," is "from heaven" and later given the title "the man of heaven" (15:48). Verses 48–49 make clear the universal nature of these two humans as representatives of those who follow them. As the one of dust, so are many of dust; as the one of heaven, so are many of heaven. According to Paul, we (using the first-person plural) are born into the image of the man of dust, but we will also bear the man of heaven's image (15:49).

Finally, whereas Jesus's humanity was of importance in 1 Corinthians 15:20–22, here his resurrected body and exalted state are in view. It is in his resurrected state that Jesus serves as a representative of humanity's future reality. In this contrast Adam represents fallen humanity, while Christ represents those resurrected from the dead. Jesus's humanity is not lost, as it remains foundational: he must be fully human, take on the image of the man of dust, in order to defeat death and usher in the resurrection of the dead. In his resurrected state, Jesus stands as the first human bringing about God's renewal of creation. Just as Adam's transgression brought about a disruption of God's original creation, so now Christ's resurrection brings about a renewal of that creation.

Other New Testament References

We have highlighted the key places in the New Testament where the figure and tradition of Adam are invoked in its presentation and understanding of Jesus. However, there are other places where Adam, or the tradition surrounding Adam, may also be evoked or assumed by the New Testament writers in their reflection on Jesus. While we remain unconvinced, James Dunn has famously argued that the hymn about Christ found in Philippians 2:5–11 contains allusions to and a contrast with Adam, as it demonstrates that "in Christ, his death and resurrection, God's original design for humanity finally achieved concrete shape and fulfillment."[44] Such an "Adam Christology" may also be reflected in Hebrews 2:5–9, as the author establishes Jesus as restoring humanity's rightful position among creation.[45]

Contribution to New Testament Christology

The New Testament's connection of Jesus to Adam provides several significant insights into how the early church understood the person and work of

---

44. Dunn, "Christ, Adam, and Preexistence," 79.
45. First Timothy appeals to Adam and Eve in its discussion of the proper conduct of women within the worshiping community. This passage has historically led to numerous misinterpretations of the text. Since it does not contribute to the New Testament's Christology, we will not treat it here. For a close examination of this text, arguing that it refers to a disruption of the created order, see Porter, *Pastoral Epistles*, in the discussion of 1 Tim. 2:11–14.

Christ. This connection links the work of Jesus to the very beginning of the biblical narrative. Genesis describes God's good creation being ravaged by the effects of sin. Sin brings death into the world and, importantly, disrupts humanity's ability to bear the image of God (*imago Dei*) to its fullness. Humanity's sin has corrupted its relationship with creation, each other, and God. In some ways, the biblical narrative is a story of God's response to sin and the disharmony it brings. The Old and New Testaments describe God's reconciling work to restore his relationship with sinful humanity and repair the damage done to his creation. The New Testament writers understood Jesus as a continuation and culmination of the reconciling work of God throughout history. As Paul describes in his writings, Jesus is the agent through whom the lethal effects of Adam's sin are reversed and life is made available to God's people.

The theme of creation becomes especially important as Jesus is presented as an Adam-like figure. Through Jesus Christ, God has inaugurated a "new creation," as was promised by the prophet Isaiah. Paul writes that the entire creation, which has been held in "bondage to decay" because of humanity's sin, eagerly awaits the new creation brought through Christ and the children of God (Rom. 8:19–23). The book of Revelation has as its climax a vision of the new heaven and the new earth, with God declaring, "See, I am making all things new" (Rev. 21:5). This idea is applied to the believer as Paul uses this metaphor to describe a person's new status in Christ (2 Cor. 5:16–17). The believer's old ways are left behind as the new creation takes hold in their life. In his Letter to the Galatians, Paul states, "Neither circumcision nor uncircumcision is anything; but a new creation is everything!" (Gal. 6:15).

Humanity's new creation through Christ is a restoration of humanity's creation in the image of God. While sin corrupted humanity's ability to bear God's image fully, Christ is understood as fully bearing God's image. Through Christ, humans are now able to fully bear the image of God as they were always created to do. Ephesians encourages believers to "clothe yourselves with the new self, created according to the likeness of God in true righteousness and holiness" (Eph. 4:24).

Christ, as the last Adam, inaugurates the new creation of both the cosmos and the individual. This is possible because Jesus is not only an Adam-like figure but also the creator and sustainer of the universe. The author of Hebrews writes that it is through Jesus that God created the worlds and that Jesus "sustains all things by his powerful word" (Heb. 1:3). Colossians states that in Christ "all things in heaven and on earth were created, things visible and invisible, whether thrones or dominions or rulers or powers—all things have been created through him and for him" (Col. 1:16).

> ## IRENAEUS ON RECAPITULATION
>
> Irenaeus of Lyons, a second-century theologian, articulates his notion of Jesus "recapitulating," or essentially reliving, the life of Adam. For Irenaeus, this supports the doctrine of Christ's preexistence.
>
>> Now it has been clearly shown that the Word which exists from the beginning with God, through whom all things were made, who was also always present with the human race, has in these last times, according to the time appointed by the Father, been united to his own creation and has been made a human being capable of suffering. This disposes of the objection of those who say, "If he was born at that time, it follows that Christ did not exist before then." For we have shown that the Son of God did not begin to exist at that point, because he had always existed with the Father. But when he was incarnate and became a human being, he recapitulated in himself the long history of the human race, obtaining salvation for us, so that we might regain in Jesus Christ what we had lost in Adam, that is, being in the image and likeness of God.[a]
>
> a. Irenaeus, *Against Heresies* 5.1.1. Translation from McGrath, *Christian Theology Reader*, 286.

Christ as the last Adam also emphasizes the life of Jesus in his identity and reconciling work. Without neglecting the events surrounding Jesus's passion, understanding Jesus as the last Adam brings the entirety of his life to bear upon his salvific work. By leading a life of perfect obedience, Jesus demonstrates the obedience that the first Adam was unable to achieve. The second-century theologian Irenaeus of Lyons picks up on this motif in his theory of "recapitulation." Irenaeus understands Jesus, as the last Adam, to have relived the life of the first Adam but without giving in to temptation or sin. In this way, Jesus not only modeled how to live but also sanctified each stage of life, making it possible for humanity to follow his example. Further, this perfect obedience, according to Irenaeus, brought about the destruction of sin and death.

Irenaeus's theology contributes to a larger tradition of understanding Jesus's life, death, and resurrection as offering something new for humanity that they would not have been able to obtain on their own. Jesus as the last Adam places proper significance in both Jesus's full humanity and his whole life of obedience. Jesus succeeds where the first Adam failed. Sin and death entered the world through the disobedience of Adam. Yet since Jesus as the last Adam remained faithful to God, he has opened a new way for reconciliation between God and his people. Through Jesus, they are a "new creation," one that harks back to the original creation of the cosmos and humanity's being made in the image of God.

CHAPTER 10

JESUS THE WORD

Introduction

Of all the vivid and creative imagery in the book of Revelation, one of the most striking is the presentation of Jesus at the parousia found in the nineteenth chapter (Rev. 19:11–16). Christ is described as a rider on a white horse coming down from heaven. His eyes are like flames, his tongue is like a sword, and numerous diadems are on his head. The author offers several names for this rider ("Faithful and True" in 19:11; "King of kings and Lord of lords" in 19:16), including one that only the rider himself knows (19:12). One name that the author gives to Jesus is "Word of God"—using the Greek term λόγος for "Word."[1] This phrase is used elsewhere in John's Apocalypse (1:2, 9; 6:9; 17:17; 19:9; 20:4), often in reference to the proclamation of the gospel and frequently connected to the "testimony of Jesus." In Revelation 19:13, however, the phrase ὁ λόγος τοῦ θεοῦ is a name given to Jesus—he is the "Word of God."

The name given to Jesus in Revelation 19 immediately conjures up the famous prologue to John's Gospel, which uses the term λόγος for Jesus (John 1:1–18). A lot of ink has been spilled on the contextual background for the Gospel writer's use of this term in the prologue and elsewhere in the Johannine literature.[2] As we will see, the term λόγος was common in Hellenistic

---

1. We acknowledge that this chapter's exploration of *Logos* and *Sophia* may be the most susceptible to the issue of conflating a term with a concept that we discussed in the introduction. We have attempted to use the Greek terms (λόγος; σοφία) when those terms are being used or discussed. We then retain *Logos* and *Sophia* for references to a particular concept or tradition (i.e., the Wisdom tradition) or when they are being used as titles (e.g., Jesus as the *Logos*).
2. On some of this literature, see Porter, *John, His Gospel, and Jesus*, 89–119.

culture—particularly in Stoic philosophical thought. Some scholars, particularly in the early twentieth century, identify this notion from Greek philosophy mediated through Alexandrian Judaism as the backdrop to John's prologue.[3] A second line of interpretation identifies the closest parallel to John's use in the Old Testament Wisdom tradition, in which God's σοφία (wisdom) is personified and an active participant in the creation of the world.[4] While these and other traditions are important for understanding the use of λόγος for Jesus in the New Testament, the early Christian writers developed these traditions into something entirely new when applied to Christ.

Among the various traditions examined in this study, Jesus as the *Logos* finds some parallels with the use of the title "Savior" (see chap. 8 above). Both titles for Jesus are not used frequently in the New Testament but do offer something unique to early christological thought. As we will see, Jesus as the *Logos* communicates the early Christian notion of who Jesus is in relation to God. It also is a helpful term for the New Testament understanding of Jesus's preexistence. As with Savior, both the Hellenistic and the Jewish backgrounds are vitally important for understanding the New Testament's use of λόγος. In the first century, λόγος was a common term used in a variety of contexts that illuminate how early Christians applied the term to Jesus. This chapter will also examine the Wisdom tradition found in early Jewish writings. Jesus is never explicitly called *Sophia* (Wisdom), but this sacred tradition does inform the New Testament treatment of him. As we will see, the *Sophia* and *Logos* traditions overlap in significant ways, and so Jesus as *Sophia* will be explored alongside presentations of him as *Logos*.

Logos in Jewish and Greco-Roman Contexts

Modern readers of the New Testament come to the passages referring to the personified *Logos* without any frame of reference for such a concept. This was not the case in the ancient world. The *Logos* concept was widespread in both Greco-Roman and Jewish literature and culture.[5] There is no doubt that the New Testament writers are using a notion that would have been familiar to their audiences. Yet exactly because λόγος was so widespread in the ancient world, no single use or understanding of the concept exists across cultures. To better understand how the term is applied to Jesus in the New Testament, we must explore how λόγος was utilized in the ancient world.

---

3. See Kleinknecht, "The Logos in the Greek and Hellenistic World."
4. See esp. Harris, *Origin of the Prologue to St. John's Gospel*, 1–66; Dodd, *Interpretation of the Fourth Gospel*, esp. 263–85.
5. Cullmann, *Christology of the New Testament*, 253–54.

> ## PLUTARCH ON *LOGOS*
>
> In his *To an Uneducated Ruler*, Plutarch, a late first-century Greek philosopher, uses λόγος to refer to reason indwelling all mortals as opposed to law being written in books.
>
>> For one who is falling cannot hold others up, nor can one who is ignorant teach, nor the uncultivated impart culture, nor the disorderly make order, nor can he rule who is under no rule. But most people foolishly believe that the first advantage of ruling is freedom from being ruled. And indeed the King of the Persians used to think that everyone was a slave except his own wife, whose master he ought to have been most of all.
>> Who, then, shall rule the ruler? The
>>
>> Law, the king of all,
>>   Both mortals and immortals,
>>
>> as Pindar says—not law written outside him in books or on wooden tablets or the like, but reason [λόγος] endowed with life within him, always abiding with him and watching over him and never leaving his soul without its leadership.[a]
>
> a. Plutarch, *Ad principem ineruditum* 780c. Translation by H. N. Fowler (LCL).

The Greek word λόγος indicates something being expressed, so it was used to convey a wide range of meanings in Greek literature that pertain to expression. It could indicate a calculation, explanation, account, saying, definition, or oration, among others. More significant for Greek philosophy was the use of λόγος for human reasoning or the rationality behind the world.[6] For Heraclitus, λόγος conveys a universal law and a principle that holds the world together.[7] Further, the λόγος is eternal, and "everything comes to pass in accordance" with it.[8] Aristotle uses λόγος to refer to reasoning, which sets humans apart from the animals: "But man lives by reason [λόγος] also, for he alone of animals possesses reason [λόγος]" (*Politics* 1332b).[9] For the Stoics,

---

6. See Tobin, "Logos."
7. *Fragment* 83. Greek text available in Diels, *Die Fragmente der Vorsokratiker*.
8. *Fragment* 1. Translation from Burnet, *Early Greek Philosophy*, 133. Aristotle notes the ambiguity of whether the *Logos* is "forever" or whether humans cannot comprehend it "forever" (*Rhetoric* 3.1407b).
9. Translation by H. Rackham (LCL).

λόγος describes the orienting principle behind the cosmos (Diogenes Laertius, *Lives of Eminent Philosophers* 7.149), and it is even compared to God (7.134). Plutarch, a Middle Platonist philosopher, describes the crocodile as a living representation of God because it has no tongue. This is because "the Divine Logos has no voice" (*De Iside et Osiride* 381B).[10]

This use was not uniform, but there is clear evidence that within Greek philosophical thought, λόγος was frequently used to describe the universal principle or reason that stands behind the world and holds it together. Sometimes this concept was compared to the divine; other times it refers to human logic or understanding.

Foundational to Hellenistic Jewish uses of λόγος is an understanding of the "word of God" in the Jewish Scriptures.[11] Frequently, God's "word" refers to his commandments (Deut. 4:10; 1 Kings 13:21; Tob. 14:4). God's word is true and worthy of praise (Ps. 56:4, 10; Prov. 30:5). God's word also refers to his promises, which can be fully relied upon (2 Sam. 7:28; 1 Kings 8:26). The divine message spoken by the prophets is described as the "words of the Lord" (Isa. 1:10; 40:8; Jer. 43:1; Ezek. 6:3; Hosea 4:1). More significant, sometimes God's word is personified (Ps. 33:4; Isa. 55:11; *1 En.* 14.24; Wis. 18:15) and even connected to the creation of the heavens (Ps. 33:6).

An important text for understanding the background of λόγος in the New Testament is Wisdom of Solomon 9:

> O God of my ancestors and Lord of mercy,
> who made all things by your word [λόγος],
> and by your wisdom [σοφία] have formed humankind
> to have dominion over the creatures you have made. (Wis. 9:1–2)

Not only is God's λόγος personified as acting, including taking a role in creation, but it is also connected to God's wisdom. This is representative of the Wisdom tradition found in Jewish literature that offers a helpful glimpse into the use of λόγος in the New Testament. God's wisdom is personified in the Old Testament (Prov. 8:22–31; 9:9–10) and later Jewish literature (Wis. 6:12–16; Sir. 15:1–10).[12] Wisdom is portrayed as a woman and is often referred to using a feminine pronoun because the Hebrew חכמה and the Greek σοφία are feminine nouns. Wisdom of Solomon confirms that Wisdom was present at creation (Wis. 9:9) and played an important role in biblical events (10:1–21).

---

10. See Keener, *Gospel of John*, 342.
11. For an examination of *Logos* theology within Jewish religious imagination, see Boyarin, "Gospel of the Memra."
12. See Gathercole, "Wisdom (Personified)."

Like the *Logos* in Stoic thought, Wisdom is presented as "the fashioner of all things" who "renews all things" (7:22, 27).

In Sirach 24, Wisdom speaks in the assembly of God, proclaiming that she came forth from God. She was created before the ages and will not cease to exist (Sir. 24:3, 9). Wisdom recalls being instructed to make her tent and dwelling among Israel (24:8) and in the Jerusalem temple. Similarly, in Baruch 3, God gives wisdom/knowledge to Israel, and "she appeared on earth and lived with humankind" (Bar. 3:36–37). Further, in both Sirach and Baruch, Wisdom is identified with Torah (Sir. 24:23; Bar. 3:9; 4:1).

The Similitudes of Enoch offers an interesting description of Wisdom that parallels Sirach 24:

> Wisdom could not find a place in which she could dwell;
> but a place was found (for her) in the heavens.
> Then Wisdom went out to dwell with the children of the people,
> but she found no dwelling place.
> (So) Wisdom returned to her place
> and she settled permanently among the angels.
> Then Iniquity went out of her rooms,
> and found whom she did not expect.
> And she dwelt with them,
> like rain in a desert,
> like dew in a thirsty land. (*1 En.* 42)[13]

This text, like Sirach 24, assumes a preexistent Wisdom who is sent to dwell among humanity but is rejected.[14]

Some Hellenistic Jewish thinkers picked up on the notion of reason as a governing force within philosophical discourse. Aristobulus of Alexandria (second century BCE) is believed to have written that Moses called the creation of the world the "words" (λόγοι) of God.[15] A fragment of Aristobulus also states that wisdom existed before heaven and earth (*Fragment* 5.3). The author of 4 Maccabees states that the purpose of his composition is to establish that "devout reason" (ὁ εὐσεβὴς λογισμός) is sovereign over the emotions (4 Macc. 1:1). For the author, "rational judgment" is the highest virtue (1:2). This is compatible with the Jewish law, since the law expresses such rational judgment and keeps one's emotions in check (2:1–23). In the *Letter to Aristeas*, the author similarly describes how the Jewish law establishes a morality that is embraced by Greek philosophy. In a discussion of the law, the high priest

---

13. Translation by E. Isaac in *OTP* 1:33.
14. See Loader, "Wisdom and Logos Traditions in Judaism and John's Christology."
15. Eusebius, *Preparation for the Gospel* 13.12.

states that generally all things are governed by "natural reason" (τὸν φυσικὸν λόγον) and that the specifics of the law are overseen by "profound reason" (λόγον βασθύν) (143).

This combination of Hellenistic philosophical thought and the Jewish Wisdom tradition is most clearly present in the writings of Philo of Alexandria. Philo makes extensive use of the personified *Logos* and *Sophia* traditions. At times the *Logos* and *Sophia* traditions merge so that the two are related to each other.[16] As with other Jewish writings, σοφία is personified and understood as present at the creation of the universe.[17] However, it is the concept of the *Logos* that takes on great significance in Philo's writings.[18] The *Logos* is connected to reason[19] and is "the most ancient of all the objects of intellect in the whole world."[20] Philo frequently refers to the "Divine Word."[21] The *Logos* is the image of God through whom all the world was made.[22] Interestingly, the *Logos* is also the model for the creation of human intellect.[23] According to Philo, humans were created "after the pattern of a second deity, who is the Word of the supreme Being" in respect to their rational nature. The human mind is "the similitude and form" of God's *Logos*.[24]

Further, the *Logos* serves as an intermediary between God and his creation for Philo. In *Who Is the Heir?* 205, he writes that the Father gave the "ancient Word" (πρεσβυτάτῳ λόγῳ) to stand between the Creator and that which has been created. He continues,

> And this same Word is continually a suppliant to the immortal God on behalf of the human race, which is exposed to affliction and misery; and is also the ambassador, sent by the Ruler of all, to the subject race.

Similarly, in *On Agriculture* 51, Philo explains how God oversees all of creation and has set up an "immediate superintendent, his own [λόγος], his first-born son, who is to receive the charge of this sacred company."

The Greek term λόγος was used in different ways within Greco-Roman and Jewish literature. In Greek philosophy, it commonly conveyed a concept

---

16. Philo, *On Flight and Finding* 108–9; *On Dreams* 2.242, 245.
17. Philo, *On Flight and Finding* 109; *On Drunkenness* 30–31.
18. See Winston, *Logos and Mystical Theology in Philo of Alexandria*.
19. Philo, *Questions and Answers on Genesis* 2.62.
20. Philo, *On Flight and Finding* 101.
21. Philo, *On Flight and Finding* 5; *On the Migration of Abraham* 244.
22. Philo, *Allegorical Interpretation* 1.81; 3.96; cf. *On the Confusion of Tongues* 147; *On Flight and Finding* 101.
23. Philo, *On the Creation of the World* 24–25.
24. Philo, *Questions and Answers on Genesis* 2.62. Translations of Philo are from Yonge, *Works of Philo*.

connected to rational thought or reasoning. Elsewhere, especially among the Stoics, the *Logos* was a universal principle that held the universe together. In Israel's Scriptures, God's *Logos* metaphorically referred to his commandments and relationship with his creation. By the time of Hellenization, the Word (λόγος) began to take on the characteristics of Wisdom, as personified in various texts.

Jesus as the *Logos* in the New Testament

In this section we will examine how the *Logos* tradition was utilized by New Testament writers—especially the author of the Fourth Gospel—and in the next we will explore the Wisdom tradition. Jesus is identified as λόγος in only a handful of places, but these passages are highly significant for early Christology. Connected to this title is the concept of Jesus as the true revealer of the Father—a theme that is found in numerous places in the New Testament.

John's Prologue

Instead of beginning with a birth narrative (like Matthew and Luke) or an account of John the Baptist's ministry (like Mark), John's Gospel begins by stating, "In the beginning was the Word [λόγος]" (John 1:1). In the following seventeen verses, the Gospel writer describes how the *Logos*—later identified as the person Jesus Christ—was involved in the creation of the world, dwelled among that creation, and serves as a mediator between God and creation. It is a powerful opening section that sets the stage for the narrative that follows. John clearly pulls from traditions regarding a divine *Logos*, and a great deal of scholarship has focused on the backdrop for John's *Logos* prologue. Before engaging the question of the prologue's background, we will first examine how the Gospel utilizes the notion of God's *Logos* in John 1:1–18.

First, we must embrace a paradox in John's presentation of the *Logos* and the divine.[25] In one sense, the *Logos* and God are equated with each other ("the Word was God," θεὸς ἦν ὁ λόγος; John 1:1). The *Logos* is given characteristics reserved for God: he was present in the beginning of time, and all creation came into being through him (1:1–3). On the other hand, the author parallels these statements by saying that the *Logos* was *with* God. This parallel is obvious in John 1:1–2:

> In the beginning was the Word,
> and the Word was with God,

---

25. See Cullmann, *Christology of the New Testament*, 266.

and the Word was God.
He was in the beginning with God.

So, is the Word God, or is the Word *with* God? The author seems to be saying yes to both. As the prologue continues, the author discusses God and the *Logos* using the language of Father and Son (1:14–18). While designating two different participants in a Father-Son relationship, John continues to maintain that the Word/Son is God: "No one has ever seen God. The *only God* who is in the bosom of the father has made him known" (1:18 AT). The italicized phrase represents a textual issue in the manuscript evidence of John's Gospel. The earliest manuscripts read μονογενὴς θεός (unique/only God), while later manuscripts replaced θεός with the term for "son" (υἱός), so that it reads "the only Son."[26] The interpretive issue is whether the Gospel writer here uses θεός (God) to refer to the *Logos* figure. On the basis of the best external evidence, this seems to be the case.

Second, the author uses a variety of images to describe the Word and its actions. One is the dualism of light/darkness, which is found frequently in Greek philosophical, Jewish, and later Gnostic literature.[27] The Gospel writer identifies the *Logos* as "true light" (τὸ φῶς τὸ ἀληθινόν; John 1:9) that "enlightens everyone" (1:9), shines into the darkness (1:5), and is coming into the world. The image of light is used alongside the image of the *Logos* as life (1:4–5). Both images are introduced here but are used extensively throughout the rest of the Gospel (3:19–21; 5:26, 35, 40; 6:33, 63; 8:12; 11:9–10, 25; 12:35–36; 20:31). Later in the Gospel, Jesus declares, "I am the bread of life" (6:35, 48) and "I am the light of the world" (9:5; cf. 12:46). Also of interest is the image of the cosmos—representing both the physical world and the people who dwell in it. The *Logos* is in the world, and even though the world came into existence through the *Logos*, the world did not recognize it (1:10).

Finally, we should consider the actions given to the *Logos* in John's prologue. As already mentioned, the *Logos* is described as active in the creation of the cosmos and life. It was present in the beginning, and everything that came into being came through it (John 1:3). The *Logos* is also described as entering the creation. It "became flesh" and "lived among us" (1:14) and was rejected (1:11). In addition, the *Logos* reveals God to the creation, acting as a mediator between the two (1:18).

---

26. See the section devoted to this issue in Metzger, *Textual Commentary on the Greek New Testament*, 169–70.
27. See Keener, *Gospel of John*, 383–85.

Background to John 1

These images and descriptions of the *Logos*'s actions recall earlier uses of the *Logos* and *Sophia* traditions. As in some Greek philosophical thought, the *Logos* holds the cosmos together and is compared to a divine being. As in the Jewish Wisdom tradition, *Sophia* is involved in creation, dwells on earth, and is ultimately rejected. There are points of contact with numerous sacred traditions, and it may be that the author intended to appeal to various traditions for his readers. As Udo Schnelle points out, "The [*Logos*] concept intentionally opens up a broad cultural vista: the worlds of Greco-Roman philosophy and education and of Hellenistic Judaism of the Alexandrian type."[28] In what follows, we will examine four key sources for the Fourth Gospel's use of the divine *Logos* concept: the Genesis creation narrative, the Wisdom tradition, Philo, and the Greco-Roman philosophical *Logos*.

First, the Gospel writer uses language from the creation narratives in Genesis 1 and 2 in the prologue.[29] The opening words "In the beginning" (Ἐν ἀρχῇ; identical to Gen. 1:1 in the LXX) clearly reflect the creation text. Whereas the Genesis account states that God was in the beginning, John's Gospel emphasizes the presence of the *Logos* in the beginning. Other parallels include the act of creation (John 1:3, 10) and the discussion of light/darkness (Gen. 1:3–4; John 1:5). The Genesis account also depicts the Creator *speaking* the world into existence. In John's Gospel, the divine *Logos* (word) is active in bringing everything into being.

Second, the Jewish Wisdom tradition, especially Sirach 24, serves as a significant background to the prologue of John 1. The Gospel writer uses some of the same themes and language for *Logos* that the Wisdom tradition uses for *Sophia* (see the table on p. 198).[30]

One can find parallels for nearly every claim in John 1:1–18 in the Wisdom tradition.[31] The Gospel writer's presentation of Jesus the *Logos* is informed by the tradition of *Sophia* in early Jewish literature. However, we must acknowledge that Jesus here is not *Sophia* but *Logos*. The author adapts many of the themes from this tradition but applies them to a personified *Logos*. Clearly, John uses the traditions of both *Sophia* and *Logos* in his description of Jesus in his opening chapter.

---

28. Schnelle, *Theology of the New Testament*, 688–89.
29. Evans, *Word and Glory*, 77–79.
30. For a fuller examination, see Evans, *Word and Glory*, 83–94.
31. Dodd, *Interpretation of the Fourth Gospel*, 335; Evans, *Word and Glory*, 92; Keener, *Gospel of John*, 352.

John 1	Sirach 24	Other Wisdom Passages
"In the beginning ['Εν ἀρχῇ]" (v. 1a)	"... in the beginning [ἀπ' ἀρχῆς], he created me" (v. 9)	"I was set up in the beginning [ἐν ἀρχῇ]" (Prov. 8:23 AT)
"The Word was with God" (v. 1b)		"I was beside him" (Prov. 8:30)
"All things [πάντα] came into being through him" (v. 3)		"[Wisdom] was present when you made the world" (Wis. 9:9)
"The life [ζωή] was the light [φῶς] of all people" (v. 4)	"It pours forth instruction like light [φῶς]" (v. 27 AT)	"All who hold her fast [Wisdom] will live [ζωή] ... walk toward the shining of her light [φῶς]" (Bar. 4:1–2)
"The light shines [φαίνει] in the darkness" (v. 5)	"I will make it shine [ἐκφαίνω] from far away" (v. 32b AT)	
"The true light, which enlightens [φωτίζει] everyone" (v. 9)	"I will again make instruction shine forth [φωτίζω] like the dawn" (v. 32a)	"All light [φῶς] shines through [wisdom]" (Aristobulus, *Fragment 5.2*)
"The world did not know [γινώσκω] him" (v. 10)	"The first man did not know [γινώσκω] wisdom fully" (v. 28)	
"He gave authority [ἐξουσία]" (v. 12)	"In Jerusalem was my authority [ἐξουσία]" (v. 11 AT)	
"The Word became flesh [σάρξ] and lived [σκηνόω] among us" (v. 14a)	"My Creator chose the place for my tent [σκηνή]. He said, 'Make your dwelling [κατασκηνόω] in Jacob'" (v. 8)	"[Wisdom] dwells with all flesh [μετὰ πάσης σαρκὸς]" (Sir. 1:10)
		"[Wisdom] appeared on earth and lived with humankind" (Bar. 3:37)
		"Then Wisdom went out to dwell with the children of the people" (*1 En.* 42.2)
"We have seen his glory [δόξα] ... full of grace [χάρις] and truth" (v. 14b)	"My branches are branches of glory [δόξα] and grace [χάρις]" (v. 16 AT)	
"The law [νόμος] indeed was given through Moses" (v. 17)	"The law [νόμος] that Moses commanded us" (v. 23)	
"No one has ever seen [ὁράω] God.... [The only God] has made him known [ἐξηγέομαι]" (v. 18)		"Who has seen [ὁράω] him and can describe [ἐκδιηγέομαι] him?" (Sir. 43:31)

Third, Philo's writings offer an interesting parallel to John's prologue. It is unclear whether the Gospel writer drew his *Logos* theology from Philo, but both authors use the *Logos* tradition similarly. "Philo and the Fourth Gospel are indeed both riffs on a common theme: two intimately related, but distinct articulations of a common exegetical and theological impulse."[32] One can trace similar themes in the two authors' portrayal of the *Logos*: light/darkness, significance of the name (ὄνομα), divine begetting, mediator with creation. Significantly, Philo connects the *Logos* with Wisdom.[33] Especially in places where John seems to go beyond the Wisdom tradition in his depiction of the *Logos*, Philo offers parallel hermeneutical movements.[34]

Finally, Greco-Roman philosophical traditions should not be ignored when considering John's prologue.[35] It is true that Jewish literature and traditions can explain the various language and themes utilized by the Gospel writer. Yet the notion of *Logos* was so prevalent in Hellenistic culture that John would have at least known that the image of the personified *Logos* would have provoked certain connotations. In philosophical literature, the *Logos* was a concept—often connected to reasoning—that permeated all things. For the Gospel of John, the *Logos* is Jesus Christ, who is implicitly the supreme philosophical notion. He holds the creation together and is the ultimate revelation of the divine. While the author pulls directly from the Jewish Wisdom tradition, his identification of Jesus as the *Logos* makes a bold claim to a Hellenized audience familiar with the *Logos* as a philosophical concept.

The Unique Contribution of John 1

An examination of the *Logos* and *Sophia* traditions that informed the Fourth Gospel's prologue should in no way suggest that the author does not offer his own unique presentation of those traditions. The simple fact that the Gospel writer connects the *Logos* to a historical figure is exceptional. In earlier traditions, *Logos* and *Sophia* remained concepts or mysterious figures, even when understood as dwelling on the earth. In John's prologue, the *Logos* is the person Jesus Christ. The diverse characteristics and actions attributed to the personified *Logos* or *Sophia* are found in the person Jesus. Also unique is that the author emphasizes that the *Logos* and God are not to be separated. The *Logos* is not simply compared to the divine (as in some Greek philosophical

---

32. Attridge, "Philo and John," 117.
33. Philo, *On Flight and Finding* 97, 108–9; *On Dreams* 2.242, 245.
34. See esp. Tobin, "Prologue of John and Hellenistic Jewish Speculation."
35. For a recent study on the influence of Stoic ideas of *Logos* in the prologue of John's Gospel, see Engberg-Pedersen, *John and Philosophy*, esp. chap. 2.

literature) or only said to be *with* God (as in the Wisdom tradition). In John 1 the author stresses that the *Logos is* God.[36] We may further note that unique to the prologue is the idea that Jesus the *Logos* is the definitive revelation of God to creation. As the author writes, no one has seen God, but it is through the *Logos* in flesh that he has revealed himself.

Jesus as God's Divine Word

Outside of John's prologue, the designation of Jesus as the *Logos* is absent. In 1 John 1:1, Jesus is the "word of life" (τοῦ λόγου τῆς ζωῆς), and, as we have seen, in Revelation he is referred to as the "Word of God" (ὁ λόγος τοῦ θεοῦ; 19:13). The opening of 1 John recalls the prologue of John's Gospel by referring to that which was "from the beginning" (Ἐν ἀρχῇ). It is what has been heard concerning the "word of life" that is from the beginning. However, this is more than a message that is heard. The author describes it as something "we have seen with our eyes" and "touched with our hands." This message of the word of life is about Jesus but here is also understood *as* Jesus. The message takes concrete form in Jesus.[37] In Revelation 19:13, the designation "Word of God" is clearly a title given to Jesus—it is the only place in the New Testament where this title appears. The phrase "word of God" is also found in Revelation 1:2, 9; 6:9; 17:17; 19:9; and 20:4 and refers to Christian testimony or proclamation.[38] The meaning may be similar in 19:13, as Jesus is not necessarily the revealer (as in John 1) but rather the embodied testimony of the Christian message.

Even though Jesus is rarely given the title *Logos*, throughout the New Testament the authors make a connection between God's word and God's revelation through Jesus. John's Gospel frequently uses the term λόγος in reference to Jesus's spoken word, and this is understood as God's word (John 17:14). Those who hear the word are called to believe in it (4:41; 5:24), for the word is truth (17:17). There are also appeals to "continue in my word" (8:31) and to "keep my word" (8:51, 55), which point to active fidelity to God's revelation in Jesus. Paul also says that God's word is the message of Jesus (2 Cor. 5:19; Eph. 1:13; Phil. 2:16; Col. 1:25), although this language is less frequent in his letters. In Revelation the "word of God" and the "testimony of Jesus" (τὴν μαρτυρίαν Ἰησοῦ) are recurrently paired together (Rev. 1:2, 9; 20:4).

Hebrews 4:12–13 presents a personified ὁ λόγος τοῦ θεοῦ (word of God) that is "living" (ζάω) and "active" (ἐνεργής) (cf. 1 Pet. 1:23). It pierces (δίστομος)

---

36. On this see Cullmann, *Christology of the New Testament*, 265–66.
37. Marshall, *Epistles of John*, 102.
38. Osborne, *Revelation*, 683.

and judges (κριτικός) and is sharper than a double-edged sword. Some early Christian interpreters understood the λόγος here to be a reference to the Son,[39] but Hebrews lacks the *Logos* Christology that is found in John 1. Instead, the ὁ λόγος τοῦ θεοῦ in this passage refers to God's message, harking back to God speaking through Psalm 95 in Hebrews 4:7. This λόγος, like a sharp sword, can penetrate the deepest parts of a person.

Jesus and Wisdom

Since the *Logos* and Wisdom traditions converge in the christologically rich prologue of John's Gospel, we treat the two together in this chapter. This section is devoted to how the New Testament writers incorporated the Wisdom tradition into their portrayals of Jesus separately from the *Logos* tradition. We will first examine passages that connect Jesus and *Sophia*. We will then turn to two significant christological passages that draw from the Wisdom tradition (Col. 1:15–20 and Heb. 1:1–4).

Jesus and Sophia

The Gospels at several places represent Jesus as having wisdom, although this can be generally understood as knowledge (Matt. 13:54; Mark 6:2; Luke 2:40, 52). At other places the Gospels apply characteristics of the personified *Sophia* to Jesus or identify Jesus as Wisdom. In Matthew 11, Jesus responds to John the Baptist's inquiry about his identity by pointing to his miraculous deeds. He then begins to speak to the crowd and concludes by saying, "For John came neither eating nor drinking, and they say, 'He has a demon'; the Son of Man came eating and drinking, and they say, 'Look, a glutton and a drunkard, a friend of tax collectors and sinners!' Yet wisdom [σοφία] is vindicated by her deeds" (Matt. 11:18–19). The Gospel writer here identifies Jesus as σοφία, as it is his deeds that are being referred to.[40] Luke changes this last line so that it reads "wisdom is vindicated by all her children" (Luke 7:35). In this account Jesus is identified not as Wisdom but, together with John, as a child of Wisdom.

Matthew's and Luke's Gospels also contain an account of Jesus confronting the Pharisees and describing how God sent prophets and others who were persecuted and killed (Matt. 23:34–39; Luke 11:49–51). The implication is that the Pharisees are acting like the generations before them, opposing God's

---

39. See Swetnam, "Jesus as Λόγος in Hebrews 4,12–13."
40. Dunn, *Christology in the Making*, 197.

messengers, and will be held accountable. In Luke's version, the statement is a quotation spoken by the "Wisdom of God" (ἡ σοφία τοῦ θεοῦ): "Therefore also the Wisdom of God said, 'I will send them prophets and apostles, some of whom they will kill and persecute'" (Luke 11:49). There is no clear source for this quotation, but its content is consistent with the theme found in Wisdom literature of God sending *Sophia* into the world only to be rejected. In Matthew's version, Jesus himself says, "Therefore I send you prophets, sages, and scribes, some of whom you will kill and crucify, and some you will flog in your synagogues and pursue from town to town" (Matt. 23:34). Both Gospels seem to be drawing on a shared source, but the direction of the influence is unclear. Either Matthew adopted words attributed to Wisdom (from either Luke's Gospel or a shared source [Q material]) and put them in Jesus's mouth, or Luke took Jesus's words (from Matthew or Q) and identified them as from Wisdom. In either scenario, Jesus and Wisdom are tightly linked.

Nowhere is Jesus more clearly portrayed as God's true revealer of wisdom than in Matthew 11:25–27//Luke 10:21–22. In this saying, Jesus thanks God for revealing his ways to young children while keeping them hidden from the wise and intelligent. Further, he states that "all things have been handed over to me by my Father" and that the Father is revealed only to those whom the Son chooses. These words are reminiscent of John 1, in which the author states that no one has seen God but only the Son has made him known (John 1:18).

In several places in the writings attributed to Paul, Jesus represents a heavenly wisdom that counters any earthly wisdom (1 Cor. 1:17–24; 2:6; 2 Cor. 1:12). In fact, God's work through Jesus is seen as foolishness to those who value earthly wisdom (1 Cor. 1:20–21). True wisdom, according to Paul, is found in Jesus, who "became for us wisdom from God" (1:30; cf. 1:24). The wisdom of God is made known through the church and in accordance with the Father's work in Jesus (Eph. 3:10–11). In Christ are "hidden all the treasures of wisdom [σοφία] and knowledge [γνῶσις]" (Col. 2:3). There is no sense here of a preexistent, personified Wisdom; rather, the message of Jesus is equated with *divine* wisdom, even if it seems unwise by earthly standards.

Two Key Wisdom Christology Texts

This exploration of how the Jewish Wisdom tradition influenced the New Testament writers' presentations of Jesus includes two significant passages for New Testament Christology: Colossians 1:15–20 and Hebrews 1:1–4. In both passages, the influence of the Wisdom tradition on the New Testament writers is obvious.

Colossians 1:15–20

Most biblical scholars identify all or most of Colossians 1:15–20 as an early Christian hymn.[41] The verses can be divided into two strophes (vv. 15–18a; 18b–20) and include poetic lines and parallelism. It is impossible to know whether the hymn existed prior to the composition of Colossians or if it originates here. Yet it is clear that the hymn invokes imagery from the Wisdom tradition and may well be modeled after such Wisdom hymns.[42] While the author draws from the Wisdom tradition, this is a hymn in celebration of Christ, and it offers its own unique contribution to New Testament Christology.

The first half of the hymn (Col. 1:15–18a) uses language that highly exalts Jesus as the source and agent of creation. The statement that he is the "image" (εἰκών) of God may hark back to the Genesis account and contribute to an understanding of Jesus as a new Adam (see chap. 9). However, *Sophia* is also described as God's "image" (Wis. 7:26; Philo, *Allegorical Interpretation* 1.43). As the hymn goes on to describe Christ as active in the world's creation, the Wisdom tradition is in view. Jesus is the "firstborn" (πρωτότοκος) of creation (Col. 1:15), a concept that is clearly expressed of Wisdom elsewhere (Prov. 8:22; Philo, *On Drunkenness* 30–31). The concept of all creation being made through Wisdom (Ps. 104:24; Wis. 8:5; 9:9) is also found. The exalted language in the hymn continues in the statement that Jesus is "before all things" (Col. 1:17). The poetic language is unclear whether Jesus is presented as the first among created things (as πρωτότοκος can be taken) or the agent of that creation. Certainly, the patristic interpreters confirmed the latter option, which can be supported by the writer's use of prepositions and the parallelism within the strophe. Colossians 1:16a states that all things were created *in* him (ἐν αὐτῷ), followed by several parallels: all things in the heavens and on the earth; the seen and the unseen; either thrones or powers or rulers or authorities. Then the author states that all things have been created *through* him (δι'αὐτοῦ) and *for* him (εἰς αὐτόν). This may be too much theological weight for these prepositions to carry, but the overall sense of this first strophe is that creation has come about because of Jesus rather than that Jesus is among the created order. These are divine actions reserved for God and applied to Jesus. Further, the author's comment that all things have been created *for* him (εἰς αὐτόν) points to Jesus as the goal of creation—a concept that Paul

---

41. The secondary literature on this passage is overwhelming. A good introduction to early Christian hymns and this one in particular is Gordley, *New Testament Christological Hymns*, esp. 111–43, on Col. 1:15–20.

42. Dunn, *Epistles to the Colossians and Philemon*, 85. See also McKnight, *Letter to the Colossians*, 139–43.

elsewhere reserves for God (Rom. 11:36; 1 Cor. 8:6).[43] The notion that "all things hold together" in Christ recalls philosophical discussions of the *Logos* as the rationality that lies behind the universe. Wisdom too is described as holding all things together (Wis. 1:7).

Also interesting in the first strophe is the emphasis on the visible and the invisible. Jesus is the image of the "invisible God" (τοῦ θεοῦ τοῦ ἀοράτου), and all things invisible or visible were created in him. It is impossible to see God (Sir. 43:31), but in Christ he is made known. This coheres with the role of *Sophia* or *Logos* as revealing who God is and serving as his mediator with creation. The reference to the visible and the invisible things is a poetic expression of completeness: all things—not just what one can see—were created in Jesus. The author is also articulating a dualism that finds further expression by the reference to things in heaven and on earth (Col. 1:16; cf. 1:20). God is among the invisible things of heaven that are unknown to those on earth. However, Jesus serves as the visible manifestation of God on earth and bridges the two.

The second strophe focuses on Christ's redemptive work on the cross and its implications for creation. Colossians 1:18b states that Jesus is the "beginning" (ἀρχή), a term found in Genesis 1:1 but also applied to *Sophia* (Prov. 8:22; Philo, *Allegorical Interpretation* 1.43). This line is intended to parallel Colossians 1:16. Here again Jesus is the πρωτότοκος, but instead of being the firstborn of creation, he is the firstborn of the dead—a reference to his resurrection. Whereas Jesus was described in the first strophe as Wisdom among creation, here he is the resurrected one among the new creation.[44] The author is building on and moving beyond the Wisdom tradition in presenting Jesus as the one through whom creation is restored and reconciled to God. Colossians 1:19 powerfully states that in Jesus "all the fullness of God was pleased to dwell." Whereas Wisdom was instructed to "dwell" among the creation, here the "fullness" is said to "dwell" in Christ. It is unclear within the text to what the "fullness" refers, although most translations and commentators understand that the "fullness" of God is intended.[45] Such a notion can be supported by the context of the hymn and finds support in Colossians 2:9, where the author states (using similar structure and vocabulary), "For in him [Christ] the whole fullness of deity dwells bodily." This is reminiscent of the Johannine motif that the Father is in Jesus and Jesus is in the Father (cf. John 17:21).

---

43. Tuckett, *Christology and the New Testament*, 77.
44. Dunn, *Epistles to the Colossians and Philemon*, 97.
45. See Bruce, *Epistles to the Colossians, to Philemon, and to the Ephesians*, 72–74.

The Colossians hymn depicts Jesus as the source, agent, and goal of creation. Especially in the first strophe, the author draws from the Wisdom tradition to clearly state that Jesus should be identified as what earlier Wisdom texts identified as *Sophia*. He was present at creation, and it is through him that all things hold together. However, the hymn goes beyond this tradition in its praise of Christ. Unlike Wisdom, Christ is not understood as a part of the created order.[46] The writer clearly identifies Christ as fully divine and the active expression of God in creation. Further, the hymn presents Christ not only as the Wisdom-like figure of creation but also as the resurrected one who restores and reconciles the creation to God. In this way, Christ fulfills and completes Wisdom's task of revealing the Father. Not only should Christ be identified as Wisdom, according to the writer, but he also more completely represents God in his restoration of creation.

Hebrews 1:1–4

Like the Colossians hymn, the opening exordium of the Epistle to the Hebrews (1:1–4) draws from the Wisdom tradition in its portrayal of Jesus. The author states that in previous times God spoke by the prophets, but now he has spoken to us by his Son (1:1–2). These verses speak of two ages in which God has spoken. In the previous age, he spoke by the prophets "on many occasions" and "in many ways" to the ancestors (1:1). In the present age—described as "in these final days" (ἐπ'ἐσχάτου τῶν ἡμερῶν)—he has spoken to us by a Son (1:2).

The remaining verses in the exordium go on to describe the Son, later identified as Jesus (Heb. 2:9). Similar to Wisdom, the Son was present at creation and was the means through which God created the universe (1:2; cf. Prov. 8:27; Wis. 9:9). The term for what God created, αἰῶνας, may be understood temporally ("ages") or spatially ("worlds"). Elsewhere in Hebrews it is used in both senses (spatially: 11:3; temporally: 6:5; 9:26), and both could fit the context here.[47] The term is not used in Wisdom texts to describe the created order, but its spatial sense communicates the same idea that *Sophia* was present at the creation of the world (κόσμος; Wis. 9:9) and heavens (οὐρανόν; Prov. 8:27). However, the temporal sense also fits the Wisdom tradition, as *Sophia* is said to be created "before the ages" (πρὸ τοῦ αἰῶνος; Sir. 24:9). The author may be playing with the ambiguity of the term, but the point is that the Son was the means through which God created *everything*.

---

46. See Fee, *Pauline Christology*, 300n31.
47. So Koester, *Hebrews*, 178.

Verses 3 and 4 make up a carefully crafted section that contains some of the characteristics of other early Christian hymns (such as Col. 1:15–20). It appears that hymnic materials inspired the verses, but the author clearly modified any such sources for his own purposes.[48] The Son is described as the "reflection of [God's] glory" (ἀπαύγασμα τῆς δόξης) and the "exact representation of his nature" (χαρακτὴρ τῆς ὑποστάσεως αὐτοῦ) (1:3). An interesting parallel is Wisdom 7:26, in which *Sophia* is described as the "reflection" of God's light and then a "mirror" of God's working and the "image" of his goodness. The term χαρακτήρ appears only here in the New Testament and infrequently in the Septuagint, but the idea is the same as that of *Sophia* in the Wisdom tradition: Jesus is the pure representation of the divine. Philo speaks of the *Logos* being the "seal" (σφραγίς) of God upon the human mind. The "eternal Logos" is the "impression" (χαρακτήρ) of this seal (*On Planting* 18). This Son not only is involved in creation but also "sustains all things" by his word (Heb. 1:3). This recalls the description of *Sophia* as one who "pervades and penetrates all things" (Wis. 7:24) and "orders all things" (8:1) and of *Logos* as the "bond of every thing" (Philo, *On Flight and Finding* 112).

As in other early Christian hymns, the focus shifts from Christ's work at creation to his salvific activity (Heb. 1:3b–4; cf. Phil. 2:9–11; Col. 1:20). The reference to "purification for sins" recalls cultic purification language. It implies that Jesus's death on the cross was a sacrificial offering—something described later in greater detail (Heb. 9:11–22). The passage envisions Christ's exaltation at the right hand of "the Majesty on high" (1:3).

Summary

The Wisdom tradition is clearly behind these two early Christian hymns. This has led to speculation as to whether the authors adopted earlier hymns written of *Sophia* or crafted their own. Regardless, these two texts demonstrate how early Christian thinkers adapted language and ideas that were reserved for *Sophia* and applied them to Jesus. Just as some earlier Jewish writers identified the divine Wisdom with Torah (Bar. 4:1), so these early Christians identified *Sophia* with Jesus. As James Dunn points out, this is still within the monotheistic worldview of early Judaism, which held that God revealed himself through his creative power.[49] Identifying Jesus as *Sophia* is, of course, unique, but so is the focus on Jesus's salvific activity. Like *Sophia*, Jesus was present and active at the creation of the world, and he holds all things together. However, these Christian writers move beyond this to

---

48. Attridge, *Hebrews*, 41–42.
49. Dunn, *Christology in the Making*, 89.

demonstrate how Jesus, as the true revealer of God and his activity, reconciled the creation to God.

Contribution to New Testament Christology

The *Logos* and *Sophia* traditions provided the New Testament writers with language and imagery to articulate aspects of the person Jesus. In addition, it is highly significant that the early Christian writers identified the figures of *Logos* and *Sophia* as Christ. Especially in the Hellenistic context, recognizing Christ as the true divine *Logos* places him above other sources of intellect and rationality. Compared to the *Logos* as the universal principle behind the cosmos, which was the view of philosophical schools, especially the Stoics, Jesus as the *Logos* is the true sustainer of the world. Similarly, by describing Christ in terms reserved for Wisdom, the New Testament writers revealed that he was the one those texts were describing. Jesus is the preexistent divine figure who fully reveals the divine and was active in the creation of the world.

> ### JUSTIN MARTYR ON JESUS THE *LOGOS*
>
> In the following passage, Justin Martyr, a second-century Christian theologian, discusses the notion of Jesus as the Word within a larger concept of Greek philosophy and human reasoning.
>
>> We have been taught that Christ was First-begotten of God [the Father] and we have indicated above that He is the Word of whom all mankind partakes. Those who lived by reason are Christians, even though they have been considered atheists: such as, among the Greeks, Socrates, Heraclitus, and others like them; and among the foreigners, Abraham, Elias, Ananias, Azarias, Misael, and many others whose deeds or names we now forbear to enumerate, for we think it would be too long. So, also, they who lived before Christ and did not live by reason were useless men, enemies of Christ, and murderers of those who did live by reason. But those who have lived reasonably, and still do, are Christians, and are fearless and untroubled. From all that has been said an intelligent man can understand why, through the power of the Word, in accordance with the will of God, the Father and Lord of all, He was born as a man of a virgin, was named Jesus, was crucified, died, rose again, and ascended to Heaven.[a]
>
> a. Justin Martyr, *First Apology* 46. Translation from Falls, *Saint Justin Martyr*, 83–84.

Revealer

At the heart of the christological use of the *Logos* and Wisdom traditions is the belief that God has revealed himself fully in the person Jesus. Whereas the *Logos* served as an expression of the divine will and *Sophia* revealed divine action, Christ in the flesh is the whole of divine revelation. The language is robust, and it was hotly debated in the earliest centuries of Christianity. Jesus is the "reflection" (ἀπαύγασμα; Heb. 1:3), "exact imprint" (χαρακτήρ; 1:3), "form" (μορφή; Phil. 2:6), and "image" (εἰκών; Col. 1:15) of God. These terms may communicate the reality of Christ's divinity, but at the very least they express the idea that God has fully revealed himself in Christ.

The statement in the Colossians hymn that Christ is the "image of the invisible God" (Col. 1:15) communicates that Christ is the physical, visible display of what is unseen. The prologue of John says that no one has seen God, but that the Son alone has made him known (John 1:18). This is incredible when considering that the *Logos* and *Sophia* remained ambiguous and mysterious figures. That the *Logos* took on flesh and could be seen with one's eyes is a remarkable declaration. The early Christian witness, then, concerns what they had seen with their eyes and touched with their hands (1 John 1:1; cf. John 1:14). God has been revealed in a physical and tangible way.

Creator and Sustainer

These traditions also helped the New Testament writers express Christ's role in the creation of the universe. Like the *Logos* and *Sophia* in the Wisdom tradition, Jesus is an agent of creation and was present when the world was made. The language is not precise, but God creates, while Christ is the means through which he creates. This does not negate the importance of Christ's role. All things came about through Jesus, and without Jesus they would not have come about (John 1:3). The New Testament writers emphasize Jesus's role not just in the creation of the physical world but in the creation of everything. The exordium of Hebrews states that, through the Son, God created the universe—a term with temporal and spatial aspects (Heb. 1:2). The Colossians hymn states that *all things* in heaven and on earth, invisible or visible, were created through Christ (Col. 1:16). Elsewhere, Paul writes that all things exist through Christ (1 Cor. 8:6).

Christ is also the one who upholds the creation and sustains it. In Greek philosophical thought, the *Logos* was sometimes understood as the rationality that stood behind the universe holding it together. The New Testament writers give this role to Christ, who "sustains all things" (Heb. 1:3) and holds all things together (Col. 1:17). Connected to this is the idea that Jesus's redemptive work reconciles the created order to God. Through Christ, the Colossians hymn states, "God was pleased to reconcile to himself all things" (1:20).

Preexistence

Several New Testament writers articulate a view of the preexistence of Christ. Beyond the language of Jesus being sent by God (as would be a prophet or messenger), these writers describe the prehistory of Jesus prior to his appearance on earth. Paul expresses this notion in Philippians 2:6–7, stating that Jesus, who was in the form of God, took on the form of a human (cf. 1 Cor. 8:6; Gal. 4:4). In Colossians, Christ is said to be the "firstborn" of creation (Col. 1:15) and "before all things" (1:17). He existed "in the beginning" according to John's prologue (John 1:1), and later in the Gospel Jesus declares, "I came from the Father and have come into the world" (16:28). In the next chapter of John's Gospel, Jesus prays to the Father, seeking to be glorified with the "glory that I had in your presence before the world existed" (17:5).

CHAPTER II

JESUS THE HIGH PRIEST

Introduction

The Epistle to the Hebrews was written to a community in the middle of a crisis. Its author details the community's previous trial of great suffering, which included public humiliation, imprisonment, and persecution (Heb. 10:32–36). While this event happened in the past, it is clear that the author speaks to a community facing a current crisis—either one of physical persecution as in their past or one of a crisis of faith. Whatever the current crisis, many are abandoning the community because of it (10:25). Faced with this dilemma, the author of Hebrews offers a key christological concept to motivate and encourage his audience: Jesus as the great high priest.

At the end of the epistle's fourth chapter, the author writes, "Since, then, we have a great high priest who has passed through the heavens, Jesus, the Son of God, let us hold fast to our confession" (Heb. 4:14). The author goes on to develop the idea of Jesus's high priesthood, but here we can see that one significant function of this christological concept is to encourage a weary audience to remain faithful to their faith and community.

One can imagine that an audience familiar with Jewish thought and practice would immediately raise the issue of Jesus's genealogy. According to Israel's Scriptures, the high priest was to come from the line of Levites. It is likely that the high priests of the first century were appointed for more political reasons, but a Levitical high priesthood remained the biblical ideal. If Jesus came from the line of Judah, and not Levi, how could the author of Hebrews say that he is a high priest? The author anticipates this objection (see Heb. 7:14) and finds his justification in the Old Testament figure of

Melchizedek. By establishing a precedent using an obscure figure (mentioned only twice in the Hebrew Bible), the author of Hebrews builds his case for Jesus's high priesthood—one of the most significant christological concepts of the early Christians.

The High Priest in Israel's Sacred Scriptures

Before we can fully appreciate the significance of Jesus as a high priest, we must first understand the role of the priests, and the high priesthood specifically, in the religious life of Israel.[1] The Hebrew Bible speaks frequently of the priesthood and its numerous responsibilities. The book of Leviticus lays out the requirements and cultic duties of Israel's priests. Literature of the Second Temple period also frequently describes the actions of the priests and reflects the developed thinking within Judaism of that time. First-century Jewish writers such as Josephus likewise describe the contemporary priesthood and priests' function within a Roman-occupied land. Second Temple literature also looks ahead to a new priest—one with kingly characteristics who plays a significant role in the end times. The figure of Melchizedek, who appears so infrequently in the Old Testament, becomes an example of just such an eschatological priest-king.

The Priesthood in the Old Testament

Israel's priests find their earliest predecessor in Aaron, the brother of Moses, and his sons (the Levites).[2] In the book of Leviticus, God separates Aaron and his line from the rest of the Israelites to serve as their priests. Much of the book is devoted to descriptions of the priestly practices and their various sacrifices and offerings. In Leviticus 8, Moses anoints and consecrates the Levites as priests. As Israel was called to be separate and holy from its neighboring nations, so too the priests were to be uniquely set apart among the Israelites. They, for example, were not allowed to be near a dead body (even a family member!), could marry only a specific

---

1. The Greco-Roman world also had priests, with the *pontifex maximus* (greatest priest) likely being the closest thing to the Jewish high priest. However, the New Testament writers so clearly draw from the Jewish role and tradition of the high priesthood that we will not examine the Greco-Roman history here. For a study of priests especially in the Roman Empire, see Rüpke, *From Jupiter to Christ*, esp. chap. 12.

2. While the priesthood finds its origin with Aaron, it is unclear whether they were active in the life of Israel as early as the days of the tabernacle. Scholars often debate whether these texts, written during the monarchy, were intended to lend credibility to the priesthood of the Jerusalem temple. See Milgrom, *Leviticus 17–22*, 3–35.

type of woman, and had limitations on their physical appearance (esp. Lev. 9:10–15).

The priesthood was passed down among the Levites. Uniquely called by God for this role, only the Levites were to serve as priests within the religious life of Israel. Since they were entrusted with this task, the Levites were given no allotment of land or inheritance in Israel. Therefore, the other tribes of Israel were required to set apart a portion of their crops and offerings for them. This is because, as Deuteronomy puts it, "the LORD your God has chosen Levi out of all your tribes, to stand and minister in the name of the LORD, him and his sons for all time" (Deut. 18:5).

The priests were charged with the operation of Israel's cultic worship in the Old Testament—in the tabernacle, specific religious locations, and eventually the Jerusalem temple. This involved overseeing the various sacrifices and offerings on behalf of the people. Only a priest from the tribe of Levi could offer a sacrifice, since they were understood as the only people holy enough to handle such a task. Detailed descriptions of different sacrificial offerings are described in Leviticus (esp. chaps. 1–4), and the priests' functions included burning sacrificial animals and sprinkling their blood on the altar. The priests also served as communicators of God's law and interpreters of God's will (see Deut. 17:8–12). Only a priest could take an offering before the Lord; they brought such offerings on behalf of those who offered them. The priests served as necessary mediators between sinful people in need of atonement and a holy God.

The Role of the High Priest

In preexilic times, the priest stationed at the helm of a community's priesthood was often referred to simply as "the priest" or "head priest." The term "high priest" (הכהן הגדול) was used in reference to Aaron and was used more frequently of the head priest during the time of the first Jerusalem temple.[3] In Leviticus, Aaron is described as the first high priest of Israel and given the responsibilities that generations of high priests would assume up until the time of the Second Temple's destruction in 70 CE. Aaron was followed by his son Eleazer. This line within the Levites was believed by the ancient Israelites to have been preserved up to the building of the Jerusalem temple during the reign of King Solomon. The high priest at the first temple's dedication was Zadok, from whom the family line of high priests ("Zadokites") took its name. The Zadokites served as Israel's high priests up until the Hasmonean

---

3. See Gafni, "High Priest."

dynasty of the second century BCE. Under the Herodian dynasty, the high priesthood was returned to the Zadokite line—although in a much more limited capacity. By the first century CE, the high priesthood was dictated by the Roman client king, who often appointed and dropped high priests according to his interests.[4] During the time of the Second Temple, the high priest took on a dual role as the leader of Israel's cultic life and the head of the state. In the time of Jesus's ministry, the high priest was Caiaphas, who plays an important role in the Gospels' passion narratives.[5]

The high priest had a unique role among the Levitical priests. He was responsible for the operation and care of the temple and the cultic life of Israel. The high priest wore special vestments and clothing and was held to a stricter code of cleanliness than ordinary priests. Only the high priest could enter the holy of holies, where God's presence was said to reside. The high priest oversaw temple ceremonies on specific dates and important religious ceremonies.[6] One such ceremony in which the high priest played a significant role was the yearly Day of Atonement (or Yom Kippur).

The Day of Atonement was the only time during the year when the high priest entered the holy of holies. Leviticus 16 contains the instructions for this ceremony, which had two phases. In the first phase, the high priest offered sacrifices to cleanse the holy of holies. The second phase involved an atonement offering for the sins of the people. Only the high priest could present these offerings in the holy of holies—essentially functioning as the people's surrogate before God.

The Priest-King

In addition to the high priest, we can identify a tradition within Jewish literature of an ideal priest-king. An important figure in this regard is Melchizedek, who appears briefly in Genesis 14 but becomes a highly speculated-upon character in later Jewish writings. In Genesis 14:18–20, Abraham has an encounter with Melchizedek, who is described as both the king of Salem and a priest of God Most High. He blesses Abraham, and in return Abraham gives him a tenth of his possessions. This meeting takes up only three verses, and the Pentateuch tells us nothing else about this mysterious figure. While brief, this passage is significant, as Melchizedek is the first priest mentioned

---

4. This created the necessary category of "chief priests," who appear frequently in the Gospels and Acts, which consisted of former high priests and the families of former and current high priests.

5. See Bond, *Caiaphas*, esp. 64–72.

6. See Josephus, *J.W.* 5.230–36.

in the biblical narrative, and he offers the first blessing to Abraham (apart from God's own promise in Gen. 12).

Melchizedek appears again in the Old Testament only in Psalm 110, a royal psalm celebrating the capture of Jerusalem and enthronement of King David. In verse 4 the psalmist writes, "The LORD has sworn and will not change his mind, 'You are a priest forever according to the order of Melchizedek.'"[7] As in Genesis 14, Melchizedek is described as a priest. Because this is a royal psalm, we can discern a relationship between Melchizedek's priesthood and his kingship—although this is not explicitly stated as it is in Genesis. Unique to this psalm, however, is the implication that Melchizedek's priesthood is eternal.

The High Priest in Second Temple Literature

Upon returning from exile and after the rebuilding of the temple, Joshua— the grandson of Seraiah, the last high priest before the Babylonian exile— served as high priest.[8] During this time under Persian control, Jerusalem again became the center of the Jewish religion, and the high priest belonged to the ruling class—both religiously and politically.[9] When Alexander the Great conquered the Persians, Hellenism increasingly influenced Jerusalem. While in some ways curbed by the Greek authorities, the high priest was the leader in Jerusalem. He was not only the priest but also a prince whose power was consolidated by the principles of life-tenure and inheritability.[10] However, by the time of Roman occupation, the high priest was chosen and controlled by the occupying authorities. These appointments rarely lasted more than a few years and often were made for personal or political reasons. Nearly a century passed during this period, and twenty-seven high priests were appointed (compared to twenty-four during the previous five centuries from the rebuilding of the temple to the Roman occupation).[11] While the Hellenistic and Roman influences downgraded the position of high priest, the priesthood retained respect among Second Temple Jews.[12] Even if the man who filled the role did not warrant respect, the fact that he was the high priest certainly did. A certain dignity continued to be granted to the office, if not the man.[13]

---

7. On the interpretation of this psalm, see Allen, *Psalms 101–150*, 78–87.
8. For a thorough examination of the relevant Joshua materials, see VanderKam, *From Joshua to Caiaphas*, 1–42.
9. Levine, *Jerusalem*, 42.
10. Schürer, *History of the Jewish People*, 227.
11. Based on figures in VanderKam, *From Joshua to Caiaphas*, 491–92.
12. Sanders, *Judaism*, 327; Schürer, *History of the Jewish People*, 228.
13. Skarsaune, *Shadow of the Temple*, 99.

Josephus discusses the high priesthood in numerous places in his writings. He presents Aaron as the ideal high priest, called by God for the honor because of his virtue.[14] In *Jewish Antiquities*, Josephus portrays Moses telling the Israelites, "[Aaron] is to have the care of the altars, and to make provision for the sacrifices; and he it is that must put prayers for you to God, who will readily hear them . . . because he will receive them as offered by one that he hath himself chosen to this office" (*Ant.* 3.191).[15] Here Josephus emphasizes the high priestly function of serving as a representative of the people to God. Further, God will listen to the people's prayers because they come through Aaron, the high priest. Josephus also discusses the attire and function of the high priest in great detail (*Ant.* 3.159–79; *J.W.* 5.230–35), emphasizing their significance within first-century Judaism.

While Josephus's depiction of the high priesthood is generally positive, there are indications within the Second Temple period of a more critical appraisal. The Maccabean literature is especially negative in its treatment of the high priests. It strongly opposes the priesthoods of Jason (2 Macc. 4:7–17), Menelaus (2 Macc. 4:32–34, 50), and Alcimus (1 Macc. 7:5–9). When the Hasmoneans took over the high priesthood, they replaced the line of the Zadokites with that of the Maccabean family. The Herodian dynasty returned the high priesthood to the Zadokite line, although with significantly less power.

The Qumran literature also portrays a negative critique of the high priesthood—most likely a response to the Hasmonean high priestly line.[16] The best example of this is found in the Pesher on Habakkuk.[17] This Habakkuk commentary speaks of a "Wicked Priest" whose "heart became proud, and he forsook God and betrayed the precepts for the sake of riches. He robbed and amassed the riches of the men of violence who rebelled against God, and he took the wealth of the peoples, heaping sinful iniquity upon himself. And he lived in the ways of abominations amidst every unclean defilement."[18] The wicked priest, the text continues, "did not circumcise the foreskin of his heart" and "walked in the ways of drunkenness,"[19] taking advantage of the poor and defiling the temple of God.[20]

---

14. See Josephus, *Ant.* 3.188–91.
15. Translation from Whiston, *Works of Flavius Josephus*, 91.
16. See Murphy-O'Connor, "Essenes and Their History."
17. Other DSS examples of a negative view of the high priesthood include 4Q169 1.5; CD 6.12–17; 1QS 5.5–6; 8.8–9; 9.6.
18. 1QpHab 8.8–13. Translation from Vermes, *Complete Dead Sea Scrolls in English*, 513.
19. 1QpHab 11.12–15 (Vermes, *Complete Dead Sea Scrolls in English*, 515).
20. 1QpHab 12.1–10.

> ## HIGH PRIESTS MORE IMPORTANT THAN KINGS
>
> In this passage from the first-century Jewish philosopher Philo of Alexandria, the role of the high priest is understood to have more power than the role of the king.
>
> > And I am, as you know, a Jew; and Jerusalem is my country, in which there is erected the holy temple of the most high God. And I have kings for my grandfathers and for my ancestors, the greater part of whom have been called high priests, looking upon their royal power as inferior to their office as priests; and thinking that the high priesthood is as much superior to the power of a king, as God is superior to man; for that the one is occupied in rendering service to God, and the other has only the care of governing them.[a]
>
> a. Philo, *On the Embassy to Gaius* 278. Translation from Yonge, *Works of Philo*, 782.

Discussing Hasmonean high priests around the time of Pompey's invasion, the *Psalms of Solomon* blames them for provoking God to anger.[21] They "stole from the sanctuary of God,"[22] "walked on the place of sacrifice of the Lord," and "defiled the sacrifices."[23] Furthermore, "there was no sin they left undone in which they did not surpass the gentiles."[24] The *Psalms of Solomon* responds to the capture of Jerusalem by the Romans by highlighting the corruption of the temple and its sanctuary by the priests who seized power illegally.

These negative criticisms of the high priest, it should be noted, were not directed at the role itself but rather at what it had become by the first century. As Josephus demonstrates, Aaron remained the ideal high priest, and those modeled after him were revered. Philo is a good example of this, as he often writes about the ideal high priest in a positive way. The high priest is "a perfect man" and "is a sort of nature bordering on God, inferior indeed to him, but superior to man" (*On Dreams* 2.185, 188).

Frustration with the high priesthood during the Second Temple period may explain an emphasis in the literature on a future priest-king, sometimes connected with anticipation of Israel's messiah. The literature from Qumran indicates such an expectation. *Rule of the Community* contains a reference

---

21. *Pss. Sol.* 8.9. Translations of *Psalms of Solomon* are by R. B. Wright in *OTP* 2:639–70.
22. *Pss. Sol.* 8.11; see also 1.8; 2.3.
23. *Pss. Sol.* 8.12.
24. *Pss. Sol.* 8.13.

to "the coming of the prophet and the Messiahs of Aaron and Israel" (1QS 9.11).[25] Scholarship is divided on this passage, but there seems to be some expectation of a priestly messiah, possibly alongside a royal messiah.[26] In *Rule of the Congregation*, a future priestly figure enters the eschatological banquet before the Messiah and must bless the food before the Messiah can partake (1QSa 2.11–22).[27] Similarly, the *Testament of Levi* declares that "the Lord will raise up a new priest" (18.2). This new priest will have kingly characteristics ("His star shall rise to heaven like a king"; 18.3), and his priesthood will last forever (18.8).[28]

Melchizedek emerges in Second Temple literature within discussions of an eternal priesthood and an expected messiah. Several writers, such as Josephus and Philo, discuss Melchizedek while retelling the biblical narrative of Genesis 14.[29] He is presented as an early—sometimes the very first—high priest but also as one having a royal position. From the Qumran literature, 11QMelchizedek understands Melchizedek as an eschatological figure who carries out God's judgment and deliverance. There is no emphasis on his priesthood, although it does appear to portray Melchizedek as overseeing an eschatological Day of Atonement sacrifice.[30] This text offers a fully formed articulation of Melchizedek as a future priestly figure bringing God's judgment in the end times.

The high priest served an important function in the cultic life of ancient Israel, and his significance and tasks developed over time. The Old Testament offers details of the responsibilities of the high priest—which included being the only individual allowed in the holy of holies on the Day of Atonement. The high priest functioned as a mediator between Israel and Yahweh, offering sacrifices on the people's behalf and often being God's mouthpiece to the nation. Aaron was the first and ideal high priest, and this role continued into the Second Temple period. By the first century, the high priesthood had a more distinct political function under the occupation of the Roman Empire. The perceived corruption of the high priesthood likely contributed to a growing expectation of a future priest who would serve a royal and a messianic role and who would have an eternal priesthood. In some circles the

---

25. Translations in this section are from J. Charlesworth, *Dead Sea Scrolls*.

26. On the discussion of this passage, see Attridge, "How the Scrolls Impacted Scholarship on Hebrews," esp. 341.

27. Several other documents from Qumran point to the expectation of a future priestly messiah figure alongside a royal figure. For a discussion of these texts, see Mason, *"You Are a Priest Forever,"* 83–111.

28. Translation by H. C. Kee in *OTP* 1:794.

29. See Josephus, *Ant.* 1.179–81; Philo, *On the Embassy to Gaius* 3.79–82.

30. See Mason, *"You Are a Priest Forever,"* 184.

figure of Melchizedek was viewed as a precursor for this coming, everlasting priest-king.

The High Priest in the New Testament

The high priest appears numerous times in the Gospels and Acts, usually as the leader of the Jewish people and in opposition to Jesus and Paul. In the Gospels of Matthew, Mark, and John, Jesus is led before Caiaphas, the high priest, during his trial. Matthew and Mark describe the interaction between Jesus and the high priest, resulting in Jesus being accused of blasphemy and sentenced to death. An interesting encounter occurs in Acts 23 when Paul unknowingly insults the high priest. After identifying his mistake, Paul states, "I did not realize, brothers, that he was high priest; for it is written, 'You shall not speak evil of a leader of your people'" (Acts 23:5). In these narrative accounts, the high priest functions as the leader of the Jewish people. We see little of his cultic responsibilities or his role as a messenger of God.

Jesus as Priest

Our earliest Christian documents do not use priestly imagery for Jesus. Jesus's crucifixion is described as an atoning sacrifice in Paul's Letters and the Synoptic Gospels (see esp. Matt. 26:26–29; Rom. 5:6–8; 2 Cor. 5:14–15; 1 Thess. 5:9–10), but Jesus himself is not explicitly labeled a priest. However, some key texts in the Synoptic tradition may be infused with priestly significance. In a recent study, Nicholas Perrin has argued that in the Synoptic Gospels Jesus identifies his movement as a priestly movement and himself as the eschatological high priest.[31] Perrin reveals how key texts from the Gospels—the Lord's Prayer, Jesus's baptism, Jesus's teaching on the kingdom—are marked with cultic imagery. Further, Jesus and his disciples introduce practices that are "intended to mimic and ultimately supplant the liturgical practices of the Jerusalem cultus."[32] If Perrin is right—and this is yet to be seen—then the Synoptics portray Jesus as the eschatological high priest who initiates a new cultic reality.

In addition, Jesus is also probably depicted as functioning as a priest in the Gospel of John. Jesus's farewell prayer in John 17, sometimes referred to as his "high priestly prayer," seems to draw on priestly traditions—especially those surrounding the Day of Atonement.[33] Mirroring the responsibilities of

---

31. Perrin, *Jesus the Priest*.
32. Perrin, *Jesus the Priest*, 207.
33. On the history of the designation "high priestly prayer," see Attridge, "How Priestly Is the 'High Priestly Prayer' of John 17?"

the high priest on the Day of Atonement, Jesus first prays for himself (John 17:1–5; "Father, glorify your Son"), then for his disciples (17:6–19; "I am asking on their behalf. . . . Sanctify them"), and finally for those who will come to faith through the disciples (17:20–21). In Leviticus 16, the high priest is said to make atonement for himself, for his house, and for all of Israel (16:17). This structure, along with the language of "glorify" (δοξάζω) and "sanctify" (ἁγιάζω), points to a priestly backdrop for this prayer. However, while these allusions seem clear, the concept of Jesus as a high priest is not fully developed in the Gospel of John. In the words of Harold Attridge, the presentation of Jesus's prayer in John 17 "remains a gesture, not a fully developed symbolic reading of Jesus' actions in priestly terms."[34] For a fully developed articulation of Jesus as a high priest, we must turn to the Epistle to the Hebrews.

Jesus the High Priest in the Epistle to the Hebrews

The title "high priest" (ἀρχιερεύς) is first given to Jesus in Hebrews 2:17 and is used nine more times to describe him (3:1; 4:14–15; 5:5, 10; 6:20; 7:26; 8:1; 9:11). The author also uses the title "priest" (ἱερεύς) for Jesus, specifically within the context of quoting Psalm 110:4 (Heb. 5:6; 7:17, 20), sometimes qualifying it as "another priest" (7:11, 15) or "a great priest" (10:21).[35] In addition to the use of these titles, the author of Hebrews develops a sustained argument for the qualifications, benefits, and superior nature of Jesus's high priesthood.

In Hebrews 2:17–18, the author introduces the concept of Jesus as a high priest as a result of his becoming like his brothers and sisters—a reference to Jesus's incarnation. For the author, these two things are related to each other. Jesus, whom the author previously describes using divine attributes ("reflection of God's glory," "exact imprint of God's very being," "sustains all things by his powerful word"; Heb. 1:3), became human *so that* (ἵνα) he might be "a merciful and faithful high priest" (2:17). Hebrews then offers two benefits of this high priestly role: (1) Jesus offers a sacrifice of atonement for the sins of the people (2:17); and (2) he can help those in their present need (2:18). A main function of Israel's high priests, as we have seen, was to offer sacrifices for the sins of the people. In this section of Hebrews, Jesus is similarly described as "bringing many children to glory" (2:10) and as "the one who sanctifies" (2:11). Less pronounced in Jewish literature is the role that the high priest played in caring for his people. Certainly, the high priest was a leader of Israel, but Hebrews emphasizes that Jesus is a high priest who

---

34. Attridge, "How Priestly Is the 'High Priestly Prayer' of John 17?," 12.
35. Ellingworth, *Epistle to the Hebrews*, 183–84.

empathizes with the people he leads. Repeatedly, the author establishes that Jesus became "like his brothers and sisters" (2:17), shared flesh and blood with his people (2:14), and is "not ashamed to call them brothers and sisters" (2:11). Put succinctly in verse 18, "because [Jesus] himself was tested by what he suffered, he is able to help those who are being tested."

Hebrews 4:14–16 combines many of these same elements while transitioning into the next section about Jesus's high priestly requirements in chapter 5. A few aspects of this passage are worth highlighting. First, Jesus as a high priest is connected to the title "Son of God" (τὸν υἱὸν τοῦ θεοῦ). Jesus's sonship is vitally important for the author of Hebrews, and the title "Son of God" is used two other times for Jesus—both occurrences appear within references to Jesus's sacrifice and the punishment that those who profane his name will face (Heb. 6:6; 10:29). Elsewhere, Melchizedek is described as "resembling the Son of God" while also being a priest forever (7:3). Jesus is the Son of God, and this designation is combined with his high priestly role. Second, this passage stresses Jesus's ability to empathize with those he represents as high priest. Here the author includes the community as those Jesus serves: he is able to "sympathize with *our* weaknesses" and has "been tested as *we* are, yet without sin" (4:15). Third, this leads the author to encourage his audience to "approach the throne of grace with boldness" in order that they might find "help in time of need" (4:16).

Jesus's qualifications to be a high priest are taken up in Hebrews 5:1–10. In 5:1–4 the author provides a description of the biblical priesthood and establishes the requirements of a high priest: he must be able to empathize with those he represents (5:1–3) and must be called by God (5:4).[36] The author responds to these criteria in the reverse order. Through quotations from the Psalms, Hebrews shows that Jesus was specifically called by God to be a high priest. To make this calling clear, the author introduces the quotations by saying, "[Jesus] was appointed by the one who said to him . . ." In Hebrews 5:6, the author quotes from Psalm 110 and applies the words to Jesus: "You are a priest forever, according to the order of Melchizedek" (also 5:10; 6:20; 7:11, 15, 17). The author will develop the connection to Melchizedek, but here it is important to note that by quoting Psalm 110 as direct speech from God to Jesus, the author of Hebrews demonstrates Jesus's divine calling to be a high priest. In 5:7–10 the author responds to the second criterion by establishing that Jesus is able to empathize with those he represents as priest.

---

36. Attridge notes three general points of comparison being made between Heb. 5:1–4 and vv. 5–10, adding that the high priest's basic function is to make atonement for sin. This is expressed at the end of 5:1 and compared to Jesus's salvific function expressed in vv. 9–10 (Attridge, *Hebrews*, 143).

To do this, he emphasizes Jesus's humanity ("in the days of his flesh"; 5:7) and the weaknesses and vulnerability that come with the human condition.

Even though Jesus meets the two requirements for high priesthood laid out by the author of Hebrews, he fails to meet another important requirement: he is not a Levite. The author indirectly addresses this issue in Hebrews 5 by stating that each high priest is "called by God, just as Aaron was" (5:4). In demonstrating Jesus's divine calling in 5:6–7, the author indicates that this direct divine call is equivalent to that of the first and ideal high priest, Aaron. However, Jesus's lineage does appear to be a stumbling block for the author's argument. The author identifies this issue in chapter 7: "[Jesus] belonged to another tribe, from which no one has ever served at the altar. For it is evident that our Lord was descended from Judah, and in connection with that tribe Moses said nothing about priests" (7:13–14). The solution to this problem comes in the figure of Melchizedek.

Having already introduced Melchizedek by quoting Psalm 110:4 in chapter 5, the author now retells the account from Genesis of Abraham encountering this mysterious figure (Heb. 7:1–10). In his retelling, the author of Hebrews makes two important points regarding Melchizedek and his priesthood. First, since the biblical account tells us nothing of Melchizedek's genealogy or death, one can assume that his priesthood has no beginning or end (7:3). His priesthood is eternal, and he remains a priest forever. Second, drawing from the fact that Abraham (and through him the entire line of Levites) gave Melchizedek a tenth of his spoils, the author reasons that Melchizedek's priesthood is both prior to that of the Levites and superior to their priesthood (7:4–10). Thus, in the figure of Melchizedek, the author establishes a precedent for a priest outside of the Levitical line while arguing that such a priest is superior to the Levites. He then states that Jesus resembles Melchizedek and "has become a priest, not through a legal requirement concerning physical descent, but through the power of an indestructible life" (7:16).

Before moving further into the argument of Hebrews, we should pause here to consider the importance of Melchizedek for understanding the epistle's presentation of Jesus as a high priest. When Melchizedek emerges in Second Temple Jewish literature, there is a stress on his dual role as a priest-king. The author of Hebrews introduces Melchizedek as "king" when quoting from Genesis 4. He then contemplates the meaning of his name ("king of righteousness") and interprets the phrase "king of Salem" to mean "king of peace" (Heb. 7:2). Clearly, Hebrews sees Melchizedek as a priest-king, so it is curious that the author does not reflect much on Jesus's kingship. Jesus is given the title "Lord" in Hebrews (7:14; 13:20), but the author seems more interested in establishing his priesthood. By stating that Jesus is a priest "in the order of Melchizedek," the author reveals several aspects of Jesus's priesthood. First, he is a priest outside of the traditional lineage of the Levites. Like that of Melchizedek, Jesus's legitimacy as a high priest comes not from human descent but from the power of his indestructible life—a phrase much debated but that likely refers to his eternal nature.[37] This leads to the second aspect of Jesus's priesthood: his is an eternal priesthood. The notion that Melchizedek served as an eternal priest was already hinted at in Psalm 110. In Hebrews, Melchizedek is interpreted as having no beginning or end, and therefore his priesthood continues indefinitely. So too Jesus serves as a priest forever. Finally, through his connection to Melchizedek, Jesus has a priesthood that is superior to that of the Levitical priests. This is an important point for the author, and he spends the bulk of chapters 8–10 developing this idea.

The author of Hebrews goes to great lengths to show how Jesus's high priesthood is superior to that of the Levitical priests. His argument is introduced in the statement "Now if perfection had been attainable through the Levitical priesthood, . . . what further need would there have been to speak of another priest arising according to the order of Melchizedek, rather than one according to the order of Aaron?" (Heb. 7:11). This statement implies that there was an irreconcilable weakness with the Levitical priesthood and that to overcome this weakness a new priest had to arise outside of that line. This sets off a series of arguments for how Jesus's priesthood is more effectual than the Levitical priesthood. Whereas the total number of Levite high priests is high (since no priest lived forever), Jesus the high priest is not susceptible to death and so his priesthood continues forever (7:24). Unlike the earlier high priests, Jesus does not need to offer sacrifices for his own sins—a necessary offering for the Levites (7:27). The author further argues that Jesus, the superior high priest, made his offering at an altar superior to that of the Levites. Jesus is the exalted high priest, currently situated in heaven in the heavenly sanctuary (8:2). The Levitical priests offered their sacrifices in the earthly sanctuary, one made by human hands. According to the author of Hebrews, this earthly sanctuary is a "mere copy of the true one" (9:24). Jesus, by comparison, did not enter an earthly sanctuary but rather entered "heaven itself." He offered his sacrifice directly in the presence of God and continues to intercede for his people from the heavenly throne.

In Hebrews, not only is Jesus a superior priest who offered a sacrifice at a superior altar, but his sacrifice is also of a vastly superior nature compared to the Levitical priests' sacrifices. Whereas the earlier priests offered the blood of animals to God, Jesus offered his own blood. The author writes, "For if the

37. See Moffitt, *Atonement and the Logic of Resurrection*, 203.

blood of goats and bulls . . . sanctifies those who have been defiled so that their flesh is purified, how much more will the blood of Christ, who through the eternal Spirit offered himself without blemish to God, purify our conscience from dead works to worship the living God!" (Heb. 9:13–14). The sacrificial blood of animals is limited, since "it is impossible for the blood of bulls and goats to take away sins" (10:4). Animal blood does not permanently remove sin—priests needed to repeatedly make sacrifices for the people's sins. In comparison, Jesus offered a single sacrifice "for all time" and "once and for all" (10:10, 12). Put simply: "By a single offering he has perfected for all time those who are sanctified" (10:14). According to Hebrews, Jesus is not only our great high priest but also our superior sacrifice.

In summary, Jesus's high priesthood is superior to that of earthly high priests because he does not share their limitations (Heb. 7:27–28), he serves in the true sanctuary (8:1–2; 9:11–12, 24), and he offered a once-and-for-all sacrifice of himself (7:27; 9:25–28; 10:12). There is no longer any need for repeated sacrifices by human high priests on behalf of God's people. In his one-time sacrifice of himself and offering of his blood before the heavenly altar, Jesus as a high priest secured permanent atonement for the people of God.[38] Now seated at the right hand of God's throne, Jesus continues to serve as our high priest and mediate on our behalf.

Contribution to New Testament Christology

The title and presentation of Jesus as high priest offer several important contributions to our examination of how the New Testament writers understood his person and nature. First, for the early church, Jesus fulfilled the expectation of a future priest who would finally bring atonement for God's people. The priesthood was an integral aspect of Israel's worship life, with the priests serving as mediators between God and the people. As the early Christians began to move away from these cultic practices—likely because the temple in Jerusalem had been destroyed—the image of Jesus as a final and eternal high priest satisfied the need for heavenly mediation. In addition, early Christians understood this priestly function of Jesus as an important component of his identity as the Messiah—something well established within Jewish literature. The anticipated figure of the Messiah, while often understood in diverse ways, was commonly understood to have both kingly (Davidic) and priestly aspects.

---

38. For a survey of recent research on atonement in Hebrews, see Laansma, Guthrie, and Westfall, *So Great a Salvation*.

> ## JESUS THE HIGH PRIEST IN *1 CLEMENT*
>
> Written at the end of the first century, *1 Clement* is one of the earliest Christian apocryphal writings that we have. In this passage its author reflects on Jesus as our high priest and is clearly influenced by the Epistle to the Hebrews.
>
>> This is the way, dear friends, in which we found our salvation, namely Jesus Christ, the high priest of our offerings, the benefactor and helper of our weakness. Through him we look steadily into the heights of heaven; through him we see as in a mirror his faultless and transcendent face; through him the eyes of our hearts have been opened; through him our foolish and darkened mind springs up into the light; through him the Master has willed that we should taste immortal knowledge, for he, being the radiance of his majesty, is as much superior to angels as the name he has inherited is more excellent.[a]
>
> a. *1 Clement* 36.1-2. Translation from Holmes, *Apostolic Fathers*, 93.

Second, the identification of Jesus as an eternal high priest in Hebrews also highlights Jesus's role as the sacrifice made on behalf of the people. Jesus is not only the great high priest but also the perfect sacrifice that—unlike the sacrifices of calves or goats—obtains eternal redemption (Heb. 9:12). In chapter 6 we examined the tradition of the Passover Lamb and how Jesus is portrayed as a substitutionary sacrifice on behalf of his people as a means of forgiveness of sins. Whereas the image of Jesus as the sacrificial lamb invokes the Passover, the imagery in Hebrews is more reminiscent of the Day of Atonement festival and sacrifice. Both images—Jesus as the Passover Lamb and as the Day of Atonement sacrifice—present Jesus's sacrificial offering of himself on behalf of his people as achieving complete and lasting sanctification (10:10).

Third, Jesus's role as high priest articulates an understanding of his current ministry in the lives of God's people. Hebrews is clear that Jesus's sacrifice and offering of his blood was a one-time event that permanently atones for the sins of those he represents, but Jesus is also an active high priest who continues to intercede for his people. He is a high priest who can empathize with his people and continues to help them in their distress from his heavenly position. Jesus is a priest forever, exalted at the right hand of the Father. This notion of Jesus's ongoing ministry is expressed elsewhere in the New Testament apart from his role as high priest. Paul similarly identifies Jesus's present place at the right hand of God as a position from which he continues to intercede for his people (Rom. 8:34). The author of 1 John encourages the recipients that "we have an advocate with the Father, Jesus Christ the righteous; and he is the atoning sacrifice for our sins, and not for ours only but also for the sins of the whole world" (1 John 2:1–2).

Finally, we return to where this chapter began. The notion of Jesus as a merciful and eternal priest was meant to inspire confidence and motivation for a community in crisis. Amid affliction and possibly fearing for their safety, this community was encouraged to envision Jesus as he truly is: seated at the right hand of the Father, ready to intercede on their behalf. This image of Jesus as a high priest gives believers confidence that their sins have been forgiven by Jesus's once-and-for-all sacrifice. This is not some distant or impersonal high priest. Jesus, who became just like his human brothers and sisters, can empathize with their weaknesses and will one day lead them on to glory.

CONCLUSION
JESUS AS GOD

Introduction

A Christology of the New Testament may be written in various ways. We chose to emphasize titles and traditions. We recognize that there are other types of Christologies, including narrative Christologies that emphasize Jesus as he is depicted in discursive passages in the New Testament. Nevertheless, the tradition-based approach of this volume allowed us to focus on a number of titles and attributions that play a significant role in the New Testament as a means of arriving at a full appreciation of who Jesus is. In this conclusion we wish to bring some of the major findings of this volume together to form an overall perspective on what we know about Jesus and about the Christology of the New Testament. To do this, we place discussion of New Testament Christology within its current context so our study can be properly situated.

History of the Question(s) of Christology

Questions regarding the Godhead were present in Christianity from its earliest times. Christians focused on several major issues, including the members of the Godhead and their relationships to one another. A discussion of the rise of trinitarianism and its relationship to the New Testament goes beyond the scope of this conclusion. We here focus on discussions regarding Jesus—who he is and how he is related to God the Father. Some of the earliest controversies were christological; that is, the question of the nature of Jesus as the

Christ was debated.[1] Was Jesus divine or not? His divinity is often defined in different ways—for example, ontologically, functionally, or relationally—sometimes to the point of confusing the issue unnecessarily by straying into more philosophical rather than biblical categories. Throughout this book, we defined Jesus's divinity this way: he is one with the God of Israel.

The debate over Jesus's divinity reached one of its high points during the period of the church councils, as early Christians attempted to define more clearly Jesus's nature and his relation to God the Father. To oversimplify, two major positions emerged. The first was what we might call the divine nature view, and the second was the developmental view. The first view, which came to represent Christian orthodoxy, held that there is a divine nature that encompasses the eternal preexistence of the Son and the Father. This orthodox view was cemented at the Council of Chalcedon (451 CE), which declared that Christ is one person in two natures—fully divine and fully human. The second view, the developmental view, took a number of different forms but is often equated with various adoptionist Christologies. Adoptionists believe that somewhere along a temporal continuum, the man Jesus either was "adopted by" or came to be viewed as God, whether at his baptism, transfiguration, resurrection, or ascension, or sometime after that, at some point in the early church. The classic articulation of adoptionism comes from Paul of Samosata, a third-century bishop and theologian. He contended that Jesus was human by nature but that at his baptism the divine *Logos* indwelled him. As a result, Jesus was adopted into divinity and tasked with the status of Messiah, but he did not possess full divinity because he was not eternally begotten.[2]

The Council of Nicaea of 325 CE asserted that Jesus Christ is of the same essence as God the Father. The word that was used to describe this relationship is ὁμοούσιος (same in being/essence), a word not found in the Greek New Testament.[3] There were many other disputes in the church, and the Nicene Creed (later amended at Constantinople in 381 and then finalized in 451) did not entirely solve the issue, as questions remained regarding what it meant for Jesus to be both fully human and fully God. However, Western orthodox Christianity generally accepted Jesus Christ's divinity as Christian doctrine until it was subjected to intense critical scrutiny beginning especially in the nineteenth century with the development of historical-critical scholarship

---

1. See Norris, *Christological Controversy*.
2. See Plantinga, Thompson, and Lundberg, *Introduction to Christian Theology*, esp. 236.
3. See Schaff, *Creeds of the Greek and Latin Churches*, 60 (for the Nicene Creed of 325 CE), 57–58 (for the Niceno-Constantinopolitan Creed of 381 CE), and 62–63 (for the Chalcedonian Creed of 451 CE). All use ὁμοούσιος. The last also uses the word of Christ's relationship with humanity, an issue we do not discuss here.

and the rise of theological liberalism. A focal point of such discussion was the history of religions school, which reflected many of the major tenets of both the historical-critical method and liberalism's emphasis on Jesus as a highly ethical and representative human being. The result was serious doubt about the reliability of the New Testament and its depiction of Jesus, including the traditionally held belief that Jesus is a divine being with the same essence as God who existed in relationship with God the Father since before his incarnation.

Two Important Questions regarding Christology

Discussion of the nature of Jesus, including the depiction of his nature in the New Testament, has been a major issue in New Testament study since at least the nineteenth century. A variety of explanations of how Jesus emerged as not just *a* god but *the* God have been proposed. Some of these explanations affirm and reinforce the traditional orthodox view, and others reflect the developmental view mentioned above. The developmental view brought to the fore two important questions regarding Christology: *When* did Jesus become divine, and *how* did Jesus become divine? These are two separate but interrelated questions that require examination. The traditional orthodox answer is that Jesus was preexistent as God, shared God's nature from eternity, and had that nature when he was incarnated. For those who raised these two questions in light of the rise of historical criticism and theological liberalism, there were a range of answers.

As for the question of *when* Jesus became God, contemporary scholarship has offered two major answers. One is the reaffirmation of Jesus as God. Not only has this been the traditional orthodox view, but it has also been reiterated by some contemporary New Testament scholars.[4] The other major response has been the revival of forms of developmentalism that focus on a time when Jesus "became" God. These forms of adoptionism contend that Jesus became God, at least in the view of his followers, at some time after his birth as a human. Adoptionism continues to remain significant within theological views that wish to identify a time when Jesus was designated as having a divine nature, some arguing that such recognition may have happened shortly after Jesus's life and others that it was a more prolonged process—some seeing signs of adoptionism in the New Testament itself (e.g., Rom. 1:3–4 or John's Gospel as the earliest text with a divine Christology)

---

4. See, e.g., Gathercole, *Pre-existent Son*; Bird, *Jesus the Eternal Son*. See also, but from a slightly less traditional view, O'Neill, *Who Did Jesus Think He Was?*; and O'Neill, *Point of It All*.

and others seeing the process as occurring within the post–New Testament early church.[5]

The other question concerns *how* Jesus came to be God. One of the factors often overlooked in this discussion is that the two questions of when and how Jesus became God have a significant amount of overlap. Even some of those who provide explanations of how Jesus became God with a view to arguing for a high Christology in the New Testament sometimes seem to reflect a view that does not necessarily endorse Jesus's preexistence and that apparently has some developmental characteristics. Hence, such views—because they do not overtly accept that Jesus was preexistently God, only that there are plausible reasons why early Christians, especially Jewish Christians, were willing to accept Jesus as having a divine nature or essence—are themselves arguably forms of adoptionism.

Numerous attempts to describe how Jesus came to be God emerged within critical scholarship, many of them influenced by scholars associated with the history of religions school of the late nineteenth and early twentieth centuries.[6] The history of religions school, a loose association of scholars, was interested in the study of religion, with Christianity being one prominent example of it. Hence, they wished to study Christianity in terms of its being a product of human development in which Jesus was elevated to the position of God by his later followers. To do so, they looked to cultural influences that might account for such a development. In other words, what is sometimes referred to as the "high" Christology of the New Testament, in which Jesus is seen to be one with God, is the result of an upgrading of an earlier low Christology. One of the best-known of these theories is that of the German scholar Wilhelm Bousset, who argued that the Christology of the New Testament was the result of the development of a Hellenistic and gentile Lord-cult, one that was heavily influenced by the divinization of rulers that spread from the east to the west and that heavily influenced emerging Christianity.[7]

This resurgence of adoptionism has led some to identify a new history of religions school. One of the major differences is that this approach looks more to Judaism than it does to Hellenism, as its earlier forms did. The scholar who led the way in this new history of religions approach was the Tübingen

---

5. Some major modern adoptionists are Bultmann, *Theology of the New Testament*; Dunn, *Christology in the Making*; Dunn, *Did the First Christians Worship Jesus?*; Casey, *From Jewish Prophet to Gentile God*; Ehrman, *How Jesus Became God*; Litwa, *Iesus Deus*; and Kirk, *Man Attested by God*. Many others could be mentioned.

6. See Baird, *History of New Testament Research*, 222–53.

7. Bousset, *Kyrios Christos*. Cf. Reitzenstein, *Hellenistic Mystery-Religions*, for an alternative developmental hypothesis that emerged from the history of religion.

New Testament scholar Martin Hengel, who found an early high Christology in the New Testament.[8] His work, beginning in the early 1970s, has had a major impact on this discussion as well as giving warrant for exploration of the topic. Even for those who accept the traditional position, a recurring question is how a Jewish man, within Jewish monotheism, could come to be recognized as God without threatening that monotheism. Several proposals that have been made in recent scholarship are worth mentioning briefly.

The first stage in recent discussion seems to have begun with recognition of the role of angels and other intermediary figures within Judaism. These theories flourished mostly in the 1980s and 1990s. However, angels have been a constant in the debate and have readily been discussed, and their role has been suggested as a means of explaining the emergence of a high Christology. There was a precedent for competing divine figures on the basis of mediating figures, such as angels, who were in God's presence and acted on God's behalf.[9] However, because such mediating figures do not seem to have risen to the level of identity with God in being or action and were not worshiped as such, this theory has not satisfied most scholars and has been disputed.

Three other views on how Jesus came to be understood as God without disrupting monotheism have been argued with more sustaining power. The first of these is divine identity, proposed by Richard Bauckham.[10] According to this proposal, there is an identity created within the New Testament so that what is said of God's unique identity in a monotheistic Jewish context is also said of Jesus Christ's identity. Bauckham points to Jesus's sovereignty, exaltation, being given the divine name, worship, and preexistence as indicating that this is not just a functional or even simply an "ontic" Christology but one of genuine identity. The second view concerns the devotion and worship given to Jesus that is reserved elsewhere in the Bible only for God. This position is argued by Larry Hurtado.[11] This view has been identified with what

---

8. Hengel, *Between Jesus and Paul*, esp. 30–47, "Christology and the New Testament Chronology" (1972); Hengel, *Cross of the Son of God*; Hengel, *Studies in Early Christology*, as well as other studies. See Pitts, "Martin Hengel, the New Tübingen School, and the Study of Christian Origins."

9. Some of the major advocates for such a position are Fossum, *Name of God and the Angel of the Lord*; Stuckenbruck, *Angel Veneration and Christology*; Carrell, *Jesus and the Angels*; Fletcher-Louis, *Luke–Acts*; and Gieschen, *Angelomorphic Christology*.

10. Bauckham, *Jesus and the God of Israel*, esp. 1–59 for "God Crucified," which first appeared in 1998; followed in differing ways by Capes, *Old Testament Yahweh Texts in Paul's Christology*; Capes, *Divine Christ*; and Fletcher-Louis, *Jesus Monotheism*. A further extension by means of what is called prosopological exegesis is found in Bates, *Hermeneutics of the Apostolic Proclamation*; and Bates, *Birth of the Trinity*.

11. Hurtado has written on this topic more than any other scholar we know of. His works include *One God, One Lord*; *At the Origins of Christian Worship*; *Lord Jesus Christ*; *How*

was early called a binitarian and later called a dyadic perspective—that is, for early Christians, two beings were identified and worshiped as God, as is evidenced in such things as prayers, confessions, baptism, the Lord's Supper, early Christian hymns, and prophecy. The third and final of these views is the relational view of Chris Tilling.[12] On the basis of the previous exegetical work of Gordon Fee,[13] as well as of Bauckham and Hurtado, Tilling argues that the relationship between Israel and its God, Yahweh, is arguably the same kind of relationship as between Christ followers and the risen Christ. Tilling's emphasis is on a relational equivalence that demonstrates how believers viewed Christ in light of their Jewish monotheistic heritage.

Even though each of these proposals has been subject to criticism, not least by those holding competing views, there is much merit to each of them because each arrives at a divine or high Christology. As several have observed, however, even though each of these three major positions (and similar views) ultimately endorses a high Christology, ostensibly providing a basis for it within Jewish monotheism, the relationship of such belief to the figure of Jesus and his own realization of his divinity is open to further examination. Those views that focus on Paul, such as those of Hengel and Tilling, would need to see a high Christology by the time of Paul's writings and thus some of the earliest writings in the New Testament; others would not necessarily need to find it that early, but could posit such a realization by the next generation of Christian believers.

The Contribution of This Study

In this volume we have not directly addressed these questions regarding when and how Jesus became God. Instead, we have indirectly addressed both questions by discussing various christological titles and how they are understood in the New Testament. We have found a high Christology to be present in all the titles we have examined, to varying degrees. Many of these are titles used of Jesus with the possibility that Jesus himself saw himself as divine in light of what these titles represented. Whereas "lord" is a term used of respect for another, it can be expanded in its semantic scope to indicate one worthy of supreme respect, even God. Jesus is called Lord in the same way that God is often called Lord in the Greek Old Testament and in opposition to divinized

---

on Earth Did Jesus Become a God?; Ancient Jewish Monotheism and Early Christian Jesus-Devotion, including his first essay on the topic from 1979; Honoring the Son.

12. Tilling, *Paul's Divine Christology*, with a helpful critical summary of the previous positions (11–62), as well as a helpful foreword by Douglas Campbell (x–xix).

13. Fee, *Pauline Christology*.

rulers in the Hellenistic world. Paul recognizes this and speaks of Jesus in this way in his letters, but Jesus is also depicted in the Gospels in this way. Jesus is Lord as Yahweh is Lord.

Just as the Old Testament and the prophets pronounced God's word to his people, calling out their unfaithfulness and provoking them to covenant faithfulness, so Jesus calls people to repentance. However, Jesus is not just another prophet; he is *the* prophet anticipated by John the Baptist and expected after the type of Moses. The eschatological prophet was to arrive and bring the end of days, as the crowds recognized and as Jesus himself expresses in his proclamations.

The Son of Man is a humanlike figure in the Old Testament who is depicted in a unique way in the book of Daniel. Following after the Danielic Son of Man, Jesus in the New Testament not only performs human functions in his earthly ministry and suffers at the hands of others; he also fulfills God's eschatological purposes by declaring his coming enthronement by God to judge humanity. The Son of Man exercises the same divine functions as God himself.

There was a surprising abundance of "Son of God" language in the ancient world. Hellenistic rulers were given this title, and it is used in the Old Testament and in later Jewish literature such as that found at Qumran. Jesus uses this same language to refer to himself and to his Father, God, as do others. While this language is adoptionist in the extra–New Testament sources, in that human beings such as emperors are declared or proclaimed "sons of god," Jesus is depicted in the New Testament as being the Son of God from before creation and thus not a created or adopted being. The New Testament declares that Jesus, as the Son of God, enjoys a unique filial relationship in which he is of one being with God himself.

The Suffering Servant of Isaiah represents one who suffers on behalf of the people. In the New Testament, Jesus is the Suffering Servant who offers himself as an atoning substitutionary sacrifice and who, through suffering, restores the covenant relationship between God and his people. Jesus appears to have seen himself as this anointed sufferer, beginning with his public ministry and baptism and continuing to its end, including the Last Supper. The Suffering Servant is a messianic figure who offers himself as a ransom for the redemption of God's people.

Jesus is depicted as the Passover Lamb primarily in John's Gospel and Revelation. One of the major themes in the Gospel of John is Jesus as the Lamb who offers himself as an atoning sacrifice for the people. However, in Revelation he is not just the Lamb who was slain, like the Suffering Servant, for the people, but the apocalyptic Divine Lamb who sits on the divine throne in judgment.

Ancient Israel knew many messianic figures, both secular and sacred. There was varied expectation of a Davidic king, a prophet, and a priest who would one day fulfill God's eschatological purposes. Many false messiahs appeared on the scene, attempting to liberate the Jewish people. Most of them were rejected by these same people. Jesus was anticipated as the Christ from before the outset of his ministry and then not only was embraced in this messianic role by his followers such as Paul, who never lost sight of Jesus as the Messiah, but also embraced it himself.

Other titles were probably later attributed to Jesus Christ as a means of recognizing who he is and the role he plays in God's salvific economy. The title "Savior" is found in both ancient Jewish and Hellenistic writings and is attributed to a variety of figures who were expected to deliver their people and establish peace for them. This title was probably used by some of the earliest interpreters of the person and work of Jesus, especially Paul, who sees Jesus as the one who atoned for the sins of his people.

Paul also depicts Jesus as the second or last Adam, although the relationship of Jesus to Adam is also described elsewhere in the New Testament. Adam is an intriguing figure in Israelite religion and early Judaism. The word אדם (*adam* or human) indicates humanity before it is bifurcated into man and woman. The first Adam is depicted as the one who introduces sin and death into the world. However, all that Adam did to create the human sinful condition, Jesus Christ countered through his death and resurrection, providing a means for humanity to be reconciled to God.

The Word concept is found in both Jewish and Greco-Roman contexts. On the one hand, it represents God's creative word, while on the other it may indicate the rational principle that governs the universe, with a range of views in between. John's Gospel depicts the preincarnate Word that becomes the man Jesus. Even those who argue for a low Christology in the New Testament until the writing of the book of John are usually willing to concede that John describes the human Jesus as the incarnate Word, with preexistence and divine being together.[14]

Finally, Jesus the high priest takes upon himself one of the important cultic roles within ancient Judaism. The Jewish high priest was inaugurated in the Pentateuch and continued to function, although with politically and religiously motivated fluctuations in role, until the time of Jesus. The high priest occupied a central position in Israelite worship, but in other traditions he was often seen as a priest-king, like Melchizedek. Jesus appropriates for himself many of the functions of the high priest in his own ministry, including

---

14. See Dunn, *Christology in the Making*, 213–50.

his teaching on the kingdom of God. Jesus's role as high priest is especially important in the book of Hebrews, with its substitutionary theology in which Jesus replaces the cult practices and is seen as a priest forever, seated at God's right hand and interceding for his people.

This short summary shows that there are several titles used of Jesus that point to his divinity. We have tried to show that the depiction of Jesus as divine was not a later event but a reflection of how Jesus was seen by his first and earliest followers. These titles occur within the New Testament, whether in the letters of Paul or in the Johannine literature or elsewhere. Thus the question of *when* Jesus became God must, we think, be answered this way: it did not just happen early—for example, in the earliest writings of the New Testament—but was a fact built into the very fabric of the New Testament from its earliest traditions. Some of these titles go back to Jesus himself, and if not to Jesus then to his earliest associates and followers, from John the Baptist to Paul and other New Testament writers.

The question of *how* Jesus came to be God is arguably a potentially misleading question to ask, especially in light of what we have just stated above. The question may imply that there was a movement from Jesus not being God to Jesus becoming God. The New Testament, we believe, never depicts a time when Jesus was not God or not thought of as God. As our study has illustrated, the cultural and religious background of the christological titles is grounded in a complex of both Jewish and Greco-Roman concepts, none of which can be categorically excluded as pertinent and informative and forming the background for Jesus and the New Testament writers' usage. Further, the religious world of first-century Judaism was fully immersed within the highly complex Greco-Roman religious world. This was a world of Jewish monotheism, but this monotheism was embedded within and forced to compete with other religions with multiple gods of different sorts. The Roman pantheon was full of anthropomorphic gods, not least the divinized Hellenistic rulers and the emperors. We may agree that in some instances Jesus is identified with God, that other instances show devotion to him as a god, and that still other instances reveal a parallel relationship of God to Jesus with Yahweh to his people. However, we believe that even that formulation of the issue is too narrow. The question is how Jesus, who we believe was God from before his incarnation, as is shown and believed in the New Testament, could be recognized and depicted as God, and how even Jesus could recognize himself as God in the Jewish environment in which he lived.

As a result, we describe our contribution to New Testament Christology as one of selective divine precedent or appropriation of sacred tradition. In other words, the New Testament authors—and we must also include

Jesus—selectively appropriated precedents within Judaism and the Greco-Roman sacred traditions in their depiction of Jesus as divine. Therefore, it is not necessarily appropriate or needed, we believe, to ask the question of how Jesus became divine. The question is, how did Jesus and his followers express his divinity by means of these sacred traditions? They did so by finding appropriate language, wordings, depictions, figures, and characters within the complex religious world of the first century to express their personal (in the case of Jesus) and confessional (in the case of his followers) belief that Jesus never *became* God because he already *was* God. They needed to express his divine character in appropriate ways that would resonate with the world in which they lived. Each of the titles we studied in this book contributes to a high Christology by revealing, sometimes forcefully and sometimes more subtly, that Jesus is seen by the New Testament writers—and even sometimes by himself—as having divine character and functioning in redemptive and salvific ways for God's people. The New Testament authors did not subordinate Jesus to the limitations of the titles they appropriated. Rather, by drawing upon the precedents of sacred traditions, they provided a suitable language for a fuller and more resonant expression of the unique divine character of Jesus.

BIBLIOGRAPHY

Abegg, Martin G., and Craig A. Evans. "Messianic Passages in the Dead Sea Scrolls." In *Qumran-Messianism*, edited by James H. Charlesworth, Hermann Lichtenberger, and Gerbern S. Oegema, 191–203. Tübingen: Mohr Siebeck, 1998.

Achtemeier, Paul J. *1 Peter*. Hermeneia. Minneapolis: Fortress, 1996.

Allen, Leslie C. *Psalms 101–150*. WBC 21. Waco: Word, 1983.

Allison, Dale C., Jr. *Constructing Jesus: Memory, Imagination, and History*. Grand Rapids: Baker Academic, 2010.

———. "Matthew's First Two Words." In *Studies in Matthew: Interpretation Past and Present*, 157–62. Grand Rapids: Baker Academic, 2005.

———. *The New Moses: A Matthean Typology*. Minneapolis: Fortress, 1993.

Attridge, Harold W. *Hebrews*. Hermeneia. Philadelphia: Fortress, 1989.

———. "How Priestly Is the 'High Priestly Prayer' of John 17?" *CBQ* 75 (2013): 1–14.

———. "How the Scrolls Impacted Scholarship on Hebrews." In *Essays on John and Hebrews*, 331–55. WUNT 264. Tübingen: Mohr Siebeck, 2010.

———. "Philo and John: Two Riffs on One Logos." *SPhiloA* 17 (2005): 103–17.

Aune, David E. *Prophecy in Early Christianity and the Ancient Mediterranean World*. Grand Rapids: Eerdmans, 1983.

———. *Revelation*. 3 vols. WBC 52. Dallas: Word, 1999.

Baird, William. *History of New Testament Research*. Vol. 2, *From Jonathan Edwards to Rudolf Bultmann*. Minneapolis: Fortress, 2003.

Barrett, C. K. "The Background of Mark 10:45." In *New Testament Essays: Studies in Memory of Thomas Walter Mason*, edited by A. J. B. Higgins, 1–18. Manchester: Manchester University Press, 1959.

———. *The First Epistle to the Corinthians*. 2nd ed. BNTC. London: A&C Black, 1971.

———. *From First Adam to Last: A Study in Pauline Theology*. New York: Scribner, 1962.

———. *The Gospel according to St. John: An Introduction with Commentary and Notes on the Greek Text*. 2nd ed. Philadelphia: Westminster, 1978.

———. "The Old Testament in the Fourth Gospel." *JTS* 48 (1947): 155–69.

Bates, Matthew W. *The Birth of the Trinity: Jesus, God, and Spirit in New Testament and Early Christian Interpretation of the Old Testament*. Oxford: Oxford University Press, 2015.

———. "A Christology of Incarnation and Enthronement: Romans 1:3–4 as Unified, Nonadoptionist, and Nonconciliatory." *CBQ* 77 (2015): 107–27.

———. *The Hermeneutics of the Apostolic Proclamation: The Center of Paul's Method of Scriptural Interpretation*. Waco: Baylor University Press, 2012.

———. *Salvation by Allegiance Alone: Rethinking Faith, Works, and the Gospel of Jesus the King*. Grand Rapids: Baker Academic, 2017.

Bauckham, Richard. *The Climax of Prophecy: Studies on the Book of Revelation*. London: T&T Clark, 1993.

———. "The Divinity of Jesus Christ in the Epistle to the Hebrews." In *The Epistle to the Hebrews and Christian Theology*, edited by Richard Bauckham et al., 15–36. Grand Rapids: Eerdmans, 2009.

———. *Jesus and the God of Israel: "God Crucified" and Other Studies on the New Testament's Christology of Divine Identity*. Grand Rapids: Eerdmans, 2008.

———. "Jesus and the Wild Animals (Mark 1:13): A Christological Image for an Ecological Age." In *Jesus of Nazareth, Lord and Christ: Essays on the Historical Jesus and New Testament Christology*, edited by Joel B. Green and Max Turner, 3–21. Grand Rapids: Eerdmans, 1994.

———. *The Jewish World around the New Testament: Collected Essays I*. WUNT 233. Tübingen: Mohr Siebeck, 2008. Reprint, Grand Rapids: Baker Academic, 2010.

Beale, G. K. *The Book of Revelation*. NIGTC. Grand Rapids: Eerdmans, 1999.

Beard, Mary, John North, and Simon Price. *Religions of Rome*. 2 vols. Cambridge: Cambridge University Press, 1998.

Beasley-Murray, George. *The Book of Revelation*. Rev. ed. NCB. Grand Rapids: Eerdmans, 1981.

———. *John*. 2nd ed. WBC 36. Waco: Word, 1999.

Beattie, Gillian. *Women and Marriage in Paul and His Early Interpreters*. LNTS 296. London: T&T Clark, 2005.

Bellinger, William H., Jr., and William R. Farmer, eds. *Jesus and the Suffering Servant: Isaiah 53 and Christian Origins*. Harrisburg, PA: Trinity Press International, 1998.

Bernard, John H. *A Critical and Exegetical Commentary on the Gospel according to St. John*. Edited by A. H. McNeile. 2 vols. ICC. Edinburgh: T&T Clark, 1928.

Best, Ernest. *1 Peter*. NCB. London: Oliphants, 1971.

Bigg, Charles. *A Critical and Exegetical Commentary on the Epistles of Peter and Jude*. 2nd ed. ICC. Edinburgh: T&T Clark, 1910.

Bird, Michael F. *Are You the One Who Is to Come? The Historical Jesus and the Messianic Question*. Grand Rapids: Baker Academic, 2009.

———. *Jesus Is the Christ: The Messianic Testimony of the Gospels*. Downers Grove, IL: IVP Academic, 2012.

———. *Jesus the Eternal Son: Answering Adoptionist Christology*. Grand Rapids: Eerdmans, 2017.

Blomberg, Craig L. "Matthew." In *Commentary on the New Testament Use of the Old Testament*, edited by G. K. Beale and D. A. Carson, 1–110. Grand Rapids: Baker Academic, 2007.

Bond, Helen K. *Caiaphas: Friend of Rome and Judge of Jesus?* Louisville: Westminster John Knox, 2004.

Borchert, Gerald L. *John*. 2 vols. NAC. Nashville: Broadman & Holman, 1996–2002.

———. "Passover and the Narrative Cycles in John." In *Perspectives on John: Method and Interpretation in the Fourth Gospel*, edited by Robert B. Sloan and Mikeal C. Parsons, 303–16. Lewiston, NY: Edwin Mellen, 1993.

Borgen, Peder. *Bread from Heaven: An Exegetical Study of the Concept of Manna in the Gospel of John and the Writings of Philo*. NovTSup 10. Leiden: Brill, 1965.

Borsch, Frederick Houk. *The Christian and the Gnostic Son of Man*. London: SCM, 1970.

Bousset, Wilhelm. *Kyrios Christos: A History of the Belief in Christ from the Beginnings of Christianity to Irenaeus*. Translated by John E. Steely. Nashville: Abingdon, 1970.

Boxall, Ian. *The Revelation of Saint John*. BNTC. Peabody, MA: Hendrickson, 2006.

Boyarin, Daniel. "Gospel of the Memra: Jewish Binitarianism and the Prologue of John." *HTR* 94 (2001): 243–84.

Braun, Herbert. "The Meaning of New Testament Christology." In *God and Christ: Existence and Province*, edited by Robert W. Funk with Gerhard Ebeling, 89–127. New York: Harper & Row, 1968.

Brayford, Susan. *Genesis*. Septuagint Commentary Series. Leiden: Brill, 2007.

Bremmer, Jan N. *Greek Religion*. 2nd ed. Cambridge: Cambridge University Press, 2021.

Brennan, Nick. *Divine Christology in the Epistle to the Hebrews: The Son as God*. LNTS 656. London: T&T Clark, 2021.

Brooke, George J. "Luke–Acts and the Qumran Scrolls." In *Luke's Literary Achievement: Collected Essays*, edited by C. M. Tuckett, 72–90. JSNTSup 116. Sheffield: Sheffield Academic, 1995.

Brown, Jeannine K. "Creation's Renewal in the Gospel of John." *CBQ* 72 (2010): 275–90.

Brown, Raymond E. *The Birth of the Messiah: A Commentary on the Infancy Narratives in the Gospels of Matthew and Luke.* New updated ed. New York: Doubleday, 1999.

———. *The Gospel according to John.* 2 vols. AB 29–29A. Garden City, NY: Doubleday, 1966–70.

Bruce, F. F. *The Epistles to the Colossians, to Philemon, and to the Ephesians.* Grand Rapids: Eerdmans, 1984.

Brunt, P. A., and J. M. Moore. *Res Gestae Divi Augusti: The Achievements of the Divine Augustus.* Oxford: Oxford University Press, 1967.

Bultmann, Rudolf. *The Gospel of John: A Commentary.* Translated by G. R. Beasley-Murray et al. Philadelphia: Westminster, 1971.

———. *Theology of the New Testament.* Translated by Kendrik Grobel. 2 vols. London: SCM, 1952–55.

Burkert, Walter. *Greek Religion.* Translated by John Raffan. Cambridge, MA: Harvard University Press, 1985.

Burkett, Delbert R. *The Son of Man Debate: A History and Evaluation.* Cambridge: Cambridge University Press, 1999.

———. *The Son of Man in the Gospel of John.* JSNTSup 56. Sheffield: JSOT Press, 1991.

Burnet, John. *Early Greek Philosophy.* 3rd ed. London: A&C Black, 1920.

Burrows, E. W. "Did John the Baptist Call Jesus 'The Lamb of God'?" *ExpTim* 85 (1973–74): 245–47.

Byrne, Brendan. "Jesus as Messiah in the Gospel of Luke: Discerning a Pattern of Correction." *CBQ* 65 (2003): 80–95.

Capes, David B. *The Divine Christ: Paul, the Lord Jesus, and the Scriptures of Israel.* Grand Rapids: Baker Academic, 2018.

———. "New Testament Christology." In *The State of New Testament Studies: A Survey of Recent Research*, edited by Scot McKnight and Nijay K. Gupta, 161–81. Grand Rapids: Baker Academic, 2019.

———. *Old Testament Yahweh Texts in Paul's Christology.* WUNT 2/47. Tübingen: Mohr Siebeck, 1992.

Caragounis, Chrys C. *The Son of Man: Vision and Interpretation.* WUNT 38. Tübingen: Mohr Siebeck, 1986.

Carey, G. L. "The Lamb of God and Atonement Theories." *TynBul* 32 (1981): 97–122.

Carrell, Peter R. *Jesus and the Angels: Angelology and the Christology of the Apocalypse of John.* SNTSMS 95. Cambridge: Cambridge University Press, 1997.

Carroll, John T. *Luke: A Commentary.* Louisville: Westminster John Knox, 2012.

Carson, D. A. *The Gospel according to John.* PNTC. Grand Rapids: Eerdmans, 1991.

Casey, P. M. *From Jewish Prophet to Gentile God: The Origins and Development of New Testament Christology.* Cambridge: James Clarke, 1991.

———. *The Solution to the "Son of Man" Problem*. LNTS 343. New York: T&T Clark, 2007.

Charlesworth, James H. "Can We Discern the Composition Date of the Parables of Enoch?" In *Enoch and the Messiah Son of Man: Revisiting the Book of Parables*, edited by Gabriele Boccaccini, 450–68. Grand Rapids: Eerdmans, 2007.

———, ed. *The Dead Sea Scrolls*. 10 vols. Tübingen: Mohr Siebeck, 1994–2018.

Charlesworth, M. P. *Documents Illustrating the Reigns of Claudius and Nero*. Cambridge: Cambridge University Press, 1939.

Childs, Brevard S. *Biblical Theology of the Old and New Testaments: Theological Reflection on the Christian Bible*. Minneapolis: Fortress, 1992.

———. *Exodus: A Commentary*. London: SCM, 1974.

Cirafesi, Wally V. "The Priestly Portrait of Jesus in the Gospel of John in the Light of 1QS, 1QSa and 1QSb." *JGRChJ* 8 (2011–12): 83–105.

Cohick, Lynn. "Philippians and Empire." In *Jesus Is Lord, Caesar Is Not: Evaluating Empire in New Testament Studies*, edited by Scot McKnight and Joseph B. Modica, 166–82. Downers Grove, IL: IVP Academic, 2013.

Collins, Adela Yarbro. "Establishing the Text: Mark 1:1." In *Texts and Contexts: The Function of Biblical Texts in Their Textual and Situational Contexts*, edited by Tord Fornberg and David Hellholm, 111–27. Oslo: Scandinavian University Press, 1995.

Collins, Adela Yarbro, and John J. Collins. *King and Messiah as Son of God: Divine, Human, and Angelic Messianic Figures in Biblical and Related Literature*. Grand Rapids: Eerdmans, 2008.

Collins, John J. *Daniel*. Hermeneia. Minneapolis: Fortress, 1993.

———. *The Scepter and the Star: The Messiahs of the Dead Sea Scrolls and Other Ancient Literature*. New York: Doubleday, 1995.

———. "The 'Son of God' Text from Qumran." In *From Jesus to John: Essays on Jesus and New Testament Christology in Honour of Marinus de Jonge*, edited by Martinus C. de Boer, 65–82. JSNTSup 84. Sheffield: Sheffield Academic, 1993.

Cousar, Charles B. *Philippians and Philemon: A Commentary*. Louisville: Westminster John Knox, 2009.

Cranfield, C. E. B. *The Gospel according to Saint Mark*. Cambridge: Cambridge University Press, 1959.

Crowe, Brandon D. *The Last Adam: A Theology of the Obedient Life of Jesus in the Gospels*. Grand Rapids: Baker Academic, 2017.

Cullmann, Oscar. *The Christology of the New Testament*. Translated by Shirley C. Guthrie and Charles A. M. Hall. Rev. ed. London: SCM, 1963.

Culpepper, R. Alan. *Anatomy of the Fourth Gospel: A Study in Literary Design*. Philadelphia: Fortress, 1983.

Dahl, Nils Alstrup. "The Messiahship of Jesus in Paul" (1953). In *The Crucified Messiah*, 37–47. Minneapolis: Augsburg, 1974.

Daise, Michael A. *Feasts in John*. WUNT 2/229. Tübingen: Mohr Siebeck, 2007.

———. *Quotations in John: Studies on Jewish Scripture in the Fourth Gospel*. LNTS 610. London: T&T Clark, 2020.

Davids, Peter H. *The First Epistle of Peter*. NICNT. Grand Rapids: Eerdmans, 1990.

Davies, Margaret. *Rhetoric and Reference in the Fourth Gospel*. Sheffield: JSOT Press, 1992.

Davies, W. D. *The Gospel and the Land: Early Christianity and Jewish Territorial Doctrine*. Berkeley: University of California Press, 1974.

Davis, Carl J. *The Name and Way of the Lord: Old Testament Themes, New Testament Christology*. JSNTSup 129. Sheffield: Sheffield Academic, 1996.

de Boer, Martinus C. *The Defeat of Death: Apocalyptic Eschatology in 1 Corinthians 15 and Romans 5*. JSNTSup 22. Sheffield: JSOT Press, 1988.

Deferrari, Roy J., trans. *Eusebius Pamphili: Ecclesiastical History, Books 1–5*. FC 19. Washington, DC: Catholic University of America Press, 1953.

Deissmann, Adolf. *Bible Studies*. Translated by A. J. Grieve. 2nd ed. Edinburgh: T&T Clark, 1909.

———. *Light from the Ancient East: The New Testament Illustrated by Recently Discovered Texts of the Graeco-Roman World*. Translated by Lionel R. M. Strachan. Rev. ed. London: Hodder & Stoughton, 1927.

Diels, Hermann. *Die Fragmente der Vorsokratiker*. Vol. 1. Edited by Walther Kranz. Berlin: Weidmannsche Verlagsbuchhandlung, 1960.

Dodd, C. H. *The Interpretation of the Fourth Gospel*. Cambridge: Cambridge University Press, 1953.

———. "Jesus as Teacher and Prophet." In *Mysterium Christi*, edited by George K. A. Bell and G. Adolf Deissmann, 53–66. London: Longmans, Green, 1931.

Driver, S. R., and A. D. Neubauer, trans. *The Fifty-Third Chapter of Isaiah according to the Jewish Interpreters*. Oxford: James Parker, 1877.

Dunn, James D. G. "Adam and Christ." In *Reading Paul's Letter to the Romans*, edited by Jerry Sumney, 125–38. Atlanta: Society of Biblical Literature, 2010.

———. "Christ, Adam, and Preexistence." In *Where Christology Began: Essays on Philippians 2*, edited by Ralph P. Martin and Brian J. Dodd, 74–83. Louisville: Westminster John Knox, 1998.

———. *Christology in the Making: A New Testament Inquiry into the Origins of the Doctrine of the Incarnation*. 2nd ed. Grand Rapids: Eerdmans, 1989.

———. *Did the First Christians Worship Jesus? The New Testament Evidence*. London: SPCK, 2010.

———. *The Epistles to the Colossians and Philemon: A Commentary on the Greek Text*. NIGTC. Grand Rapids: Eerdmans, 1996.

———. *Jesus Remembered*. Christianity in the Making 1. Grand Rapids: Eerdmans, 2003.

Edwards, J. Christopher. *The Ransom Logion in Mark and Matthew: Its Reception and Its Significance for the Study of the Gospels*. WUNT 2/327. Tübingen: Mohr Siebeck, 2012.

Ehrenberg, Victor, and A. H. M. Jones, eds. *Documents Illustrating the Reigns of Augustus and Tiberius*. 2nd ed. Oxford: Clarendon, 1955.

Ehrman, Bart D. *How Jesus Became God: The Exaltation of a Jewish Preacher from Galilee*. New York: HarperOne, 2014.

Elledge, Roderick. *Use of the Third Person for Self-Reference by Jesus and Yahweh: A Study of Illeism in the Bible and Ancient Near Eastern Texts and Its Implications for Christology*. LNTS 575. London: Bloomsbury, 2017.

Ellingworth, Paul. *The Epistle to the Hebrews*. NIGTC. Grand Rapids: Eerdmans, 1993.

Engberg-Pedersen, Troels. *John and Philosophy: A New Reading of the Fourth Gospel*. Oxford: Oxford University Press, 2017.

Evans, Craig A. "The Historical Jesus and the Deified Christ: How Did the One Lead to the Other?" In *The Nature of Religious Language: A Colloquium*, edited by Stanley E. Porter, 47–67. Roehampton Institute London Papers 1. Sheffield: Sheffield Academic, 1996.

———. *Jesus and His Contemporaries: Comparative Studies*. AGJU 25. Leiden: Brill, 1995.

———. *Mark 8:27–16:20*. WBC 34B. Nashville: Nelson, 2001.

———. "Mark's Incipit and the Priene Calendar Inscription: From Jewish Gospel to Greco-Roman Gospel." *JGRChJ* 1 (2000): 67–81.

———. "Messianic Hopes and Messianic Figures in Late Antiquity." *JGRChJ* 3 (2006): 9–40.

———. "Prophet, Sage, Healer, Messiah, and Martyr: Types and Identities of Jesus." In *Handbook for the Study of the Historical Jesus*, edited by Tom Holmén and Stanley E. Porter, 1217–43. Leiden: Brill, 2010.

———. *Word and Glory: On the Exegetical and Theological Background of John's Prologue*. JSNTSup 89. Sheffield: Sheffield Academic, 1993.

Falls, Thomas B., trans. *Saint Justin Martyr: The First Apology, the Second Apology, Dialogue with Trypho, Exhortations to the Greeks, Discourse to the Greeks, The Monarchy or The Rule of God*. FC 6. Washington, DC: Catholic University of America Press, 1948.

Fantin, Joseph D. *The Lord of the Entire World: Lord Jesus, a Challenge to Lord Caesar?* NTM 31. Sheffield: Sheffield Phoenix, 2011.

Fee, Gordon D. *The First Epistle to the Corinthians*. Rev. ed. NICNT. Grand Rapids: Eerdmans, 2014.

———. *Pauline Christology: An Exegetical-Theological Study*. Peabody, MA: Hendrickson, 2007. Reprint, Grand Rapids: Baker Academic, 2013.

———. *Paul's Letter to the Philippians*. NICNT. Grand Rapids: Eerdmans, 1995.
Feldmeier, Reinhard. *The First Letter of Peter*. Waco: Baylor University Press, 2008.
Ferguson, John. *The Religions of the Roman Empire*. Ithaca, NY: Cornell University Press, 1970.
Fewster, Gregory P. "The Philippians 'Christ Hymn': Trends in Critical Scholarship." *CurBR* 13 (2015): 191–206.
Fitzmyer, Joseph A. "The Contribution of Qumran Aramaic to the Study of the New Testament." Reprinted in *A Wandering Aramean: Collected Aramaic Essays*, 85–113. Chico, CA: Scholars Press, 1979.
———. *First Corinthians*. AYB 32. New Haven: Yale University Press, 2008.
———. *The Gospel according to Luke: Introduction, Translation, and Notes*. 2 vols. Garden City, NY: Doubleday, 1981–85.
———. "κύριος, etc." In *Exegetical Dictionary of the New Testament*, edited by Horst Balz and Gerhard Schneider, 2:328–31. 3 vols. Grand Rapids: Eerdmans, 1990–93.
Fletcher-Louis, Crispin. *Jesus Monotheism*. Vol. 1, *Christological Origins: The Emerging Consensus and Beyond*. Eugene, OR: Cascade Books, 2015.
———. *Luke–Acts: Angels, Christology and Soteriology*. WUNT 2/94. Tübingen: Mohr Siebeck, 1997.
Fossum, Jarl E. *The Name of God and the Angel of the Lord: Samaritan and Jewish Concepts of Intermediation and the Origin of Gnosticism*. Reprint, Waco: Baylor University Press, 2017.
France, R. T. *Jesus and the Old Testament: His Application of Old Testament Passages to Himself and His Mission*. Downers Grove, IL: InterVarsity, 1971.
Fredriksen, Paula. *Paul: The Pagans' Apostle*. New Haven: Yale University Press, 2017.
Freed, Edwin D. *Old Testament Quotations in the Gospel of John*. NovTSup 11. Leiden: Brill, 1965.
Gafni, Isaiah. "High Priest." In *Encyclopedia Judaica*, edited by Fred Skolnik, 9:99–100. 22 vols. Detroit: Macmillan, 2007.
Garland, David E. *1 Corinthians*. BECNT. Grand Rapids: Baker Academic, 2003.
Gathercole, Simon J. *The Pre-existent Son: Recovering the Christologies of Matthew, Mark, and Luke*. Grand Rapids: Eerdmans, 2006.
———. "The Son of Man in Mark's Gospel." *ExpTim* 115, no. 11 (2004): 366–72.
———. "Wisdom (Personified)." In *The Eerdmans Dictionary of Early Judaism*, edited by John J. Collins and Daniel C. Harlow, 1339. Grand Rapids: Eerdmans, 2010.
Gieschen, Charles A. *Angelomorphic Christology: Antecedents and Early Evidence*. Reprint, Waco: Baylor University Press, 2017.
Gilbert, Gary. "Roman Propaganda and Christian Identity in the Worldview of Luke–Acts." In *Contextualizing Acts: Lukan Narrative and Greco-Roman Discourse*,

edited by T. Penner and C. Vander Stichele, 233–56. SBLSS 20. Atlanta: Society of Biblical Literature, 2003.

Glasson, Thomas F. *Moses in the Fourth Gospel*. SBT 40. London: SCM, 1963.

Goldingay, John E. *Daniel*. WBC 30. Dallas: Word, 1987.

Goppelt, Leonhard. *A Commentary on 1 Peter*. Translated by John E. Alsup. Edited by Ferdinand Hahn. Grand Rapids: Eerdmans, 1993.

———. *Theology of the New Testament*. Edited by Jürgen Roloff. Translated by John E. Alsup. 2 vols. Grand Rapids: Eerdmans, 1981–82.

Gordley, Matthew E. *New Testament Christological Hymns: Exploring Texts, Contexts, and Significance*. Downers Grove, IL: IVP Academic, 2018.

Goulder, Michael D., ed. *Incarnation and Myth: The Debate Continued*. London: SCM, 1979.

Gray, George Buchanan. *Sacrifice in the Old Testament: Its Theory and Practice*. Oxford: Clarendon, 1925.

Green, Joel B. *The Gospel of Luke*. NICNT. Grand Rapids: Eerdmans, 1997.

Gregorovius, Ferdinand. *The Emperor Hadrian: A Picture of the Graeco-Roman World in His Time*. Translated by M. E. Robinson. London: Macmillan, 1898.

Grigsby, Bruce H. "The Cross as an Expiatory Sacrifice in the Fourth Gospel." *JSNT* 5 (1982): 51–80.

Grindheim, Sigurd. *Christology in the Synoptic Gospels: God or God's Servant?* New York: T&T Clark, 2012.

———. *God's Equal: What Can We Know about Jesus' Self-Understanding in the Synoptic Gospels?* LNTS 446. New York: T&T Clark, 2011.

Grudem, Wayne. *1 Peter*. TNTC. London: Inter-Varsity, 1988.

Guelich, Robert A. *Mark 1–8:26*. WBC 34A. Dallas: Word, 1989.

Gurtner, Daniel. *Introducing the Pseudepigrapha of Second Temple Judaism*. Grand Rapids: Baker Academic, 2020.

Hahn, Ferdinand. *The Titles of Jesus in Christology: Their History in Early Christianity*. London: Lutterworth, 1969.

Hannah, Darrell D. "The Elect Son of Man of the *Parables of Enoch*." In *"Who Is This Son of Man?": The Latest Scholarship on a Puzzling Expression of the Historical Jesus*, edited by Larry Hurtado and Paul Owen, 130–58. LNTS 390. London: T&T Clark, 2011.

Harris, J. Rendel. "The Early Christian Interpretation of the Passover." *ExpTim* 38 (1926–27): 88–90.

———. *The Origin of the Prologue to St. John's Gospel*. Cambridge: Cambridge University Press, 1917.

Hawthorne, Gerald F. "A New English Translation of Melito's Paschal Homily." In *Current Issues in Biblical and Patristic Interpretation*, edited by Gerald F. Hawthorne, 147–74. Grand Rapids: Eerdmans, 1975.

Hays, Richard B. *Echoes of Scripture in the Gospels*. Waco: Baylor University Press, 2016.

Hengel, Martin. *Between Jesus and Paul*. Translated by John Bowden. Philadelphia: Fortress, 1983.

———. *The Cross of the Son of God*. Translated by John Bowden. London: SCM, 1986.

———. *Judaism and Hellenism: Studies in Their Encounter in Palestine during the Early Hellenistic Period*. Translated by John Bowden. Philadelphia: Fortress, 1974.

———. *Studies in Early Christology*. Edinburgh: T&T Clark, 1995.

———. *Studies in the Gospel of Mark*. Translated by John Bowden. Philadelphia: Fortress, 1985.

Hengel, Martin, with Daniel P. Bailey. "The Effective History of Isaiah 53 in the Pre-Christian Period." In *The Suffering Servant: Isaiah 53 in Jewish and Christian Sources*. Edited by Peter Stuhlmacher and Bernd Janowski, 75–146. Grand Rapids: Eerdmans, 2004.

Hengel, Martin, and Anna Maria Schwemer. *Jesus and Judaism*. Translated by Wayne Coppins. Waco: Baylor University Press, 2019.

Henrichs-Tarasenkova, Nina. *Luke's Christology of Divine Identity*. LNTS 542. London: Bloomsbury, 2016.

Hess, Richard S. "The Image of the Messiah in the Old Testament." In *Images of Christ: Ancient and Modern*, edited by Stanley E. Porter, Michael A. Hayes, and David Tombs, 22–33. Roehampton Institute London Papers 2. Sheffield: Sheffield Academic, 1997.

Hick, John, ed. *The Myth of God Incarnate*. London: SCM, 1977.

Holmes, Michael, ed. *The Apostolic Fathers: Greek Texts and English Translations*. 3rd ed. Grand Rapids: Baker Academic, 2007.

Hooker, Morna D. *Jesus and the Servant: The Influence of the Servant Concept of Deutero-Isaiah in the New Testament*. London: SPCK, 1959.

———. *The Signs of a Prophet: The Prophetic Actions of Jesus*. Reprint, Eugene, OR: Wipf & Stock, 2010 [1997].

———. *The Son of Man in Mark: A Study of the Background of the Term "Son of Man" and Its Use in St. Mark's Gospel*. London: SPCK, 1967.

Horbury, William. *Jewish Messianism and the Cult of Christ*. London: SCM, 1998.

Hoskins, Paul M. "Deliverance from Death by the True Passover Lamb: A Significant Aspect of the Fulfillment of the Passover in the Gospel of John." *JETS* 52, no. 2 (2009): 285–99.

———. "Freedom from Slavery to Sin and the Devil: John 8:31–47 and the Passover Theme of the Gospel of John." *TJ* 31 (2010): 47–63.

Hoskyns, Edwyn C. *The Fourth Gospel*. Edited by Francis Noel Davey. 2 vols. London: Faber and Faber, 1947.

Howard, James Keir. "Passover and Eucharist in the Fourth Gospel." *SJT* 20 (1967): 329–37.

Hurtado, Larry W. *Ancient Jewish Monotheism and Early Christian Jesus-Devotion: The Context and Character of Christological Faith.* Waco: Baylor University Press, 2017.

———. *At the Origins of Christian Worship: The Context and Character of Earliest Christian Devotion.* Carlisle: Paternoster, 1999.

———. *Honoring the Son: Jesus in Earliest Christian Devotional Practice.* Bellingham, WA: Lexham, 2018.

———. *How on Earth Did Jesus Become a God? Historical Questions about Earliest Devotion to Jesus.* Grand Rapids: Eerdmans, 2005.

———. "Lord." In *Dictionary of Paul and His Letters*, edited by Gerald F. Hawthorne, Ralph P. Martin, and Daniel G. Reid, 560–69. Downers Grove, IL: InterVarsity, 1993.

———. *Lord Jesus Christ: Devotion to Jesus in Earliest Christianity.* Grand Rapids: Eerdmans, 2003.

———. *One God, One Lord: Early Christian Devotion and Ancient Jewish Monotheism.* London: SCM, 1988.

Hurtado, Larry W., and Paul L. Owen, eds. *"Who Is This Son of Man?": The Latest Scholarship on a Puzzling Expression of the Historical Jesus.* LNTS 390. New York: T&T Clark, 2011.

Jamieson, R. B. *The Paradox of Sonship: Christology in the Epistle to the Hebrews.* Downers Grove, IL: IVP Academic, 2021.

Janowski, Bernd, and Peter Stuhlmacher, eds. *The Suffering Servant: Isaiah 53 in Jewish and Christian Sources.* Translated by Daniel P. Bailey. Grand Rapids: Eerdmans, 2004.

Jeremias, Joachim. "Ἀδάμ." In *TDNT* 1:141–43.

———. *The Eucharistic Words of Jesus.* Translated by Norman Perrin. Philadelphia: Fortress, 1966.

Jipp, Joshua W. *Christ Is King: Paul's Royal Ideology.* Minneapolis: Fortress, 2015.

———. *The Messianic Theology of the New Testament.* Grand Rapids: Eerdmans, 2020.

Jobes, Karen. *1 Peter.* BECNT. Grand Rapids: Baker Academic, 2005.

Johnson, Luke Timothy. *The Acts of the Apostles.* SP 5. Collegeville, MN: Liturgical Press, 1992.

———. *Miracles: God's Presence and Power in Creation.* Interpretation. Louisville: Westminster John Knox, 2018.

———. *Prophetic Jesus, Prophetic Church: The Challenge of Luke–Acts to Contemporary Christians.* Grand Rapids: Eerdmans, 2011.

Johnson, Marshall D. *The Purpose of the Biblical Genealogies with Special Reference to the Setting of the Genealogies of Jesus.* SNTSMS 8. Cambridge: Cambridge University Press, 1969.

Joynes, Christine E. "Elijah." In *The Eerdmans Dictionary of Early Judaism*, edited by John J. Collins and Daniel C. Harlow, 577–78. Grand Rapids: Eerdmans, 2010.

Kaiser, Walter C. "The Identity and Mission of the Servant of the Lord." In *The Gospel according to Isaiah 53: Encountering the Suffering Servant in Jewish and Christian Theology*, edited by Darrell L. Bock and Mitch Glaser, 87–107. Grand Rapids: Kregel, 2012.

Keener, Craig S. *Acts: An Exegetical Commentary.* 4 vols. Grand Rapids: Baker Academic, 2012–15.

———. *A Commentary on the Gospel of Matthew.* Grand Rapids: Eerdmans, 1999.

———. *1 Peter: A Commentary.* Grand Rapids: Baker Academic, 2021.

———. *The Gospel of John: A Commentary.* 2 vols. Peabody, MA: Hendrickson, 2003. Reprint, Grand Rapids: Baker Academic, 2012.

Keil, C. F., and F. Delitzsch. *Commentary on the Old Testament in Ten Volumes.* Reprint, Grand Rapids: Eerdmans, 1983.

Kelly, J. N. D. *A Commentary on the Epistles of Peter and Jude.* BNTC. London: A&C Black, 1969.

Kerényi, C. *The Heroes of the Greeks.* Translated by H. J. Rose. London: Thames and Hudson, 1959.

Kim, Seyoon. "Jesus, Sayings of." In *Dictionary of Paul and His Letters*, edited by Gerald F. Hawthorne, Ralph P. Martin, and Daniel G. Reid, 474–92. Downers Grove, IL: InterVarsity, 1993.

Kirk, J. R. Daniel. *A Man Attested by God: The Human Jesus of the Synoptic Gospels.* Grand Rapids: Eerdmans, 2016.

———. *Unlocking Romans: Resurrection and the Justification of God.* Grand Rapids: Eerdmans, 2008.

Kleinknecht, H. "The Logos in the Greek and Hellenistic World." In *TDNT* 4:77–91.

Koester, Craig R. *Hebrews.* AB 36. New York: Doubleday, 2001.

———. "'Savior of the World' (John 4:42)." *JBL* 109 (1990): 665–80.

———. *The Word of Life: A Theology of John's Gospel.* Grand Rapids: Eerdmans, 2008.

Kraeling, Carl H. *Anthropos and Son of Man: A Study in the Religious Syncretism of the Hellenistic Orient.* New York: Columbia University Press, 1927.

Kreider, Glenn R. "Jesus the Messiah as Prophet, Priest, and King." *BSac* 176 (2019): 174–87.

Kreitzer, Larry J. "Adam and Christ." In *Dictionary of Paul and His Letters*, edited by Gerald F. Hawthorne, Ralph P. Martin, and Daniel G. Reid, 9–15. Downers Grove, IL: InterVarsity, 1993.

———. *Jesus and God in Paul's Eschatology.* JSNTSup 19. Sheffield: JSOT Press, 1987.

Kümmel, Werner Georg. *The Theology of the New Testament according to Its Major Witnesses: Jesus–Paul–John.* Translated by John E. Steely. Nashville: Abingdon, 1973.

Laansma, Jon C., George H. Guthrie, and Cynthia Long Westfall, eds. *So Great a Salvation: A Dialogue on the Atonement in Hebrews.* LNTS 516. London: T&T Clark, 2019.

Ladd, George Eldon. *A Commentary on the Revelation of John.* Grand Rapids: Eerdmans, 1972.

Lane, William L. *The Gospel according to Mark.* NICNT. Grand Rapids: Eerdmans, 1974.

Lattey, C., ed. *Texts Illustrating Ancient Ruler-Worship.* London: SPCK, 1924.

Lee, Dorothy. "Paschal Imagery in the Gospel of John: A Narrative and Symbolic Reading." *Pacifica* 24 (2011): 13–28.

Lessing, R. Reed. "Isaiah's Servants in Chapters 40–55: Clearing Up the Confusion." *Concordia Journal* 37 (2011): 130–34.

Levine, Lee I. *Jerusalem: Portrait of the City in the Second Temple Period (538 BCE–70 CE).* Philadelphia: Jewish Publication Society, 2002.

Levison, John R. "Adam and Eve." In *The Eerdmans Dictionary of Early Judaism*, edited by John J. Collins and Daniel C. Harlow, 300–302. Grand Rapids: Eerdmans, 2010.

———. *Portraits of Adam in Early Judaism from Sirach to 2 Baruch.* Sheffield: Sheffield Academic, 1988.

Lewis, Naphtali, and Meyer Reinhold, eds. *Roman Civilization.* Vol. 2. New York: Columbia University Press, 1955.

Liebeschuetz, J. H. W. G. *Continuity and Change in Roman Religion.* Oxford: Clarendon, 1979.

Lindars, Barnabas. *The Gospel of John.* NCB. London: Marshall, Morgan & Scott, 1981.

———. *New Testament Apologetic: The Doctrinal Significance of the Old Testament Quotations.* London: SCM, 1961.

Litwa, M. David. "Behold Adam: A Reading of John 19:5." *HBT* 32 (2010): 129–43.

———. *Iesus Deus: The Early Christian Depiction of Jesus as a Mediterranean God.* Minneapolis: Fortress, 2014.

———, trans. *Refutation of All Heresies.* Writings from the Greco-Roman World. Atlanta: SBL Press, 2016.

Loader, William. "Wisdom and Logos Traditions in Judaism and John's Christology." In *Reading the Gospel of John's Christology as Jewish Messianism*, edited by Benjamin E. Reynolds and Gabriele Boccaccini, 303–34. Leiden: Brill, 2018.

Longenecker, Richard N. *The Christology of Early Jewish Christianity.* London: SCM, 1970.

———. *Studies in Hermeneutics, Christology, and Discipleship*. NTM 3. Sheffield: Sheffield Phoenix, 2004.

Louw, Johannes P., and Eugene A. Nida. *Greek-English Lexicon of the New Testament Based on Semantic Domains*. 2 vols. New York: United Bible Societies, 1988.

Luter, A. B., Jr. "Savior." In *Dictionary of Paul and His Letters*, edited by Gerald F. Hawthorne, Ralph P. Martin, and Daniel G. Reid, 867–69. Downers Grove, IL: InterVarsity, 1993.

Malbon, Elizabeth Struthers. *Mark's Jesus: Characterization as Narrative Christology*. Waco: Baylor University Press, 2009.

Manson, T. W. *The Teaching of Jesus: Studies in Its Form and Content*. Cambridge: Cambridge University Press, 1967.

Marcus, Joel. *Mark 1–8*. AB 27. New York: Doubleday, 2000.

———. "Son of Man as Son of Adam." *RB* 110 (2003): 38–61.

Marshall, I. Howard. *The Epistles of John*. NICNT. Grand Rapids: Eerdmans, 1978.

———. *The Gospel of Luke*. NIGTC. Grand Rapids: Eerdmans, 1978.

———. *The Origins of New Testament Christology*. Downers Grove, IL: InterVarsity, 1976.

———. "The Synoptic 'Son of Man' Sayings in the Light of Linguistic Study." In *To Tell the Mystery: Essays on New Testament Eschatology in Honor of Robert H. Gundry*, edited by Thomas E. Schmidt and Moisés Silva, 72–94. JSNTSup 100. Sheffield: Sheffield Academic, 1994.

Mason, Eric F. *"You Are a Priest Forever": Second Temple Jewish Messianism and the Priestly Christology of the Epistle to the Hebrews*. STDJ 74. Leiden: Brill, 2008.

Matera, Frank J. *New Testament Christology*. Louisville: Westminster John Knox, 1999.

Mattingly, H. *Augustus to Vitellius*. Vol. 1 of *Coins of the Roman Empire in the British Museum*. London: British Museum, 1965.

McCaulley, Esau. *Sharing in the Son's Inheritance: Davidic Messianism and Paul's Worldwide Interpretation of the Abrahamic Land Promise in Galatians*. LNTS 608. London: T&T Clark, 2019.

McCrum, M., and A. G. Woodhead, eds. *Select Documents of the Principates of the Flavian Emperors Including the Year of Revolution A.D. 68–96*. Cambridge: Cambridge University Press, 1966.

McDonough, Sean M. *Christ as Creator: Origins of a New Testament Doctrine*. Oxford: Oxford University Press, 2009.

McGrath, Alister E. *Christian Theology: An Introduction*. 3rd ed. Oxford: Blackwell, 2001.

———, ed. *The Christian Theology Reader*. 5th ed. Malden, MA: Wiley Blackwell, 2017.

McKnight, Scot. *Jesus and His Death: Historiography, the Historical Jesus, and Atonement Theory*. Waco: Baylor University Press, 2005.

———. *The Letter to the Colossians.* NICNT. Grand Rapids: Eerdmans, 2018.

———. *Sermon on the Mount.* The Story of God Bible Commentary. Grand Rapids: Zondervan, 2013.

McKnight, Scot, and Joseph B. Modica, eds. *Jesus Is Lord, Caesar Is Not: Evaluating Empire in New Testament Studies.* Downers Grove, IL: IVP Academic, 2013.

McWhirter, Jocelyn. *Rejected Prophets: Jesus and His Witnesses in Luke–Acts.* Minneapolis: Fortress, 2013.

Mead, James K. "The Biblical Prophets in Historiography." In *Ancient Israel's History: An Introduction to Issues and Sources,* edited by Bill T. Arnold and Richard S. Hess, 262–87. Grand Rapids: Baker Academic, 2014.

Meeks, Wayne A. *The Prophet-King: Moses Traditions and the Johannine Christology.* NovTSup 14. Leiden: Brill, 1967.

Meier, John P. *A Marginal Jew: Rethinking the Historical Jesus.* Vol. 2, *Mentor, Message, and Miracles.* New Haven: Yale University Press, 1994.

Mettinger, Tryggve N. D. *A Farewell to the Servant Songs: A Critical Examination of an Exegetical Axiom.* Lund: C. W. K. Gleerup, 1983.

Metzger, Bruce M. *A Textual Commentary on the Greek New Testament.* 2nd ed. Stuttgart: Deutsche Bibelgesellschaft, 1994.

Michaels, J. Ramsey. *1 Peter.* WBC 49. Waco: Word, 1988.

———. *The Gospel of John.* NICNT. Grand Rapids: Eerdmans, 2010.

Middleton, Paul. *The Violence of the Lamb: Martyrs as Agents of Divine Judgement in the Book of Revelation.* LNTS 586. London: T&T Clark, 2018.

Milgrom, Jacob. *Leviticus 17–22: A New Translation with Introduction and Commentary.* AYB 3A. New Haven: Yale University Press, 2000.

Miller, Donald G. *On This Rock: A Commentary on First Peter.* PTMS 34. Allison Park, PA: Pickwick, 1993.

Minear, Paul S. *To Heal and to Reveal: The Prophetic Vocation according to Luke.* New York: Seabury, 1976.

Moffitt, David M. *Atonement and the Logic of Resurrection in the Epistle to the Hebrews.* NovTSup 141. Leiden: Brill, 2011.

Moloney, Francis J. *The Johannine Son of Man.* Rome: LAS, 1978.

Moo, Douglas J. *The Old Testament in the Gospel Passion Narratives.* Sheffield: Almond Press, 1983.

Morris, Leon. *The Apostolic Preaching of the Cross.* 3rd ed. Grand Rapids: Eerdmans, 1965.

———. "Salvation." In *Dictionary of Paul and His Letters,* edited by Gerald F. Hawthorne, Ralph P. Martin, and Daniel G. Reid, 858–62. Downers Grove, IL: InterVarsity, 1993.

Moule, C. F. D. *The Origin of Christology.* Cambridge: Cambridge University Press, 1977.

Moulton, James Hope. *Prolegomena*. Vol. 1 of *A Grammar of New Testament Greek*. 3rd ed. Edinburgh: T&T Clark, 1908.

Mounce, Robert H. *The Book of Revelation*. Rev. ed. NICNT. Grand Rapids: Eerdmans, 1998.

Murphy-O'Connor, Jerome. "The Essenes and Their History." *RB* 81 (1974): 215–44.

Myers, Alicia D. "Isaiah 42 and the Characterization of Jesus in Matthew 12:17–21." In *"What Does Scripture Say?": Studies in the Function of Scripture in Early Judaism and Christianity*. Vol. 1, *Synoptic Gospels*, edited by Craig A. Evans and H. Daniel Zacharias, 70–89. LNTS 469. London: T&T Clark, 2012.

———. "Jesus the Son of God in John's Gospel: The Life-Making Logos." In *Portraits of Jesus in John's Gospel*, edited by Craig Koester, 141–55. LNTS 589. London: T&T Clark, 2019.

Nicholson, G. C. *Death as Departure: The Johannine Descent-Ascent Scheme*. SBLDS 63. Chico, CA: Scholars Press, 1983.

Nielsen, Jesper Tang. "The Lamb of God: The Cognitive Structure of a Johannine Metaphor." In *Imagery in the Gospel of John: Terms, Forms, Themes, and Theology of Johannine Figurative Language*, edited by Jörg Frey et al., 217–56. WUNT 200. Tübingen: Mohr Siebeck, 2006.

Nolland, John. "What Kind of Genesis Do We Have in Matt. 1.1?" *NTS* 42 (1996): 463–71.

Nongbri, Brent. *Before Religion: A History of a Modern Concept*. New Haven: Yale University Press, 2013.

Norris, Richard A., Jr., ed. *The Christological Controversy*. Sources of Early Christian Thought. Minneapolis: Fortress, 1980.

North, Christopher R. *The Suffering Servant in Deutero-Isaiah: An Historical and Critical Study*. London: Oxford University Press, 1948.

Novenson, Matthew V. *Christ among the Messiahs: Christ Language in Paul and Messiah Language in Ancient Judaism*. Oxford: Oxford University Press, 2012.

———. *The Grammar of Messianism: An Ancient Jewish Political Idiom and Its Users*. Oxford: Oxford University Press, 2017.

Oakes, Peter S. *Philippians: From People to Letter*. SNTSMS 110. Cambridge: Cambridge University Press, 2001.

Oegema, Gerbern S. *The Anointed and His People: Messianic Expectations from the Maccabees to Bar Kochba*. JSPSup 27. Sheffield: Sheffield Academic, 1998.

O'Neill, J. C. *The Point of It All: Essays on Jesus Christ*. London: Deo, 2000.

———. *Who Did Jesus Think He Was?* Biblical Interpretation Series 11. Leiden: Brill, 1996.

Osborne, Grant. *Revelation*. BECNT. Grand Rapids: Baker Academic, 2002.

Pao, David W., and Eckhard J. Schnabel. "Luke." In *Commentary on the New Testament Use of the Old Testament*, edited by G. K. Beale and D. A. Carson, 251–414. Grand Rapids: Baker Academic, 2007.

Pate, Marvin C. *Apostle of the Last Days: The Life, Letters, and Theology of Paul.* Grand Rapids: Kregel, 2013.

Pearson, Brook W. R. "The Book of the Twelve, Aqiba's Messianic Interpretations, and the Refuge Caves of the Second Jewish War." In *The Scrolls and the Scriptures: Qumran Fifty Years After,* edited by Stanley E. Porter and Craig A. Evans, 221–39. Roehampton Institute London Papers 3. Sheffield: Sheffield Academic, 1997.

Peeler, Amy L. B. *You Are My Son: The Family of God in the Epistle to the Hebrews.* LNTS 486. London: Bloomsbury, 2014.

Pennington, Jonathan T. *The Sermon on the Mount and Human Flourishing: A Theological Commentary.* Grand Rapids: Baker Academic, 2017.

Peppard, Michael. "Adopted and Begotten Sons of God: Paul and John on Divine Sonship." *CBQ* 73, no. 1 (2011): 92–110.

———. *The Son of God in the Roman World: Divine Sonship in Its Social and Political Context.* New York: Oxford University Press, 2011.

Perrin, Nicholas. *Jesus the Priest.* Grand Rapids: Baker Academic, 2018.

Petersen, David L. *The Prophetic Literature: An Introduction.* Louisville: Westminster John Knox, 2002.

Pitre, Brant J. *Jesus and the Last Supper.* Grand Rapids: Eerdmans, 2015.

Pitts, Andrew W. "Martin Hengel, the New Tübingen School, and the Study of Christian Origins." In *Pillars in the History of Biblical Interpretation.* Vol. 2, *Prevailing Methods after 1980,* edited by Stanley E. Porter and Sean A. Adams, 137–57. MBSS 2. Eugene, OR: Pickwick, 2016.

Plantinga, Richard J., Thomas R. Thompson, and Matthew D. Lundberg. *An Introduction to Christian Theology.* Cambridge: Cambridge University Press, 2010.

Porter, Stanley E. "The Adjectival Attributive Genitive in the New Testament: A Grammatical Study." *TJ,* n.s., 4 (1983): 3–17.

———. *The Apostle Paul: His Life, Thought, and Letters.* Grand Rapids: Eerdmans, 2016.

———. "The Greek Papyri of the Judaean Desert and the World of the Roman East." In *The Scrolls and the Scriptures: Qumran Fifty Years After,* edited by Stanley E. Porter and Craig A. Evans, 293–316. Roehampton Institute London Papers 3. Sheffield: Sheffield Academic, 1997.

———. *Idioms of the Greek New Testament.* 2nd ed. Sheffield: Sheffield Academic, 1994.

———. "Introduction: The Messiah in the Old and New Testaments." In Porter, *Messiah in the Old and New Testaments,* 1–9.

———. *John, His Gospel, and Jesus: In Pursuit of the Johannine Voice.* Grand Rapids: Eerdmans, 2015.

———. *The Letter to the Romans: A Linguistic and Literary Commentary.* NTM 37. Sheffield: Sheffield Academic, 2015.

———. *Linguistic Analysis of the Greek New Testament: Studies in Tools, Methods, and Practice*. Grand Rapids: Baker Academic, 2015.

———. "Literary Approaches to the New Testament: From Formalism to Deconstruction and Back." In *Approaches to New Testament Study*, edited by Stanley E. Porter and David Tombs, 77–128. JSNTSup 120. Sheffield: Sheffield Academic, 1995.

———. "The Messiah in Luke and Acts: Forgiveness for the Captives." In Porter, *Messiah in the Old and New Testaments*, 144–64.

———, ed. *The Messiah in the Old and New Testaments*. Grand Rapids: Eerdmans, 2007.

———. *The Pastoral Epistles*. Grand Rapids: Baker Academic, 2023.

———. "Paul Confronts Caesar with the Good News." In Porter and Westfall, *Empire in the New Testament*, 164–96.

———. *Sacred Tradition in the New Testament: Tracing Old Testament Themes in the Gospels and Epistles*. Grand Rapids: Baker Academic, 2016.

———. *When Paul Met Jesus: How an Idea Got Lost in History*. Cambridge: Cambridge University Press, 2016.

Porter, Stanley E., and Cynthia Long Westfall, eds. *Empire in the New Testament*. MNTS. Eugene, OR: Pickwick, 2011.

Price, Simon. *Religions of the Ancient Greeks*. Cambridge: Cambridge University Press, 1999.

Puech, Emile. "Fragment d'une apocalypse en Araméen (4Q246 = pseudo-Dan^d) et le 'royaume de Dieu.'" *RB* 99 (1992): 98–131.

Pummer, Reinhard. *The Samaritans: A Profile*. Grand Rapids: Eerdmans, 2016.

Rainbow, Paul A. *Johannine Theology: The Gospel, the Epistles and the Apocalypse*. Downers Grove, IL: IVP Academic, 2014.

Reitzenstein, Richard. *Hellenistic Mystery-Religions: Their Basic Ideas and Significance*. Translated by John E. Steely. Reprint, Waco: Baylor University Press, 2018.

Reynolds, Benjamin E. *The Apocalyptic Son of Man in the Gospel of John*. WUNT 2/249. Tübingen: Mohr Siebeck, 2008.

———. "Jesus the Son of Man: Apocalyptic Interpretations and Johannine Christology." In *Portraits of Jesus in the Gospel of John*, edited by Craig Koester, 125–39. LNTS 589. London: T&T Clark, 2019.

Riesenfeld, Harald. "ὑπέρ." In *TDNT* 8:507–16.

Robertson, A. T. "The Use of ΥΠΕΡ in Business Documents in the Papyri." *The Expositor*, 8th series, 18 (1919): 321–27.

Robertson, Archibald, and Alfred Plummer. *A Critical and Exegetical Commentary on the First Epistle of St Paul to the Corinthians*. 2nd ed. ICC. Edinburgh: T&T Clark, 1914.

Rose, H. J. *Religion in Greece and Rome*. New York: Harper and Brothers, 1959.

Rosenberg, Roy A. "Jesus, Isaac, and the Suffering Servant." *JBL* 84 (1965): 381–88.

Rowe, C. Kavin. *Early Narrative Christology: The Lord in the Gospel of Luke*. Reprint, Grand Rapids: Baker Academic, 2009.

Rowe, Robert D. *God's Kingdom and God's Son: The Background to Mark's Christology from Concepts of Kingship in the Psalms*. Leiden: Brill, 2002.

Rüpke, Jörg. *From Jupiter to Christ: On the History of Religion in the Roman Imperial Period*. Oxford: Oxford University Press, 2014.

Said, Edward W. *Orientalism*. New York: Vintage, 1978.

Sanders, E. P. *Judaism: Practice and Belief, 63 BCE–66 CE*. London: SCM, 1992.

Sandy, D. Brent. "John the Baptist's 'Lamb of God' Affirmation in Its Canonical and Apocalyptic Milieu." *JETS* 34 (1991): 447–60.

Satterthwaite, Philip E., Richard S. Hess, and Gordon J. Wenham, eds. *The Lord's Anointed: Interpretation of Old Testament Messianic Texts*. Grand Rapids: Baker, 1995.

Schaff, Philip. *The Creeds of the Greek and Latin Churches, with Translations*. London: Hodder & Stoughton, 1878.

Schaser, Nicholas J. "Inverting Eden: The Reversal of Genesis 1–3 in John's Passion." *Word & World* 40, no. 3 (2020): 263–70.

Scheck, Thomas P., trans. *Origen: Commentary on the Epistle to the Romans, Books 1–5*. FC 103. Washington, DC: Catholic University of America Press, 2001.

Schelkle, Karl H. "σωτήρ, ῆρος, ὁ." In *Exegetical Dictionary of the New Testament*, edited by Horst Balz and Gerhard Schneider, 3:325–27. 3 vols. Grand Rapids: Eerdmans, 1990–93.

Schnackenburg, Rudolf. *The Gospel according to St John*. Translated by K. Smyth et al. 3 vols. New York: Crossroad, 1968–82.

Schnelle, Udo. *Theology of the New Testament*. Translated by M. Eugene Boring. Grand Rapids: Baker Academic, 2009.

Schuchard, Bruce G. *Scripture within Scripture: The Interrelationship of Form and Function in the Explicit Old Testament Citations in the Gospel of John*. SBLDS 133. Atlanta: Scholars Press, 1992.

Schürer, Emil. *The History of the Jewish People in the Age of Jesus Christ (175 BC–AD 135)*. Vol. 2. Rev. English ed. Edinburgh: T&T Clark, 1979.

Schweitzer, Albert. *The Mysticism of Paul the Apostle*. Translated by William Montgomery. London: A&C Black, 1931.

Scott, James M. *Adoption as Sons of God: An Exegetical Investigation into the Background of υἱοθεσία in the Pauline Corpus*. WUNT 2/48. Tübingen: Mohr Siebeck, 1992.

Scroggs, Robin. *The Last Adam: A Study in Pauline Anthropology*. Philadelphia: Fortress, 1966.

Selwyn, Edward Gordon. *The First Epistle of St. Peter*. 2nd ed. London: Macmillan, 1947.

Skarsaune, Oskar. *In the Shadow of the Temple: Jewish Influences on Early Christianity*. Downers Grove, IL: InterVarsity, 2002.

Skinner, Christopher W. "Another Look at 'The Lamb of God.'" *BSac* 161 (2004): 89–104.

Smalley, Stephen S. *The Revelation to John: A Commentary on the Greek Text of the Apocalypse*. Downers Grove, IL: InterVarsity, 2005.

Smallwood, E. Mary. *Documents Illustrating the Principates of Gaius, Claudius and Nero*. Cambridge: Cambridge University Press, 1967.

Spieckermann, Hermann. "The Conception and Prehistory of the Idea of Vicarious Suffering in the Old Testament." In *The Suffering Servant: Isaiah 53 in Jewish and Christian Sources*, edited by Peter Stuhlmacher and Bernd Janowski, 1–15. Grand Rapids: Eerdmans, 2004.

Stein, Robert H. *Mark*. BECNT. Grand Rapids: Baker Academic, 2008.

Stibbe, Mark W. G. *John's Gospel*. New Testament Readings. London: Routledge, 1994.

Stone, Michael Edward. *Fourth Ezra*. Hermeneia. Minneapolis: Fortress, 1990.

Stone, Michael E., and Matthias Henze. *4 Ezra and 2 Baruch: Translations, Introductions, and Notes*. Minneapolis: Fortress, 2013.

Stuckenbruck, Loren T. *Angel Veneration and Christology: A Study in Early Judaism and in the Christology of the Apocalypse of John*. Reprint, Waco: Baylor University Press, 2017.

Swetnam, James. "Jesus as Λόγος in Hebrews 4,12–13." *Biblica* 62 (1981): 214–24.

Taylor, Lily R. *The Divinity of the Roman Emperor*. Middletown, CT: American Philological Association, 1931.

Taylor, Vincent. *Jesus and His Sacrifice: A Study of the Passion-Sayings in the Gospels*. London: Macmillan, 1937.

———. *The Names of Jesus*. London: Macmillan, 1953.

Teeple, Howard Merle. *The Mosaic Eschatological Prophet*. SBLMS 10. Atlanta: Society of Biblical Literature, 2006.

Thiessen, Matthew. *Paul and the Gentile Problem*. Oxford: Oxford University Press, 2016.

Thiselton, Anthony C. *The First Epistle to the Corinthians*. NIGTC. Grand Rapids: Eerdmans, 2000.

Tilling, Chris. *Paul's Divine Christology*. Reprint, Grand Rapids: Eerdmans, 2015.

Tobin, Thomas H. "Logos." In *The Eerdmans Dictionary of Early Judaism*, edited by John J. Collins and David C. Harlow, 894–96. Grand Rapids: Eerdmans, 2010.

———. "The Prologue of John and Hellenistic Jewish Speculation." *CBQ* 52 (1990): 252–69.

Tuckett, Christopher M. *Christology and the New Testament: Jesus and His Earliest Followers*. Louisville: Westminster John Knox, 2001.

Turner, C. H. *The Gospel according to St. Mark*. London: SPCK, 1931.
VanderKam, James C. *The Book of Jubilees*. Sheffield: Sheffield Academic, 2001.
———. *From Joshua to Caiaphas: High Priests after the Exile*. Minneapolis: Fortress, 2004.
Vermes, Geza. *The Complete Dead Sea Scrolls in English*. Rev. ed. London: Penguin, 2004.
———. *The Dead Sea Scrolls in English*. 4th ed. Sheffield: Sheffield Academic, 1995.
———. "The 'Son of Man' Debate." *JSNT* 11 (1978): 19–32.
Veyne, Paul. *Did the Greeks Believe in Their Myths? An Essay on the Constitutive Imagination*. Translated by Paula Wissing. Chicago: University of Chicago Press, 1988.
Watts, R. E. "Jesus' Death, Isaiah 53, and Mark 10.45: A Crux Revisited." In *Jesus and the Suffering Servant: Isaiah 53 and Christian Origins*, edited by William H. Bellinger Jr. and William R. Farmer, 125–51. Harrisburg, PA: Trinity Press International, 1998.
———. "Mark." In *Commentary on the New Testament Use of the Old Testament*, edited by G. K. Beale and D. A. Carson, 111–250. Grand Rapids: Baker Academic, 2007.
Wendland, Paul. "Σωτήρ: Eine religionsgeschichtliche Untersuchung." *ZNW* 5 (1904): 335–53.
Wenham, David. *Paul: Follower of Jesus or Founder of Christianity?* Grand Rapids: Eerdmans, 1995.
Westcott, Brooke Foss. *The Gospel according to St. John: The Authorized Version with Introduction and Notes*. London: John Murray, 1894.
Westermann, Claus. *Isaiah 40–66: A Commentary*. Translated by David M. G. Stalker. OTL. Philadelphia: Westminster, 1969.
Westfall, Cynthia Long. "Messianic Themes of Temple, Enthronement, and Victory in Hebrews and the General Epistles." In Porter, *Messiah in the Old and New Testaments*, 210–29.
Whiston, William. *The Works of Flavius Josephus*. Reprint, Peabody, MA: Hendrickson, 1987.
Wilamowitz-Moellendorff, Ulrich von. "Alexandrinische Inschriften." *Sitzungsberichte der königlich preussischen Akademie der Wissenschaften zu Berlin* (1902): 1093–99.
Wilcken, U., ed. *Griechische Ostraka aus Ägypten und Nubien*. 2 vols. Leipzig: Giesecke & Devrient, 1899.
Wilcken, U., and L. Mitteis, eds. *Grundzüge und Chrestomathie der Papyruskunde*. 2 vols. in 4. Leipzig and Berlin: Teubner, 1912.
Williams, Catrin H. "Composite Citations in the Gospel of John." In *Composite Citations in Antiquity*. Vol. 2, *New Testament Uses*, edited by Sean A. Adams and Seth M. Ehorn, 94–127. LNTS 593. London: T&T Clark, 2018.

———. "Jesus the Prophet: Crossing the Boundaries of Prophetic Beliefs and Expectations in the Gospel of John." In *Portraits of Jesus in the Gospel of John*, edited by Craig R. Koester, 91–108. LNTS 589. London: T&T Clark, 2019.

Wills, Lawrence M. "Wisdom and Word among the Hellenistic Saviors: The Function of Literacy." *JSP* 24 (2014): 118–48.

Winston, David. *Logos and Mystical Theology in Philo of Alexandria*. Cincinnati: Hebrew Union College Press, 1985.

Winter, Bruce W. *Divine Honours for the Caesars: The First Christians' Responses*. Grand Rapids: Eerdmans, 2015.

Wrede, William. *The Messianic Secret*. Translated by J. C. G. Greig. London: Clarke, 1971.

Wright, N. T. *Jesus and the Victory of God*. Minneapolis: Fortress, 1996.

———. *Paul and the Faithfulness of God*. 2 vols. Minneapolis: Fortress, 2013.

Yonge, C. D. *The Works of Philo*. Peabody, MA: Hendrickson, 1993.

Zacharias, H. Daniel. "Old Greek Daniel 7:13–14 and Matthew's Son of Man." *BBR* 21, no. 4 (2011): 453–66.

MODERN AUTHORS INDEX

Achtemeier, Paul J., 129n69
Allen, Leslie C., 215n7
Allison, Dale C., Jr., 28, 28n10, 28n12, 28n15, 36n34, 39nn38–40, 40n41, 41nn42–43, 42n44, 42n47, 43n48, 175, 175n12
Attridge, Harold W., 17n51, 38n37, 199n32, 206n48, 218n26, 219n33, 220, 220n34, 221n36
Aune, David E., 25n1, 29n16, 34nn24–25, 35n32, 130n73

Bailey, Daniel P., 97n8
Baird, William, 230n6
Barrett, C. K., 106, 106n28, 107n33, 122n40, 123n43, 124n54, 126n58, 128n65, 172n2
Bates, Matthew W., 14n40, 84n47, 137, 137n6, 231n10
Bauckham, Richard, 48n6, 50n13, 86n53, 137n5, 176n22, 177nn23–24, 231, 231n10, 232
Baur, Ferdinand Christian, 149
Beale, G. K., 131n75
Beard, Mary, 70n15
Beasley-Murray, George, 123n44, 131n76
Beattie, Gillian, 11n35
Bellinger, William H., Jr., 92n1
Bernard, John H., 116n8, 122n37
Best, Ernest, 129n71
Bigg, Charles, 129n71
Bird, Michael, 69n14, 83n45, 136n2, 137, 137n6, 144n20, 229n4
Blomberg, Craig L., 93n6
Bond, Helen K., 214n5
Borchert, Gerald L., 118n16, 124n54

Borgen, Peder, 119n22
Borsch, Frederick Houk, 48n7
Bousset, Wilhelm, 4, 4nn6–8, 6, 7, 7n28, 8, 15n46, 66, 66n5, 73n25, 161n17, 230n7
Boxall, Ian, 131n77
Boyarin, Daniel, 192n11
Braun, Herbert, 48n5
Brayford, Susan, 170n1
Bremmer, Jan N., 70n15
Brennan, Nick, 86n54
Brooke, George J., 74n34
Brown, Jeannine K., 178n30, 179n33
Brown, Raymond E., 39n40, 42n45, 123n43, 126n58
Bruce, F. F., 204n45
Brunt, P. A., 68 note *a*
Bultmann, Rudolf, 55n29, 123, 124n52, 166, 166n35, 230n5
Burkett, Delbert R., 50n13, 57n33, 70n15
Burnet, John, 191n8
Burrows, E. W., 116n10
Byrne, Brendan, 144n22

Capes, David B., xxi, xxi n10, 14nn40–41, 19n53, 73n25, 231n10
Caragounis, Chrys C., 49n8, 49n10, 50, 50nn11–12, 50n14, 51, 51n15, 58, 58n37
Carey, G. L., 116n9, 126n58
Carrell, Peter R., 231n9
Carroll, John T., 164n26
Carson, D. A., 119n27, 126n58
Casey, P. M., 58n36, 230n5
Charlesworth, James H., 53n19, 218n25

Charlesworth, M. P., 67n9, 68n10
Childs, Brevard S., 92, 92n2, 114n3
Cirafesi, Wally V., 118n18
Cohick, Lynn, 165n30
Cohoon, J. W., 161n16
Collins, Adela Yarbro, 53n23, 137, 137n6
Collins, John J., 52n18, 53n21, 53n23, 74nn33–34, 75n35, 137, 137n6
Cousar, Charles B., 165n33
Cranfield, C. E. B., 71n18, 105n26
Crosby, H. L., 161n16
Crowe, Brandon D., 174, 174nn10–11, 176nn20–21, 177n26
Cullmann, Oscar, xix n7, xxi, xxi n8, 4n3, 15n46, 17n50, 19n53, 30, 30n18, 48n4, 65n1, 82n39, 84n48, 87n60, 97n7, 98n12, 99n14, 100n16, 106n28, 108, 108n42, 145nn24–25, 147n31, 149n35, 159, 159n4, 161n17, 165n34, 189n5, 195n25, 200n36
Culpepper, R. Alan, 121n33

Dahl, Nils Alstrup, 149, 149n35
Daise, Michael A., 117n13, 119n23
Davies, Margaret, 117n11, 124n50, 126n58
Davies, W. D., 118, 118n18
Davis, Carl J., 13n39
de Boer, Martinus C., 15n44
Deferrari, Roy J., 33 note *a*
Deissmann, Adolf, 4, 4n8, 6, 6n25, 7, 7nn26–27, 68n10, 71, 72, 72n20, 72n24, 73n25, 162n22
Delitzsch, F., 114n3
Diels, Hermann, 191n7
Dodd, C. H., 34n23, 34n26, 124n52, 189n4, 197n31
Driver, S. R., 98 note *a*
Dunn, James, xix n6, 26n6, 59n39, 66n2, 75n37, 82n40, 85n51, 106n29, 179n35, 180n39, 185, 185n44, 201n40, 203n42, 204n44, 206n49, 230n5

Edwards, J. Christopher, 106n29
Ehrenberg, Victor, 67n9, 68n10
Ehrman, Bart D., 88n62, 230n5
Elledge, Roderick, 48n2
Ellingworth, Paul, 220n35
Engberg-Pedersen, Troels, 199n35
Evans, Craig A., 4n8, 32, 32n21, 60n44, 61nn45–46, 62nn48–49, 71n18, 73n27, 74n34, 75n36, 122n38, 126n58, 136n2, 138n10, 141n15, 142n16, 143n18, 197nn28–30

Falls, Thomas B., 207 note *a*
Fantin, Joseph D., 5n8, 19n54

Farmer, William R., 92n1
Fee, Gordon D., 82n43, 84n46, 105, 105n27, 149n35, 150n41, 151n43, 165n31, 165n33, 179n34, 180n37, 182n41, 183n43, 205n46, 232n13
Feldmeier, Reinhard, 129n69
Ferguson, John, 70n15
Fewster, Gregory P., 13n38
Fitzmyer, Joseph A., 3n2, 4, 4n5, 12n37, 19n53, 73n25, 73n27, 74n32, 74n34, 128n67, 163n24
Fletcher-Louis, Crispin, 231nn9–10
Fossum, Jarl E., 231n9
Fowler, H. N., 191 note *a*
France, R. T., 107n35
Fredriksen, Paula, 137, 137n6
Freed, Edwin D., 124n53, 124n56

Gafni, Isaiah, 213n3
Garland, David E., 128n64
Gathercole, Simon J., 59n41, 192n12, 229n4
Gieschen, Charles A., 231n9
Gilbert, Gray, 161n10, 162n20, 164n26
Glasson, Thomas F., 115n5, 122n36
Godley, A. D., 161n13
Goldingay, John E., 52n18
Goppelt, Leonhard, 13n39, 129n70
Gordley, Matthew E., 203n41
Goulder, Michael D., 66n2
Gray, George Buchanan, 123n41, 123n43
Green, Joel B., 163nn24–25, 164n26, 176n18
Gregorovius, Ferdinand, 162n22
Grigsby, Bruce H., 123n47
Grindheim, Sigurd, 55n28, 82n40, 138n9, 144n23
Grudem, Wayne, 128n69
Guelich, Robert A., 70n17
Gurtner, Daniel, 53n24
Guthrie, George H., 224n38

Hahn, Ferdinand, xxi, xxi n8
Hannah, Darrell D., 53n20
Harris, J. Rendel, 122n36, 189n4
Hawthorne, Gerald F., 133 note *a*
Hays, Richard B., 175n13
Hengel, Martin, 54n26, 58n35, 61n47, 70n17, 73n26, 84n48, 85n49, 97n8, 144n21, 231n8
Henze, Matthias, 173n8
Hess, Richard S., 136n2, 138, 138n10, 139n11
Hick, John, 66n2
Holmes, Michael, 20 note *a*, 41 note *a*, 109 note *a*, 156 note *a*, 168 note *a*, 225 note *a*
Hooker, Morna D., 26n7, 34, 35nn28–31, 48n1, 92n1, 106, 106n31, 107, 107n33

Horbury, William, 138n8
Hoskins, Paul M., 115n4, 116n7, 120, 120n28, 120n30
Hoskyns, Edwyn C., 122n37
Howard, J. K., 117, 117n12, 119n26, 122n37, 122n39
Hurtardo, Larry W., 11n36, 14n41, 15n42, 48n3, 49n8, 69n14, 105n26, 144n23, 149n35, 231n11, 232

Isaac, E., 53n22, 54 note *a*, 61, 193n13

Jamieson, R. B., 17n50, 86, 86n55, 87, 87n56, 87nn58–59
Janowski, Bernd, 92n1
Jeremias, Joachim, 103n21, 121n35, 126n59, 129n69, 176n19
Jipp, Joshua W., 136n3, 137, 137nn6–7
Johnson, Luke Timothy, 31n19, 42n44, 148n34
Johnson, Marshall D., 176n19
Jones, A. H. M., 67n9, 68n10
Jones, W. H. S., 161n14
Joynes, Christine E., 28n9

Kaiser, Walter C., 97n10
Kee, H. C., 218n27
Keener, Craig S., 32n22, 38n35, 104n24, 126n58, 129n69, 192n10, 196n27, 197n31
Keil, C. F., 114n3
Kelly, J. N. D., 129n71
Kerényi, C., 70n16
Kim, Seyoon, 11n35
Kirk, J. R. Daniel, 56n32, 83n45, 230n5
Kleinknecht, H., 189n3
Klijn, A. F. J., 26n5
Koester, Craig, 162n22, 164, 164nn27–28, 205n47
Kraeling, Carl H., 49n9
Kreider, Glenn R., 138n10
Kreitzer, Larry J., 15, 15n43, 15n47, 16, 16nn48–49, 182n42
Kümmel, Werner Georg, 72n24

Laansma, Jon C., 224n38
Ladd, George Eldon, 130n74
Lane, William L., 70n17
Lattey, C., 67n7
Lee, Dorothy, 116n7
Lessing, R. Reed, 97n10
Levine, Lee I., 215n9
Levison, John R., 172nn3–4, 172nn6–7, 173n9
Lewis, Naphtali, 162n19
Liebeschuetz, J. H. W. G., 70n15

Lindars, Barnabas, 118n21, 124n54, 126n58
Litwa, M. David, 88 note *a*, 178n31, 230n5
Loader, William, 193n14
Longenecker, Richard N., xxii n11, 48n7, 69n14, 82n39, 82nn41–42, 84n46, 85n50, 99nn14–15, 140n12, 146n27
Louw, Johannes P., 108nn39–40
Lundberg, Matthew D., 228n2
Luter, A. B., Jr., 165n30

Malbon, Elizabeth Struthers, xxiv n13, 56n32
Manson, T. W., 147n28
Marcus, Joel, 59n40, 176n21, 177n25
Marshall, I. Howard, xxi n8, 59n42, 163n24, 175n14, 175n17, 200n37
Mason, Eric F., 218n27, 218n30
Matera, Frank J., xix n5
McCaulley, Esau, 137, 137n6
McCrum, M., 67n9
McDonough, Sean, 83n44, 87n56, 137, 137n6
McGrath, Alister E., xix n3, 187 note *a*
McKnight, Scot, 19n54, 36, 36n33, 40n41, 42n46, 43n48, 92n1, 102n18, 104n23, 106n28, 107nn35–36, 203n42
McWhirter, Jocelyn, 31n19
Mead, James K., 25nn3–4
Meeks, Wayne A., 28nn12–13, 115n5
Meier, John P., 29n16
Metzger, Bruce M., 196n26
Michaels, J. Ramsey, 38n36, 42n45, 117n14, 129n70
Middleton, Paul, 131n77
Milgrom, Jacob, 212n2
Miller, Donald G., 128n68
Minear, Paul S., 31n19
Mitteis, L., 5n11
Modica, Joseph B., 19n54
Moffitt, David M., 54n27, 223n37
Moloney, Francis J., 57n33
Moo, Douglas J., 126n58
Moore, J. M., 68 note *a*
Morris, Leon, 15n45, 164n29
Moule, C. F. D., 4n3, 8n31, 59n40
Moulton, James Hope, 107n37
Mounce, Robert H., 131n76
Murphy-O'Connor, Jerome, 216n16
Myers, Alicia D., 85n50, 93n6

Neubauer, A. D., 98 note *a*
Nicholson, G. C., 119n27
Nida, Eugene A., 108nn39–40
Nielsen, Jesper Tang, 115n4

Nolland, John, 175n13
Nongbri, Brent, 67n6
Norris, Richard A., Jr., xix n2, 228n1
North, Christopher R., 70n15, 97n9
Novenson, Matthew V., 136–37, 137n4, 149n35, 150, 150nn38–40

Oakes, Peter S., 165nn32–33
Oegema, Gerbern S., 142n16, 144n19
O'Neill, J. C., 229n4
Osborne, Grant R., 130n74, 200n38
Owen, Paul, 49n8

Pao, David W., 103, 103n19
Pate, Marvin C., 15n44
Pearson, Brook W. R., 143n18
Peeler, Amy L. B., 86n52
Pennington, Jonathan T., 40n41
Peppard, Michael, 67n8, 72n21
Perrin, B., 162n18
Perrin, Nicholas, 219, 219nn31–32
Petersen, David L., 25nn2–3
Pitre, Brant J., 36n34, 42n44, 43, 43nn48–49, 112n1, 121nn34–35, 126nn60–62, 127n63
Pitts, Andrew W., 231n8
Plantinga, Richard J., 228n2
Plummer, Alfred, 128n66
Porter, Stanley E., 19n54, 55n28, 59n40, 68n11, 71n19, 72nn22–23, 73n27, 83n45, 99n13, 103n22, 107n38, 118n20, 120n29, 125n57, 136n2, 138n10, 143n18, 147nn29–30, 148n33, 150n41, 151n43, 154n48, 157n2, 180n38, 181n40, 185n45, 189n2
Price, Simon, 70n15
Pummer, Reinhard, 28n14

Rackham, H., 191n9
Rainbow, Paul A., 10n33, 18n52, 115nn4–5, 116n7, 146n26
Reinhold, Meyer, 162n19
Reitzenstein, Richard, 230n7
Reynolds, Benjamin E., 57n33
Riesenfeld, Harald, 103n21
Robertson, A. T., 103n22, 128n66
Rose, H. J., 70n15
Rosenberg, Roy A., 97n11
Rowe, C. Kavin, xxiv, xxiv n14, 2n1
Rowe, R., 138n10
Rüpke, Jörg, 212n1

Said, Edward W., 7n28
Sanders, E. P., 215n12

Sandy, D. Brent, 116n9
Satterthwaite, Philip E., 136n2
Schaff, Philip E., 228n3
Schaser, Nicholas J., 178n27, 178n31
Scheck, Thomas P., 182 note *a*
Schelkle, Karl H., 160n5
Schnabel, Eckhard, 103, 103n19
Schnackenburg, Rudolf, 119n24
Schnelle, Udo, 197, 197n28
Schuchard, Bruce G., 124n54
Schürer, Emil, 215n12
Schweitzer, Albert, 15n44
Schwemer, Anna Maria, 58n35
Scott, James M., 67n7, 73n25
Scroggs, Robin, 172n2
Selwyn, Edward Gordon, 129n71
Shipley, F. W., 162n21
Skarsaune, Oskar, 215n13
Skinner, Christopher W., 116n9
Smalley, Stephen S., 131n76
Smallwood, E. Mary, 67n9, 68n10
Sommerstein, A. H., 161n15
Spieckermann, Hermann, 92n3
Stein, Robert H., 176n21
Stibbe, Mark W. G., 117n15, 118n19, 121n31
Stone, Michael E., 54n25, 173n8
Stuckenbruck, Loren T., 231n9
Stuhlmacher, Peter, 92n1
Swetnam, James, 201n39

Taylor, Lily R., 67n9, 68n10, 69n12
Taylor, Vincent, xxi, xxi n8, 99n14, 126n58
Teeple, Howard Merle, 28n13
Thiessen, Matthew, 137, 137n6
Thiselton, Anthony C., 128n64
Thompson, Thomas R., 228n2
Tilling, Chris, 15n42, 232, 232n12
Tobin, Thomas H., 191n6, 199n34
Tuckett, Christopher M., xix n5, xxi n9, 204n43
Turner, C. H., 70n17

VanderKam, James C., 172n5, 215n8
Vermes, Geza, 28n11, 58n36, 74n31, 216nn18–19
Veyne, Paul, 69n13

Watts, R. E., 106n28, 106n32, 107n33
Wendland, Paul, 161n11
Wenham, David, 11n35, 136n2
Westcott, Brooke Foss, 119n25
Westermann, Claus, 93n5
Westfall, Cynthia L., 19n54, 152n44, 153, 153n47, 154n49, 224n38

Whiston, William, 5 note *a*, 161n9, 216n15
Wilamowitz-Moellendorff, Ulrich von, 5n10, 69n12
Wilcken, U., 5n11, 6n16, 6n18, 6n24
Williams, Catrin H., 30n18, 32n20, 124n51
Wills, Lawrence M., 161n12
Winston, David, 194n18
Winter, Bruce, 162n23

Woodhead, A. G., 67n9
Wrede, William, 147n28
Wright, N. T., 14n40, 34n27, 137, 137n6
Wright, R. B., 217n21

Yonge, C. D., 194n24, 217 note *a*

Zacharias, H. Daniel, 59n43

ANCIENT SOURCES INDEX

Old Testament

Genesis
1 170, 197
1–3 170, 173, 178–79, 181
1:1 197, 204
1:1 LXX 197
1:2 178
1:3–4 197
1:20 179
1:21 179
1:22 179
1:23 179
1:25 179
1:26–27 170
1:27 171
1:28 171
2 170, 197
2:4 175
2:7 171, 184
2:7 LXX 178
2:15 171
2:16 170n1
2:17 171
2:19 171
2:19–20 177
2:22 170
2:22–23 171
3 173
3:1–7 171
3:22 178
3:24 176
4:7 171
4:25 170
5:1 175
5:1–32 175n16
5:5 171
5:22–24 27n8
6:2 80
6:5 3
11:5 50, 63
12 215
12:3 168
14 214–15, 218
14:18 140
14:18–20 214
18:3 3
18:12 3
20:7 25
22:1–19 176

Exodus
1:16 39
2:15 39
3:2 8
3:5 39
4:19 39
6:14–25 175n16
8:19 42
12 112, 116, 118
12:2 113
12:3 118n17
12:3–5 112, 112n2
12:4 118n17
12:5 118n17, 129
12:6 123
12:7 119n27, 124
12:8–11 126
12:10 124–25
12:12–13 113
12:14 113
12:17 113
12:19 124
12:21 112n2, 113, 118n17
12:21 LXX 128
12:21–22 125 note *a*
12:22 113, 119n27, 123–24
12:23 113
12:24–27 113
12:29–42 113
12:32 112n2, 118n17
12:42 113
12:43 113
12:43–50 113
12:46 113
12:46 LXX 124–25
13:3 159
13:14 159
15:18 154
16 40
18:25 42
20:2 159
20:21 140
24 42
24:1 43
24:6 LXX 43
24:8 37–43
24:11 43
24:12 42
24:15–18 42
24:16 42–43
24:18 40
24:29–30 42
24:35 42
25:30 43
29:6–7 140
29:38–41 117n11
30:30 43
32 179n36
33:11 37
33:17–23 38
34 42
34:3 42
34:5 42
34:6–7 38
34:29 41
34:29–30 43
34:34 14

Leviticus
4:3 140
4:5 140
4:16 140
6:22 140
8 212
9:3 117n11
9:10–15 213

Ancient Sources Index

12:6 117n11
14:6–7 124n49
14:10 117n11
16 213
16:17 220
16:32 140
18:3 159
19:23–25 183
23:9–14 183

Numbers

1:4–16 41
6:14 128
9:1–14 113
9:11–13 126
9:12 124
10:11–22:1 176
15:41 159
16:5 14
16:26 14
19:6 124n49
23:19 50
24:15–17 28
28:3 128
28:9 128
28:19 116–17

Deuteronomy

4:10 192
5:6 159
6:5 8n32
6:13 8n32, 40
6:16 8n32, 40
6:21 159
8:3 40
9:18 40
10:17 18
16:1–8 113
17:8–12 213
18 32–33
18:5 213
18:15 25, 28
18:18 25, 28, 32
18:18–19 28, 32
18:19 32
32:8 50
32:21 14
33:1 25
33:3 140
33:8–11 28
34:1–4 40

Joshua

3:9–17 39
3:12 41
5:10–12 113
5:13–15 39
5:15 39
24:25 39
24:26 39

Judges

3:9 160
4:1–10 25
6:8 159
9:11 160

1 Samuel

2:1 163
2:27 25
9:1 175n16
9:8 25
9:9 25
9:16 139
10:1 139
10:18 159
15:1 139
15:17 139
16:3 139
16:12 139
16:13 139
24:6 139
24:10 139
26:9 139
26:11 139
26:16 139
26:19 50
26:23 139

2 Samuel

1:14 139
1:16 139
2:4 139
2:7 139
3:39 139
5:3 139
5:17 139
7:2–17 25
7:11 141
7:11–14 141
7:11–16 139
7:12 141
7:13 141
7:14 12, 50, 73, 80, 141
7:28 192
12:7 139
19:10 LXX 139
19:11 139
19:21 139
22:2–3 159
22:5 25
22:51 139
23:1 139
24:11 25

1 Kings

1:34 139
1:39 139
1:45 139
5:1 139
8:26 192
8:39 50, 63
12:22 25
13:1 25
13:21 192
19:1 12
19:4–8 176
19:8–18 43
19:15 139
19:15–16 139
19:16 139
20:28 25
22:27–28 35

2 Kings

1:8 29
1:10 25
2:8 39
2:11 27
4:7 25
9:1 60
9:3 139
9:6 139
9:12 139
11:12 139
13:5 158
18:37 60
23:6 39
23:22 114
23:30 139

1 Chronicles

3:10–24 175n16
6:16–30 175n16
11:3 139
14:8 139
29:22 139–40
29:23 73

2 Chronicles

6:30 50
22:7 139
23:11 139
24:21 35
35 114
35:6 114

Ezra

6 114

Nehemiah

9:18 159
9:27 158

Job

1:6 177
15 171
15:7 171
16:21 50
25:6 50
35:8 50

Psalms

1:1 140
2:2 73, 141
2:7 61, 73, 79–80, 141, 148
6:8 14
8 54
8:4 50
10:16 154
12:1–2 50
14 50
16:8–11 148
16:10 LXX 148
18:50 139
22:28 154
24:1 14
25:5 163

31:2 LXX 12
31:19–20 50
32:2 12
33:4 192
33:6 192
33:21 LXX 124
34:8 17
34:20 124
35:9 163
45:2 40
45:6 86
45:7 LXX 139
45:8 139
49:2 50
50:9 124n49
53:1–2 50
56:4 192
56:10 192
62:9 50
78:25 40
80:8–16 122n37
80:17 50
81:10 159
82:7 171
89:20 LXX 139
89:21 139
89:26 73
89:27 73
89:47 50
90:3 50
94:2 14
94:11 12
95 201
102:6 16
102:25–26 87
104:24 203
106:20 179n36
106:21 159
109:1 LXX 61
110 215, 221
110:1 9, 61, 73, 86, 147–48
110:4 215, 220
117:1 12
144:3 50
146:3 50

Proverbs

8:22 203–4
8:22–31 192
8:23 198

8:27 205
9:9–10 192
15:11 50
30:5 192

Ecclesiastes

8:11 50
9:3 50
9:12 50

Isaiah

1:9 12
1:10 192
2:10 14
2:19 14
2:21 14
5:1–7 122n37
6:10 117, 125
8:13 17
9:1–7 163
11:3–5 143
11:6–9 177n24
12:2 160
19:19 4–5
19:20 158–59
26:13 14
27:2–11 122n37
28:11 12
28:22 12
35:4 159
38:1 25
40:3 8, 29, 117
40:8 192
40:13 12–13
42 102
42:1 93, 97, 104
42:1–4 92–93, 97
42:3 93
42:4 98
42:6 97–98
43:3 159
45:1 139
45:17 159
45:22 159
45:23 13, 15
49:1 94, 97
49:1–7 92, 94
49:2 97
49:3 94, 97, 107
49:5 94, 97, 107

49:5–6 97–98
49:5–7 94
49:6 94, 148, 168
49:7 94, 107
49:8 97, 104
49:18 13
49:26 159
50:4–5 97
50:4–11 92, 95
50:6 95
50:6–8 95
50:7–8 95
50:7–9 97
50:8 95
50:8–9 95
51–52 15
51:12 50, 63
52:11 12, 14
52:13 105
52:13–53:12 92–93, 96
52:14 50
52:14–15 107
52:15 96
53 92, 98, 104, 106, 106n28, 107–9, 122, 129n70, 149
53:1 12, 96, 117, 125
53:3 96
53:4 102, 117, 146
53:4–5 104
53:4–6 96, 105
53:4–8 117
53:5 96
53:6 96, 105
53:7 96–97, 117, 129, 129n69
53:7–8 91
53:7–8 LXX 127
53:8 96
53:9 96, 105
53:10 117
53:10–12 106
53:11 107
53:11 LXX 107
53:11–12 96, 104–5
53:12 97, 103, 105, 107, 108n40, 117
53:12 LXX 107
55:3 148
55:11 192
56:2 50

59:17 16
61:1 140
65 180
66:4–6 16
66:5 14
66:15 14, 16

Jeremiah

1:1 26
1:5 25
1:5–16 39
2:1 29
2:21 122n37
9:24 13
12:10–13 122n37
20:2 35
26:20–23 35
31 43
31:31–34 41, 43
32:19 50
34:13 159
43:1 192
49:18 50
49:33 50
50:40 50
51:43 50

Ezekiel

1:4–28 51
2:1 51
2:3 51
3:16 29
6:3 192
15:1–8 122n37
16:59–63 43
19:10–14 122n37
29:9 168
34:23–24 99
37:24–25 99

Daniel

2:44 154
2:44–45 53
2:47 18
7 xviii, 48, 52–54, 58–59, 61–63, 108–9
7:1–8 53
7:1–14 51
7:9 51

Ancient Sources Index

7:13 48, 51–53,
  59–62, 86
7:13–14 52 note *a*,
  59
7:14 154
7:18 52
8:17 51, 51n16, 52
10:16 51n16
10:18 51, 51n16

Hosea
1:1 29
4:1 192
6:7 171
10:1 122n37
11:1 40, 77
13:4 159

Joel
1:12 50
2:28 26
2:28–32 148
2:32 13
3:1–5 LXX 148

Amos
9:11 141
9:11–12 LXX 148

Obadiah
21 154

Jonah
1:1 29

Micah
1:1 29
5:6 50
5:7 50

Habakkuk
1:5 148
3:18 163

Zephaniah
1:1 175n16

Haggai
1:15–2:9 26

Zechariah
2:11 168
3:8 99
8:1–8 26
9:11–17 43
12:10 124–25
14:5 14–15
14:9 154

Malachi
1:6–2:17 26
1:7 14
1:12 14
3:1 27, 29
4:5 27
4:6 30

Old Testament Apocrypha

Baruch
2:11 159
2:28 37
3 193
3:9 193
3:36–37 193
3:37 198
4:1 193, 206
4:1–2 198
4:22 160

Judith
9:11 160
9:11–12 160

1 Maccabees
4:30 160
4:46 27
7:5–9 216
9:27 26
14:41 27

2 Maccabees
3–4 140
4:7–17 216
4:32–34 216
4:50 216
7:30 37

3 Maccabees
6:29 160
6:32 160
7:16 160

4 Maccabees
1:1 193
1:2 193
2:1–23 193
17:19 37

Sirach
1:10 198
4:10 73
15:1–10 192
15:13–15 173
15:13–20 173
17:2–4 177n23
24 193, 197–98
24:3 193
24:8 193, 198
24:9 193, 198, 205
24:11 198
24:16 198
24:23 37, 193, 198
24:27 198
24:28 198
24:32 198
25:24 172
33:7–15 173
40:1–11 173
43:31 198, 204
46:1 160
48:4 27 note *a*
48:8–10 27 note *a*
48:10 27–28
49:16 172
51:8 160

Tobit
1:1 175n16
8:6 172
14:4 192

Wisdom of Solomon
1:7 204
2:18 73
2:23–24 173
2:24 172, 177
6:12–16 192
7:22 193
7:24 206
7:26 203, 206
7:27 193
8:1 206
8:5 203
9 192
9:1–2 192
9:2–3 177n23
9:9 192, 198, 203, 205
10:1–2 172
10:1–21 192
10:3–4 172
18:15 192

Old Testament Pseudepigrapha

Apocalypse of Moses
10.1–11.1 177n23
17.4 177

Aristobulus
Fragment 5.2 198
Fragment 5.3 193

2 Baruch
17.3 173
23.4 173
54.19 173
56.6 173
73.3–74.3 173
73.6 177n24
85.1 26
85.3 26

1 Enoch
10.9 4
14.24 192

37–71 62
42 193
42.2 198
46.1–2 53
46.4–5 53, 63
48.2 53, 63, 142
48.2–6 54 note *a*
48.3 53, 63
48.6 53, 63, 142
48.10 53, 63, 142
49.2 53, 142
51.3 53, 62
51.3–4 61 note *a*
51.4 142
52.4 53, 142
52.6 53, 142
52.8–9 53
53.6 53, 142
55.4 53, 142
61.8 53, 142
62.1 53, 142
62.9 142
62.11 53, 63
69.27–29 53, 63
69.29 53
71.17 53
90.37 27n8

2 Enoch

31.1–6 172
58.3 177n23

4 Ezra

1.7 159
3.4–11 173
6.26 27–28
6.45–59 172n7
6.54 177n23
7.11–14 172n3
7.26 28
7.118 173
12.11 53
12.31–34 141
13.3 54
13.25–38 54
15.10 159

Jubilees

1.14 177n23
2.23 172

3.9 177
3.23–25 172
3.27 172
4.25 172
6.1–3 172
16.24 172

Letter of Aristeas

143 193–94

Life of Adam and Eve

6.1–3 177
21.1–6 172

Psalms of Solomon

1.8 217n22
2.3 217n22
8.9 217n21
8.11 217n22
8.12 217n23
8.13 217n24
8.33 160
17.4 141–42
17.21 141–42
17.26 142
17.28 142

Sibylline Oracles

1.22–64 172
1.33–34 172
1.41 172
1.63 172
3.35 160
3.788–95 177n24

Testament of Joseph

19.6 140n13

Testament of Judah

21.2 140n13

Testament of Levi

18.2 4, 218
18.3 218

18.8 218
8.11–19 140

Testament of Moses

1.14 140

Testament of Simeon

72 140n13

New Testament

Matthew

1:1 9
1:1–17 175
1:18–2:23 39
1:20 1, 8–9
1:21 163
1:22 2
1:24 2, 8
2:13 2, 8
2:13–14 39
2:15 2, 8, 40, 77, 104
2:16–18 39
2:18 104
2:19 2, 8
2:19–20 39
3:1–12 29
3:3 2, 8, 30
3:11 30
3:13–17 104
3:15 104
3:17 9, 77, 85, 93
4:1–11 40, 177
4:2 40
4:3 9, 78
4:4 40
4:6 9, 78
4:7 2, 8n32, 40
4:8–9 40
4:10 2, 8n32, 40
4:11 40
4:17 34
5:11 58n38
5:11–12 35
5:17 40
5:17–20 40
5:21–48 40
5:33 2

7 2
7:21 77
7:21–23 1
8:1 41
8:5 1
8:5–13 10
8:6 10
8:17 102, 146
8:20 55
8:25 8n29
8:27 174
8:29 9, 78
8:31 58n38
9:2 167
9:2–8 174
9:6 55
9:14–15 100
9:27 9
10 1
10:1–4 41
10:23 56
10:24 1
10:32 58n38
10:32–33 77
11 201
11:2 145
11:2–4 xvii n1
11:2–6 135
11:3 xvii, 135
11:4–6 135
11:7–10 145
11:9 29
11:10 29
11:13–15 30
11:18–19 201
11:19 55
11:21–22 34
11:25–27 77, 202
11:27 76, 84
11:28 174
12:8 55
12:17 102
12:17–21 93
12:18–21 102
12:23 9
12:31–32 58
12:32 55
12:39 35
12:39–40 101
12:40 56, 101
12:50 77
13:37 55

Ancient Sources Index

13:41 56, 59
13:54 201
13:57 33
14:1–12 23
14:5 23, 29
14:22–32 10
14:28 8n30, 10
14:30 8n30, 10
14:33 9, 65, 78
15:13–21 42
15:22 9–10
15:25 10
15:30 77
16:4 35
16:13 58
16:13–17 xviii
16:13–20 44, 101
16:14 24
16:16 xviii, 78, 146
16:17 77
16:20 147
16:21 58n38
16:22 8n30
16:23 101
16:27 77
16:28 56
17:1–8 42
17:4 8n30
17:5 9, 78, 80, 93
17:13 30
17:22–23 101
18:10 77
18:19 77
18:21 8n30
18:35 77
19:6–8 37
19:25 163
19:28 56
20:17–19 101
20:20–28 106n30
20:23 77
20:28 56, 106, 106n30
20:30 9
20:31 9
21:9 8–9
21:10 xviii
21:11 32
21:15 9
21:18–22 35
21:33–46 102
21:46 32
22:37 8n32

22:42 145, 147
22:44 9, 20
22:45 9
23:2–28 34
23:34 202
23:34–36 35
23:34–39 201
23:37 36
23:37–24:2 35
24:1–36 34
24:2 34
24:5 145
24:23 145
24:27 56
24:30 56
24:36 76, 84
24:37 56
24:39 56
24:44 56
25:31 56
25:34 77
26:2 55n30
26:6–13 102
26:14–16 102
26:17–30 126
26:20–29 35
26:22 8n29
26:26 126
26:26–29 43, 219
26:28 43
26:28–29 103
26:29 77
26:38 126
26:39 77
26:42 77
26:53 77
26:57 47
26:57–68 47
26:63 47, 60, 78, 145
26:63–64 76n38, 85
26:64 60
26:67–68 32
26:68 145
27:11 145
27:17 146
27:22 146
27:29 146
27:37 146
27:40 78
27:43 78
27:54 9, 78
28:18 21

28:19 76, 84
28:19–20 168

Mark

1:1 66, 66n3, 71, 78, 144
1:2–8 29
1:3 30
1:6 29
1:7–8 30
1:9–11 104
1:11 9, 77, 85, 93
1:12–13 176
1:15 34, 71
1:16 144
1:17 144
1:18 144
1:35 176
2:1 55
2:4 144
2:6–8 xvii n1
2:10 58
2:18–20 100
2:27–28 58
2:28 55
3:11 9, 78
3:14–16 41
4:41 174
5:7 78
5:19 9
5:20 9
6:2 201
6:4 33
6:14–15 31
6:14–16 23
6:31 176
6:40 42
7:9 37
8:27 58
8:27–30 xviii, 44
8:27–33 101
8:27–16:30 5n8
8:29 xviii, 146
8:29–33 56n32
8:30 147
8:31 55n30, 101
8:33 101
8:35 71
8:38 56, 59, 77
9:2 42–43
9:2–3 42

9:2–8 42
9:6 43
9:7 9, 42, 78, 80, 104n23
9:9 55n30
9:10–17 42
9:11–13 30
9:12 55n30
9:13 30
9:31 55, 101
9:32 101
9:41 147
10:20 71
10:26 163
10:32–34 101
10:33 55n30
10:33–34 34
10:35–37 106
10:38 104
10:45 55, 106, 106n28, 107, 107n37, 108, 128, 129n70
10:47 9
10:48 9
11:12–21 35
11:27–28 xvii n1
12:29 8n32
12:30 8n32
12:35 9, 147
12:36 9, 20
12:37 9
13:1–32 34
13:2 34
13:10 71
13:11 65
13:21 145
13:26 56, 59
13:32 76, 84
14:3–9 102
14:8 102
14:9 71
14:10–11 102
14:12 126, 127n63
14:12–25 126
14:17–25 35
14:21 55n30
14:22 126
14:22–25 43
14:24 43, 126
14:24–25 103
14:36 77

14:41 55n30
14:53–65 47
14:55 47
14:61 47, 60, 145
14:61–62 76, 85
14:62 48, 56, 56n32, 60–61
14:65 32
15:2 145
15:18 146
15:26 62, 146
15:32 146
15:39 9, 71, 78

Luke

1:6 8
1:9 8
1:11 8
1:16 8n32
1:17 9, 30
1:28 75
1:32 8n32, 75, 78, 85
1:32–35 75
1:33 75
1:35 9, 75, 78, 85
1:46–47 8
1:47 163, 167
1:68 8
1:69 163
1:76 29
2 167
2:1 164
2:9 8, 19
2:10–11 163
2:11 19, 146, 168
2:14 163
2:24 8
2:26 146
2:39 8
2:40 201
2:49 77
2:52 201
3 177
3:1–20 29
3:2 29
3:4 8, 30
3:5 144
3:16 30
3:21–22 104
3:22 9, 77, 85, 175
3:23–28 175

3:38 177
4:1–12 176
4:1–13 40, 177
4:2 177
4:3 40, 78
4:7 40
4:8 8n32
4:9 78, 177
4:12 8n32, 40, 164
4:14 65
4:16–30 32
4:24 32–33
4:41 78, 146
5:1–11 35
5:8 8n30
5:12–15 10
5:24 55
5:31 164
5:33–36 100
6:5 55
6:13 41
6:22 55, 58n38
6:22–23 35
6:24–26 34
7:16 31
7:18–23 135
7:19 xvii, 145
7:20 135
7:22–23 135
7:26 29
7:27 29
7:34 55
7:35 201
7:36–50 xvii
7:39 31
7:49 xvii
7:50 167
8:25 174
8:28 9, 78
8:39 10
9:7–9 23–24
9:8 24
9:9 xvii
9:14 42
9:18–20 xviii, 24
9:18–21 44, 101
9:20 xviii, 24, 146
9:22 58n38
9:28–36 42
9:35 9, 78, 80
9:43–45 101
9:54 10

9:58 55
10:17 8n29
10:18 34
10:21–22 77, 202
10:22 76, 84
11:1 8n29
11:20 42
11:29 35
11:30 56
11:49 202
11:49–51 35, 201
12:8 56, 58n38
12:10 55
12:40 56
12:41 8n30
12:50 100, 104
13:31–35 33, 100
13:32 100
13:33 33, 36, 100
13:34 36
17:22 56
17:24 56
17:26 56
17:26–30 34
17:29–30 56
17:37 8n29
18:8 56
18:26 163
18:31–34 101
18:38 9
18:39 9
19:9 9, 163
19:10 55
19:41–44 34
20:37 8n32
20:41 147
20:42 9
21:5–33 34
21:6 34
21:36 56
22:3–6 102
22:7 126, 127n63
22:7–23 126
22:11 127n63
22:14–20 43
22:14–23 35
22:19 126
22:20 126
22:20–23 103
22:29 77
22:30 8n30
22:37 103–4

22:38 8n29
22:42 77
22:48 56
22:49 8n29
22:63–71 47
22:64 32
22:67 145
22:69 60
22:70 9, 47, 60, 76, 78, 85
23:2 145
23:3 145
23:34 77
23:35 104n23, 146
23:39 xvii n1
23:46 77
24:7 55, 55n30
24:13–35 32
24:19 32
24:26 147
24:40 148
24:49 77

John

1 116, 197–202
1–12 121
1:1 178, 195, 198, 209
1:1–2 195
1:1–3 195
1:1–18 38, 189, 195, 197
1:3 196–98, 208
1:4 198
1:4–5 196
1:5 196–98
1:6–9 30
1:9 198
1:10 196–98
1:11 196
1:12 198
1:14 38, 78, 196, 198, 208
1:14–18 140, 196
1:17 37–38, 115, 148, 198
1:18 38, 78, 196, 198, 202, 208
1:19 196
1:19–28 29
1:19–12:16 116
1:20 145

Ancient Sources Index

1:21 23, 30
1:23 8, 30, 117
1:25 145
1:25–28 30
1:26–27 30
1:29 105n25, 111, 116–17, 119n25, 122, 129, 131, 131n76
1:29–36 116, 127
1:31 128n69
1:34 78
1:36 116, 119n25, 122, 129, 131
1:41 146
1:45 115
1:49 78
1:51 57
2:1 154
2:13 116n6, 117–18
2:13–25 117–18, 131
2:14–15 129
2:16 77
2:19 118
2:21 118
2:23 116n6, 118
3:13–14 57
3:14 115
3:16–18 78
3:17 164, 166
3:19–21 196
3:25–30 30
3:28 145
3:35–36 78
4:19 32
4:22 164
4:25 28, 146
4:26 146–47
4:29 146
4:41 146, 200
4:42 163–64, 167
4:45 116n6
5:1 116n6
5:19 76–77
5:19–26 76
5:20 76
5:21 76
5:22 76
5:23 76
5:24 200
5:25 76
5:26 76, 196

5:27 57
5:35 196
5:37 59
5:40 196
5:43 77
5:45 115
5:45–47 42
5:46 115
6 118
6:1–13 42
6:1–14 118, 131
6:3 42
6:4 116n6, 118
6:4–5 119
6:14 32, 42
6:14–15 42
6:15 42
6:22–70 57
6:22–71 118
6:27 57
6:31–33 119
6:32 77, 115
6:33 119nn25–26, 196
6:34 8n29
6:34–38 119
6:35 196
6:40 77
6:48 196
6:48–51 119
6:51 119
6:53 57
6:53–58 119
6:54 119n26
6:56 119n26
6:57 119n26
6:58 119n26
6:62 57
6:63 196
6:68 8n30
6:70 41
7:2 120
7:19 115
7:22 115
7:23 115
7:25–31 xvii n1
7:26 145
7:27 145
7:40 32
7:41 145
7:42 145
8:5 115
8:12 196

8:19 77
8:25 xviii
8:28 57
8:31 200
8:31–32 120
8:31–47 120, 131
8:34–38 120
8:36 120
8:38 77
8:42–47 120
8:49 77
8:51 200
8:53 xviii
8:54 77
8:55 200
8:58 147
9:5 196
9:17 32
9:19 146
9:22 147
9:28 115
9:29 115
9:35 57
10 129n72
10:17–18 77
10:24 147
10:25 77
10:29 77
10:36 76, 85
10:37 77
11 120
11:4 76, 85
11:9–10 196
11:12 8n29
11:25 196
11:27 19, 78, 147
11:47–12:8 120, 131
11:50 120
11:51–52 120
11:55 116n6, 121
11:56 116n6
12:1 116n6, 121
12:1–8 121
12:7 121
12:12 116n6
12:16 122
12:20 116n6
12:23 57, 122
12:26 77
12:27 77
12:28 122
12:32 101

12:33 101
12:34 55, 57, 101, 145
12:35–36 196
12:38 117, 122, 125
12:40 117, 125
12:41 122
12:46 196
13–17 121–22
13–19 121
13:1 116n6, 121, 122n36
13:1–17:26 131
13:2 122
13:4 122
13:6 8n30
13:9 8n30
13:18 119n26
13:26 122
13:29 116n6
13:30 122
13:31 57
13:31–32 122
13:36 8n30
13:37 8n30
14:2 77
14:7 77
14:13 76–77
14:20–21 77
14:23 77
14:31 77
15–17 122
15:1 77
15:1–10 122
15:8 77
15:10 77
15:15 77
15:23–24 77
16:10 77
16:23 77
16:25 77
16:28 209
16:32 77
17 219–20
17:1 76–77
17:1–5 220
17:3 148
17:5 77, 122, 209
17:6–19 220
17:11 77
17:14 200
17:17 200
17:20–21 220

17:21 77, 204
17:24–25 77
18:1 178
18:11 77
18:26 178
18:28 116n6, 122, 127n63
18:33 145
18:33–38 xvii n1
18:39 116n6, 122–23
19 112, 116, 123–25
19–20 178
19:3 146
19:5 178
19:7 78
19:12 20n55
19:13–42 122, 131
19:14 116n6, 122, 122n40, 123, 131n76
19:14–15 146
19:28–30 125 note b
19:29 123
19:31 122, 122n40, 123–24
19:31–36 131n76
19:34 124
19:36 124–25, 129
19:36–37 122, 124–25
19:37 124–25
19:38 124
19:41 178
19:42 122, 122n40, 123
20:1 178
20:15 178
20:17 77
20:19 178
20:21 77
20:22 178
20:24–29 19
20:28 8n32, 19
20:31 66, 78, 147, 154, 196
21:12 10n33
21:15 10n33, 129
21:15–17 8n30
21:16 10n33
21:17 10n33
21:20 10n33
21:21 8n30, 10n33

Acts

1:4 79
1:6 10n33
1:21 10n34
1:24 10n33
2:14–36 148
2:17–21 148
2:21 8
2:25–28 10
2:30–31 148
2:31 148
2:33–35 9
2:34–35 148
2:36 148
2:38 148, 148n32
3:6 148n32
3:11–26 32
3:12–26 148
3:13 79
3:18 148
3:20 148, 148n32
3:22 32
3:22–23 32, 140
3:26 79
4:6 148
4:10 148n32
4:33 148n32
5:31 167
5:42 148n32
7 36
7:37 32, 140
7:51–52 36
7:56 54–55
7:59 10nn33–34
7:60 10n33
8 91
8:5 148
8:12 148n32
8:16 10n34
8:31 91
8:32 116–17, 129
8:32–33 91, 127
8:37 148n32
9 148
9:10 10n33
9:13 10n33
9:20 66, 79, 148
9:22 148
9:34 148n32
10:36 148n32
10:48 148n32

11:17 10n34, 148n32
11:20 10n34
13:21–40 148
13:23 164
13:33 79
13:47 94
15:11 10n34
15:13–21 148
15:26 10n34, 148n32
16:18 148n32
16:31 10n34
17:2 149
17:3 148–49
17:7 20n55
18:5 148n32
18:28 148n32
19:4 29
19:5 10n34
19:13 10n34
19:17 10n34
20:21 148n32
20:24 10n34
20:35 10n34
21:13 10n34
22:19 10n33
23 219
23:5 219
24:24 148n32
25:26 6
26:22–23 149
26:23 148
28:31 148n32

Romans

1:1 72, 83
1:1–4 71
1:3 72, 79, 83
1:3–4 83, 229
1:4 xxiv, 11n36, 19, 66, 72, 79, 83
1:7 11n36
1:9 79
1:18 15
1:18–25 179
1:24 11
2:5 15
3:5 15
3:19–31 38
3:24–25 151
4:8 12
4:25 105

5 169
5:1 11n36, 169, 181
5:1–11 169, 180
5:4 179
5:6 149
5:6–8 151, 219
5:6–11 169
5:8 149
5:9 15, 164, 169
5:10 79, 169
5:11 11n36, 181
5:12 169, 180–81, 183
5:12–21 179–80, 182
5:13 180–81
5:13–18 181
5:14 169–70, 179–80
5:15–17 170
5:15–18 180
5:18 181
5:19 105, 180–81
5:20 181
5:21 11n36, 181
6:3 151
6:4 149
6:8 149
6:9 149
6:17 170
6:23 11n36
7:25 11n36
8:3 79
8:19–23 186
8:20–21 180
8:22–23 180
8:29 79
8:32 79
8:34 151, 226
8:38–39 21
8:39 11n36
9:5 151
9:28–29 12
10:9 13, 18
10:9–13 165
10:10 96
10:13 13, 15
10:16 12
11:3 12, 35
11:34 12
11:36 204
12:19 12
13:14 11n36
14:9 13, 151
14:11 13

14:15 151
15:6 11n36, 79, 83
15:11 12
15:14 183
15:18–19 183
15:20 183
15:20–22 183
15:21 96
15:30 11n36
15:35 183
15:45–49 183
16:24 11n36

1 Corinthians

1:2 11n36, 13
1:3 11n36
1:7 11n36
1:8 11n36
1:9 11n36, 79
1:10 11n36
1:17 151
1:17–24 202
1:18 128
1:20–21 202
1:23 151
1:24 202
1:30 202
1:31 13
2:6 202
2:16 13
3:20 12
5:6–8 128
5:7 127, 128n69
5:10 79
6:11 11n36
7:10 11, 11n35
7:12 11
8:6 11n36, 204, 208–9
8:11 151
9:1 150n42
9:14 11
10:3–4 119
10:6 170
10:6–22 119n27
10:21 14
10:22 14
10:26 14
11:8–9 179
11:23–26 35, 43
11:24–25 11, 103
11:25–27 126
12:3 13, 18
14:21 12
15 182, 184
15:1–2 164
15:1–19 182
15:3–5 151
15:3–7 150
15:20–22 179, 182, 184–85
15:21 183
15:21–22 183
15:22 179, 183
15:25 20–21
15:28 79
15:31 11n36
15:35 184
15:40 184
15:44 184
15:45 179
15:45–49 179, 182, 184
15:47 184
15:47–49 184
15:48 185
15:48–49 185
15:49 185
15:57 11n36
16:22 15

2 Corinthians

1:2 11n36
1:3 11n36, 79, 83
1:12 202
1:19 79
3:16 14
5:14–15 219
5:16 150n42
5:16–17 180, 186
5:19 200
5:21 179
6:17–18 12
10:17 14
11:31 80
13:13 11n36
13:31 83

Galatians

1:3 11n36
1:11–24 150
1:16 79
2:20 79
3:10–14 38
4:4 79, 209
4:6 79
6:12 151
6:15 180, 186
6:18 11n36

Ephesians

1:1 151
1:2 11n36
1:3 11n36, 79, 83
1:9–10 168
1:13 200
1:17 11n36
1:22 21
2:13–16 151
3:10–11 202
3:11 11n36
3:14 11n36
4:13 79
4:24 186
5:6 15
5:20 11n36
5:20–22 179
5:23 157, 165
6:23 11n36
6:24 11n36

Philippians

1:1 157
1:2 11n36, 157
1:6 157
1:8 157
1:11 157
1:14 157
1:15 157
1:18 157
1:26 157
2 20
2:1 157
2:5 157
2:5–11 179, 185
2:6 208
2:6–7 209
2:6–8 105
2:6–11 13
2:7–8 105
2:9–11 206
2:10 20
2:10–11 15
2:11 11n36, 13, 18, 157
2:16 200
2:19 157
2:21 157
2:24 157
2:29 157
3:1 157
3:3 157
3:8 157
3:8–10 157
3:17 170
3:18 151, 165
3:20 157, 165, 168
3:21 165
4:1 157, 165
4:2 157
4:4 157
4:7 157
4:10 157
4:19 157
4:21 157
4:23 11n36, 157

Colossians

1:3 11n36
1:13 79
1:15 79, 83, 203, 208–9
1:15–18 203
1:15–20 20, 83, 201–3, 203n41, 206
1:16 21, 186, 203–4, 208
1:17 20, 203, 208–9
1:18 204
1:18–20 203
1:19 204
1:20 204, 206, 209
1:25 200
1:28 21
2:3 202
2:6 11n36
2:9 204
2:10 20
3 180
3:6 15
3:9–10 180

1 Thessalonians

1:1 11n36
1:3 11n36

1:7 170
1:10 15, 79, 152, 164
2:15 36
3:13 14–15
4:6 14
4:14 152
5:1 16
5:8 16
5:9 11n36
5:9–10 219
5:23 11n36
5:28 11n36

2 Thessalonians

1:1 11n36
1:2 11n36
1:6–12 16
1:7–8 14
1:9 14
1:12 11n36, 14
2:1 11n36
2:14 11n36
2:16 11n36
3:9 170
3:12 11n36
3:18 11n36

1 Timothy

1:1 163
1:2 11n36
1:12 11n36
1:15 164
2:3 163
2:4 165
2:6 107n37
2:11–14 185n45
2:13–14 179
6:3 11n36
6:14 11n36
6:15 21

2 Timothy

1:2 11n36
1:10 157, 165, 168
2:19 14

Titus

1:3 163, 166
1:4 157, 166

2:10 166
2:13 157, 166
2:13–14 168
3:4 166
3:6 157, 166
3:17–21 157
3:20 157

Philemon

3 11n36
25 11n36

Hebrews

1 87
1:1 205
1:1–2 205
1:1–4 201–2, 205
1:2 80, 86, 205, 208
1:3 86, 186, 206, 208, 220
1:3–4 206
1:4 206
1:5 80, 86
1:5–14 86
1:8 16–17, 80, 86, 87
1:8–12 86
1:10 16, 87
1:10–11 87
1:13 20
2:3 17
2:5–9 185
2:6 54, 152
2:6–8 54
2:9 205
2:10 220
2:11 220–21
2:14 221
2:17 220–21
2:17–18 220
2:18 220
3:1 220
3:1–6 140
3:3 38
3:3–6 37
3:5 153
3:5–6 38
3:6 80, 152
3:6–4:16 38
3:14 153
3:16 38, 153

4:5 221
4:7 201
4:12–13 200
4:14 66, 80, 211
4:14–15 220
4:14–16 221
4:15 221
4:16 221
5 222
5:1 221n36
5:1–3 221
5:1–4 221, 221n36
5:1–10 221
5:4 221–22
5:5 80, 153, 220
5:5–10 221n36
5:6 153, 220–21
5:6–7 222
5:7 222
5:7–10 221
5:8 80
5:9–10 221n36
5:10 220–21
6 225
6:5 205
6:6 221
6:20 220–21
7 222
7–10 38
7:1–10 222
7:2 222
7:3 80, 221–22
7:11 220–21, 223
7:13–14 222
7:14 17, 211, 222
7:15 220–21
7:16 222
7:17 220–21
7:20 220
7:24 223
7:26 220
7:27 223–24
7:27–28 224
7:28 80
8–10 223
8:1 220
8:1–2 224
8:1–7 38
8:2 223
8:5–6 140
8:6–7 44
9 153

9:11 153, 220
9:11–12 224
9:11–22 206
9:12 225
9:13–14 224
9:14 153
9:19 123n48
9:19–23 38
9:23–28 38
9:24 153, 223–24
9:25–28 224
9:26 205
10:1 39
10:4 224
10:10 153, 224–25
10:12 224
10:13 20
10:14 224
10:21 220
10:25 211
10:29 80, 221
10:32–36 211
11:3 205
11:26 153
11:36–38 35
12:9 86
13:20 222
13:20–21 17

James

1:1 17, 153
1:7 17
2:1 17, 153
3:9 17
4:10 17
4:15 17
5:4 17
5:7 17
5:8 17
5:10 17, 35
5:11 17

1 Peter

1:2 153
1:3 17, 80, 83, 153
1:7 153
1:11 153
1:13 153
1:18–19 128, 132
1:19 116, 129, 153

1:23 200
1:25 17
2:3 17
2:5 153
2:21 153
2:21–22 105
2:23–25 105
3:12 17
3:15 17, 153
3:16 153
3:18 153
3:21 153
4:1 153
4:13 153
4:14 153
5:1 153
5:10 152n45, 153
5:13 66

2 Peter

1:1 153, 166
1:2 17, 166
1:3 166
1:5 166
1:6 166
1:8 17, 153, 166
1:11 17, 153, 166
1:14 17
1:16 17, 153
1:16–18 42
1:16–19 153
1:17 80
2:9 17
2:11 17
2:20 17, 153, 166
3:2 17, 166
3:8 17
3:9 17
3:10 17
3:16 166
3:17 166
3:18 17, 153, 166

1 John

1:1 200, 208
1:3 80, 154
1:7 80
2:1–2 226
2:2 154
2:22 154
2:22–24 80

3:8 80
3:9 154
3:23 80, 154
4:7 154
4:9 80
4:10 80
4:14 80, 166–67
4:15 66, 80, 154
4:42 166
5:1 154
5:4 154
5:5 80
5:6 154
5:9–13 80
5:20 80, 154

2 John

3 66, 80, 154
7 154
9 80, 154

Jude

4 17, 153
5 17
9 17
14 17
17 17, 153
21 17, 153
25 17, 153, 163, 167

Revelation

1:1–2 154, 200
1:2 189, 200
1:5 20
1:6 80
1:8 18
1:9 189, 200
1:13 54–55
1:17–18 55
2:18 66, 79
2:28 79
3:5 79
3:21 79
4:8 18
4:11 18
5 129
5:5 130
5:6 130
5:8 130
5:12 130

5:13 130
6:1 130
6:9 189, 200
6:16 130
7:9–10 130
7:14 18, 130
7:17 130
11:4 18
11:8 18
11:15 18, 21, 154
11:17 18
12:10 155
12:11 130
13:8 130
13:11 129
14 55
14:1 130
14:4 130
14:10 130
14:13 18
14:14 54–55
14:14–16 55
15:3 18, 130
15:4 18
16:7 18
17:14 18, 21, 130
17:17 189, 200
18:8 18
18:24 35
19 189
19:6 18
19:7 130
19:9 130, 189, 200
19:11 189
19:11–16 189
19:12 189
19:13 189, 200
19:16 18, 21, 189
20:4 155, 189, 200
20:6 155
21–22 168
21:5 186
21:9 130
21:14 130
21:22 18
21:23 130
21:27 130
22:1 130
22:3 130
22:5 18
22:6 18
22:20 18
22:21 18

Dead Sea Scrolls

1Q39

1 21 142n16

1QapGen

20.12–13 4n4

1QM

11.7–8 142n16

1QpHab

8.8–13 216n18
11.12–15 216n19
12.1–10 216n20

1QS

5.5–6 216n17
8.8–9 216n17
9.6 216n17
9.11 28, 37, 142, 218

1QSa

2.1–12 141
2.11–22 218

4Q169

1.5 216n17

4Q252

5,3–4 142n16

4Q266

10 i 12 142

4Q270

2 ii 13–14 142n16

4Q375

1 i 9 142n16

4Q376

1 i 1 142n16

4Q426
1.2–2.1 74 note *a*
1.7 74
1.9 74
2.1 74

4Q458
2 ii 6 142n16

4Q521
1 ii 1 141, 142n16
8 9 142n16

4QEn^b
1,iv.5 4n4

4QFlorilegium
1.10–13 141

11QMelch
2.18 142n16

11QPs^a
28.7–8 4n4

11QtgJob
24.6–7 4n4

CD
6.12–17 216n17
12.23–13.1 142
14.19 142
19.10–11 142
20.1 142

Philo and Josephus

Philo

Allegorical Interpretation
1.43 203, 204
1.81 194n22
2.56 158n3

3.27 158n3
3.96 194n22

On Agriculture
51 194
80 160n7

On the Confusion of Tongues
93 160n7
147 194n22

On the Creation of the World
24–25 194n23

On Dreams
2.185 217
2.188 217
2.242 194n16, 199n33
2.245 194n16, 199n33

On Drunkenness
30–31 194n16, 203

On the Embassy to Gaius
3.79–82 218n29
278 217 note *a*

On Flight and Finding
5 194n21
97 199n33
101 62, 194n20, 194n22
108–9 194n16, 199n33
109 194n16
112 206
162 158n3, 160n8

On the Life of Moses
2.3–4 37, 42

On the Migration of Abraham
21 194n21
25 158n3, 160n6

On Planting
18 206

On the Preliminary Studies
171 160n6

On the Sacrifices of Cain and Abel
70 160n6
70–71 158n3

On the Special Laws
2.198 160n8

Questions and Answers on Genesis
2.62 194n19, 194n24

That God Is Unchangeable
137 160n7
156 160n8

Who Is the Heir?
60 160n7
205 194

Josephus

Against Apion
1.40 26

Jewish Antiquities
1.2 175n15
1.179–81 218n29
2.94 161
2.229 175n15
3.159–79 216
3.188–91 216n14
3.191 216
11.278 161
12.223 161
12.265 175n15
13.67–68 5 note *a*
13.68 4
13.222 161
13.271 161
13.301 140

13.320 140
14.444 161
18.116–19 29n16
20.90 4
20.97 26

Jewish War
1.70 140
2.261 26
5.230–35 216
5.230–36 214n6
7.418–19 6

Rabbinic Works

Babylonian Talmud

Sanhedrin
59 177
93 143

Jerusalem Talmud

Ta'anit
4:5 143

Mekilta

Exod. 20:21 140

Midrash on Psalms

1.2 140
2.9 61

Mishnah

Bava Metzi'a
1:8 28
2:8 28
3:4–5 28

Sanhedrin
6:4 60
7:5 60
7:8 60
7:10 60

Sotah
9:15 28

Ancient Sources Index

Sifre on Deuteronomy
344   140

Targums
Isa. 61:1   140

Apostolic Fathers

Barnabas
5.1–3   109 note *a*
14.2   41 note *a*
14.4–5   41 note *a*

1 Clement
36.1–2   225 note *a*
59.3–61.3   105

2 Clement
20.5   168a

Didache
9.2   105
10.2   105

Ignatius

To the Ephesians
1.1   167n36
18.2   156 note *a*

To the Smyrnaeans
1.1   20 note *a*

Martyrdom of Polycarp
8.2   6n24
19.2   167n36

Patristic Sources

Athanasius

On the Incarnation
10   167n36

Eusebius

Ecclesiastical History
1.3.6   33 note *a*

Preparation for the Gospel
13.12   193n15

Hippolytus

Philosophumena
7.35.1–2   88 note *a*

Irenaeus

Against Heresies
5.1.1   187 note *a*

Justin Martyr

First Apology
46   207 note *a*

Origen

Commentary on the Epistle to the Romans
5.2.2   182

Other Greek and Latin Sources

Aeschylus

Suppliant Women
980–82   161

Aristotle

Politics
1332   191

Rhetoric
3.1407   191n8

Dio Chrysostom

To the People of Alexandria
32.18   161

Diodorus

Library of History
16.20   161

Diogenes Laertius

Lives of Eminent Philosophers
7.134   192
7.149   192

Heraclitus
Fragment 1   191n8
Fragment 83   191n7

Herodotus

Histories
7.192–93   161

Pausanias

Description of Greece
8.30.10   161n14

Plutarch

Ad principem ineruditum
780   191 note *a*

Alexander
28.1   67

De Iside et Osiride
381   192

Life of Dion
46.1   161

Life of Titus Flamininus
16.4   162n18

Velleius Paterculus
2.126   162n21

Papyri and Inscriptions

BGU
423.6   6n23

IG
VII.1836   162

IGR
III.719   162

OGIS
90.1   4
186.8   5n9
415   5n13
418   5n13
423   5n13
425   5n13
426   5n13
458   72n23, 162
606   5n14

O.Petr.
209   6n17
288   6n20

P.Faud.
266   3n2

P.Hamb.
4.14–15   103

P.Lond.
1215   6n18

P.Meyer II
22.2–3   6n18
23.3–4   6n18
24.2–3   6n18
25.2–3   6n18
36a.3   6n18

37.3–4 6n18
39.4 6n19
76.4–5 6n18

P.Oxy.

37.6 6n15
110.2–3 6n23

246.30 6n18
246.36–37 6n20
1143.4 5n12
1439 6n24

P.Teb.

104.39–40 103

Res Gestae Divi Augusti

10.1 68

Rosetta Stone

line 10 68

SB

1927 6n24

SIG³

814.31 6n21
814.55 6n22

www.ingramcontent.com/pod-product-compliance
Lightning Source LLC
Chambersburg PA
CBHW031724230426
43669CB00007B/229